FIELDS OF BLOOD

CIVIL WAR AMERICA Gary W. Gallagher, editor

FIELDS OF BLOOD

THE PRAIRIE GROVE CAMPAIGN

William L. Shea

THE UNIVERSITY OF NORTH CAROLINA PRESS

Chapel Hill

Designed by Courtney Leigh Baker and set in Arno Pro and Bodoni Classic Deco One by Tseng Information Systems, Inc.
Manufactured in the United States of America

The University of North Carolina Press has been a member of the Green Press Initiative since 2003.

The paper in this book meets the guidelines for permanence and durability of the Committee on Production Guidelines for Book Longevity of the Council on Library Resources.

Library of Congress Cataloging-in-Publication Data
Shea, William L.
Fields of blood : the Prairie Grove Campaign / William L. Shea.
p. cm. — (CIVIL WAR AMERICA)
Includes bibliographical references and index.
ISBN 978-0-8078-3315-5 (cloth: alk. paper)
ISBN 978-0-8078-6602-3 (large print pbk.)
1. Prairie Grove, Battle of, Ark., 1862. I. Title.
E474.92.S54 2009
973.7'32—dc22
2009011469

13 12 11 10 09 5 4 3 2

Contents

Maps

Illustrations

Preface

> Why so many monuments at Gettysburg when no stone marks the spot
> where the 37th like a wall of fire rolled back the waves of treason and rebellion;
> no stone where Little, Miller and Hickey died; no stone nor song to tell the story
> of where we stood before the Angel of Death on the field of Prairie Grove.
> —MAJOR HENRY N. FRISBIE, Thirty-seventh Illinois

THE PRAIRIE GROVE CAMPAIGN WAS THE CULMINATION OF THE DRAMATIC struggle for control of Arkansas, Missouri, Kansas, and the Indian Territory during the Civil War. Union forces gained the upper hand in Missouri soon after the war broke out but suffered a severe setback at Wilson's Creek in the summer of 1861. The Confederate resurgence was, in turn, cut short by a smashing Union victory at Pea Ridge in early 1862. For a time secession west of the Mississippi River seemed on the verge of collapse, but everything changed when a remarkable figure arrived on the scene and singlehandedly revived Confederate fortunes.

The story of the Prairie Grove campaign is, to a large extent, the story of Thomas C. Hindman and his extraordinary effort to reverse the course of the war in the trans-Mississippi. Hindman restored order and morale, raised an army from scratch, and launched a bold attempt to recover Missouri for the Confederacy. The Union response to Hindman's challenge was impressive in its own right. Overcoming personal differences, Samuel R. Curtis, John M. Schofield, and James G. Blunt created an army of their own. The ensuing duel between the Confederate Trans-Mississippi Army and the Union Army of the Frontier was one of the Civil War's most intriguing contests and, until now, one of its best-kept secrets. After months of intricate maneuvering marked by hard marching, sharp clashes, and a flurry of thrusts and counterthrusts, the armies finally collided on a wooded hillside in northwest Arkansas called "Prairie Grove." There, on a frigid Sunday in December 1862, the fate of the trans-Mississippi was settled. Hindman's bold gambit failed but only by the slimmest of margins. Had it succeeded, the history of the Civil War in the West would have been very different.

DOZENS OF PEOPLE helped make this book possible. I am in debt to Bruce Allardice, Frank Arey, Bob Besom, John Bradbury, William Droessler, Bill Gurley, Earl Hess, Bryan Howerton, Kip Lindberg, Howard Mann, Jim Martin, Matt Matthews, James McGhee, Ron Newberry, Danny Odom, Jeff Patrick, Linda Russell, Kim Allen Scott, Bryce Suderow, Tom and Karen Sweeney, Steve Warren, Dale West, Jeremy Wilder, Gary Zellar, and many others for their advice, assistance, and generosity. Alan Thompson and Don Montgomery at Prairie Grove Battlefield State Park deserve special thanks, as do Linda Forrest and Mary Heady of the University of Arkansas at Monticello.

A FEW WORDS of explanation. The term "trans-Mississippi" refers to the geographical area west of the Great River, while "Trans-Mississippi" is reserved for official usage, as in Trans-Mississippi Army. As customary, Union unit designations are capitalized only in formal usage, thus Tenney's First Kansas Battery but Tenney's battery; Confederate unit designations are capitalized in both formal and informal usage, thus Blocher's Arkansas Battery or Blocher's Battery (but not Blocher's battery). Finally, an intersection is a four-way crossing; a junction is not.

1 HINDMAN

BY THE SUMMER OF 1862 THE CONFEDERACY WAS IN SERIOUS TROUBLE. Southern military and naval forces west of the Appalachian Mountains had suffered an unrelieved string of defeats and disasters. Significant portions of Arkansas, Louisiana, Tennessee, and Mississippi had fallen under Union control, and the Stars and Stripes flew over two state capitals, Nashville and Baton Rouge. All of the bustling commercial centers along the Mississippi River had been lost except Vicksburg, and it was uncertain whether the reeling Confederates could maintain their grip on that beleaguered citadel.

The situation was particularly grim in the trans-Mississippi Confederacy, an immense region composed of Arkansas, Louisiana, Texas, the Indian Territory, the Arizona Territory, and, after a fashion, Missouri. Most Missourians were loyal to the Union, but a substantial minority favored secession and made a vigorous effort to bring the state into the southern fold. The secessionists suffered several early setbacks and were pushed into the southwest corner of the state around Springfield. There they rallied and won small but heartening victories at Carthage, Wilson's Creek, and Lexington in the summer and early fall of 1861. The leader of the secessionist faction in Missouri, Governor Claiborne F. Jackson, was so encouraged by this turn of events that he convened a rump session of the state legislature in Neosho. To no one's surprise, the legislators voted to leave the Union and join the Confederacy. By the close of 1861, the secessionists appeared to be gaining momentum. Then came a series of calamities from which the Confederate cause in the trans-Mississippi never recovered.

In early 1862, a Union army commanded by Major General Samuel R. Curtis drove into southwest Missouri. Sterling Price, commander of the secessionist Missouri State Guard, fled south with the Federals in hot pursuit. The Missourians joined forces with Brigadier General Benjamin McCulloch's

Confederate army in northwest Arkansas and withdrew into the Boston Mountains. Curtis halted just inside Arkansas. He was satisfied at having rid Missouri of its Rebels and was determined not to let them return. The Confederates, of course, were equally determined to do exactly that. Major General Earl Van Dorn arrived from the East and combined Price's and McCulloch's forces into a single army under his overall command. He struck Curtis at Pea Ridge on 7–8 March 1862, but the outnumbered Federals stood their ground and won a decisive victory. Van Dorn retreated to the Arkansas River, his army wrecked and demoralized. Pea Ridge seemingly settled the fate of Missouri but left open the future of Arkansas and the Indian Territory.

Dispirited by his failure to recover Missouri, Van Dorn decided to try his luck elsewhere. Without consulting or even informing his superiors, he moved his entire force, along with all the arms, ammunition, stores, equipment, animals, and machinery that he could lay his hands on, to the east side of the Mississippi River. By the end of April the only Confederate forces left in Arkansas, Missouri, and the Indian Territory were a handful of cavalry regiments and a few hundred irregulars.[1]

Arkansas was thrown into turmoil by this stunning development. Howls of outrage from political leaders and prominent citizens soon reached General Pierre G. T. Beauregard, who exercised nominal authority over the trans-Mississippi from his headquarters in Corinth, Mississippi. Under normal circumstances Beauregard would have referred a problem of this magnitude to the Confederate government in Richmond, but the urgency of the situation compelled him to act at once. Beauregard needed manpower after the recent bloodletting at Shiloh, so he decided against sending Van Dorn and his men back across the Mississippi. Instead, he appointed an interim commander for the abandoned trans-Mississippi. The man he chose was Major General Thomas C. Hindman Jr.

Thomas Hindman was a southerner to the core. Born in 1828 to a prosperous Tennessee family, he attended the Lawrenceville Classical Institute in New Jersey and was salutatorian of the class of 1843. He moved to Mississippi where he raised cotton and studied law. When the Mexican War broke out, Hindman joined the Second Mississippi and served capably as a junior officer. The regiment was ravaged by disease and saw no action, but after the war Hindman found his true calling in the arena of political combat.[2]

In 1854 Hindman left Mississippi to seek his fortune in the neighboring state of Arkansas. He must have found what he was looking for as soon as he set foot on Arkansas soil, for he settled in the port of Helena on the west bank of the Mississippi River. Hindman plunged into politics and quickly became a leading figure in the Democratic Party. His meteoric rise threw the state's political establishment into turmoil and generated scores of enemies. Elected to Congress in 1858 and again in 1860, he was an uncompromising advocate of state's rights and, ultimately, secession. Hindman was blessed with boundless energy and a remarkable gift for oratory. "I must say that as a speaker for the masses I never heard his superior," recalled an acquaintance. His most memorable quality was a fiery temper. "Hindman had a wonderful talent to get into fusses," said a friend, "from which he always came off either victor or with credit." Friends and enemies alike—and he had plenty of both—described him as outspoken and confrontational. He rarely backed away from a scrape, and his political career was marked by a number of violent incidents.[3]

Hindman was short, slight, and fair-complexioned. He had blue eyes and his hair was a "light auburn, almost golden color, very fine, and worn long, combed, like a girl's, carefully behind his ears." As Hindman grew older he let his wavy locks grow longer, probably to compensate for a receding hairline. He dressed stylishly—he had a penchant for pastels—and undoubtedly was regarded as a dandy by many Arkansans. While campaigning for Congress in 1858, Hindman broke his left leg in a carriage accident; the bones did not heal properly, and the injured leg became two inches shorter than the other. Thereafter he wore a boot with a built-up heel and carried a cane.[4]

Hindman became close friends with another newcomer to Arkansas, an Anglo-Irish immigrant named Patrick R. Cleburne. In 1856 the two men engaged in a shootout with three members of the Know-Nothing Party on a Helena street in broad daylight. Both Hindman and Cleburne suffered serious chest wounds. Hindman recovered quickly but Cleburne lingered near death for several days. One member of the opposing group was killed, apparently by Hindman, but no charges were filed and everyone seemed to take the incident in stride. Politics in antebellum Arkansas clearly was not for sissies.[5]

When the Civil War began, Hindman resigned his seat in Congress and hurried home to organize military forces for the nascent Confederacy. He and Cleburne each led a brigade in Major General William J. Hardee's corps at Shiloh in April 1862. Both men survived the hail of fire unscathed, but Hindman suffered another fractured leg when his horse went down. He was promoted to major general upon his recovery and given command of a division. In war as in politics, Hindman seemed destined for great things. Then came Beauregard's request, made at the "earnest solicitation of the people of Arkansas," that Hindman return to his adopted state and prevent the trans-Mississippi from going under. Hindman was reluctant to leave the Army of

Thomas C. Hindman (Museum of the Confederacy, Richmond, Va.)

Tennessee where his star was in the ascendant, but after talking things over with Cleburne he accepted the challenge and set out for Arkansas. "In the existing condition of things General Beauregard could not spare me a soldier, a gun, a pound of powder, nor a single dollar of money," Hindman recalled. He may have been flattered by the thought that Beauregard considered him a one-man army.[6]

On 31 May 1862 Hindman arrived in Little Rock and assumed command of the newly created Trans-Mississippi District, which consisted of Arkansas, Missouri, and the Indian Territory. The desperate state of affairs in the district came as a profound shock. "I found here almost nothing," Hindman informed the War Department in Richmond. "Nearly everything of value was taken away by General Van Dorn." Undaunted, Hindman set to work. His first act was to issue a ringing declaration that began: "I have come here to drive out the invader or to perish in the attempt." That statement was no rhetorical flourish; Hindman meant every word of it.[7]

The Trans-Mississippi District was under attack from two directions when Hindman assumed command. Following his victory at Pea Ridge in the spring, Curtis carried the war deep into Arkansas. He advanced to within forty miles of Little Rock before his line of communications broke down, then turned toward the Mississippi River where he could obtain supplies by way of the Union navy. Hindman appealed to Arkansans in Curtis's path to burn their crops and poison their wells, but his call for a "scorched earth" campaign was largely ignored. In mid-July Curtis occupied Helena. For the rest of the war the town was a Union enclave, and the handsome new Hindman residence was Union headquarters.[8]

While Curtis headed toward Helena, Colonel William Weer advanced into the Indian Territory from Kansas. A resounding Union victory at Locust Grove convinced more than a thousand disillusioned Cherokees, many of whom had fought in Van Dorn's ranks at Pea Ridge, to change sides. The swelling Union force reached Fort Gibson and Tahlequah in mid-July but could go no farther because of a brutal drought that dried up springs and reduced rivers to a trickle. Weer was removed from command by his subordinates, who promptly fell to squabbling among themselves. Parched and paralyzed, the Federals gave up and returned to Kansas.[9]

Curtis and Weer marched almost at will across large swatches of Arkansas and the Indian Territory during the summer of 1862. Their forces overran thousands of square miles of Confederate territory and seized or destroyed property worth tens of millions of dollars, much of it in the form of slaves who followed the blue columns to an uncertain freedom. The incursions were hindered more by distance and nature than by organized resistance. Confederate forces, such as they were, achieved little except to annoy the Federals. But when the dust settled and the fires burned out, the only permanent territorial loss suffered by the Confederacy was Helena, which would have fallen to Union gunboats had Curtis not gotten there first. Hindman could hardly believe his good fortune, though his relief was tempered by the certainty that the Federals would resume offensive operations in the near future. It was imperative that the Confederates meet them on more equal terms.

A more immediate problem was the breakdown in public order. The presence of Union forces in Arkansas and the Indian Territory generated a resurgence of Unionist sentiment that led to widespread disaffection. Judges, sheriffs, tax collectors, jailers, and other officials failed to carry out their duties or were prevented from doing so. With courts closed, jails open, and law enforcement suspended, some areas teetered on the verge of anarchy barely a year after the start of the war. Arkansas governor Henry M. Rector and the state legislature proved incapable of dealing with the situation. Conditions were even worse in the Indian Territory, where the Cherokee tribal government ceased to function altogether.[10]

Alarmed by what he described as the "virtual abdication of the civil authorities," Hindman declared martial law throughout the Trans-Mississippi District. "Immediately he commenced issuing military orders, which under his vigorous government had all the force of Imperial decrees," recalled an Arkansas industrialist named Henry Merrell. "Bad as it seems that there should ever be so much power in one man, it was in General Hindman's case a very great improvement upon the state of things before his coming, and quiet citizens in our part of the country breathed freely once more." Not everyone agreed, of course. There was the usual overheated rhetoric decrying "tyrannical acts" and "military despotism," but most Arkansans discovered that Hindman's heavy-handed approach got results. The *Little Rock True Democrat*, the state's largest and most influential newspaper, supported the temporary imposition of martial law as a necessary evil. "It is the only means at hand to afford protection, and every good citizen should lend his earnest assistance to promote its success," opined editor Richard H. Johnson.[11]

In his dual roles as district commander and (self-appointed) military governor, Hindman demonstrated what diligence, determination, and a disregard for legalities could accomplish. "*His genius was especially administrative*," remarked a Confederate officer who knew Hindman well. "Nothing escaped his vigilance and his energy. Resources, arms, supplies and army sprang into being almost by the magic of his will." Merrell noticed that after Hindman assumed control, a "kind of nervous energy was infused into every department of Government within his reach" and that no corner of the state was unaffected. "The whole country was taught that she could clothe, subsist and manufacture for her own necessities," marveled another officer. Acting on his own authority, Hindman awarded military contracts and established facilities to manufacture arms, ammunition, clothing, shoes, camp equipment, medicines, harnesses, and wagons. He set price controls to stamp out profiteering and minimize inflation. He burned tons of cotton to prevent it from falling into enemy hands. He pared away incompetent and inefficient officers regardless of their political connections. He rigorously enforced the Conscription Act and established camps of instruction. He interpreted the Partisan Ranger Act in the broadest possible fashion and authorized the formation of irregular bands to harass Union forces and Unionists. All the while he badgered authorities in Richmond for more men, more arms, more supplies, more funds, more of everything.[12]

The barrage of appeals, requests, and demands produced results. A large number of Missouri State Guard troops had refused to transfer to Confederate service during the Pea Ridge campaign. Van Dorn carried them off to Mississippi despite their status as civilian militiamen. The irate Missourians clamored to return to their state or at least to their side of the Mississippi River, a demand that Hindman strongly seconded. The War Department finally gave in. In late summer Brigadier General Mosby M. Parsons and nine hundred veterans of Wilson's Creek and Pea Ridge made their way back to Arkansas. This was the only occasion during the Civil War when a Confederate force of any size crossed the Mississippi from east to west.[13]

Hindman envisioned Parsons's command as the nucleus of a strong Missouri component in the army he was cobbling together. The Conscription Act could not be enforced in Missouri because a Unionist administration was in control of the state government, so Hindman launched a recruiting drive unique in Confederate history. During the summer of 1862 he sent dozens of Missouri State Guard and Confederate officers back to their home state. Some traveled alone or with a handful of companions, others were accompanied by small cavalry forces. They spread the news that Hindman was assembling an army in Arkansas capable of restoring Missouri to the Confederacy, and they encouraged fellow secessionists to take part in the climactic struggle by enlisting in regular forces or joining irregular bands on their home ground.[14]

The recruiters found receptive audiences, particularly in the "Little Dixie" region of west-central Missouri where sympathy for secession was wide and deep. Thousands of men took off for camps of instruction in Arkansas; thousands more took to the brush in Missouri. Emboldened by larger numbers and the promise of regular military support in the near future, guerrillas swarmed out of their hiding places and threw the state into turmoil. Ambushes, skirmishes, and small battles flared all across Missouri. Union authorities from St. Louis to Kansas City were caught off guard by the sudden shift in the military situation.[15]

When Hindman reached Little Rock at the end of May, Missouri was gone and Arkansas and the Indian Territory were practically defenseless. Union military forces were on the move from the Mississippi River to the Great Plains. Ten weeks later everything had changed. Federal offensive operations had come to a standstill. More than 20,000 Confederate troops—forty regiments of infantry and cavalry and a dozen batteries of artillery—were in the field or in camps of instruction in Arkansas and the Indian Territory. Thousands more were in irregular service, mostly in Missouri. The Confederacy west of the Mississippi River had come back from the dead.[16]

In only seventy days Hindman had created an embryonic army and a rudimentary logistical base in the least populous and least developed part of the Confederacy. It was an achievement without parallel in the Civil War.

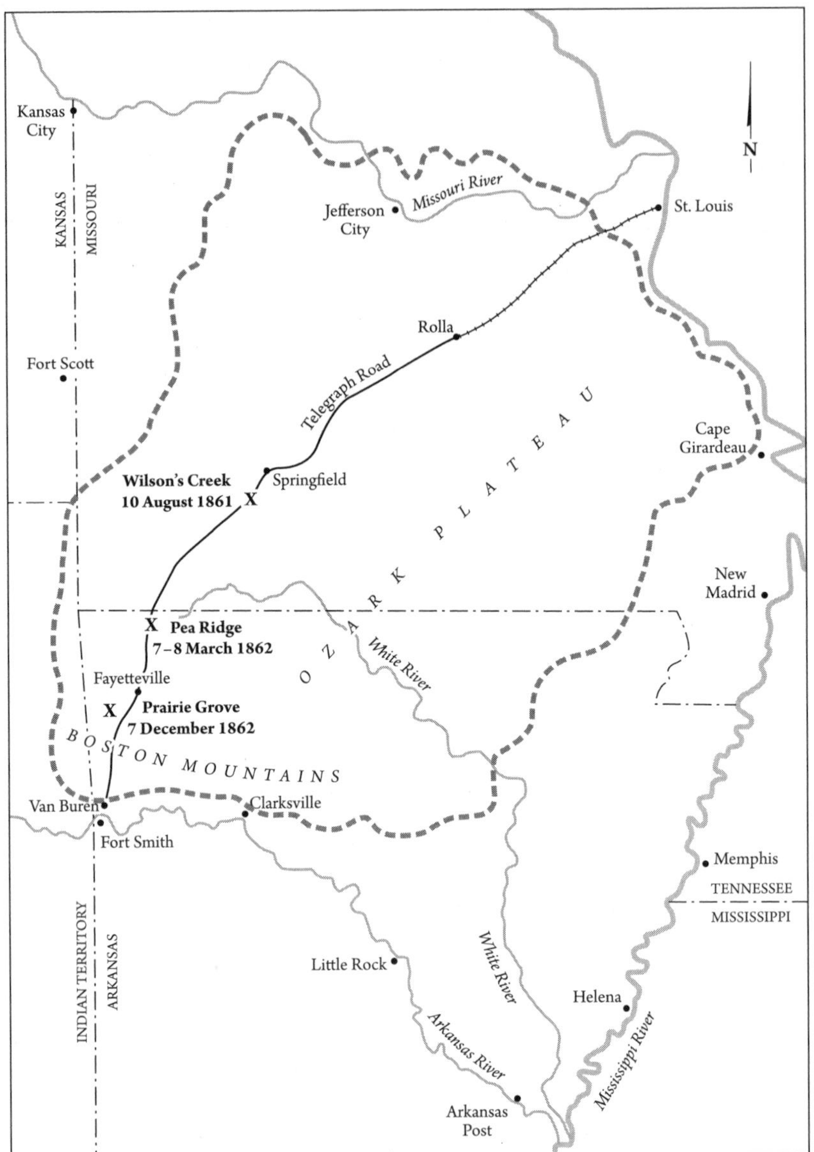

Southern Missouri and northern Arkansas in 1861–62

Nevertheless, his accomplishments were overshadowed by the rigorous and sometimes extralegal methods he employed. Hindman viewed war as a serious business. From the day he assumed command in Little Rock he made it clear that he expected everyone to make sacrifices to achieve victory. In short, Hindman demanded a level of commitment to the cause of southern independence that not every southerner was willing to make. Most Confederate citizens supported secession and independence in the abstract, but the harsh reality of war—shortages, inflation, hardships, destruction, and death—was more than many had bargained for.

The political and economic elites in Arkansas were particularly outraged by Hindman's insistence that they make sacrifices like everyone else. Wealthy planters and merchants saw no reason to place national goals above their own interests. When, for example, Hindman burned their cotton or impressed their slaves to construct fortifications, the elites resisted him at every turn. "These measures made General Hindman very unpopular with a certain very clamorous class of people," noted a Confederate officer. That was an understatement. Hindman himself observed that his actions "greatly embittered the disaffected population against me. That population controlled the political demagogues of the State. They made war on me." Well-placed Arkansans bombarded the distant Confederate government with exaggerated and often baseless complaints about Hindman's alleged autocratic methods. "It was the clamor of politicians and disappointed aspirants for military preferment—not the wish or request of the intelligent, patriotic citizenship of the State—that prevailed upon the authorities at Richmond" to remove Hindman, declared a disgusted Confederate officer.[17]

President Jefferson Davis usually responded to political pressure by digging in his heels, but on this occasion he capitulated to the "clamors of the rich men" of Arkansas. Davis rejected demands that Hindman be removed and decided instead to place the fiery Arkansan under the authority of a more moderate officer. This seemed the best way to temper Hindman's zeal while still making use of his talents. Davis gathered Arkansas, Missouri, Louisiana west of the Mississippi River, Texas, the Indian Territory, and the Arizona Territory into an immense new entity named the "Trans-Mississippi Department." Then he looked for someone to run it.[18]

Davis quickly settled on Major General Theophilus H. Holmes, a schoolmate from his West Point days and a veteran of the Mexican and Seminole wars. Holmes was fifty-seven years old, but because of his stooped appearance and fretful manner he struck people as being older. During the early days of the war he had picked up the unfortunate nickname "Granny." Holmes was six feet tall but lacked a soldierly bearing, a matter of considerable importance in the mid-nineteenth century. "He is hunchbacked, and makes a very ungraceful appearance, either on foot or on a horse," noted a disappointed observer. Physical shortcomings aside, Holmes had not distinguished himself during the first year of the war in Virginia. He turned in such a lackluster performance at First Manassas and Seven Days that he was reassigned to command the Department of North Carolina. Holmes soon informed Davis that the burdens of departmental command were "entirely too comprehensive for my capacity" and begged the president to send "someone more able" to take his place. "Whatever is effected here must be done by a stern and firm will that can make itself respected and feared. Such a one I am not nor can I make myself," Holmes acknowledged. Davis was unfazed by this painfully honest self-appraisal from his old friend. Instead, he came to the remarkable conclusion that Holmes was just the man to set things right on the far side of the Mississippi River. Holmes attempted to decline the appointment, but Davis insisted and that settled the matter.[19]

Holmes was promoted to lieutenant general and sent on his way. Traveling west by railroad and steamboat, he reached Little Rock on 11 August. He soon discovered that Hindman had worked wonders during his seventy days of independent command. Instead of repudiating Hindman, as many expected and some hoped, Holmes publicly embraced him. He told Davis that when Hindman arrived "there was absolutely no law in Arkansas and no Troops to resist Curtis who was threatning this city and could have come here without fireing a gun." Hindman "assumed control of every thing civil and military and exercised his power with a success that places the State in a condition of tolerable order, and security." Holmes not only endorsed Hindman's controversial actions, he asked Davis to restore Hindman's sullied reputation. "As I am certain all this has been done with a single eye to the public interest, and in a manner perfectly wreckless of his own popularity I respectfully request that you will confirm all that he has done." Davis did not like being told that he had made a mistake. He gracelessly acknowledged that Hindman might have done some good but insisted that martial law be terminated. Holmes complied but changed little else that Hindman had wrought.[20]

"I have resolved to take the army as I found it," Holmes informed Davis, and "to make no changes in its organization or construction." His only significant contribution was to divide the sprawling Trans-Mississippi Department into three districts. Hindman continued in charge of military affairs in Arkansas, Missouri, and the Indian Territory, now renamed the "District of Arkansas." From the very beginning of his tenure Holmes focused his attention on affairs in Arkansas. In retrospect, it would have been better had he established his headquarters in a more central location, such as Shreveport, Louisiana, and allowed Hindman the same freedom of action enjoyed by the other district commanders. This view was shared by Lieutenant General Edmund Kirby Smith, Holmes's successor and the only other man to head

Theophilus H. Holmes (Library of Congress)

the unwieldy department. Smith believed that Holmes erred when he set up shop in Little Rock and attempted to exercise "solely the functions of a district commander." Holmes never explained why he maintained his headquarters in Arkansas, but he may have felt that his place was there given the unsettled conditions and the absence of a viable state government.[21]

Holmes threw himself into his new assignment with all the energy and ability he could muster. "General Holmes is a plain, quiet man, makes no show, but works hard," observed a Missouri officer. Holmes was conscientious to a fault, but he simply was not up to the demands of the job, as he would have been the first to admit. Holmes was a mediocre administrator who shied away from difficult decisions and meddled in the affairs of his subordinates. An exasperated staff officer described him as "excellently inefficient." Henry Merrell, who also worked closely with Holmes, concluded that he did not have "enough of the 'mustang' in him to deal with Wild Western men."[22]

Holmes and Hindman worked together for more than six months in the Trans-Mississippi Department. They made an odd pair, as nearly opposite in appearance, experience, personality, and temperament as two human beings could be. But despite disagreements on matters of strategy, there is no record of any personal discord between the two men. Hindman swallowed his pride and tried to be a model subordinate. He provided Holmes with advice and assistance when in Little Rock and sent him a stream of telegrams and letters when in the field. For his part, Holmes recognized that his hard-driving subordinate had the "stern and firm will" he so conspicuously lacked. He allowed Hindman wide freedom of action and sought his opinion on all important issues.

Meanwhile, glowing reports about the success of the recruiting campaign and guerrilla uprising in Missouri were flowing into Little Rock. Hindman believed the time had come to seize the initiative and "push forward toward the Missouri River with the greatest vigor." Although Holmes would have liked nothing better than to plant the Confederate flag on the banks of the Missouri, he insisted that no offensive take place without proper preparation. To that end, on 21 August, only ten days after his arrival in Little Rock, Holmes ordered Hindman to proceed up the Arkansas River to Fort Smith and organize an army capable of liberating Missouri. Hindman wasted no time. He was on his way within an hour.[23]

Roughly half of the 20,000 or so newly raised troops in the District of Arkansas were in camps of instruction around Fort Smith, which was located on the Arkansas River near the border with the Indian Territory. The impressive numbers were offset by ineffective leadership, inadequate training, and crippling deficiencies of every description. Food and forage were in short supply, ammunition was almost nonexistent, and, according to Hindman, the "small arms scarcely deserved the name." Colonel Charles A. Carroll, the Fort Smith post commander, did not exaggerate when he lamented that "we are short of every thing necessary to equip a command."[24]

Carroll would not have gotten any argument from the men in the ranks. "We have in our Regiment no conveniences of any kind scarcely," complained David W. Moore of Carroll's Arkansas Cavalry, which was stationed in Fort Smith. "Very few tents or any of the equipment necessary for a Regiment other than those furnished by the men themselves." Moore waxed indignant as he warmed to his subject. "I have seen enough service to know how a Regiment should be equipped and never have I seen one as poorly provided for as this. No tents, no clothing, no cooking utensils and in fact scarcely anything have been issued by the Government to the men." Conditions were even worse a few miles to the west in the Indian Territory. "We are having a hard time," reported Lucian D. Gilbert of Alexander's Texas Cavalry near Tahlequah. "Provisions are very scarce and as for clothing it is folly to think of it for there is none here and a great many of our men are nearly naked and barefooted." If these descriptions are accurate, the Confederates must have looked more like refugees than fighting men.[25]

Despite the difficulties inherent in assembling and maintaining a large military force on the frontier, Fort Smith was the logical jumping-off point for a push into Missouri. The reason is geography. Twenty miles north of town the Ozark Plateau abruptly rises 2,500 feet above sea level. The massive limestone dome is more than two hundred miles wide and occupies most of southern Missouri and northern Arkansas. The eastern three-fourths of the plateau, hollowed out by the White River and other streams, is a maze of narrow, winding valleys. Travel across this area was extremely difficult in the nineteenth century and is not easy even today. The narrow stretch of bottomland between the plateau and the Mississippi River was also effectively impassible. Before the creation of the modern levee system, the swampy terrain might be underwater for months at a time.

The only place in the trans-Mississippi where Civil War armies could move north and south without encountering insurmountable natural obstacles was the western rim of the Ozark Plateau, a rolling tableland called the "Springfield Plain." This narrow strategic corridor stretches from Kansas City in the north to Fayetteville in the south, a distance of 260 miles. South of Fayetteville, however, the Springfield Plain gives way to the Boston Mountains, a rugged mass of sandstone and shale that crowns the southern edge of the plateau. The mountains, which can be seen from Fort Smith on a clear day, were both boon and barrier. On the one hand, they shielded the Confederates in the Arkansas Valley from Union forces on the Springfield Plain. On the other, they impeded Confederate efforts to reach the Springfield Plain and operate effectively against those Union forces. Cavalry, infantry, and artillery could pass through the mountains in both directions, but heavily laden supply wagons found the crude roads and steep inclines difficult to overcome. In the approaching campaign, the Springfield Plain and Boston Mountains would play vital and ever-changing roles.

Hindman traveled up the Arkansas River on a light-draft steamboat. Reaching Fort Smith on 24 August, he tackled his new assignment with typical energy and enthusiasm. He traveled tirelessly from camp to camp to see problems for himself and to encourage his demoralized soldiers. As a general rule, Hindman made a favorable impression. An Arkansan wrote that the members of his regiment "had much confidence in the ability of General Hindman and the majority of men that I heard say any thing about it believed that he was a worthy officer and that he would lead them to victory." Hindman's promise of an imminent northward movement found a particularly receptive audience among the Missourians. One officer informed his family that "General Hindman promises to clear out Missouri in three months work." But cynics abounded, especially among the Texans in the Indian Territory. "General Hyndman is of the opinion that we will defeat them easily and then march for St. Louis, but I beg leave to differ with the distinguished General Hyndman," wrote Lucian Gilbert. "I have been in the army long enough to know something about it. Our Brigade is perfectly raw," he went on. "I know when they run against the Feds they will be whipped and badly, for I happened to be in a party once that jumped them up." The subsequent behavior of the Texas regiments would validate Gilbert's doubts.[26]

Hindman had doubts as well but they concerned his own limited military experience. "General Hindman did not consider himself a General fit to manage a campaign," recalled Merrell. "He once told me so. He could carry a Brigade into action gallantly and bring it out all right, but he was no master of strategy in war." Aware of his limitations, Hindman concentrated on his strengths. He applied his impressive intellectual and organizational skills to the problems of building, training, equipping, and sustaining an army on the frontier. He set about the daunting task with the same single-minded intensity that characterized all of his endeavors.[27]

Only a fraction of the Confederate troops in northwest Arkansas and the Indian Territory were prepared for service in the field, but Hindman feared the uprising in Missouri could not sustain itself without the support of regular forces. The drought-stricken summer of 1862 was fading into fall. The onset of cold weather was only two months away, and Hindman quailed at the thought of a winter campaign atop the Ozark Plateau with his troops so poorly clothed and supplied. If he was going to act, he had to act soon.

Despite misgivings, Hindman set out for Missouri in early September with a makeshift force of 6,000 Arkansas, Missouri, Texas, and Indian soldiers. The Confederates moved north in parallel columns from Fort Smith and other points along the Arkansas River. Once across the Boston Mountains, they made rapid progress across the Springfield Plain. Hindman established a forward headquarters at Pineville in the southwest corner of Missouri, eighty-five miles north of Fort Smith. This was more of a political statement than a military move. A few days earlier a Missouri officer had urged Hindman to join him there. "A move of your forces even this far into Missouri would exert a moral influence throughout the State that would be very favorable to us." Always sensitive to political considerations, Hindman acted on the suggestion.[28]

Less than two weeks after arriving in Fort Smith, Hindman reestablished nominal Confederate control over 5,000 square miles of Arkansas and the Indian Territory. He even occupied a symbolic patch of Missouri. Encouraged by the lack of Federal resistance, he decided to push deeper into Missouri and threaten Springfield. Meanwhile, back in Little Rock, Holmes worried that Hindman was attempting to do too much too soon. He also fretted over the wisdom of sending half of his meager force to Missouri while Arkansas was threatened with invasion from Union forces on the Mississippi River. Then came an unexpected calamity.

In late August the Confederate transport *Fair Play* and its cargo of 5,500 rifles and muskets and 65,000 rounds of ammunition were captured by a Union gunboat while attempting to dash up the Mississippi from Vicksburg to Little Rock. Holmes railed at the stupidity of sending an unarmed and unescorted vessel into waters patrolled by the enemy. Depressed by the loss, which seriously impacted Confederate operations in the months ahead, he penned a cautionary letter to Hindman in which he emphasized the importance of preparation and deliberation. "Until we are ready to strike a blow it will not do for us to make any demonstration on Missouri or we shall subject ourselves to the same failure that rendered General Price's labor useless to the cause. We must have our army organized and disciplined before we start or disaster will result." Holmes concluded with a gloomy assessment of the strategic situation. "You and I can do nothing for Missouri and will be particularly fortunate if we can defend Arkansas." Nevertheless, he did not order Hindman to stop.[29]

A week later, however, Holmes called Hindman back to Little Rock. This development was caused by the breakdown of the temporary command arrangement the two men had devised for the District of Arkansas. Holmes agreed to look after routine administrative matters while Hindman was in the field. What this meant in practice was that Holmes assigned the additional responsibility to Brigadier General Allison Nelson, of Texas, a very capable officer. But when Nelson fell fatally ill with typhoid, a distraught Holmes sent for Hindman. Holmes later acknowledged that he recalled Hindman at the worst possible time, but the damage was done.[30]

Hindman was preparing to advance on Springfield when he received the order to return. Mystified, he left Pineville on 10 September and hurried back to Fort Smith, where a steamboat carried him down the Arkansas to Little Rock. He later described his feelings: "I obeyed the order with forebodings of disaster, which were afterward most unfortunately realized."[31]

2 FEDERALS

HINDMAN'S COUNTERPART IN BLUE WAS BRIGADIER GENERAL JOHN M. Schofield, commander of the District of Missouri. Schofield was a highly regarded 1853 graduate of West Point whose classmates included John B. Hood, James B. McPherson, and Philip H. Sheridan. After a tour of duty in Florida and a teaching stint at his alma mater, Schofield became disillusioned with the slow pace of advancement in the peacetime army. He secured an extended leave of absence and joined the faculty of Washington University in St. Louis where he taught physics and astronomy. Schofield seemed destined for a career in academe, but he resigned after Fort Sumter and returned to active duty. Despite being a conservative Democrat, Schofield was committed to the Union cause. He served as Brigadier General Nathaniel Lyon's chief of staff during the early months of the war and earned a Medal of Honor for his "cool and conspicuous courage" at Wilson's Creek. At the age of thirty-one Schofield found himself wearing a star on each shoulder.[1]

Schofield did not cut a dashing military figure, however. He had thinning reddish hair, a wispy beard, and was prone to pudginess. A colleague described him as a "quiet, reserved man in his manners and conversation." Some contemporaries thought him better suited to scholarly pursuits than soldiering, but Schofield was no ivory-tower intellectual. He was an effective military administrator and a ruthless political infighter. He also was ambitious and unscrupulous. Like other officers in the regular army, Schofield viewed the war as an opportunity for advancement in his chosen profession. He schemed tirelessly for promotion and undercut potential competitors at every opportunity. He sometimes seemed to forget that the real enemy wore gray.[2]

In the spring of 1862 Schofield described Missouri as being in a "condition of comparative peace." He was caught off guard by the resurgence of

John M. Schofield in 1862 (Old State House Museum)

Confederate activity during the summer but responded forcefully. In July he ordered all able-bodied Missourians to take a stringent loyalty oath and join a new statewide militia. The policy compelled every male citizen of the state to choose one side or the other. The great majority dutifully took the oath and enrolled in the militia, but many with secessionist leanings found this unpalatable. In the long run, Schofield's edict provided Union forces in Missouri with the means to carry out an effective counterinsurgency program. In the short run, however, it drove thousands of men into hiding or into Hindman's ranks.[3]

With several Confederate offensives under way east of the Mississippi River, Schofield suspected that the uprising in Missouri foreshadowed a full-scale invasion from Arkansas. Hindman's rapid advance from Fort Smith in mid-September seemed to confirm that suspicion. Schofield rushed every available soldier and militiaman to Springfield, the principal town in southwest Missouri, then scrambled to find more. The nearest source of additional manpower was the adjacent Department of Kansas, commanded by Brigadier General James G. Blunt. Blunt had moved to Kansas in the 1850s to practice medicine but became caught up in the whirl of frontier politics. He was an ardent abolitionist and a supporter of James H. Lane, the dominant figure in Kansas politics and one of the most radical members of the Republican Party.

Blunt helped raise the Third Kansas after Fort Sumter and was promoted to brigadier general a few months later. In May 1862 Lane urged President Abraham Lincoln to place Blunt in command of the Department of Kansas despite his lack of military education or experience. Lincoln had a soft spot in his heart (and in his head) for Lane and approved the appointment. At the age of thirty-five Blunt became one of only a handful of Union department commanders without a West Point background.[4]

Rarely did a name so aptly fit a man. "In speech, in manners, in dress, as well as in name, the Kansas commander is Blunt all over," observed a newspaper correspondent. Blunt was stocky in build and straightforward in manner. He often wore a suit instead of a uniform and had little use for military decorum. A member of Blunt's personal escort stated that the general did not "put on half as much style as some petty captains and lieutenants." Blunt had serious personal and professional shortcomings. He drank too much, associated with men (and women) of dubious character, and was an indifferent and corrupt military administrator. But he also was a bold, resolute, and intrepid leader who liked nothing better than leading troops into battle. "He is, every inch, a fighting General," declared a fellow Kansan. Blunt's lack of pretense and love of action made him immensely popular with his men. Despite his flaws, he was well suited for the peculiar demands of the Civil War on the frontier.[5]

Admirers and detractors provided wildly divergent portraits of the physician-turned-soldier. "With an iron constitution and the energy of a steam engine, General Blunt is a man of action as well as of brains," remarked an enthusiastic supporter. "It is with him 'a word and a blow' with the blow quite likely as the word to come first. Where it may fall the enemy will not know until he receives it—full in the face." Individuals with more delicate sensibilities, such as Reverend Francis Springer, chaplain of the Tenth Illinois Cavalry, were offended by Blunt's animal appetites and ethical lapses. "Though his head is large and well proportioned to a stout chunky body, the manifestations of it in the way of brains are plainly surpassed by the man's love of good eating, intoxicating liquors, and free women." Springer acknowledged Blunt's "fighting pluck" but regarded this as merely another manifestation of his degraded moral condition. "He is not a man of reflection and reason, but only of impulse."[6]

Schofield knew Blunt only by reputation, which was hardly reassuring, but he acted immediately to secure cooperation between Union forces in Missouri and Kansas. "The enemy is advancing in large force with the evident design of attacking Springfield," Schofield telegraphed on 14 September. He

James G. Blunt in 1862 (Kansas State Historical Society)

asked Blunt to send "as large a force as you can spare" to reinforce the Springfield garrison or, better yet, to march there with his entire command. Before Blunt could reply, Schofield complained to Major General Henry W. Halleck, the Union general-in-chief in Washington, that "I can get no valuable assistance from General Blunt." The gratuitous dig at Blunt (a potential competitor for honors and advancement) was a typical underhanded Schofield tactic, but the rest of the message was all business. "I am satisfied that the main body of the rebel army in Arkansas is moving into Southwestern Missouri," Schofield reported. "I expect to go to Springfield in a few days. Shall have there from 10,000 to 12,000 men."[7]

Schofield tended to become excited in a crisis. By mid-September he had magnified Hindman's expeditionary force of 6,000 troops into an army of "probably at least 30,000 men." Schofield also convinced himself that a second Confederate army of equal size was gathering in northeast Arkansas, an army that existed only in his imagination. Not everyone in Missouri agreed with Schofield's alarmist assessment. "The reports are that the whole country is filled with secessionists, [and] that a force of an incalculable number of thousands is marching upon us from the South and West," observed Captain Robert F. Braden of the Twenty-sixth Indiana. "We don't believe a word of it." Schofield, however, was certain the fate of the trans-Mississippi hung in the balance. "Unless something be done soon, I shall lose a large part of Missouri," he predicted. In his overwrought condition Schofield even asked Major General Frederick Steele, commanding the District of Arkansas (the Union enclave at Helena), to help him defeat the phantom Confederate force threatening southeast Missouri. Schofield wanted Steele to rush his command to southeast Missouri or march directly on Little Rock and compel the Rebels to look to their rear. Steele knew nothing about a Confederate army in northeast Arkansas and was not about to abandon Helena or advance on Little Rock without permission from Washington. He properly ignored Schofield.[8]

Schofield finally concluded that he could accomplish nothing more in St. Louis and that it was time to assume personal command of the forces gathering at Springfield. "I shall be ready to advance soon," he informed Halleck, "I believe before the enemy will." On 21 September Schofield boarded a train and departed for southwest Missouri. Meanwhile, Washington was stirring.[9]

HALLECK WAS CONCERNED by the apparent lack of concert among Union commanders in the trans-Mississippi. He decided that a single guiding hand was needed in that vast region and turned to Samuel Curtis, the victor of Pea Ridge. Curtis was an 1831 West Point graduate and a Mexican War veteran who had prospered in civilian life as an engineer, attorney, land speculator, and politician. When the Civil War erupted, Curtis resigned his seat in the House of Representatives and raised the Second Iowa. A few months later he was made a brigadier general and given command of the Army of the Southwest. In a matter of weeks Curtis drove Sterling Price out of Missouri and Earl Van Dorn out of Arkansas. He was promoted to major general in April 1862.[10]

On 19 September Halleck placed Curtis in charge of the reconstituted Department of the Missouri. Stretching from the Mississippi River to the Rocky Mountains, the new department included the districts of Missouri, Kansas, and Arkansas, along with the distant Colorado and Nebraska territories. Other than the creation of a single command structure over this immense region, the only change of note was the downgrading of Kansas from department to district status. Curtis reached St. Louis on 24 September and assumed command. He now was the principal Union commander west of the Mississippi River, a position equivalent to that held by Holmes in Little Rock. Curtis was fifty-seven years old and still feeling the effects of the grueling Pea Ridge campaign. He considered going after the Rebels in person but decided

Samuel R. Curtis in September 1862 (State Historical Society of Missouri, Columbia)

to remain in St. Louis and allow his principal subordinates — Schofield, Blunt, and Steele — to handle matters in the field.[11]

Two hundred miles away in Springfield, Schofield was shocked to learn of the change in command. He professed to be humiliated by his "demotion" and threatened to resign. One of Schofield's less endearing traits was his tendency to assume the role of martyr when things did not go his way. On this occasion he was true to form. "Did I consult my personal feelings, I would not remain in the department a day," he informed Hamilton R. Gamble, the Unionist governor of Missouri. "I am, however, willing to sacrifice my personal feelings and do whatever is best for the country." Schofield had no one but himself to blame for Curtis's appointment. Most of the misleading information Halleck had received about the supposedly desperate state of affairs in the trans-Mississippi had come directly from Schofield.[12]

When Curtis asked for an overview of the military situation, Schofield repeated his belief that two powerful Confederate columns were advancing into Missouri. He assured Curtis that he could hold Springfield "against all the rebels in Arkansas," but warned that he could do nothing to assist Steele. Schofield concluded with the curious assertion that the upsurge in Confederate activity reflected waning fortunes. "Desperate measures are the only ones left to the rebels west of the Mississippi," he declared. Curtis was unconvinced. "General Schofield thinks two large armies are moving on Missouri," he telegraphed Halleck, "but I think he overrates the forces of the enemy." Intelligence sources confirmed, or at least strongly suggested, that Holmes and Hindman were in Little Rock. Curtis thought it unlikely the Rebels would be on the march without their senior commanders. Until he could get a better fix on the situation, he decided his first order of business was to reassert Union control over southwest Missouri.[13]

Schofield continued to insist that he faced up to 30,000 Rebels, but Curtis was skeptical of such an enormous number. "I do not see how Hindman could raise so large a force and subsist it when I stripped the country," he telegraphed Schofield. This was a reference to the devastation Curtis had visited upon northwest Arkansas during the Pea Ridge campaign a few months earlier. Curtis reminded Schofield that the Rebel forces at Fort Smith were in "wretched condition at last accounts" and unlikely to be a threat to anyone. Finally, he pointed out that Hindman was "sharp in deceit and pretenses" and suggested that Schofield had been taken in by a Confederate ploy. The "over-anxious" tone of Schofield's messages disturbed Curtis. He probably had Schofield in mind when he advised Halleck in late September that "I need some older or wiser generals for remote commands."[14]

Whatever the actual size of the Confederate force threatening southwest Missouri, Curtis agreed with Schofield that it was imperative to bring Blunt into the picture as quickly as possible. Blunt was doing his best, despite Schofield's insinuations to the contrary, but an enormous effort was required to launch a large-scale military operation in an embryonic frontier state where railroads were nonexistent and navigable rivers nearly so. It took time and almost all of the wagons, mules, and oxen in Kansas to transfer thousands of men and tons of supplies overland from Fort Leavenworth to Fort Scott, one hundred miles south of Kansas City. The Herculean logistical effort was complicated by an acute scarcity of weapons. "The great draw to my movements now is the want of Infantry," Blunt wrote in mid-September. "Three full regiments of new Kansas Infantry are now rendezvousing waiting for their arms, which I am informed . . . are on the way. As soon as the new regiments are armed I shall leave here with them for a campaign into Dixie and somebody has got to be *whipped*. I only regret that I am loosing too much valuable time." On 23 September Blunt learned that 5,000 rifles and muskets had arrived at Fort Leavenworth. "This is *Glorious news for me*," he exclaimed. Blunt soon informed Curtis that he had 8,000 troops "of the very best material" at Fort Scott prepared to march into southwest Missouri.[15]

Blunt's command was popularly known as the "Kansas Division." It was composed largely of Kansas regiments and batteries but also included units from Indiana, Ohio, Wisconsin, and the Indian Territory. The Kansas Division was the only Union military organization to include substantial numbers of black and Indian soldiers in 1862. The First and Second Kansas Colored had been raised despite Lincoln's initial reluctance to allow blacks to serve in the military. The fugitive slaves from Arkansas and Missouri who filled the ranks were among the first black troops to see action in the Civil War. Blunt had great faith in his "Darkee Regiments" and assigned them the critical task of protecting the mountain of supplies at Fort Scott against Rebel raiders.[16]

The Kansas Division also included the First, Second, and Third Indian Home Guard regiments. All three units were composed of men from various tribes who had been driven out of the Indian Territory by their secessionist brethren. Like their Confederate counterparts, Union Indians usually were issued whatever cast-off equipment was available. The resulting hodgepodge of weapons, uniforms, and accouterments gave the Indian troops a tatty appearance that belied their true capability. "They are a fine-looking set of men, appearing fantastic at times with their mixed uniforms, war paint and tawdry finery," remarked a Kansas officer. "But they make good soldiers." Wives, children, and aged relatives rode behind or walked alongside the combatants, giving a new meaning to the term "camp followers." Blunt assured a dubious Curtis that the Indians were reliable soldiers and took the three regiments with him on the campaign.[17]

Schofield's command was larger but less colorful. It consisted of two provisional divisions taking shape in Springfield. One division was led by Brigadier General James Totten, an 1841 West Point graduate and a veteran of the Mexican and Seminole wars. Totten had decades of regular army experience under his belt and had performed well at Wilson's Creek. Nonetheless, his boorish behavior, fueled by a steady intake of alcohol, made him unpopular with the volunteers under his command. "We don't like him at all," declared the chaplain of the Twentieth Iowa. Schofield spent a good deal of time with Totten during the opening weeks of the campaign and must have found him very hard to take. Nevertheless, Totten was one of only a handful of professional soldiers in the Department of the Missouri and he soon had his troops ready to march.[18]

The other division was commanded by Brigadier General Francis "Frank" J. Herron, a military amateur. The precocious Pennsylvania native had walked away from the University of Pittsburgh at age sixteen convinced that he had learned enough to make his way in the world. Apparently he did, for when the

James Totten (William Schultz Collection, U.S. Army Military History Institute)

war broke out he was a successful banker in Dubuque, Iowa. Herron fought at Wilson's Creek and Pea Ridge. In the latter battle he was seriously wounded and taken prisoner while trying to stem a Confederate attack. His actions earned him a promotion to brigadier general at the age of twenty-five and a Medal of Honor.[19]

Herron was tall and slim with wavy hair and bushy sideburns. He made a favorable impression on his subordinates, most of whom were senior to him in years. "The General is a pleasant, affable and courteous gentleman, and I think well fitted for his command," declared Colonel William W. Orme of the Ninety-fourth Illinois. "He has got more life and energy in him than all the other of the generals together in this army." Lieutenant George W. Root of the Twentieth Wisconsin was equally enthusiastic. "He is a bold dashing officer, a perfect Gentleman, and very popular with this Division. We all like him very much." But an enlisted man in the Nineteenth Iowa noted with a hint of disapproval that Herron was "somewhat a fancy man" who "sports the latest style and no modern hero can eclipse him in dress or its elegance." Reserved in private, dynamic in public, supremely self-assured, and dressed to kill, Herron was a commander right out of central casting.[20]

To Herron's dismay, the troops assigned to his division were slow to arrive and he was left in Springfield when the rest of the army marched off

Francis J. Herron in 1862 (Dave Charles Collection, U.S. Army Military History Institute)

to do battle with the Rebels. After stewing for several days Herron fired off an ill-advised letter to Schofield. "One year and a halfs active service in the very front, calls for something else on my part than the control of a handful of troops at a post like Springfield," he stated. "Feeling that I have not been treated with proper military courtesy in this matter, I must insist upon my *proper position*." The letter was a model of bad timing; an order to march arrived the next morning. Herron tried to recall his missive but it was too late. Two days later he received Schofield's cold reply. "The tone and substance of your letter are such as to forbid any answer on my part other than that I will willingly forward any official communication you may have to make upon the subject." Herron wisely backed down and apologized for his intemperate language. "The fact is this, my being left behind when a movement of the troops was made, created considerable talk, not only at Springfield, but elsewhere, and things were said that gave me good reason to feel sore." Schofield was piqued with Herron (another potential competitor for promotion), but he let the matter drop.[21]

The Missouri Divisions, as Schofield's command came to be known, were composed almost entirely of troops from Illinois, Iowa, Indiana, Missouri, and Wisconsin. The only anomaly was the First Arkansas Cavalry, a newly formed unit filled with Arkansans who had been driven from their homes in the northern part of the state because of their Unionist political beliefs. The "Mountain Feds" held varying opinions about slavery and emancipation but were united by their implacable hostility to the Confederacy. "They are a fierce and reckless set of fellows, made so I presume by miseries they have endured," wrote an Iowa soldier. "Being acquainted with every road and path in the country, and moreover feeling a particular interest in the extermination of these bushwacking gentry, they are making it extremely hot for that class of rebels." The loyal Arkansans proved invaluable as guides, scouts, and counterguerrilla fighters.[22]

As the Federals marched out of Springfield and Fort Scott, they learned that Lincoln intended to issue an emancipation decree on New Year's Day, 1863. The news was met with widespread approval. "The President's proclamation is considered just the thing by all the soldiers," remarked a man in the Nineteenth Iowa. "Everybody is in favor of it," acknowledged Colonel Orme. "The opinion of the army is very radical. They are for confiscation, emancipation, and everything else. You cannot be too ultra for the soldiers." If any dissenting opinions were committed to paper, they have not survived. "The talk that the President will have trouble in the army on account of his righteous proclamation, is all gotten up for home consumption," declared an indignant officer in the First Iowa Cavalry. "The most proslavery men of former times are now among the *most radical.*" On the great issue of the day the Union soldiers massing on the frontier were largely of one mind. They were as close to an army of liberation as existed in the Civil War.[23]

IN HINDMAN'S ABSENCE the Confederate forces in southwest Missouri and northwest Arkansas were commanded by Brigadier General James S. Rains, a Missouri officer conspicuously deficient in military ability. Hindman must have had his doubts about Rains, because before departing for Little Rock on 10 September he ordered Rains "to make no aggressive movement, but if assailed to hold the line occupied as long as practicable." Rains passed the next three weeks at Elkhorn Tavern on the Pea Ridge battlefield playing cards and consuming copious amounts of whiskey. In late September he emerged from his alcoholic stupor long enough to send most of his cavalry to Newtonia, thirty miles north of the Arkansas-Missouri line. Newtonia was described as a "very nice little town beautifully located in an open plain, surrounded by timber and watered by living springs." The plain was "rich in wheat and forage," and a local steam mill did a thriving business. Upon reaching Newtonia the hungry Confederates, man and beast, settled down for some serious eating.[24]

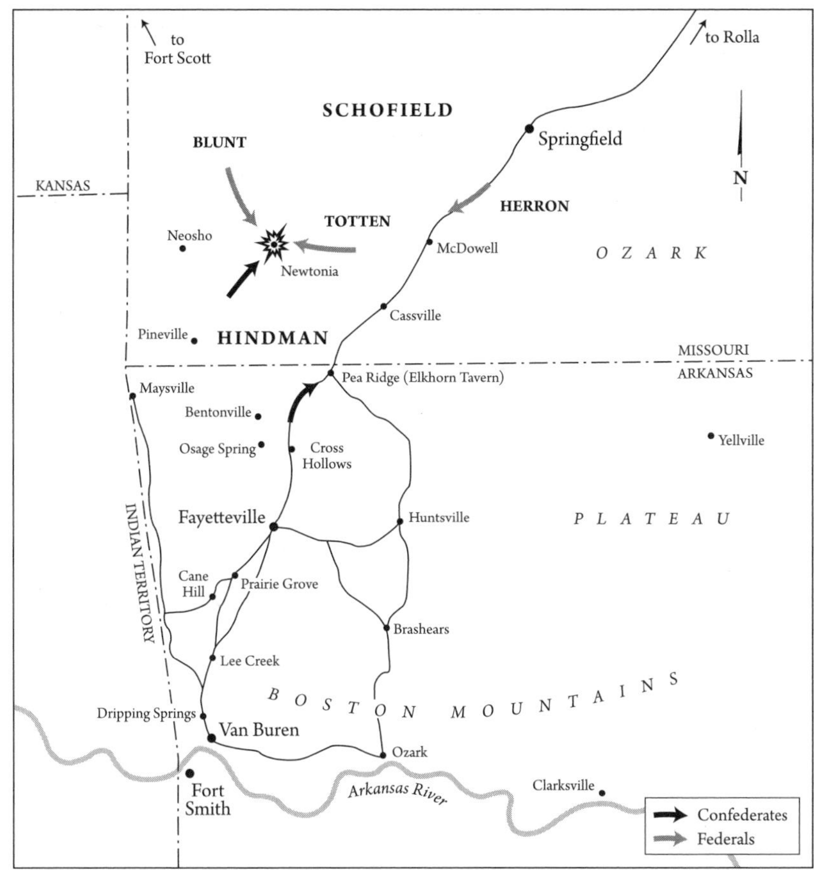

Hindman advances from the Arkansas River but is turned back by Schofield and Blunt at Newtonia.

Unknown to Rains, elements of the Kansas Division had marched out of Fort Scott a week earlier and crossed into southwest Missouri. Blunt had never directed a large-scale operation before, and his advance was slow and disorganized. The confusion was compounded when Schofield and Totten attempted to direct traffic from Springfield. Colonel William Weer, commanding one of Blunt's three brigades, expressed his exasperation: "Whether I shall run, or advance, or do anything desperate, I also do not know, as I have no less than four brigadier-generals giving me orders at the same time." Weer urged Blunt to leave Fort Scott and take the field at once. "One thing I do know, if you or somebody else do not come out here and take command of all these scattered forces we will be cut up in detail." On 30 September, six days after Weer penned his warning, another of Blunt's brigades blundered into the Confederate force at Newtonia and suffered a severe repulse. In the day-long fight nearly 250 Union soldiers in Brigadier General Frederick Salomon's command were killed, wounded, or captured, mostly the last. Rebel losses amounted to barely one-third that number.[25]

The Confederates had only a few days to savor their victory. Blunt and Schofield both hurried to the scene with reinforcements. The converging Union columns reached Newtonia on 4 October and opened an artillery bombardment that threw the Rebels into confusion. A leaderless, disorderly retreat quickly degenerated into a rout. "The men were panic stricken and nothing could be done with them," wrote a Texas cavalryman, "in fact I think the officers were in the forefront." Rains received exaggerated reports of the size of the Union force and ordered a general withdrawal. Morale plummeted as the Confederates trudged back into Arkansas. The Missourians were especially distressed by the abrupt change in their fortunes. "I do not think General Rains competent to command anything," snapped Lieutenant John B. Quesenberry. Rains lamely explained to Hindman that he planned to "await further demonstrations on the part of the enemy" before deciding on his next move, but the simple fact is that he lost his nerve and abandoned the Confederate toehold in Missouri without a fight.[26]

When Schofield learned the Confederates were falling back, he informed Curtis of his intention "to push [Rains] as far and as fast as prudence will justify." Curtis signaled his approval. "Your progress so far is highly commendable," he wrote on 7 October, "and I trust you will soon clear Missouri of the last of the invaders." Although pleased with Schofield's progress, as the days passed Curtis began to worry that the Federals might outrun their supplies. "Do not be drawn down too far," he cautioned Schofield. Curtis also fretted about the weather atop the Ozark Plateau and reminded Schofield that "we cannot keep a large army there during the winter." Schofield was annoyed at receiving unsolicited advice from someone he regarded as a usurper, but he dutifully kept Curtis apprised of logistical developments and meteorological conditions ("Weather warm").[27]

Schofield shifted his command eastward to Telegraph Road (also known as Wire Road), the principal north-south thoroughfare in the region. The road linked Springfield with Fayetteville and Fort Smith and served as a made-to-order avenue of invasion. Three days of steady rain finally broke the drought but brought Federal operations to a standstill. "Awful wet and muddy, cold and chilly," recorded an Ohio cavalryman. "Every mile wagons were in to the hubs in mud." Nevertheless, by mid-October the entire Union force was in column on Telegraph Road south of Springfield. Blunt's division was in the lead at Keetsville, only eight miles from the Arkansas-Missouri line. Totten's division occupied Cassville, seven miles farther north. Bringing up the rear at Crane Creek, another twenty-six miles to the north, was Herron's small division. Scouts reported no Confederate force of any size north of the state line.[28]

"We have driven the enemy from Missouri," Schofield announced with a mixture of pride and relief. Buoyed by his unexpectedly easy success, Schofield halved his estimate of Confederate strength from 30,000 to 15,000 men and requested permission to pursue Rains into Arkansas. "I have no doubt of my ability to whip him wherever he may stand this side of the [Boston] mountains," he told Curtis. This upbeat declaration was a far cry from Schofield's recent predictions of disaster, but Curtis wisely refrained from making any pointed remarks. Sensing that Schofield's newfound confidence was fragile, Curtis showered congratulations on his mercurial subordinate and authorized him to proceed. The news spread rapidly through the ranks. "We are at last on our way to Arkansas," exclaimed an Indiana soldier.[29]

With Schofield poised to invade the Confederacy, Curtis realized the time had come to reorganize Union forces in southwest Missouri and establish clear lines of authority. On 12 October he created the Army of the Frontier and placed Schofield in command. Blunt's force became the First Division, Totten's the Second Division, and Herron's the Third Division, though nearly everyone continued to use Kansas Division and Missouri Divisions in place of the official designations. The army consisted of nearly 20,000 troops on paper, but so many were sick, on leave, or on escort or occupation duty that Schofield probably had no more than 14,000 men with him in the field.[30]

The Army of the Frontier entered the Confederacy on 17 October. Regimental bands played patriotic and popular airs, but the occasion was marred by a minor mutiny. Soldiers in the Seventh Missouri Cavalry claimed that the terms of their enlistment prevented them from serving outside their home state and "most emphatically refused to go any farther." Colonel Daniel Huston appealed to his men "in the name of God and patriotism and the state of Missouri" to do their duty, but his impassioned oratory left a hard core of mutineers unmoved. Words having failed, four companies of the Twentieth Wisconsin were called upon to make a more pointed argument with their bayonets. All but one of the mutineers quickly "withdrew their objections" to serving in Arkansas, and the march resumed.[31]

Blunt and Totten continued south on Telegraph Road and halted on the Pea Ridge battlefield, four miles south of the Arkansas-Missouri line. When Herron arrived the next day, the Army of the Frontier was united for the only time in the campaign prior to the battle of Prairie Grove. Schofield established his headquarters in Elkhorn Tavern, only recently vacated by Rains. The two-story structure had been the focal point of two days of intense fighting the previous spring. "The old tavern itself is a dreary picture enough," noted an Iowa cavalryman. "A cannon ball or two made several breaches in the logs, and numerous rifle balls imbedded in its side gave evidence of the struggle that raged around it." Blunt, Totten, and Herron stayed with their respective commands. Life under canvas for general officers was far from primitive, even on the frontier. A soldier who visited Herron's tent jotted down a few observations in his diary: "Very pleasant. Stylish. A fur coverlet, neat stove and desk, cigars and very fine dress."[32]

The Federals remained at Pea Ridge for three days in order to bring up reinforcements and supplies and scout the country to the south. Confederate stragglers and deserters were everywhere. "The woods are full of rebles," observed an Iowan. "The Cavalry are bringing them in by the squad." Union soldiers wandered over the battlefield and gawked at the destruction. "Large trees a foot and a half and three feet through are found with holes cut clear through them and in some instances cut entirely off," marveled a man in the Eleventh Kansas. "The bullets fell in places like hail for even the smallest bushes and shrubs are all cut to pieces." Blunt lamented the missed opportunity to inflict even more violence on the landscape. "I only wish that the Rebel Army that is now trying to escape from us had made another stand here, that we might have fought the Second Battle of Pea Ridge. Notwithstanding the superiority of numbers we would have *gobbled them up clean*."[33]

Herron led his staff to the spot south of Elkhorn Tavern where he had been wounded and captured the previous March. "We found the bones of General Herron's horse just where he fell," recorded one officer. The battlefield was littered with animal bones and dotted with individual graves and burial trenches. The scene made a deep impression on Sergeant Benjamin F. McIntyre of the Nineteenth Iowa: "We rest on sacred soil, made so by a patriots blood—holy soil—for beneath it sleep martyrs who sacrificed their lives for their countrys good." Contemplating a row of Union graves only a few steps from the tavern, an officer in the First Iowa Cavalry used language prescient of Lincoln's Gettysburg Address—still a year in the future—to describe his feelings. "Their silent graves strewn over the field speak volumes to the living, and admonish us that we *see to it* that they died not in vain on that fatal day."[34]

Many soldiers took advantage of their stay at Pea Ridge to inform the folks back home of the progress of the campaign. In the two weeks since

Newtonia, the Army of the Frontier had moved from the Springfield Plain to the edge of the White River Valley. Midwesterners found the eroded jumble of hills and hollows difficult to portray and impossible to appreciate. "I would like to describe this country to you but it is so brushy and hilly and rocky and springy and creeky and so unlike what I had supposed to be Dixie that I can't for the life of me do any better than I have done," wrote Samuel Worthington of the Eleventh Kansas to his father. Captain Edmund G. Ross of the same regiment was more succinct. He told his wife that "this is the most miserable country I ever saw."[35]

The Federals also were nonplussed by the hardscrabble way of life they encountered. "We are now among Arkansas people and find some rough specimens of humanity," wrote Lieutenant William J. Steele, Twentieth Iowa. "The people are the off-shoots of the old pioneers, a hardy race, but deeply sunk in ignorance," remarked an officer on Schofield's staff. "Even the wealthier farmers are too illiterate to read anything except a Methodist newspaper." A member of Herron's staff was even less generous: "They are a tough set of people down here, and usually belong to the Ignorami." Additional details came from a soldier in the Ninety-fourth Illinois: "There are no schools here, no churches, no preachers, and civil life is but one step from barbarism." He concluded uncharitably that the region was a "thousand years behind Illinois." Captain Edward G. Miller, Twentieth Wisconsin, was not particularly disturbed by the absence of preachers, but he was sorely disappointed by the scarcity of attractive females. "Didn't see a good looking woman on the whole trip," he noted. A man in the Eleventh Kansas wrote: "It is the general sentiment of the soldiers that the country is not worth fighting for."[36]

The passage of armies during the Wilson's Creek and Pea Ridge campaigns and the breakdown of order that followed had devastated and depopulated large swatches of countryside along Telegraph Road. This was a matter of concern to every Union soldier in the Army of the Frontier from the commanding general down to the lowliest private. Civil War armies depended on foraging—officially sanctioned theft—to supplement regular means of supply, particularly when in the enemy's country, but the region had been ravaged by soldiers, guerrillas, and brigands for eighteen months and was in a sorry state. Damage wrought by man had been compounded by the drought. "I have seen ruin, waste and desolation before," wrote an Iowa cavalryman, "but never where it was so utter, complete, and without any saving feature as in Northwestern Arkansas and Southwestern Missouri." Abandoned homes, overgrown fields, and withered crops meant empty smokehouses and corn cribs. Foraging was of limited use when there was little to steal.[37]

"Now we commenced soldiering in right good earnest," observed Captain Miller. Short rations and missed meals became routine despite the best efforts of hard-pressed commissary officers. "A hard march with plenty to eat is bad enough but to march and starve is decidedly hard work," wrote one soldier. Unappealing military rations made even the most commonplace examples of home cooking seem like delicacies. "I would give most any thing for a little piece of corn bread and butter," declared a man in the Eleventh Kansas. "I have not tasted any for scarcely two months." Food, or the lack of it, was not the only problem. Clothing and equipment wore out faster than anticipated. A soldier in the Twentieth Iowa noted that "shoes furnished by the Government were good for nothing, for the purpose of marching over the sharp stones of Arkansas." He added that the "socks are equally worthless. They can't be wore a week without being out at the toes, and the heels too." As uniforms grew ragged the Federals acquired the look of veteran campaigners. A man in the Twenty-sixth Indiana reported that "we are more shabby in appearance now than at any previous time." Shortages of clothing were a matter of concern with winter approaching. Forsaking official channels, soldiers pleaded with family and friends to send everything from underwear to overcoats.[38]

Colonel Orme of the Ninety-fourth Illinois recognized the fundamental problem. "The farther the army moves, the more gigantic the scale on which trains must be kept up." A typical commissary train of two hundred wagons laden with food, forage, clothing, ammunition, and other necessities was on the road for up to four weeks, and at any given time a half-dozen such trains were in motion between railheads and river ports and the distant army in the field. The unending effort wore down animals and equipment and consumed enormous amounts of money, manpower, and material. From Illinois to Kansas and from Minnesota to Missouri, a multitude of soldiers and civilians, wheelwrights and harness makers, blacksmiths and coopers, teamsters and longshoremen, clerks and accountants struggled to keep the stores moving forward. "It is an immense task," marveled Orme.[39]

The Army of the Frontier relied on two lines of communications, one in Kansas, the other in Missouri. The Fort Leavenworth–Kansas City–Fort Scott line kept Blunt's division in the field, while the St. Louis–Rolla–Springfield line sustained Totten's and Herron's divisions. The ever-lengthening lines were extremely vulnerable. "A daring raid at any time would succeed in destroying vast amounts of stores along the roads," Orme fretted. The loss of tons of supplies would be bad enough, but the loss of the hundreds of wagons and thousands of animals that made up a single train might bring the campaign to a halt. To prevent such a calamity, a dozen cavalry and infantry regiments and scores of militia companies guarded depots and escorted trains on their endless circuits. "On an open prairie, where an enemy could be seen and easily kept away, the caravan could make its allotted ten miles in a day without hardship," wrote Albert R. Greene, Ninth Kansas Cavalry. "But in a wooded country, cut up with streams and featured by canyons and passes and rocky defiles, it was a far more difficult proposition. Every foot of that road must be scouted and inspected and combed over for a lurking enemy . . . and flankers must be stationed all along the route before the first wagon could be allowed to pass." Greene did not think the tedium and difficulty of escort duty were fully appreciated. "It is a hard service and there's precious little of the pomp and circumstance of war about it, but it's the only way to get food and supplies to an army with a base several hundred miles in the rear."[40]

No one knew how far the Union lines of communications would stretch, but they already seemed close to the breaking point as the Army of the Frontier tramped into Arkansas.

3 RETURN TO ARKANSAS

WHILE THE FEDERALS EXPLORED PEA RIDGE, THE DISPIRITED CONfederates passed the time at Cross Hollows and Elm Springs, a day's march to the south and southwest. Rains was out of ideas and under mounting criticism for falling back so far and so fast. Anxious to retrieve the situation before Hindman returned, he held a council of war. One of the officers present was Colonel Douglas H. Cooper, a hard-drinking Mexican War veteran who had raised the First Choctaw and Chickasaw Mounted Rifles at the outbreak of the war. Cooper was superintendent of Indian Affairs and de facto commander of Confederate forces in the Indian Territory. When Rains asked for suggestions, Cooper proposed that the Confederates attack Fort Scott.[1]

Cooper believed that Blunt's line of communications was vulnerable and that the weak link was the isolated depot at Fort Scott. If the Confederates overran Fort Scott and destroyed the stores intended for the Kansas Division, Blunt would have to retire. Without Blunt, Schofield most likely would fall back to Springfield. Cooper argued that his loosely organized but highly mobile force of Indians, Arkansans, Missourians, and Texans could do the job. Rains was impressed and authorized Cooper to proceed, but on the condition that he leave his four Texas cavalry regiments in Arkansas. Cooper protested the loss of nearly half his strength but Rains refused to budge. On 15 October Cooper and his much-reduced force headed west. Rains and the main body moved in the opposite direction, apparently in the hope of distracting or confusing Schofield. Rains crossed the White River and halted at Huntsville, thirty miles southeast of Pea Ridge. The orphaned Texans remained at Cross Hollows a few days longer to maintain the illusion that the Confederates were still on Telegraph Road.[2]

Rankled at the loss of his Texans, Cooper stopped in the Indian Territory to gather reinforcements before pushing on to Kansas. He called on every soldier in the Five Civilized Tribes to join him at Old Fort Wayne, an abandoned military post three miles southwest of Maysville. Two days later the only organized force to make an appearance was Colonel Stand Watie's battalion-size First Cherokee. Disappointed, Cooper put the Fort Scott raid on hold. He later explained that he was "compelled to stop until I could collect my scattered Indian forces—always difficult, but now rendered almost impossible."[3]

Confederate Indians were organized into an impressive array of regiments and battalions, but they were essentially an ill-disciplined militia. Officers obeyed orders when it suited them, and soldiers came and went as they pleased. By the fall of 1862 most Indians were tired of the war, which had brought only misery to the Indian Territory, and many were beginning to have doubts about the future of the Confederacy. Nearly all lacked tents, blankets, and heavy clothing and were wary of being caught in the open by an early winter storm. Cooper got along famously with Indians, but on this occasion he failed to comprehend the lack of enthusiasm among his charges. "I sent them order after order to come together," he told Hindman, but the "tardiness of some of the troops and disobedience of orders by others proved fatal to the command and defeated the expedition upon which we had started." Appeals to pride and promises of plunder were equally futile. Cooper fell ill and took to his bed. After several days of inactivity he finally ordered Watie to proceed to Fort Scott with whatever force was available, but before anything could be done word arrived that a Union column was fast approaching from Arkansas.[4]

The Army of the Frontier remained at Pea Ridge from 17 to 20 October. Schofield and Blunt spent much of that time at Elkhorn Tavern planning the next phase of the campaign. Blunt urged Schofield to keep the pressure on Rains and not allow him to regain the initiative. Schofield needed little encouragement. He wanted to bring the Confederates to battle, possibly at Cross Hollows, but his plans went out the window when he learned that Rains and Cooper had parted company and moved in opposite directions. Schofield was puzzled by this unorthodox development, but after talking things over with Blunt he decided to emulate the Rebels and divide his command. Blunt and the Kansas Division would pursue Cooper; Schofield and the Missouri Divisions would go after Rains.[5]

To steal a march on the elusive Rebels, the Federals waited for darkness on 20 October. Shortly after sunset Blunt led two-thirds of his division toward the Indian Territory. His immediate command consisted of Colonel William Weer's Second Brigade, Colonel William F. Cloud's Third Brigade, and a half-

Douglas H. Cooper
(Massachusetts Commandery,
U.S. Army Military History Institute)

dozen ambulances packed with ammunition and medical stores. Salomon's First Brigade remained at Pea Ridge to protect the army's trains. (Salomon was in Blunt's doghouse because of his lackluster performance at Newtonia. He spent most of the campaign in the rear.) Soldiers carried arms, ammunition, blankets, and as much food as they could stuff into haversacks, saddlebags, and pockets. As was his custom, Blunt rode near the head of the column in a carriage accompanied by an escort and preceded by a bevy of scouts. There was no moon and the Federals made their way down the winding valley of Little Sugar Creek in near total darkness. Two or three hours after midnight they halted on Little Osage Creek south of Bentonville. At some point during the tedious twelve-mile trek, a fifteen-year-old drummer boy in the Nineteenth Iowa named William Cunningham stumbled out of the column and fell asleep by the side of the road. Cherokees from the Third Indian found Cunningham the next morning and delivered him to the Tenth Kansas, where he was dubbed the "Arkansaw Traveler" and made the regimental mascot until he could be returned to his unit.[6]

The Kansas Division spent the morning and afternoon of 21 October resting along the banks of the Little Osage. Toward evening, scouts brought word that Cooper was camped at Old Fort Wayne. Blunt was delighted. He decided to make another night march and fall upon the Confederates at first light.

After sunset the Federals resumed their westward movement through a maze of ravines cut by the headwaters of Spavinaw Creek. Eight hours and fourteen miles later Blunt stopped on a broad grassland called Beaty's Prairie. It was well after midnight. "The men were weary and exhausted, and no sooner were they halted than they dropped down in the brush by the roadside and were soon fast asleep," Blunt reported. The night was cold and windy, but the Federals did without tents or campfires.[7]

At 4:00 A.M. on 22 October, Blunt awakened the nearest troops as quietly as possible for fear that the sound of drums and bugles would carry in the chill air. He then set out for the Indian Territory, confident that the Second and Third Brigades were following close behind. Blunt's sensible precaution against alerting the enemy backfired. Something went wrong and the Second Kansas Cavalry—the leading regiment in the column—was the only unit that got the word to march. Lieutenant Colonel Owen A. Bassett's troopers saddled up with a minimum of fuss and hurried after Blunt. The rest of the Kansas Division continued to slumber, blissfully unaware that their inattentive commander had rushed off without them.[8]

In his enthusiasm to close with the enemy, Blunt was oblivious to what was happening—or not happening—behind him. The small Union force clattered through Maysville (a "very insignificant little nest," sniffed one soldier) and stopped just inside the Indian Territory. "It was now near 5 o'clock," Blunt recalled, "and my desire was to attack at daylight." But when dawn broke Blunt looked over his shoulder and discovered that he was accompanied by fewer than 550 men. Momentarily flustered, Blunt sent an officer to bring up the rest of the division. Then, to everyone's astonishment, he drew his pistol and continued forward. "Gallop, was the order," recalled a flabbergasted Kansas trooper.[9]

Despite his best efforts, Blunt failed to achieve surprise. Confederate pickets spotted the approaching Union force near Maysville and informed Cooper. The Confederate commander squandered the better part of an hour before deciding to withdraw to Tahlequah, thirty-three miles to the southwest. The delay nearly proved fatal. As Cooper departed in an ambulance, he directed Lieutenant Colonel Michael W. Buster to cover the withdrawal of the train, which contained the entire supply of ammunition for Confederate forces in the Indian Territory. Buster formed the troops at hand into a makeshift rear guard and waited. The slow-moving wagons had barely cleared the camp when Blunt and the Second Kansas Cavalry came into sight. There was nothing for Buster to do but attempt to delay the Federals long enough for the train to escape.[10]

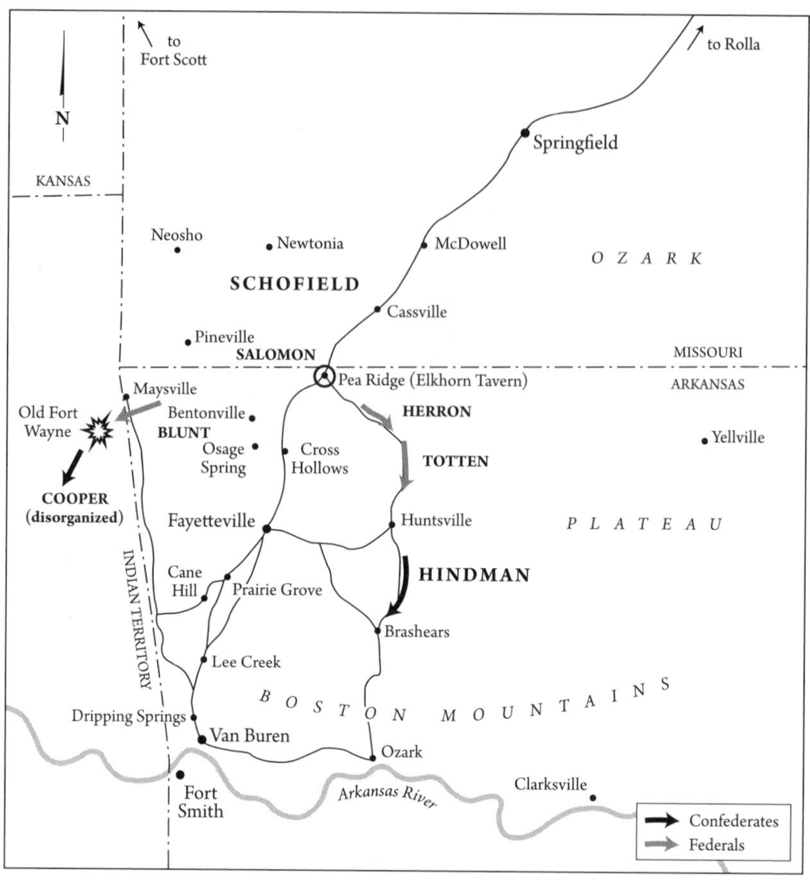

Blunt strikes Cooper at Old Fort Wayne while Schofield forces Hindman out of Huntsville.

The battlefield was a funnel-shaped extension of Beaty's Prairie. Densely wooded ravines cut by Beaty's Creek to the north and Hog Eye Creek to the south protected the Confederate flanks and rear, but the broad or open end of the funnel pointed northeast toward Maysville and provided a perfect avenue of approach for the Federals. Buster deployed his troops across a slightly narrowed section of the funnel. Captain Sylvanus Howell's Texas Battery (commanded that day by Lieutenant William A. Routh) was in the center, Buster's Battalion (an odd mix of Arkansas and Missouri infantry and cavalry) was on the left, and a battalion of Lieutenant Colonel Simpson N. Folsom's First Choctaw was on the right. Major Joel M. Bryan's Cherokee Battalion and several smaller units guarded the flanks. Watie's First Cherokee and Lieutenant Colonel Chilly McIntosh's Creek Battalion reached the field after the shooting started. They formed on Buster's left and extended the line to the trees along Beaty's Creek. The Confederate force consisted of about 250 Arkansans, Missourians, and Texans and between 1,200 and 1,400 Indians, an assortment of Choctaws, Cherokees, and Creeks.[11]

Despite being outnumbered three to one, Blunt engaged the Confederates in hopes of fixing them in place until the rest of the Kansas Division arrived. He directed Bassett to dismount his troopers and form a line opposite the Rebel center. Bassett's Kansans were well suited to the task at hand. They were armed with rifles and were really mounted infantry rather than cavalry. Blunt placed Lieutenant Elias S. Stover's Second Kansas Cavalry Battery near the trees on the right. Stover opened fire with his two 12-pounder mountain howitzers and the Texas artillerymen replied with their three 6-pounder guns. (For some reason, Routh did not bring his own mountain howitzer into action.) A Union soldier noted that the Confederate gunners "commenced blazing away at them industriously." Within a short time, however, several Texans were struck down by fragments from Union shells, and their rate of fire fell off. While the artillery dueled, Bassett advanced his dismounted cavalrymen through a sea of tall yellow grass dotted with clumps of crimson sumac. The chest-high vegetation shielded the Kansans and allowed them to get within one hundred yards of the Confederate line without suffering any losses. The Union cavalrymen found themselves in possession of the only elevated ground on the battlefield: a gentle rise twenty-five to thirty feet high. The Kansans lay down atop the rise and exchanged shots with the Confederates. Some troopers were so exhausted by the rigors of the march from Pea Ridge that they fell asleep, rifles in hand.[12]

Bassett was outnumbered and both of his flanks were exposed. Had the Confederates swept forward they could have enveloped the smaller Union force, but Buster never wavered from his decision to stand fast and buy time for the train. Buster was looking directly into the glare of the rising sun and may not have realized that he enjoyed a numerical advantage. The brief window of opportunity closed when Colonel William R. Judson's Sixth Kansas Cavalry and Colonel William A. Phillips's Third Indian reached the field and deployed to either side of the Second Kansas Cavalry. The opposing forces now were roughly equal in numbers, but the sound of bugles and drums from the direction of Maysville indicated that more Federals were approaching.[13]

Captain Samuel J. Crawford commanded five dismounted companies of the Second Kansas Cavalry on the rise in the center of the Union line. Unable to contain himself any longer, Crawford bellowed for his men to charge. The 250 Kansans got to their feet and rushed down the gentle slope shrieking at the top of their lungs. "The men went at it with a yell, and never halted for

Elias S. Stover (Kansas State Historical Society)

an instant, until they had surrounded the guns," reported another officer. "It was charge and yell," an exhilarated participant recalled. "A thousand Indians could not have set up a louder one."[14]

Crawford's unorthodox maneuver took the Confederates by surprise. The rattled Texas gunners switched from shell to canister but failed to lower their sights before firing. "The enemy shot over us or else we would have been mowed down like grass," wrote a Union cavalryman. Buster was no stranger to close-quarter combat—at Wilson's Creek he had been pinned to the ground by a bayonet—but his men were made of lesser stuff. They abandoned their guns in the face of the Union charge. Buster's Battalion and Folsom's First Choctaw joined the stampede to the rear. An amazed Kansas trooper wrote that the Confederates "broke and run for dear life." Another Kansan related that he and the men around him were "almost wild with excitement on capturing the pieces" and could barely be restrained from pursuing the fleeing Rebels on foot. A Union officer aptly summed up the charge as "sudden, energetic, and successful."[15]

Blunt remained near Stover's howitzers on the Union right throughout the engagement. He was surprised to see Crawford's battalion advance without orders and even more surprised to see the Confederate line disintegrate at the first blow. "The battle was now won," he reported, "and the enemy began flee-

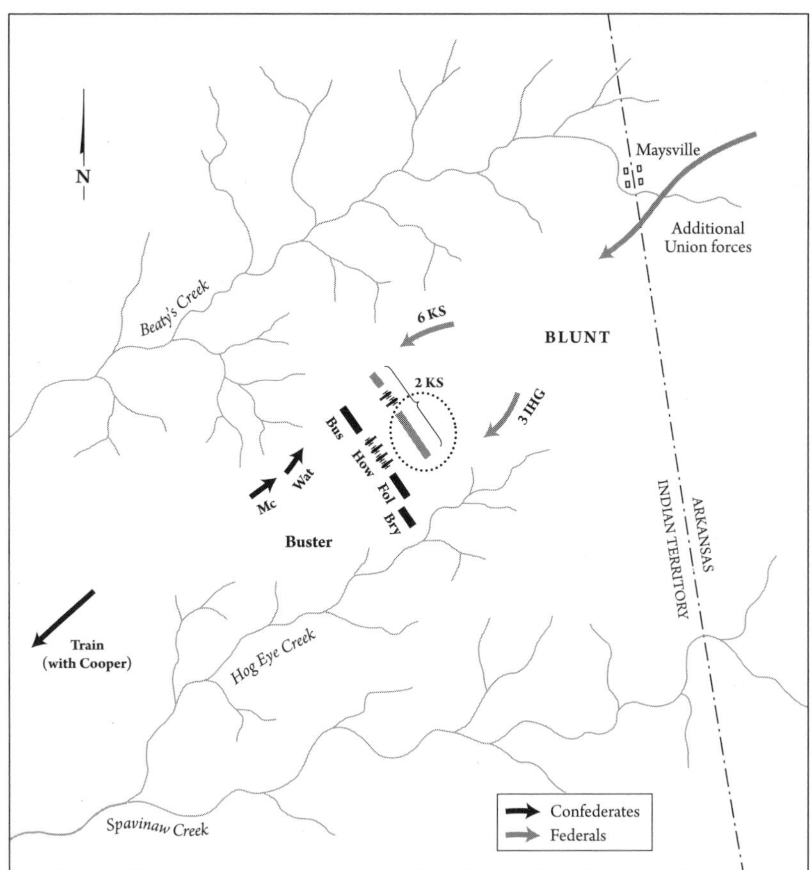

Old Fort Wayne

ing in disorder before our victorious troops." On the Confederate left, Watie's Cherokees and McIntosh's Creeks skirmished briefly with the Third Indian, but after the center of the line gave way they, too, departed in haste. As Confederates streamed away to the southwest on foot and on horseback, Captain John W. Rabb's Second Indiana Battery of four 6-pounder James rifles and two 6-pounder guns arrived on the scene and opened fire. The shriek of conical shells hastened the Rebel retreat and inflicted a few final casualties. Union infantry regiments approached the battlefield at a "pretty fast jog," recalled one winded soldier, but arrived too late to pitch in. From start to finish, the engagement at Old Fort Wayne lasted only twenty-one minutes.[16]

Blunt did his best to turn the disorderly retreat into a rout. The Sixth Kansas Cavalry and Third Indian followed the Confederates for several miles, but Cooper and the ammunition train crossed Spavinaw Creek and got away.

The pursuit was ineffective because the horses were "very tired and worn down" after the long dash to the battlefield. When the fighting sputtered out, hungry Union soldiers flocked to the Confederate camp where they found breakfast fires burning and bacon and biscuits ready to eat, if a trifle scorched. After filling their stomachs the Federals confiscated piles of "camp and garrison equipage as well as large quantities of stores of every description," material that Cooper's threadbare command could ill afford to lose.[17]

The officers and men of the Kansas Division were pleased with Blunt's hard-driving and hard-hitting approach. "The General is proving himself one of the ablest military men in the field," enthused a Union officer. "He pitches into the enemy where ever he finds them." The small number of Union casualties contributed to the widespread sense of satisfaction. Five troopers in the Second Kansas Cavalry were killed and five wounded in the charge. Blunt awarded the captured artillery to Bassett's regiment, where it was proudly dubbed the "Trophy Battery." Confederate losses were substantially greater. Incomplete returns listed sixty-three casualties: three men killed, twenty-five wounded, and thirty-five missing. Given the dismal state of Confederate record keeping in the Indian Territory, actual losses may have been closer to one hundred. A third of all Confederate casualties occurred in Howell's Battery, the smallest unit on the field. Cooper reported that "scarcely a man of the artillery company escaped without a wound or bullet-holes through his clothing." Captured Rebels were of considerable interest to the Federals, one of whom observed that the "cadaverous appearance of the prisoners we take speaks of a wretchedness unknown in our ranks."[18]

The performance of the Third Indian and of Union Indians in general did not go unnoticed. Sergeant Eli H. Gregg of the Tenth Kansas informed his hometown newspaper that the Indians were "doing a good deal of good work. They are invaluable as scouts and are by no means slow in a fight." Gregg observed that the loyal Cherokees bore a grudge against their secessionist brethren: "They hate the rebel Cherokees with a hatred that can only be appeased by blood. Stand Waitee's band is particularly obnoxious to them and they kill every one they get hold of." In the Indian Territory, as elsewhere, the Civil War provided an opportunity to settle scores.[19]

Opinions differed as to the behavior of the Confederate Indians at Old Fort Wayne. Buster placed the blame for the rout squarely on Folsom's Choctaws. "My little handful of [Arkansas and Missouri] infantry stood to the last, which I cannot say of the mounted men," he informed Cooper. Buster added that many Indians "never fired a gun," a statement that certainly corresponds with the small number of Federal casualties. Cooper was a friend of the Choctaws, and he did not allow Buster's slights to go unchallenged. Though not present at the battle, Cooper insisted that Folsom's troops gave way only after Buster's men had fallen back and Howell's Battery had been captured. Both Cooper and Buster praised Watie, despite his tardy appearance on the field, for bolstering the Confederate left flank, but it appears that Watie's principal contribution was to cover the flight of Buster's command.[20]

The disaster at Old Fort Wayne left Hindman perplexed and angry. As he confided to Holmes, "It is difficult to understand how Colonel Cooper could have been anywhere near Maysville on the day given, and still more so to believe that any sane man could have been surprised in that open country." At Hindman's request, Colonel Emmett MacDonald interviewed participants and submitted an unofficial report on the battle. "Our troops did but little fighting," MacDonald concluded. "Almost at the very onset the artillerymen abandoned their guns and [Buster's Battalion] gave back in disorder and confusion." Because MacDonald was a Missourian, his conclusion that white soldiers (many of them Missourians) gave way first seems to have the virtue of objectivity. When Hindman learned that Buster's troops had "wandered off in every direction" after the battle, he ordered the provost marshal at Fort Smith to arrest the "straggling officers and men" and "take the most energetic and prompt measures to collect the battalion again." He later ordered the battalion dissolved.[21]

The Confederate Indians also were in disarray after the debacle. From his new camp on the south side of the Arkansas River, fifty-three miles from Old Fort Wayne, Cooper finally acknowledged that his command had serious problems. He informed Hindman that the Indians "are in a destitute condition—barefooted and nearly naked. They feel that they have been abandoned by their white brethren and some regiments are almost demoralized." This marked a complete reversal for Cooper. A few days earlier he had assured Rains that the Indians could capture Fort Scott with only a modest degree of support from white troops. Now he warned Hindman that "you must not depend on them."[22]

Although the battle at Old Fort Wayne was a small affair, it had important strategic consequences. The Union victory secured Blunt's line of communications and gravely weakened Confederate power and prestige in the Indian Territory. It encouraged loyal Indians and demoralized secessionist Indians, many of whom switched sides and enrolled in Blunt's swelling Home Guard regiments. A Union wag hit the mark when he observed that the Rebels departed the battlefield with "their sensibilities and zeal in the Southern cause considerably *Blunted*. Forgive the expression."[23]

HINDMAN WAS STUCK in Little Rock from mid-September to mid-October. He persuaded Holmes to let him return to his command only after stories began to circulate in the Arkansas capital that Confederate fortunes in Missouri had taken a turn for the worst. On 10 October Hindman once again boarded a steamboat for Fort Smith. As the stern-wheeler made its way up the Arkansas River, tales of disaster grew more disturbing at every stop. Hindman reported "much confusion and no little alarm among the people—all sorts of reports in circulation." When he stepped ashore at Fort Smith five days later, his fears were confirmed. Rains had indeed fallen back into Arkansas—exactly how far no one in Fort Smith could say—and much of the territory gained in September had been lost.[24]

Dismayed at this reversal of fortune, Hindman resolved to retrieve the situation. "I shall, if it is at all practicable, resume immediately the line from which General Rains has retired," he advised Holmes. "We must hold that line, or else abandon all the country north of the Arkansas River." Hindman set out across the Boston Mountains and finally located Rains in Huntsville. A tense meeting ensued in which Rains explained that Schofield and Blunt had joined forces at Newtonia and compelled him to abandon southwest Missouri. Rains pointed out that while he had given up a lot of ground, he had brought out thousands of Missouri recruits and authorized a raid deep into Kansas.[25]

Hindman was pleased to learn of the impending attack on Fort Scott, but he wanted to do more than merely disrupt Blunt's supply line. He sent a courier racing after Cooper with orders "to make such an inroad into Kansas as will eternally be remembered, to utterly lay waste and destroy the country, making it a desert in which neither man nor beast can subsist." Hindman viewed Kansas as a base for pillaging expeditions into Missouri and the Indian Territory. He authorized Cooper to summarily execute Unionist Indians, Unionist irregulars, and any Federal soldiers found in their company. "They have proved themselves devoid of all human feeling, and are entitled to no mercy at our hands," he explained. (This from the man who only a few months earlier had authorized the formation of the infamous "partisan ranger" bands that murdered hundreds, probably thousands, of civilians and terrorized three states!) Hindman's directive was extreme even by the brutal standards of warfare in the trans-Mississippi; it was fortunate for all concerned that Cooper did not have an opportunity to put it into effect.[26]

The meeting with Rains must have convinced Hindman that things were not as bad as they seemed, because immediately afterward he announced that he "intended very soon to resume offensive operations." Hindman ordered Mosby Parsons to move his Missouri infantry brigade from Yellville to Huntsville as soon as possible, and he urged Holmes to send an Arkansas infantry division and two batteries from Little Rock. He also asked Holmes to provide 4,000 rifles and all the hard bread that he could spare. Hindman explained that he only needed enough men, arms, and supplies to get back to the granary of southwest Missouri. "Afterwards, I can take care of myself." But until help and hardtack arrived, Hindman would have to hold his ground. Schofield and Blunt were reported to be at Pea Ridge, just south of the state line. It was imperative that the Confederates prevent the Federals from pushing any deeper into Arkansas. Hindman informed his subordinates that they were "not to yield an inch without fighting and unless actually driven by superior force."[27]

Within twenty-four hours, however, Hindman concluded that a renewed offensive was out of the question. After six weeks of active campaigning the Confederates were in desperate straits. Ammunition, clothing, shoes, and other essentials were in short supply, but the most pressing problem was food. The mountainous countryside around Huntsville provided little in the way of sustenance for man and beast. Thousands of ravenous troops and animals quickly consumed the small stocks of poultry, hogs, cattle, grains, and forage in the vicinity, much to the horror of local residents who faced the prospect of winter with empty larders and smokehouses.

Not only was an immediate return to Missouri out of the question, it was not at all certain the Confederates could maintain their present position. "To enable me to stay north of the mountains," Hindman informed Holmes, "it is indispensably necessary to supply me with subsistence stores from below. I will barely be able to find forage." Not content with badgering Holmes, Hindman communicated directly with Major John C. Palmer, chief quartermaster of the Trans-Mississippi Department, and ordered him to send "with the least possible delay, by boat and by wagon, the largest quantity of supplies especially *hard bread*. This country is almost exhausted of provisions, winter is fast approaching, and it is of the greatest importance that supplies for this army should be at once provided." It was anyone's guess whether the rickety Confederate logistical system could sustain thousands of men and animals atop the Ozark Plateau. Thanks to Van Dorn, the Confederate trans-Mississippi lacked not only mules, wagons, and harnesses, but also barrels, boxes, sacks, tarpaulins, ropes, and everything else necessary to store and ship supplies. Low water in the Arkansas River could not be blamed on Van Dorn, but it contributed to the logistical nightmare.[28]

At this critical moment Confederate scouts brought alarming news: the

Union force at Pea Ridge was advancing on Huntsville. Hindman was a realist. Despite his recent directive "not to yield an inch without fighting," he knew perfectly well that his small command was unprepared for a major battle. On 21–22 October the Confederates evacuated Huntsville and fell back to Brashears, twenty-four miles to the southwest on the East Fork of the White River. The isolated hamlet was located in the heart of the Boston Mountains, but not everyone was impressed by the rugged scenery. "This is a truly godforsaken country if there is such a country in the world," grumbled a Missouri officer. Hindman established his headquarters on War Eagle Creek, eight miles closer to Huntsville. This small gesture of defiance may have been intended to demonstrate that he had not been defeated, only displaced.[29]

Hindman could not have selected a stronger defensive position than Brashears. Every approach is guarded by bluffs, narrow defiles, and steep-sided ravines. Should the Federals somehow overcome these obstacles, the Confederates had a perfect avenue of retreat. Ozark Road connects Brashears with the town of Ozark, twenty-six miles to the south in the Arkansas Valley. The road crawls over the crest of the Boston Mountains and plunges into the Mulberry River Valley. Every mile is steep, narrow, and winding. "That position has great advantages," wrote Hindman. "It cannot be turned, is very strong, and draws the enemy over two tremendous mountains, over which he must retreat when defeated." By every objective measure the tide of the campaign was flowing strongly against the Confederates, but Hindman remained optimistic and opportunistic. "I am confident of success in the fight, if the enemy comes down upon me, and then the way to Missouri will be open, for I hope to destroy him in his retreat," he told Holmes.[30]

On 20 October Schofield and the Missouri Divisions set out from Pea Ridge shortly after nightfall, barely an hour after Blunt and his command had marched off into the sunset. Everyone was in good spirits and confident of success. "General Schofield will overtake and whip them, or drive them to the wall," declared one soldier. Later that night the Federals forded the cold, waist-deep water of the White River by the light of blazing bonfires on both banks. After trying without much success to dry their clothes by the heat of the bonfires, they threaded their way through a pitch-dark labyrinth of narrow ravines that seemed to go on for miles. "It was the hardest march we have had yet," William H. Boyce of the Twentieth Iowa told his parents. "We would trip up and stumble most every step in the night. . . . It was nothing but stone and rocks. It hurt my feet like everything." Shoes went to pieces and men struggled on with bare and bleeding feet. "Missouri is a hard State to soldier in," observed another Iowan, "but it is a paradise in comparison with this mountainous portion of Arkansas." Conditions gradually improved, then the column entered a coniferous forest. The midwesterners were "pleasantly serenaded by the sighing of the wind among the pines," a novel experience for most.[31]

The next morning, 21 October, the weary Federals stopped at Van Winkle's Mill to eat and sleep. When the march resumed later in the day, they moved rapidly up the rolling valley of War Eagle Creek. If sore feet and aching muscles were not enough of a burden, the men of the Nineteenth Iowa tramped southward with empty haversacks, the result of poor staff work. "Nobody had any rations prepared and a good many had nothing to eat," a disconsolate William H. H. Clayton informed his parents. The Federals again marched through the night and entered Huntsville shortly after sunrise on 22 October. Schofield was disappointed to discover that Rains had departed. (He would have been even more disappointed had he known that at almost exactly the same hour, fifty miles to the northwest, Blunt was smashing Cooper at Old Fort Wayne.) The only Confederates left in the town were invalids, stragglers, and deserters. "All the prisoners taken are but half clothed and most of them say this war is an uphill business," observed an Iowa officer. The Rebels informed their captors that Hindman had returned from Little Rock, resumed command from Rains, and retreated to a place called Brashears.[32]

Schofield did not intend to follow Hindman into the Boston Mountains. He told Curtis that further pursuit was "impossible to any considerable extent" given the daunting terrain in his front and the precarious supply situation in his rear. The Missouri Divisions were more than one hundred miles south of Springfield, and the Kansas Division was about the same distance from Fort Scott. Hindman was free to retreat all the way to the Gulf of Mexico if he so desired, but Schofield would not, could not, follow. The Army of the Frontier had reached the end of its logistical tether. Schofield took what satisfaction he could from unconfirmed reports that the Confederates had stopped only briefly at Brashears before withdrawing into the Arkansas Valley. Most Federals probably were relieved to learn that the Rebels had decamped once again, but some professed to be disappointed. "We thought the secesh would show some spunk this time but when we got every thing ready for [a] fight thay as usual was leaving for dixie," complained Henry Crawford, Seventh Missouri State Militia Cavalry. Crawford wondered whether the Federals would ever have an opportunity to teach the Rebels a lesson.[33]

4 THE BOSTON MOUNTAINS

CONVINCED THAT HINDMAN HAD WITHDRAWN BEYOND HIS REACH into the Arkansas Valley, Schofield left Huntsville and returned to the west side of the White River. After two more days and nights of rapid marching Totten and the Second Division halted at Osage Spring, four miles south of Bentonville. Herron and the Third Division stopped six miles to the southeast in Cross Hollows. Men and animals were worn out. "We have been marching pretty hard ever since we came into Arkansas," William Clayton of the Nineteenth Iowa told his parents. "The boys are all well, but considerably footsore." Benjamin B. Sanborn of the Twentieth Wisconsin offered a typically muddled enlisted man's view of the expedition: "We crossed ridges and rivers and prairies and almost everything else, but how far we have been and where we have been, I do not know." Sanborn's bewilderment over the purpose of the grueling eighty-mile expedition was shared by many of his comrades.[1]

The Federals soon had more to grumble about than aching feet. On the night of 24 October an early winter storm dumped several inches of sleet and snow on northwest Arkansas. The army's trains were still at Pea Ridge, and the troops endured the wintry blast without shelter. Soldiers huddled around sputtering fires and cursed Schofield and the weather in equal proportion. "It seemed then like pretty rough service," recalled Lieutenant Colonel Joseph B. Leake of the Twentieth Iowa. The next day the sky cleared and the temperature rebounded. A few hardy midwesterners expressed delight at the aftermath of the storm. "The landscape is strikingly beautiful," remarked one man. "The contrast between the green, olive and deep red leaves of the woods and the pure white snow is at once singular and charming." Most Federals, however, were in no mood to enjoy the bold colors of an Ozark autumn. Two days passed before the trains arrived with tents, extra blankets, and camp equipment.[2]

Osage Spring and Cross Hollows were located on the eastern edge of the Springfield Plain, where food and forage were relatively plentiful. "Our men are scouring the country in every direction picking up all the wheat and old corn, and they have brought in considerable and we shall soon have a supply in a very few days," reported Captain Jacob D. Brewster, an officer on Herron's staff. An Iowa soldier was cavalier about how this was done. "When we want any beef or pork, geese or chickens, turkies or anything of the kind, all we have to do is go out and kill them. We are in the enemies country and we do not intend to want for anything they have got. We have got a heavy force here and we sweep the country clean or nearly so. It takes all the corn they have to feed our horses and mules and their fences furnish us with fire-wood." The Missouri Divisions contained "plenty of first class engineers and millers and, in fact, artisans of almost all descriptions," so the Federals commandeered mills and commenced grinding confiscated grain into flour and meal. Authorized foraging was supplemented by individual efforts. An Iowa officer explained that "jayhawking" became a "part of every man's duty for his own preservation for the time being." The effect of all of this on the long-suffering inhabitants, who barely had enough to keep body and soul together during the coming winter, can well be imagined.[3]

Foraging in hostile territory was dangerous business. Guerrillas wearing blue uniforms ambushed a party of Federals only three miles from Cross Hollows. One soldier was killed and another wounded in the daring attack. Herron's response was swift and ruthless. "We got very good evidence that the people in the vicinity were accessories if not principals in the murder," wrote Captain Brewster, "so the General sent down today and had four of them hung and their houses etc. burned and given orders for the same retaliation for the future which I think a good warning and will prevent repetitions of such outrages." Brewster added, perhaps unnecessarily, that "nearly all the people in this vicinity are entirely rebel and show it plainly." The casual brutality of irregular warfare made some Federals uneasy. An Illinois officer confessed to his wife that "I send out parties of cavalry here and there, and instruct men coolly to burn, kill and destroy. The invariable instruction, as against the guerrillas who infest this country, is to take no prisoners but shoot them down in their tracks. I find myself talking as flippantly about killing men as I would have done at home upon any trivial subject."[4]

Schofield returned to Elkhorn Tavern and found a stack of messages from Blunt describing the battle of Old Fort Wayne, the current location of the Kansas Division, and the general state of affairs in the Indian Territory. Schofield congratulated Blunt on his victory and expressed his disappointment at failing to win similar laurels at Huntsville. "Less fortunate than you, we did not succeed in getting a fight," he lamented. Schofield later informed Curtis that the "brilliant success" in the Indian Territory "illustrated in a high degree the energy and gallantry for which General Blunt and his division are so justly celebrated."[5]

Blunt was camped on Spavinaw Creek where it flows into the Indian Territory, three miles south of Maysville and thirty-three miles west of Elkhorn Tavern. The Kansas Division had escaped the worst of the winter storm and was engaged in vigorous foraging. "Most of my command here are out of bread, and I am thrashing out and grinding wheat." (Blunt managed to sound bellicose even when discussing food processing. He growled that living off the countryside was "a game we can play at as well as the rebels.") Blunt asked Schofield to forward Salomon's brigade and the division and commissary trains, all of which were still at Pea Ridge, and lobbied for permission to pursue Cooper into the Arkansas Valley. "I shall be in a condition to move upon Fort Smith and successfully defeat any force that can be concentrated there." Blunt was convinced that the loss of Fort Smith would throw the Confederates into turmoil. "There is no doubt that the enemy in Arkansas are much demoralized and disheartened in consequence of being driven by our forces, and we should lose as little time as possible in following up our advantages." Schofield declined to approve an advance on Fort Smith without permission from Curtis.[6]

Communication between Curtis and Schofield was nearly instantaneous because Herron had strung a telegraph line along Telegraph Road during his advance from Springfield. (The original line had been taken down following the outbreak of hostilities in the spring of 1861.) After digesting the news from Blunt, Schofield briefed Curtis on recent developments. "The whole Rebel force has fled into the Arkansas Valley very much scattered and demoralized," he reported. That statement was incorrect, as events would soon demonstrate, but Schofield believed it to be true at the time. "At present the whole country south and west of here is substantially in our possession as far as the Arkansas River." In other words, Missouri was safe and the immediate objectives of the campaign had been achieved. Curtis thought so, too. The next day he telegraphed Halleck that the Army of the Frontier had "gallantly and successfully accomplished its mission."[7]

Now the issue of Union strategy in the trans-Mississippi resurfaced. Having swept the Confederates out of southwest Missouri, northwest Arkansas, and a good part of the Indian Territory, Schofield was reluctant to simply walk away. He proposed that Blunt occupy the Indian Territory north of the Arkansas River and establish pro-Union tribal governments. "The Kansas Division," Schofield stated, "is quite strong enough to march into the Indian country and hold it." Whether the Kansas Division was strong enough to march into the Arkansas Valley was another matter, but Schofield dutifully passed on Blunt's request to advance on Fort Smith. Schofield also proposed that the Missouri Divisions remain in northwest Arkansas for a few months to protect the Unionist population and prevent a Confederate resurgence.[8]

Curtis concurred that Blunt should maintain his position on the border between Arkansas and the Indian Territory, but he did not think an advance on Fort Smith was a good idea, at least not for the present. Nor did he approve of keeping the Missouri Divisions in northwest Arkansas. "Your expedition has been successful," Curtis assured Schofield. "If, as you think, the enemy has gone beyond the Boston Mountains, your main force should immediately fall back to Cassville, as I may desire to have you move east if Blunt's division can clean out the Indian country." That same day, Curtis told Halleck: "If I can get General Schofield back to the region of Springfield I shall draw troops from that region to aid the downriver movement."[9]

The reference to a "downriver movement" explains why Curtis wanted Schofield to return to Missouri as quickly as possible. Curtis was under mounting pressure from the War Department to provide additional manpower for operations against Vicksburg. "Are you not employing more troops in Missouri than are really necessary?" snapped Halleck. "The great object now is to open and hold the Mississippi." Two months earlier not a single Union soldier in Missouri could have been spared for duty elsewhere, but the success of Schofield's campaign convinced Curtis that it was safe to comply with Halleck's demands.[10]

Schofield was agreeable to a "move east," but he repeated his proposal to "leave a sufficient force in Northwest Arkansas to protect the Union people until they can be organized and armed; otherwise much that I have gained will be lost." Curtis was sympathetic but unmoved. With Hindman on the prowl, a "sufficient force" would have to number at least 10,000 men. Anything smaller would be gobbled up in short order. The brutal truth was that loyal citizens in northwest Arkansas would have to look out for themselves for the foreseeable future. Schofield came around. "I shall be ready to move as you direct immediately," he informed Curtis. Schofield left Elkhorn Tavern and rode to Osage Spring on 27 October. He went with the intention of organizing a withdrawal, but within twenty-four hours the Army of the Frontier would be marching south once again.[11]

WHEN SCHOFIELD PULLED out of Huntsville, Hindman thought the Federals might be on their way back to Missouri. He was disappointed to learn that the Union columns had merely recrossed the White River and settled into camps at Osage Spring and Cross Hollows. Hindman's mood grew even darker when he realized that Schofield was in a perfect position to exploit the road network in northwest Arkansas and the Indian Territory. In the nineteenth century five roads crossed the western portion of the Boston Mountains. They were, from east to west, Ozark Road, Frog Bayou Road, Telegraph Road, Cove Creek Road, and the Line Road (also known as the "Old Military Road"). Four of the five roads fanned out from Fayetteville, which was only sixteen miles south of Osage Spring and Cross Hollows.

Rains uncovered Fayetteville when he left Telegraph Road and moved to Huntsville, and Hindman made things worse when he fell back to Brashears. The Confederates had bottled themselves up in a defensible but isolated valley in the heart of the Boston Mountains, thirty miles southeast of Fayetteville. They controlled Ozark Road but nothing else. If Schofield occupied Fayetteville he could push over the mountains on Frog Bayou Road, Telegraph Road, or Cove Creek Road (or any combination of the three), and Hindman would be unable to do anything about it. The situation farther west in the Indian Territory was equally alarming. In the aftermath of Cooper's defeat at Old Fort Wayne, there was nothing to prevent Blunt from marching toward Van Buren and Fort Smith on the Line Road. Schofield, of course, had no intention of invading the Arkansas Valley (though the same could not be said of Blunt), but Hindman did not know this.

Hindman was cheered by the arrival of an infantry brigade and a battery from Little Rock, but the reinforcements placed additional stress on an already overtaxed logistical system. "For the present I am very anxious to avoid a general engagement," he told Holmes. "I have not ammunition enough for two hours fighting, am barely able to subsist the troops when stationary, and would find it very difficult when moving, and there are so many of the men without shoes that it will be a distressing thing to march them any distance." Hindman obviously could not stay much longer at Brashears, but he feared the political and psychological consequences of falling back across the Boston Mountains without a fight. "It will not do to permit the enemy to reach the Arkansas river unopposed, or to escape without a battle." Casting about for some way to strike a blow, Hindman impulsively decided to lunge forward and occupy Fayetteville. If successful, the Confederates would regain control over the roads leading to the Arkansas Valley. They also would regain a measure of access to the farms and mills on the Springfield Plain that were supporting the Federals.[12]

While his staff prepared for an offensive, Hindman made a whirlwind tour of the camps around Brashears. At each stop he offered praise and encouragement and explained what he intended to do next. A Missourian named Peter D. Lane described a visit to his regiment that seemed to combine elements of a religious revival and a political rally: "General Hindman declared to us in a speech that he intended to meet the enemy and completely thrash them. This speech was delivered one night and our band played some beautiful music, the night was glorious, and we were inspired with the utmost enthusiasm." In war as in politics, Hindman's rhetorical skill was one of his most valuable assets.[13]

At this time Rains made a significant contribution to the Confederate war effort by drinking himself into a stupor. Hindman was furious. ("Drunkenness he despised and would not tolerate," recalled a staff officer.) He booted Rains out of the service and replaced him with Brigadier General John S. Marmaduke, the son of a former Missouri governor and the only man in the Trans-Mississippi Department with both an Ivy League and a West Point education. Marmaduke had performed with distinction at Shiloh and earned a general's star at the age of twenty-nine. Hindman thought highly of the tall, spare Missourian and placed him in charge of the cavalry. The rank and file withheld judgment. "He is a stranger to all here and is a young man and we will have to wait to see what he will do," opined a Rebel horseman.[14]

Marmaduke had only recently arrived from the east side of the Mississippi River and was shocked at the wretched state of his new command. "The condition of the men as to clothing is horrible," he informed Hindman. "A large number are bare footed and bare legged. As you may well imagine they get *small rations* and have the most severe duty to perform, not alone confronting danger but enduring cold hunger and fatigue." Confederate mounts were no better off than their riders. Hundreds of shoeless, emaciated, broken-down horses were "totally unfit" for further service, and nearly one-third of the men in the mounted arm actually were pedestrians. Marmaduke began his tenure as cavalry commander by bombarding Hindman with urgent appeals for arms, ammunition, uniforms, boots, coats, blankets, tents, tack, fresh horses, and all manner of camp equipment.[15]

While Hindman plotted and Marmaduke fretted, the 24 October storm swept over the Boston Mountains and pelted the Confederates with sleet and snow. Thousands of ill-clad Rebels huddled around smoky fires and

John S. Marmaduke
(Library of Congress)

tried to keep warm, just as their Union counterparts were doing forty miles to the north at Osage Spring and Cross Hollows. Hindman waited twenty-four hours for the storm to pass before setting out for Fayetteville. The skies finally cleared, and on 26 October Marmaduke advanced from Brashears to McGuire's Store, a distance of twenty-two miles. The Confederate cavalry reached the junction of Ozark and Huntsville roads, nine miles east of Fayetteville, without incident. Colonel Joseph O. Shelby's Brigade turned east and camped on Richland Creek. Colonel Jesse L. Cravens's Brigade turned west toward Fayetteville and camped on White River a short distance beyond the junction. Scouts fanned out to search for Union patrols. None were found and Marmaduke advised Hindman that the way to Fayetteville was open. The following morning, 27 October, Hindman and the infantry left Brashears and hurried after the cavalry. The Rebels tramped northward all day and well into the night, their path dimly illuminated by the light of a quarter moon.[16]

BOTH ARMY COMMANDERS were on the move that day. While Hindman marched north from Brashears, Schofield rode south from Elkhorn Tavern. Schofield wanted to discuss the impending withdrawal with Totten and Herron, but when he reached Osage Spring he found the camp buzzing with news of a different sort: a Confederate cavalry force had emerged from the

Boston Mountains and occupied McGuire's Store a few miles east of Fayetteville. Schofield believed the Confederates intended to disrupt his line of communications with Springfield, so he decided to strike first. After conferring with local Unionists who were familiar with the country, Schofield sketched out a plan that called for the Missouri Divisions to converge on McGuire's Store from the north and west and drive the Rebels back into the mountains.[17]

Schofield must have been uneasy about getting into a potentially serious "scrape" without the Kansas Division, because he instructed Blunt to move closer to Fayetteville and remain within supporting distance "for a few days at least." Blunt ignored the order. He explained that he had "just got started in the *mill business*" and did not want to move until his logistical situation had stabilized. He also noted that his camp on Spavinaw Creek was only forty-five miles from Fayetteville and that he could march rapidly to Schofield's assistance in an emergency. Schofield did not receive Blunt's mildly insubordinate message until the operation was over, which probably was just as well.[18]

Schofield, Totten, and most of the Second Division marched away from Osage Spring shortly after sunset on 27 October. The expeditionary force consisted of the Seventh Missouri Cavalry, a battalion of the Second Wisconsin Cavalry, Thirty-seventh Illinois, Twenty-sixth Indiana, Twentieth Iowa, and Battery F, First Missouri Light Artillery, a total of 3,000 men. Night marches usually were trying affairs, but the same quarter moon that illuminated Ozark Road for the Confederates also provided enough light for the Federals to find their way south on Elm Springs Road. The cavalry made good time and reached Fayetteville at sunrise the following morning. The infantry arrived during the afternoon. Schofield allowed men and animals a few hours to eat and rest, then hurried east toward McGuire's Store on Huntsville Road. He was only a few miles outside Fayetteville when he met Herron heading in his direction.[19]

Because of a breakdown in staff work, Schofield's order to march did not reach Cross Hollows until well after dark on 27 October. Most of the Third Division's cavalry was scattered far and wide on scouting and foraging duties, so Herron was forced to take the field with fewer than a thousand horsemen: two battalions of Colonel James O. Gower's First Iowa Cavalry, one battalion of Major James M. Hubbard's First Missouri Cavalry, and two battalions of Colonel John F. Phillip's Seventh Missouri State Militia Cavalry. Guided by local Unionists, Herron headed south on Telegraph Road, then turned east at Robinson's Crossroads and dropped into the White River Valley. The Union column was unencumbered by infantry or artillery and covered twenty-five

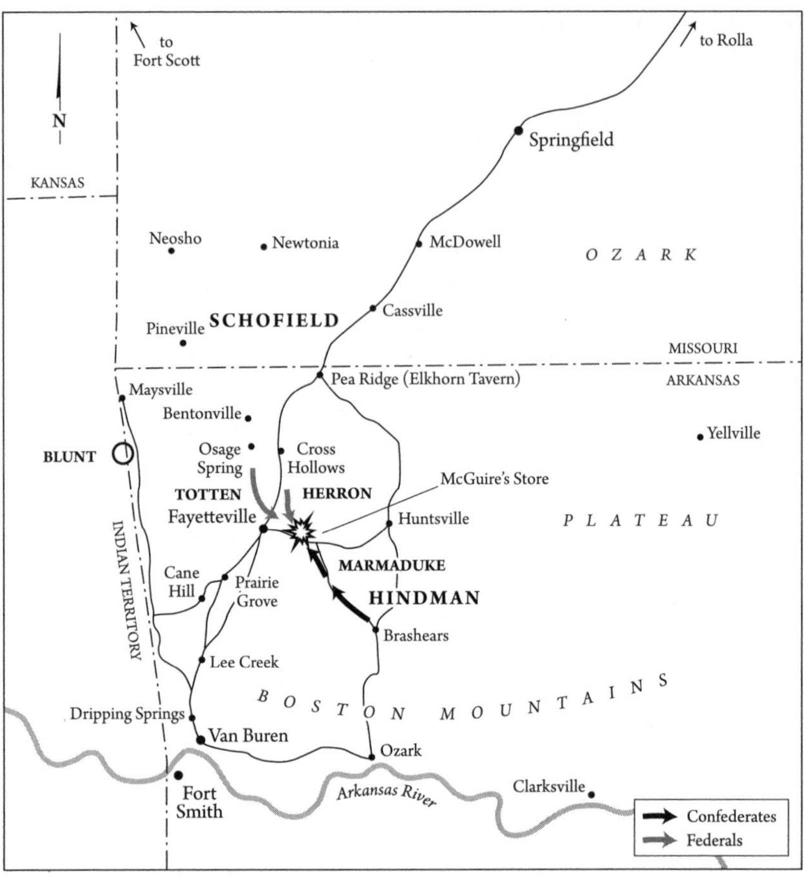

Hindman attempts to occupy Fayetteville but is checked by Schofield at White River.

miles during the night. The next morning Herron engaged the Confederates near McGuire's Store while Schofield and Totten were enjoying breakfast in Fayetteville.[20]

Although no official reports of the fight at the White River have come to light, a handful of accounts by Union participants provide an outline of events. Early on 28 October Herron's troopers exchanged shots with Confederate pickets near Oxford Bend, a settlement on the west bank of the looping White River five miles north of McGuire's Store. The pickets fled and the weary Federals pressed on. An hour later they encountered a large Confederate force. A Union trooper peered through the gray light of dawn and observed that the Rebels were "drawn up in Line to receive us."[21]

The Confederate formation was Cravens's Brigade, the four mounted regiments detached from Cooper's force eleven days earlier and recently added to

Marmaduke's command. The brigade was composed of Colonel Thomas C. Bass's Texas Cavalry, Major Robert D. Stone's Texas Cavalry, Colonel Trezevant C. Hawpe's Texas Cavalry, and Colonel Almerine M. Alexander's Texas Cavalry. Cravens and 1,200 dismounted troopers occupied the east bank of the Middle Fork of the White River; another 400 troopers waited a short distance to the rear with the horses. The Confederate line was centered on Huntsville Road and faced west toward Fayetteville. A fringe of woods along the stream provided cover, and the gravelly streambed offered an unobstructed field of fire.

Herron dismounted his command and led seven hundred troopers forward. Herron's assignment, as he understood it, was to approach McGuire's Store from the north and distract the Confederates while Totten arrived from the west on Huntsville Road and struck them in flank or rear, but something seemed amiss. Tired after a long night in the saddle and disoriented by the confusing geography of the White River Valley, Herron only gradually realized that his command was on Huntsville Road facing east. In other words, he had overshot his mark and was *in front* of Totten. Schofield's plan for a converging attack was nullified before the first shot was fired.

A noisy firefight soon erupted along the Middle Fork. Union cavalrymen popped away with pistols and carbines, and the Confederates returned the favor with carbines and shotguns. Both sides had plenty of cover and casualties were low. Herron expected Totten to arrive at any time and saw no reason to press the numerically superior Rebels. Colonel Phillips of the Seventh Missouri State Militia Cavalry either did not understand the limited role assigned to the Third Division or did not care. After thirty minutes of stationary skirmishing, Phillips ordered his bugler to sound the charge. The men of the Seventh Missouri State Militia Cavalry gave a shout and splashed across the shallow stream in their boots and spurs. The rest of the Union force followed, and the astonished Texans gave way in a scene of indescribable confusion. Cravens had the presence of mind to call on Marmaduke for help while he struggled to regain control of his brigade. He finally managed to form a second line in the middle of the Texan camp, barely a mile from the junction with Ozark Road.[22]

The Confederate side of the fight is impossible to reconstruct because of a dearth of documents. A week earlier, Colonel William R. Bradfute, Cravens's predecessor, had described the soldiers in the brigade as "thoroughly demoralized." He did not exaggerate. After months of service in the Indian Territory the Texans were not much better off than the ragtag Indian regiments. They lacked almost everything, including adequate weapons. Lieutenant

Nathaniel A. Taylor of Hawpe's regiment stated that the men in his company were armed with "utterly worthless" shotguns incapable of harming man or beast. "They will hardly stick a ball into butter at the distance of sixty paces." There was not enough ammunition to do even that much damage for very long. No wonder the Texans failed to stand their ground when pressed.[23]

Herron knew none of this. His men had performed admirably, but they were running short of ammunition and would have to withdraw unless help arrived soon. Where was Totten? The sound of small arms fire intensified as the Federals encountered the second Confederate line. A member of Herron's staff described the moment in breathless if unpunctuated prose. "We had been anxiously listening for the sound of General Totten's Division but no sound came and General Herron began to feel *blue* when the rebels gave way." The Texans mounted their horses and fled south in a disorderly mass. A disgusted Cravens followed.[24]

Herron sent a battalion of the First Iowa Cavalry in pursuit of the fleeing Texans and allowed everyone else to scavenge for spoils. "It was a complete surprise to the Rebels for we found Dough in pans just ready to bake and I saw a slice of Beef partly cut off and the knife still in it," noted a delighted Union officer. The Federals captured a dozen wagons and teams and a motley collection of camp equipment, mostly pots and pans. They were surprised to discover that the ill-equipped Texans lacked tents and slept under piles of brush.[25]

Marmaduke responded to Cravens's appeal by calling on Shelby for "immediate reinforcements." The Missourians arrived after a four-mile dash from Richland Creek and formed a line across Huntsville Road just in time to meet the First Iowa Cavalry. A brief skirmish ensued in which one Federal trooper was wounded. The appearance of a second Confederate brigade convinced Herron that it was time to go. He gathered up his command and headed west in search of Totten, who seemed to have gone missing. "About two miles from Fayetteville we met General Schofield marching out to the attack," reported Captain Brewster. Herron briefed Schofield on the situation, then led his men and horses back to Cross Hollows for a well-deserved rest. After Herron departed, Schofield advanced to within a half mile of Shelby's position and directed Totten to place his cavalry and artillery across Huntsville Road. The Union line grew longer and stronger later in the day as the infantry arrived.[26]

Hindman was five miles south of McGuire's Store when he heard the sound of gunfire. He halted the infantry in a "strong position" and hurried forward to confer with Marmaduke. By the time Hindman reached the scene,

Herron had departed and Totten had deployed his command. Hindman's heart sank as he studied the line of Union cavalry, infantry, and artillery. It was pointless to continue the operation if the Federals held Fayetteville in strength, as certainly appeared to be the case. Hindman kept Shelby's Brigade in place in the vain hope that Schofield might withdraw, as he had done at Huntsville a week earlier. Meanwhile, the Confederate infantry waited in suspense on Ozark Road. "The Feds are seemingly anxious for a fight and I hope we will satisfy them soon," a Missouri soldier confided to his diary. He was to be disappointed. Late in the afternoon Hindman received an erroneous report that the Federals were working their way around his left flank. He ordered the army back to Brashears.[27]

Around sunset Schofield realized that the Confederates had retired. He led Totten's division back to Fayetteville convinced that he had foiled a cavalry raid and nothing more. That evening Schofield advised Curtis of recent developments and praised Herron and his men for the "energy and gallantry" displayed at the White River. Curtis must have been surprised to learn of a clash east of Fayetteville when the Rebels were supposed to be in the Arkansas Valley, but he was pleased that his troops had emerged victorious. He notified Halleck that the "Army of the Frontier is again successful." One participant described the fight at the White River as a "sharp engagement," whereas another dismissed it as a "slight skirmish." The casualty list seems to support the latter characterization. One Union soldier was killed and four others wounded. Confederate casualties amounted to eight killed and perhaps twice that number wounded.[28]

Hindman's attempt to deny Schofield access to the web of roads across the Boston Mountains had backfired. When the dust settled it was the Federals, not the Confederates, who held Fayetteville. Discouraged by this turn of events, Hindman no longer spoke in terms of advancing but only of holding his ground at Brashears. "I shall be able to maintain my position if I can *subsist my command*," he told Holmes. "I need however reinforcements and the largest quantities of supplies. This entire country is almost totally exhausted of everything." But neither troops nor trains were at hand, and Hindman finally threw in the towel. On 29 October, the day after the fight at the White River, he withdrew into the Arkansas Valley on Ozark Road.[29]

While the Confederates plodded over the mountains on what one officer described as the "worst road I have yet travelled in the State of Arkansas," Hindman provided Holmes with a postmortem of recent events. He acknowledged that the Federals had "moved more rapidly than I had anticipated," but insisted that he was withdrawing only because of a lack of supplies. "I could not subsist on forage where I was," he explained. "I would have been starved from my position, if not driven from it by force." After a three-day trek the Confederates halted on the Mulberry River a few miles west of Ozark. "We have been marched over the hills in this country until I am nearly worn out," complained a Missouri officer. The new encampment was located near the Arkansas River, and steamboats loaded with food, clothing, equipment, and ammunition soon arrived from Little Rock. Additional manpower arrived as well, most notably Parsons's infantry brigade from Yellville. Hindman assured Holmes that he did not intend to tarry long on the Mulberry. My troops "will be able to live there until I can accumulate supplies sufficient for a forward movement," he asserted.[30]

About this time Hindman received a message from Emmett MacDonald, the Missouri officer charged with the investigation of the Old Fort Wayne debacle. MacDonald expressed dismay at the thought of spending another Christmas far from hearth and home. He urged Hindman to return to Missouri before the onset of winter brought campaigning to a close. "So far from going further south, I confidently expect that you will soon march *north*," declared MacDonald. Hindman may have managed a grim smile when he read those words, which perfectly reflected his own feelings. For the time being, however, the Confederates would rest and refit in the relative comfort of the Arkansas Valley. The next move was up to Schofield.[31]

5 WAR OF NERVES

LOYAL RESIDENTS OF FAYETTEVILLE MUST HAVE THOUGHT DELIVerance was at hand when they awoke on 29 October and found the streets swarming with blue-clad soldiers. But they soon learned that Union liberation was only slightly less onerous than Confederate occupation. "The stores are broke open and everything looks like the picture of ruin," wrote Aaron P. Mitchell of the Twentieth Iowa. "It is strictly against orders to destroy anything but the boys will, a great many of them, run the risk and break in and take anything they can find that they need. They have arrested quite a number for breaking into stores and shops." Most of Totten's men tried to obtain goods in a more socially acceptable manner but discovered that the handful of merchants still in business preferred Confederate script to "Lincoln greens." Whatever the method of payment, selection was limited in the war-ravaged town. "Callicoe, tea and coffee and salt are not to be bought here at any price," observed one soldier.[1]

Although bruised and battered after eighteen months of war, Fayetteville still had the power to charm, at least at a distance. "Fayetteville is the nicest country town I ever saw," enthused William Clayton of the Nineteenth Iowa. "The houses are generally frame, nicely painted, the yards enclosed with railing fences or board fences nicely whitewashed." But a closer inspection revealed that many of the houses were empty and most of the commercial buildings on the square were in ruins. Even the splendid view of the Boston Mountains to the south could not dispel the gloom. "At present desolation broods over the place," noted another Iowan. The Federals searched high and low for anything of military value, but all they found were some harness leather, a few cast-off weapons, and several makeshift hospitals filled with sick and wounded Rebels. "They are a wretched looking set, dirty and ragged, and full of vermin," observed a Union officer. The three hundred bedraggled convalescents were among the few men of military age in town. “The conscription here has been perfect,” remarked another officer. “There is not a man or boy left able to bear arms, and I am informed that the balance of the State is in the same condition.”[2]

Schofield was in no mood for shopping or sightseeing. He passed a restful night in a “quite stylish” house near the square, but morning brought unsettling, even alarming, news. The sidewalks of Fayetteville were awash with rumors that the Confederates were advancing on the town in overwhelming strength. Hindman had long since reversed course and returned to Brashears, but Schofield did not know this. Instead of attempting to confirm the rumors, Schofield lost his head and ordered the Second Division back to Osage Spring. As the Union column hurried north, an overwrought Schofield informed Blunt that the Rebels were right behind him. “They will doubtless give us battle in a few days,” he announced. “I propose to select a position near Bentonville, concentrate my forces as much as possible, and await events.” Schofield ordered Blunt to join him as soon as possible. “The Enemy must fight us soon if at all,” he explained. “They can not live long in the mountains.” On that point, at least, the rattled Union commander was correct.[3]

The alarming—not to say alarmist—tone of Schofield’s message propelled Blunt into action. The Kansas Division pulled up stakes and marched from Spavinaw Creek to Little Osage Creek, a distance of about twenty miles. By sunset on 31 October the principal components of the Army of the Frontier were arrayed within supporting distance of one another on an east-west line: Blunt’s First Division on the right a few miles south of Bentonville, Totten’s Second Division (with Schofield) in the center at Osage Springs, and Herron’s Third Division on the left at Cross Hollows. It was Halloween and the Federals braced for an attack, but the phantom Rebel army failed to materialize. Late the next day Union scouts cautiously approached Brashears and found only stragglers and abandoned equipment. They returned to Osage Spring and informed Schofield that Hindman had fallen back across the mountains after all.[4]

Relieved and mortified in equal measure, Schofield felt it was time to bring the campaign to a close. He sent Blunt a warm personal note in which he glossed over his embarrassing behavior during the past forty-eight hours. “I have hoped that the rebels would come back and give us battle where we could fight them together. But if they will not do this we must separate and follow our respective paths of duty. However this may be I shall always cherish the most pleasant recollections of the union of the armies of Kansas and Missouri.” The note demonstrated that the two generals had defied expectations and established a comfortable and effective working relationship. Unfortunately, it would not last.[5]

On 3 November Schofield and Blunt journeyed to Elkhorn Tavern for a telegraphic conference with their distant superior in St. Louis. Schofield provided Curtis with an edited version of recent events in which he avoided any mention of his unseemly flight from Fayetteville. He expressed his belief that there was "nothing more to be accomplished by my forces in this part of the country" and asked permission to withdraw in accordance with the arrangements agreed upon a few days earlier. Curtis had no objections. "Your move is right," he replied. The Elkhorn Tavern conference marked the end of offensive operations by the Army of the Frontier under Schofield's command.[6]

Blunt returned to Little Osage Creek while Schofield remained at Elkhorn Tavern to supervise the Union withdrawal. The operation was just getting under way when Curtis received an intelligence report to the effect that a Confederate force was advancing on Springfield from Yellville in north central Arkansas. Curtis would have been well advised to regard this information with his usual skepticism, but for whatever reason he thought there might be something to it and urged Schofield to hasten his return. Still on edge after the Halloween debacle, Schofield scrapped his plan for a measured withdrawal and embarked on an unnecessary three-day forced march to Springfield. The retrograde movement began on 4 November. "The march from Cross Hollows to Crane Creek was the most disagreeable one we have had yet," wrote an Iowa soldier. "The road was very dusty, it being two to three inches deep and we sometimes could not see more than ten or fifteen steps ahead. After marching all day we were about the dirtiest set of fellows imaginable." Accounts invariably mention the "stifling" cloud of gritty, whitish dust that enveloped everyone and everything.[7]

The Federals employed scorched-earth tactics as they withdrew because Curtis wanted to create a logistical desert that would hamper future Confederate incursions into southwest Missouri. "A great deal of property was destroyed before we went down there," wrote William Clayton. "On our return nearly every house was burned. The corn and forage of all kinds was used up pretty clean to feed our train. For fire wood we use rails whenever we can get them." Clayton concluded that the "secesh will not have much to live on if they return to that section of country," precisely the reason for the sanctioned destruction. William Murray, a soldier in the Twentieth Iowa, sympathized with the civilian victims of the depredations. "I don't know what the people is going to do down in this country," he told his brother. "Thay have nothing but corn and the army takes all that so I don't know what thay are going to live on. I think thay will have a hard time of it." Surveying the scene, a Union officer wrote: "Ruin stares you in the face, turn which way you may."[8]

Schofield's abrupt departure dismayed Arkansas Unionists and triggered an exodus. A trooper in the First Iowa Cavalry wrote:

> One of the saddest sights of all, was the poor refugees that followed us out, in the wake of the army, fleeing from despotism and starvation. Several hundred teams, loaded with the little that they could save from the rebels, and hauled by poor old oxen, or cows, or mules, or skeletons of horses, came slowly along after us—the women and children huddled together in their rags and wretchedness, and the men and boys, including contrabands of all ages and sexes, following the teams.

By the end of 1862 the blighted region between Springfield and Fayetteville was marked by hundreds of burned or abandoned buildings and mile after mile of overgrown fields. Years passed before the population and agricultural production returned to prewar levels.[9]

Few Union soldiers were sad to see their two-week sojourn in the Confederacy come to an end. "We are 'getting out of the wilderness' and the sensation is not a bad one," declared an officer on Schofield's staff. When the Twentieth Iowa entered Missouri, the regimental band struck up "Yankee Doodle." Gaunt and grimy soldiers "threw up their hats and gave cheers and cat calls as a farewell to Arkansas." None could have imagined that exactly one month later they would be crossing the state line in the opposite direction, bound for an obscure hamlet named Prairie Grove.[10]

Schofield reached Springfield on 6 November and informed Curtis of the current disposition of the Army of the Frontier. Blunt's First Division, 6,200 strong, remained in Arkansas. Totten's Second Division of 4,600 troops was camped on Spring River, and Herron's small Third Division, barely 2,800 men in all, was located six miles farther south on Crane Creek. Detachments of varying strength were stationed at other points along Telegraph Road. The most important of these outposts was Elkhorn Tavern, where two battalions of the First Arkansas Cavalry secured the southern terminus of the telegraph line and maintained a tenuous connection with Blunt by courier. (A third battalion of "Mountain Feds" was attached to the Kansas Division.)[11]

Curtis informed Schofield that his sojourn in Springfield would be brief. "The season is good for campaigning, and the Army of the Frontier must be marching on." Because of Halleck's demands on the Department of the Missouri for manpower, Curtis intended to send the Missouri Divisions to Helena, the southernmost Union enclave on the Mississippi and a jumping-

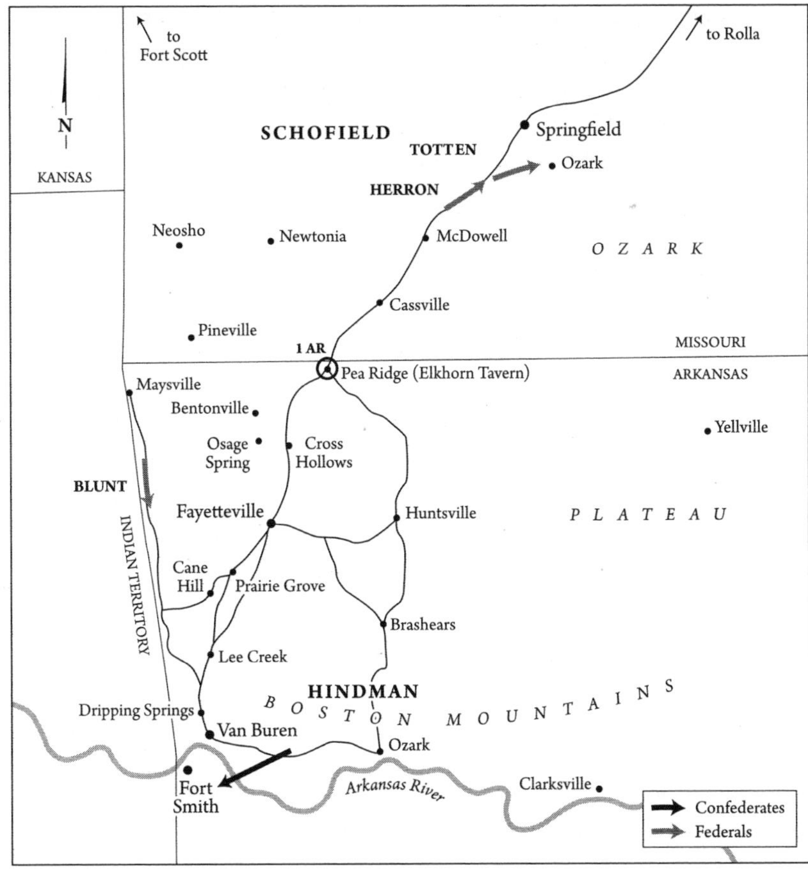

Hindman returns to Fort Smith. Schofield withdraws to Missouri.
Blunt edges closer to the Boston Mountains.

off point for operations against Vicksburg. Schofield was eager for a change of scenery. "My effective force available for a distant movement is between seven and eight thousand men, about one good Division," he replied. "This force is ready to move at any time."[12]

The officers and men of the Missouri Divisions did not share Schofield's enthusiasm for additional marching. They had experienced their fill of dust, blisters, and associated privations, not just over the past few days but for much of the campaign. Schofield described his soldiers as "inured to fatigue by constant active service," but in fact they were worn to a frazzle. Most had tramped over five hundred rough and rocky miles since the beginning of the campaign. "I am tired of marching and counter-marching over this desolate country and for no purpose that I can see," snapped Benjamin Sanborn of the

Twentieth Wisconsin. The men of the Nineteenth Iowa were particularly embittered at the brutal pace set by Schofield during the withdrawal from Arkansas. "It was a terrible tramp," wrote James E. Houghland. Two members of the regiment collapsed from "over marching" and were buried at Crane Creek. Everyone in the Ninety-fourth Illinois survived the ordeal, but Colonel Orme was outraged by the punishment inflicted on his men for no apparent reason. "They have made a long weary march to no good," he confided to his wife.[13]

The travails of the Federal soldiers were not yet over. Schofield found no sign of a Confederate force approaching Springfield. He informed Curtis that the reported offensive "seems to have been a mere feint." Curtis was not convinced. He directed Schofield to move his command to Ozark and cover the southeast approaches to Springfield. Once again Schofield responded with excessive alacrity. On 10 November he rushed both divisions to Ozark, thirty-nine and thirty-three miles east of Spring River and Crane Creek respectively. That night an exhausted soldier in the Thirty-seventh Illinois scribbled only two words in his diary: "Awful tired." The commanding officer of the Twentieth Iowa was more eloquent. Lieutenant Colonel Leake reported that the twelve-hour march "was made as rapidly as men could be forced. The whole command was very much broken up, and suffered more than from any other march we ever made." Leake was furious at the way his men were "jerked about over south Missouri."[14]

Schofield did not accompany his troops to Ozark because he was suffering from what was described as a "severe attack of bilious fever." For a day or two he continued to work on plans for the projected eastward movement. A particularly vexing problem was how much force to leave behind in Springfield. Schofield wanted to hold the town with four regiments of Enrolled Missouri Militia, but Curtis thought the plan too risky. "Enrolled militia get no pay," he observed, "and will get tired of the service as the winter comes on. It will not do to depend on them alone for garrison duty." Curtis warned that it would be a serious mistake "to leave a door open" in southwest Missouri. Schofield agreed to station the Eighteenth Iowa in Springfield to bolster the militia.[15]

Schofield's health soon declined to the point where he no longer had the strength to leave his room. "I am compelled by sickness to give up the duty and confine myself to my bed," he reported on 10 November. Curtis urged him to rest and recover his strength. "Do not bother your brains about the troops till you are quite well." Blunt also was distressed to hear of Schofield's illness and sent a get-well message from the field: "I regret to learn of your continued ill health and hope you may soon be able for active service in the field. Wether the fortunes of war shall through us together again or not, I shall always cherish the fondest recollections of the friendly intercourse—social and official—between us during our brief acquaintance."[16]

As the war did not stop while Schofield convalesced, Curtis attempted to direct the movements of the Army of the Frontier from his office in St. Louis. Operating through the bedridden Schofield and his chief of staff, Major Calvin W. Marsh, Curtis ordered Totten to take the Missouri Divisions to Cape Girardeau on the Mississippi River. (Although Herron was senior to Totten, he was suffering from an eye infection caused by the dusty conditions during the withdrawal from Arkansas. He had gone to St. Louis for medical attention, and it was uncertain when, or even if, he would return.) On 14 November Totten marched out of Ozark at the head of 6,000 troops. "If we start after the Rebs this time, we will make them suffer for having us to run after them so much," vowed a soldier in the Twenty-sixth Indiana. The head of the Federal column was only fifteen miles east of Ozark when a courier rode up with orders to halt. Something was happening in Arkansas.[17]

THE KANSAS DIVISION remained on Little Osage Creek south of Bentonville while the rest of the army withdrew, but within a few days the Federals were forced to seek greener pastures. "There is so many of us together that we cant stay in one place long on account of forage for the horses and mules," explained Sergeant Warren Day of the Thirteenth Kansas. "It is easier to move fifteen or twenty miles than to haul corn and fodder that distance to camps." Guerrillas were a constant aggravation. "*Bushwhackers* are also plenty, and our men are fired upon several times daily," wrote an officer in the First Indian. "The country is covered with thick brush and admirably adapted to their cowardly mode of warfare. Yesterday we killed one and took one prisoner. *He probably will be shot.*" On 4 November the Federals returned to their old camp on Spavinaw Creek and settled down to await developments. An infantryman in the Tenth Kansas remarked that the move required a "nice little march of twenty-three miles, far enough for a week's hard marching on the Potomac, but only an ordinary day's work for Western men."[18]

A day or two later Blunt learned that a Confederate cavalry force had crossed the Boston Mountains and occupied Cane Hill, a bountiful agricultural region thirty miles south of Spavinaw Creek. Eager to land another blow against the Rebels, Blunt assigned the task to Colonel William F. Cloud, whom he described as the "best commander I have." Cloud, a part-time Methodist minister and full-time Kansas shopkeeper, had demonstrated a talent for leading mounted forces during the first year of the war. On 7 November he set out at the head of five hundred men drawn from the Second Kansas

William F. Cloud (Kansas State Historical Society)

Cavalry, Sixth Kansas Cavalry, Second Ohio Cavalry, and First Indian; the Second Kansas Cavalry Battery provided artillery support. The Federals hurried south on the Line Road to Cincinnati, then turned east and stopped for the night near Rhea's Mill. The next morning, 8 November, they headed for Cane Hill.[19]

The Confederate force at Cane Hill was Emmett MacDonald's Missouri Cavalry Battalion. The Rebels did not expect any trouble and were busy foraging when they learned of the approaching Union column. MacDonald assembled his three hundred troopers and prepared to receive an attack. Cloud opened the fight with his mountain howitzers. The stubby 12-pounders were nicknamed "bullpups," and an officer in the First Indian wrote that the gunners "let them bark" at the Rebels. Without any artillery of their own, the Confederates were helpless. They wheeled about and fled.[20]

The Federals followed. "A charge was ordered and away we flew with loose reins and set spurs," recalled Sergeant Luman H. Tenney, Second Ohio Cavalry. With the "Fighting Preacher" out in front waving his hat and yelling like a madman, the Union horsemen followed their quarry at breakneck speed through the Boston Mountains on Cove Creek Road. "It was a rough ride," remarked a Kansas trooper, "but a nice, exciting chase." After a few miles, recorded Sergeant Tenney, "we began to see stirrups, blankets, corn and a thou-

Emmett MacDonald (Civil War Museum at Wilson's Creek National Battlefield)

sand things strewn along the road." Late in the day MacDonald reached Lee Creek on the south side of the mountains and turned to fight off his pursuers. That proved to be a mistake. The Confederates were put to flight a second time and lost their flag and train in the confusion. Fortunately for MacDonald, daylight was fading fast and the Federals broke off the pursuit. Lieutenant Horace L. Moore, Second Kansas Cavalry, retrieved the Confederate banner. He recorded that the fallen standard-bearer was a "fine looking young man of twenty-five, and it was with much difficulty that the flag staff was taken from the grip of his dead hands." After burning what they could not haul away, the Federals plodded back over the mountains to Cane Hill. With a half-dozen of his troopers dead or missing and an equal number wounded, MacDonald most likely was happy to see them go.[21]

The next morning Cloud tried his hand at subterfuge. The Federals left Cane Hill and headed toward Fayetteville with a company of the Sixth Kansas Cavalry in the lead. The Kansans carried the captured Confederate flag and wore butternut garb found in one of MacDonald's supply wagons. They nearly spoiled the ruse by singing alternating verses of "Dixie" and "John Brown's Body" as they rode into town, but apparently none of Fayetteville's secessionist residents noticed the odd mix of lyrics. Instead, they cheered the arrival of seemingly Confederate troops and denounced neighbors who had collaborated with Schofield during his brief occupation twelve days earlier. Several citizens brandished guns, including one man who announced that he had "taken an oath to shoot every [Union] picket, straggler, messenger or pilot that he could." After showing their true colors, the Federals arrested the most vocal secessionists and confiscated all the weapons they could find.[22]

Cloud continued the ruse after leaving Fayetteville. A few miles outside town a dozen Confederate guerrillas emerged from the woods and rode up to the butternut-clad Kansans. "Boys, if I didn't know better, I would take you for Feds," exclaimed the guerrilla leader. The Union soldiers pulled out their guns and ended the charade. "The look of blank surprise and embarrassing astonishment that followed, was amusing in the extreme," reported a Kansas trooper. The Federals returned to Spavinaw Creek on 11 November. (Whether the captured guerrillas made it that far is not known.) Cloud and his men were "tired out and chafed up badly" but proud that their expedition had "pushed thirty miles further into rebeldom than any previous one." In fact, they were the first Union soldiers to cross the Boston Mountains.[23]

When Hindman learned what had happened, he sent Marmaduke and his entire cavalry force (including MacDonald) back to Cane Hill. On 9–10 November a long column of Confederate horsemen and an even longer commissary train struggled over the Boston Mountains on the Line Road and turned east toward Cane Hill. The 2,000 Arkansas and Missouri troopers put their carbines and shotguns aside and commenced loading the wagons with flour, meal, hay, and meat. This foraging operation had an unforeseen impact on the course of the campaign. Marmaduke's appearance on the north side of the mountains sparked rumors that another Confederate offensive was under way. The rumors soon reached Captain Elijah D. Ham, Schofield's chief of scouts, at Elkhorn Tavern. On 14 November Ham telegraphed Schofield that Marmaduke was at Cane Hill with 5,000 men and that this was "supposed to be the advance of a general movement from Van Buren." Now it was Schofield's turn to be skeptical. He knew from recent experience how difficult it was to make sense of enemy movements in the Boston Mountains. "I do not place very much confidence in Captain Ham's report," he advised Curtis from his sickbed in Springfield. He explained that Blunt had "excellent scouts and spies and would have known and reported if as stated by Captain Ham."[24]

The next day, 15 November, Blunt confirmed Ham's warning in all particulars. A few days earlier the Kansas Division had moved from Spavinaw Creek to Flint Creek, ten miles farther south on the Line Road. A Union officer described the broad, fertile valley of Flint Creek as a "fine little bottom and well supplied with corn standing in the fields of good quality." Tents were still going up when the "excellent scouts and spies" that Schofield admired galloped into camp with alarming news: Marmaduke was at Cane Hill with Hindman close behind. "I have reliable information that the enemy are in large force in front of me," Blunt reported. He, too, estimated Confederate strength at 5,000 men and announced his intention to stand his ground regardless of the odds. "I have no doubt they mediate an attack upon me in superior force, but I am prepared to meet them and shall not retreat one inch." Major Albert C. Ellithorpe of the First Indian believed Blunt meant exactly what he said. "General Blunt is determined to fight. It makes no difference what their force is." Blunt placed his 6,200 troops in defensive positions along Flint Creek and waited for the Rebels to arrive.[25]

Now convinced that Hindman really was on the move, Schofield offered Curtis his assessment of the situation: "General Blunt is unquestionably a fighting man and has some very fine troops, but I believe he is over sanguine of his ability to whip the enemy in his front. The whole army will be none too much for the purpose." Curtis agreed, but it appeared that Blunt intended to stand his ground regardless of the odds. Curtis concluded that if the Kansas Division would not fall back, the Missouri Divisions would have to go forward. He ordered Totten to halt his eastward movement and return to Arkansas.[26]

The Missouri Divisions reversed course on 17 November. The weather was miserable. "It rained all day and it rained all night," complained a woebegone soldier in the Thirty-seventh Illinois. "We had neither overcoats blankets or food. A most *doleful* night. May I never spend another like it!" None of the cold, wet, and thoroughly unhappy Federals realized that their suffering was to no purpose. Two days earlier the Confederates had returned to the Arkansas Valley, the wagons in their commissary train piled high with food and fodder. Blunt kept a close watch on Cane Hill and soon learned that Marmaduke had departed, but he could not get a message through to Springfield for nearly forty-eight hours because the downpour caused the telegraph to malfunction. During this breakdown in communications the Missouri Divisions continued slogging south on Telegraph Road, steadily closing the gap between the two wings of the Army of the Frontier. When Totten finally received orders to halt on 18 November, the head of the Union column was near Cassville, only eighteen miles from the Arkansas state line.[27]

As soon as Schofield learned that Marmaduke had fallen back, he requested leave to convalesce at his home in St. Louis. "I do not believe [the Confederates] intend any aggressive movements," he assured Curtis. On 20

November Schofield relinquished command of the army to Blunt and departed in an ambulance. He was only a few miles outside Springfield when he encountered Herron, who was on his way back from St. Louis. Herron reported that his eyes were much improved and he was ready to return to duty. Schofield congratulated Herron on his rapid recovery and informed him that he now was in charge of the Missouri Divisions. A delighted Herron rejoined the Third Division and held a review to celebrate his unexpected elevation. "As the General passed each successive command cheer upon cheer rent the air, which made the ground shake almost," reported an officer in the Twentieth Wisconsin. With hurrahs and martial airs ringing in his ears, Herron turned to grapple with his new responsibilities.[28]

The officers and men of the Second Division also had cause for celebration. Curtis summoned Totten to St. Louis to appear as a witness in a court-martial. Totten left the Army of the Frontier on 27 November, never to return. His troops had grown weary of his churlish behavior, and there was "great rejoicing" at news of his departure. Totten's fondness for the bottle had grown stronger during the latter part of the campaign. "I do not think he has been sober in the last two weeks," wrote a disgusted officer in the Thirty-seventh Illinois. Command of the Second Division passed to Colonel Daniel Huston Jr., a West Point graduate with twelve years of experience in the regular army. Huston was an officer of no particular distinction, but his steady hand proved to be just what the division needed after three months of Totten's harsh and sometimes erratic leadership.[29]

Curtis brought Halleck up-to-date on personnel changes and other developments in the Department of the Missouri. "The Army of the Frontier has been divided, and General Schofield is here recruiting his impaired health," he wrote. After describing the disposition of his forces, Curtis explained why the Missouri Divisions were not on their way to the Mississippi River as promised: "I halted the main force near Ozark because the enemy some days since moved toward General Blunt in formidable force; but fell back, and I only wait to know how far back, in order to make further use of the force under General Herron." Curtis refrained from making any commitments about Herron's future movements.[30]

A key development in the campaign had occurred unnoticed, or at least not fully understood, by commanders on both sides. When Blunt had ordered Cloud to attack MacDonald at Cane Hill on 7 November, he set in motion a series of events that altered the strategic situation in the trans-Mississippi. Cloud sent MacDonald packing, but Hindman ordered Marmaduke to reoccupy Cane Hill and resume foraging on an even larger scale. When Marmaduke appeared north of the mountains, he startled the Federals and caused them to conclude that a Confederate offensive was under way. Blunt chose to remain at Flint Creek rather than fall back. Anxious about Blunt's safety, Curtis halted the eastward movement of the Missouri Divisions and returned them to Telegraph Road south of Springfield. Had Curtis not done so, Totten would have moved away beyond any chance of recall, and Blunt would have been without hope of succor when Hindman marched north in reality a few weeks later.

FOR THE NEXT TWO WEEKS the soldiers of the Missouri Divisions relaxed and recuperated from their recent ordeal. The Second Division camped near McCulloch's Spring while the Third Division spread out along Wilson's Creek, twelve miles to the north. The supply situation changed from one of scarcity to one of relative abundance, and not a moment too soon, for after the rigors of the campaign many soldiers were "barefooted and ragged, absolutely requiring additional clothes." Wagons loaded with uniforms, shoes, coats, blankets, and camp equipment made regular appearances. A stretch of "exceedingly agreeable" fall weather provided ample opportunity for cleaning persons, clothing, and bedding. Food was plentiful if uninspiring: coffee, flour, beans, canned goods, and that most mysterious of Union rations, desiccated vegetables (widely known, for good reason, as "desecrated vegetables"). In both a material and a physical sense, Herron's troops were ready for a new round of campaigning by the end of November.[31]

Morale was slower to recover. "They are using up men faster in their fool marches than the enemy are killing for us and it don't all amount to anything for us," declared David L. Ash of the Thirty-seventh Illinois. Everyone was frustrated by the anticlimactic end to weeks of arduous campaigning. After tramping for hundreds of miles and wearing out thousands of pairs of shoes and socks, the men of the Missouri Divisions were back where they had started. People back home were puzzled at the seemingly random movements of the Army of the Frontier. "There were enough Union soldiers in and around Arkansas to eat that State up without stopping to pin its ears back," asserted the editor of a Kansas newspaper. He spoke for many when he declared that the "whole Arkansas campaign is to us a mystery."[32]

Perhaps the heaviest burden for the Federals to bear was the belief that the rest of the country neither knew nor cared about them. "I wonder if they know in New York or Boston that there is an 'Army of the Frontier,'" mused an unhappy officer. He noted that midwestern newspapers were filled with accounts of military affairs in Virginia and Maryland, "but rarely, very rarely, is the Great West mentioned." After grumbling about the unfairness of it all, the officer comforted himself with the thought that results mattered more than recognition: "Well, we are willing to stand on our merit alone, and we shall continue to do our duty, even if we are forgotten while we are accomplishing it." In truth, most newspapers in Iowa, Illinois, Kansas, and Wisconsin kept their readers abreast of events in Arkansas and Missouri, but only an "occasional stray notice" appeared in papers published elsewhere. The regrettable tendency to celebrate events in the East, slight those in the West, and ignore the trans-Mississippi altogether was well established by 1862.[33]

The Federals found it difficult to adjust to a sedentary existence after two months of constant activity and excitement. "We are now living a regular camp life," wrote Lieutenant Albert J. Rockwell, Twentieth Wisconsin. "Nothing but eat, drill and sleep day in and day out. Oh I am so sick of this. Any thing but lying still in such a country as this. I would rather move twenty miles a day than lie here doing nothing." Boredom among the enlisted men in the Third Division, which was camped near the Wilson's Creek battlefield, led to an eruption of macabre behavior. Most Federals were content to wander over the battlefield and visit the site of Brigadier General Nathaniel Lyon's death atop Bloody Hill in August 1861, but some enterprising soldiers found a mass grave and sensed a commercial opportunity. Rockwell informed his father that for "the last three or four days mementoes in the shape of rings, charms and *teeth*, made from the bones of *our men* who fell at Wilsons Creek, have been all the rage in camp." Officers put a stop to the gruesome trade.[34]

Fearing the corrosive effects of inactivity, Herron looked for some way to keep his troops usefully employed. When he learned that the Confederate saltpeter works and storehouses at Yellville were lightly guarded, he asked Curtis for permission to make a "dash" into north central Arkansas "with a pretty strong force" and destroy the facilities. Curtis approved and Herron dispatched Colonel Dudley Wickersham with two battalions of his own Tenth Illinois Cavalry and two battalions of the First Iowa Cavalry. Guided by Unionists, the Federals made their way across 125 miles of rugged Ozark terrain without being detected. On 27 November they stormed into Yellville and took the small Confederate garrison by surprise. Wickersham and his troopers captured 60 men and twice that number of horses, paroled 150 convalescents in a military hospital, and burned the saltpeter works and storehouses. There were no fatalities on either side. "It was a complete success," exulted Herron upon Wickersham's return. "Our troops have left the place in such shape that I do not think the rebels will again attempt to make it a depot."[35]

As Wickersham returned from Yellville the rest of the Missouri Divisions celebrated a spartan Thanksgiving. "I suppose you will have a good dinner today," wrote a wistful William Boyce to his parents. "How I should like to be home to eat with you. I miss all those things here." The culinary high point of the day for Boyce and his messmates was a pot of baked beans. "I never cared much for them at home but a soldier must like most anything that is eatable," Boyce observed philosophically. "So I have learned by going to war to eat most anything." The holiday passed quietly with plenty of time for reflection. A diarist in the Nineteenth Iowa closed his daily entry with an earnest prayer: "This is my first Thanksgiving day in the Army. I pray God ere another comes Peace may be shedding its glorious influences over a rebellious and distracted people."[36]

THE KANSAS DIVISION, meanwhile, maintained its lonely vigil on the border between Arkansas and the Indian Territory. The bucolic landscape was a pleasant surprise to Sergeant Sherman Bodwell of the Eleventh Kansas: "The farms lie in the valleys, and are to my notion the best I have seen. I am continually reminded of New England." The border region had not yet been ravaged by thousands of hungry men and animals, and food was plentiful. "Hogs run wild; chickens abound; beef is plenty, and sorghum is cheap," reported a delighted officer in the Second Wisconsin Cavalry. "We have taken possession of the mills and gone into the *milling business*. We are now turning out about twenty thousand pounds of flour and meal daily, with which, together with supplies we are getting from Fort Scott, we shall soon be able to settle down to a winter's campaign." A Kansas soldier informed his hometown newspaper that occupation duty was a "good, lively, healthy business, which the boys enjoy hugely." Perhaps so, but a nomadic existence far from home had some drawbacks. Few sutlers chanced the long, dangerous journey from Fort Scott, and the troops had to do without a number of niceties, including alcoholic beverages. The result was an outbreak of temperance. "We are all sober—good reason—no whiskey," wryly observed Lieutenant Josiah B. McAfee of the Eleventh Kansas.[37]

Sutlers may have been absent but others found their way to Blunt's camp. The most numerous visitors were fugitives from bondage. "You would be astonished, mother, to see how generally the terms of the [emancipation] proclamation are known and discussed, [and] how well understood, among the slaves in this part of the country," wrote an Illinois officer. "You do not see a slave throughout the length and breadth of the land who does not brighten with joy at our approach." Many slaves did not wait for the Federals to come to them but took matters into their own hands. A Kansas officer noted that "contrabands flowed [into our camp] in a steady stream." He spoke with a young woman who had slipped away from her owner in Fayetteville and walked barefooted forty miles to reach freedom. "She seemed to be as happy as a cricket when she got among people of her own race, forgetting her torn and blistered feet." Most soldiers in the Kansas Division were abolitionist in sentiment and encouraged the influx. "We find quite an extensive colored population here," wrote Sergeant Eli H. Gregg. "All are slaves, and all are willing to be free. If we are left here, it will be something strange if Old Abe's proclamation does not go into effect immediately. It will be an easy matter to date ahead, if necessary, to cover accidents." Within a few weeks, however, slaveowners in northwest Arkansas took steps to safeguard what remained of their mobile property. In late November a Union soldier noted that "Negroes have nearly all been driven south. An able bodied Negro is as hard to find as a good serviceable horse."[38]

Slaves were not the only southerners who sought refuge with the Kansas Division. "For a wonder the people in this part of the country are all or nearly all good honest hearted Union people," marveled Samuel Worthington of the Eleventh Kansas. Hundreds of unwilling northwest Arkansas residents had been conscripted into Confederate ranks during the summer and early fall. Many deserted at the first opportunity and made their way to Union lines. To cite but one example, in November a band of fourteen men, late of Brooks's Arkansas Infantry, emerged from the brush and offered their services to the Union cause. The Arkansans carried new Enfield rifles but little else. "They are barefooted, bareheaded, and ragged and sleep on the ground without any blankets," noted a soldier in the Third Wisconsin Cavalry. Blunt enrolled some of these hardy souls in the First Arkansas Cavalry and placed others in Kansas regiments. Blunt also assisted hard-pressed Unionist farmers and storekeepers who preferred flight over fight. He purchased their crops, livestock, and inventories with promissory notes and sent them to Fort Scott under escort. Every two weeks or so dozens of families abandoned their homes and businesses and journeyed north with a returning commissary train, the wagons piled high with their clothing, furniture, and other possessions.[39]

Disloyal residents did not fare so well. Federal troops swept down on secessionist farms and businesses and confiscated or destroyed everything of value. The fate of a tannery in Cincinnati that provided shoe leather for Hindman's army was typical. "I went out with a party about eight miles and burned and destroyed a large tannery," recorded John H. Kitts of the Eleventh Kansas.

"We took the hides from the vats and threw them into the house and sheds, and set fire to the buildings." Another tannery a few miles away met a similar fate. Kitts estimated the combined loss at over $20,000, a staggering sum at that time. A more down-to-earth observation came from another Kansan. "Enough leather was destroyed to have shod ten thousand men," he wrote, "and many will be the cold toes among them the coming winter, in consequence of the loss." Depredations of this sort, repeated many times over, ground down the modest economic infrastructure of the border region and generated a stream of woebegone refugees seeking sanctuary in the Arkansas Valley. A Union officer remarked that "wherever our army goes the country becomes depopulated. Those who don't flee South beg to be taken North." Some of Blunt's men were disturbed by these developments. "By the time we leave there will not be much left for the people to live on, or come back for," concluded a Kansan. Blunt professed to be unaffected. "It is very certain that this country will afford short living for a bushwhacker when I leave it."[40]

The effects of the Union victory at Old Fort Wayne continued to ripple across the Indian Territory. Blunt informed Schofield that the Indian regiments "are fast filling up with recruits" and that the "loyal Indians are in fine spirits as to their future prospects." Seventy Creeks rode into camp in mid-November and enlisted in the First Indian. A week later one hundred Cherokees joined the Third Indian. "They are a set of hardy, athletic-looking fellows—more so than any others that have heretofore enlisted," wrote an admiring Union officer. Other tribes were represented as well. "Everything looks favorable in the Indian Territory if our advantages are followed up," wrote Blunt, who still wanted to advance to the Arkansas River "as soon as it is thought expedient to do so." Curtis was unlikely to approve such a move anytime soon, so Blunt had sent Colonel William A. Phillips and elements of the First and Third Indian on a reconnaissance-in-force into the Indian Territory on 6 November. The Indians passed through Tahlequah and Fort Gibson, then turned south and rode around the western flank of the Boston Mountains to Webber's Falls, thereby becoming the first Union soldiers to water their horses in the Arkansas River. They returned on the Line Road, brushed aside a Confederate cavalry force at Dutch Mills on 13 November, and rejoined the Kansas Division the following day without the loss of a man. The operation confirmed that the Confederacy had lost its grip on the northern half of the Indian Territory.[41]

Encouraged by Phillips's success, Blunt launched a second reconnaissance-in-force a few days later. On 20–24 November Lieutenant Colonel Lewis R. Jewell and two battalions of the Sixth Kansas Cavalry, accompanied by a battalion of the Third Indian, drove in Confederate pickets on the Line Road south of Evansville and pushed to within twenty-five miles of Van Buren. Jewell returned without incident and reported Rebel strength in the Arkansas Valley at 30,000 men. Blunt thought otherwise. "I am quite sure [Hindman's army] does not exceed 15,000 effective men, and probably not over 12,000," he told Schofield. "I would not hesitate to attack them on the other side of the mountains, and do not doubt of my ability to occupy and hold Van Buren and Fort Smith, provided General Steele [in Helena] occupies the attention of General Holmes, so that re-enforcements cannot be sent from Little Rock." Schofield forwarded the message to Curtis, who cautioned Blunt to keep a close eye on Hindman but not, under any circumstances, to attempt to cross the Boston Mountains in force.[42]

Officers and men of the Kansas Division quickly adjusted to the routine of camp life on the border. They enjoyed the pleasant fall weather and caught up with their correspondence, laundry, and sleep. "Bushwhackers are about the only enlivening element we have," reported a Wisconsin cavalryman in a light-hearted vein. "A volley from the thick jungles of brush now and then only serves to keep the boys' eyes open, and, though it is a little vexatious, it keep us on the alert." In fact, the danger posed by guerrillas, while diminished, was still very real. On 20 November a foraging party from the Eleventh Kansas was ambushed six miles from camp. One soldier was killed and another wounded.[43]

Occasional clashes with irregulars did not disguise the fact that the Confederates no longer seemed able or willing to contest the Union incursion. A Kansan made sport of the Rebel tendency to run when pressed. "As yet we have not been able to find the Southern Confederacy—only the Skedaderacy," he scoffed. More thoughtful Federals wondered why the Union offensive had come to a standstill. "'Strategy' is at work now," remarked a restless Kansas soldier, "and the army is sunning itself within a four days' march of the Arkansas river, where all had hoped to winter, and wondering why these cloudless days and mudless roads are not put to marching use." Blunt wondered the same thing. Forbidden to cross the Boston Mountains, he prowled restlessly around his sprawling camp on Flint Creek and waited for the Rebels to come to him.[44]

6 DOWN IN THE VALLEY

HINDMAN WAS ON THE MULBERRY RIVER WHEN HE LEARNED THAT Schofield had evacuated Fayetteville "in great haste." A few days later he received word that the Federals had pulled out of Osage Spring and Cross Hollows and returned to Missouri in a cloud of dust. Hindman could not believe his good fortune; the Union turnaround seemed a miracle. From his vantage point in Little Rock, Holmes offered a more prosaic explanation. He believed Schofield had misinterpreted Parsons's movement from Yellville to the Mulberry as a threat to his flank and acted accordingly. Also, Holmes wondered whether Schofield might have fewer men than previously thought, which might explain his skittish behavior. Revealing a previously unsuspected aggressive streak, Holmes expressed the hope that "when we are ready we will, I trust, be able to go after him."[1]

Hindman would have liked nothing better, but recent events had demonstrated that even his iron will could not overcome the deficiencies that plagued Confederate forces in Arkansas and the Indian Territory. "The troops and animals are much worn, having been marched over rough roads, almost in a starving condition," he wrote. "Time is needed for rest, repairs, the accumulation of subsistence and forage, and for effecting a complete organization." Hindman decided to remain in the Arkansas Valley and complete the process of creating a real army, a task he had only begun the previous summer. "I shall be able soon to organize this force and make it effective. At present it is the reverse, though the material is generally remarkably good." Hindman was buoyed by the realization that the Union counteroffensive had not significantly altered the strategic situation. "Affairs are now almost precisely as they were when I came to Fort Smith on August 24."[2]

In early November the Confederates moved up the Arkansas River to Fort Smith. Hindman picked up where he had left off three months earlier. Acting as his own inspector general, he traveled from camp to camp, evaluating officers, inspecting troops, and visiting hospitals. He was not pleased with what he found in many of the newly formed regiments. "The ignorance of many of the officers is almost *bestial*," he informed Holmes. "The indifference of others to the public good is indescribable. Such material must slough off, or be pruned away, or these troops will never become soldiers." The officer corps mirrored the poor quality of the men in the ranks, which was not surprising since many of the latter had been forced into the army at the point of a gun. Hindman acknowledged that the "class of men brought into service under the Conscription [Act] has infinitely less intelligence and soldierly spirit than that of which the volunteer regiments are composed." He established mandatory classes of instruction for officers and a rigorous program of drill for soldiers of all ranks. There was no time to produce ninety-day wonders. Thirty-day wonders would have to suffice.[3]

Food remained the most pressing problem. "The question of staying here or starving out, will very soon settle itself," Hindman predicted. Thousands of men and animals had been living off the countryside for months, and the local population was in desperate straits. "Many families are almost starving now," Hindman warned. "Beggary is becoming universal." He urged Holmes to hurry forward a thirty-day supply of beef, bread, and salt. Two weeks later he warned that "unless you send supplies in greater numbers, and far more rapidly, God only knows what I am to do." Hindman also called for shoes, uniforms, blankets, tents, and camp equipment and demanded $500,000 to pay his soldiers because the "families of many of them are in great need of it." In a lightheaded moment he even asked Holmes for a fully equipped infantry division, adding the "sooner sent the better." Fairly or unfairly, the notion that Holmes was dragging his feet gained currency, as evidenced by a letter from Colonel Asa S. Morgan to his wife. "You have no idea how poor we are and General Holmes has I think been too slow in hurrying up arms and equipment."[4]

The truth was that commissary and quartermaster personnel labored tirelessly to gather stores and get them to where they were needed, but everything was in short supply and low water in the Arkansas River hampered traffic. Transports blocked by sand and gravel bars unloaded their cargoes at the nearest convenient point and returned to Little Rock. This led to surpluses at some places along the river and shortages at others. At Clarksville, midway between Little Rock and Fort Smith, rations were adequate if uninspiring. "We have plenty of corn bread and poor beef to eat," reported a Missouri officer. But only a handful of light-draft steamboats reached the camps farther upstream. Hungry soldiers stationed near Fort Smith probably would have regarded corn bread and stringy beef as a feast. Lieutenant Colonel George W. Guess reported that his Texas cavalry regiment was "without any bread or meal" and that his troopers were reduced to "panking corn in the ashes and eating it for breakfast." The Missourians on Mazzard Prairie, just below Fort Smith, were in much the same fix. Artilleryman William H. Hoskin observed that food was "so scarse that we are eating parched corn and it is hard to get that." Animals suffered as well as men. When a train loaded with hay rolled into camp, Hoskins noted that it was the "first feed our horses has had for five days. They hav eaten the hitch reins up and several of them got away and [are] gone for good." Years later an Arkansan recalled with sardonic humor that the meager rations kept everyone "good and lean, so as to be in fine condition for dodging bullets."[5]

Hindman also struggled to equip his command with arms, ammunition, and accouterments. In early November he reported that the infantry had fewer than twenty rounds per man "and not guns enough by several thousand." The shortage of firearms, flints, caps, and cartridges was matched by a scarcity of bayonets, belts, cap pouches, and cartridge boxes. Hindman urged Colonel John V. Dunnington, the chief ordnance officer in the Trans-Mississippi Department, to hurry forward whatever weaponry was available whenever it became available. "As soon as you get fifty guns fit for use, send them, and so continue until my unarmed men have something to fight with." Ordnance personnel shipped more than 5,000 firearms of both American and European manufacture up the Arkansas in November. Near the end of the month an officer watched Arkansas and Missouri troops drill with new British-made Enfield rifles near Fort Smith. He concluded that the infantry as a whole was "pretty well armed" and that "some of the regiments are most splendidly armed." The loss of the transport *Fair Play* and its cargo of arms and ammunition the previous August continued to haunt the Rebels. Several regiments were still awaiting weapons when the army set out for Prairie Grove in early December. One day Hindman received a pathetic appeal from one of his subordinates: "If *it is possible* that shoes and arms can be furnished to my Missourians I am sure that they would be well used in the service of the Government." But the requested items were unavailable.[6]

The shiny Enfields contrasted strongly with the tattered garments worn by many of Hindman's troops. No soldiers in the Confederacy were more woebegone in appearance than those camped along the Arkansas River in the fall of 1862. "They are the ragedist lot of men that I ever saw, a great many of them barefooted and bareheaded and almost naked," wrote a Missouri officer. "When men grumble here it is chiefly about clothing, and surely they have a right to grumble, and I most vigorously do grumble with them," declared a threadbare Lieutenant Nathaniel Taylor, a Texas cavalryman. "Our clothes are nearly all worn out and we look more like a great army of beggars than anything else." Taylor had all but given up on the Confederate supply system. "The relatives of the boys had better do the best they can for them," he cautioned. Like their counterparts in blue, the Rebels called on family, friends, and patriotic citizens to send warm clothing, or any clothing at all, as temperatures drifted downward. It was still early in the war, and appeals of this sort were successful more often than not. Before the year was out Colonel Guess published a letter in several newspapers thanking the "ladies of Texas" for the "promptness and liberality with which they have furnished us with good warm clothing."[7]

Contrary to myth, the trans-Mississippi Confederacy received few manufactured goods by way of blockade-running in the western Gulf of Mexico. Nearly all factory-made items, whether firearms from Britain or footwear from Georgia, reached Arkansas via the railhead and waterfront at Vicksburg. As the war progressed, however, the presence of Union gunboats on the Mississippi severed the direct connection between Vicksburg and Little Rock. The Confederates established an indirect connection through Louisiana via the Ouachita River, but this route was longer, slower, and less reliable. By the fall of 1862 the arrival of any shipment from the eastern Confederacy was cause for celebration in Arkansas and the Indian Territory.

One such joyous event occurred in late November, when 7,000 uniforms reached Little Rock after a circuitous journey. The news raised expectations among the ragged Rebels and led Hindman to announce that he would personally oversee a "fair and just distribution" of the new uniforms. "There shall be no unfairness in this; all shall share alike, whether Missourians, Texans, Arkansians or Indians." Hindman went to great lengths to avoid even the appearance of favoritism. He made it clear that officers found "fomenting dissatisfaction" over the distribution of uniforms would be "severely dealt with, whatever may be their rank." The uniforms (a mix of gray and butternut colors) were issued as quickly as possible, and by the end of November much of Hindman's command had taken on the muted hues typical of other Confederate armies.[8]

The hardships caused by inadequate food and clothing were exacerbated by a shortage of tents and blankets. "Very disagreeable in camp without tents," commented Captain Eathan A. Pinnell, a Missouri officer, after spending a cold, rainy night under a tree. "When, if ever, we will get a supply of tents, I know not," he confided to his diary. "Without some better camp accommodations this winter, we will undoubtedly feel some of the chilling effects of frost." As fall faded into winter, soldiers weakened by malnourishment and exposure fell victim to a host of diseases.[9]

Hindman was especially concerned about medical care, a reflection of his experience in the Mexican War when the Second Mississippi was decimated by disease. "It was with him a hobby to look after the comforts of the sick and wounded," recalled a staff officer. "No general officer ever more closely inspected hospitals. Woe to the surgeon whose selfishness, drunkenness, incompetency or ignorance was brought to his knowledge." The army's medical director, Surgeon James M. Keller, shared Hindman's zeal. The quality of Confederate medical care in Arkansas and the Indian Territory was a disgrace, but both men worked diligently to improve conditions in the overcrowded, understaffed, and ill-equipped hospitals. Keller was in constant motion from one hospital to another up and down the Arkansas River. He informed Hindman that "bad weather, bad shelters, lack of bedding and clothing, and the impossibility of procuring suitable diet" was proving fatal to far too many patients. Three-fourths of the nearly nine hundred men crowded into one facility were afflicted with pneumonia. At Keller's urging, Hindman made the distribution of food, blankets, and camp equipment to hospitals a top priority, but conditions remained abysmal.[10]

In spite of Hindman's personal attention and Keller's heroic efforts, the Confederates experienced a medical crisis of staggering proportions during the final months of 1862. The first hints of disaster appeared soon after the Rebels reached the Mulberry River. "It was here that sickness began to manifest itself to a deplorable degree, for although there had been considerable chills and other light sickness before, yet there had been nothing in comparison to what we now experienced," wrote Missourian Peter Lane. Men fell ill by the thousands and filled the spartan hospitals to overflowing. Diseases proliferated as sanitary conditions deteriorated. The situation worsened after the Confederates moved to Fort Smith. "Sickness prevailed here to an alarming extent, mostly a Typhoid or Camp Fever and Diarhoea. The 'hospitals' as they were called at Fort Smith were the most awful and loathsome places imaginable," continued Lane. "Fifteen hundred or two thousand sick and dying humans continually filled those places, besides thousands in their tents at the camps." Texan John C. Williams reported tersely that a "great many of our men were taken sick, and many of them died" while the army was in the Arkansas Valley. Fort Smith, he concluded sadly, was the "unhealthiest camp we were placed in during the war." No one will ever know how many men were swept away in this maelstrom, but in military terms the loss of manpower could not have been less than a brigade.[11]

Hindman's depleted ranks were partially filled by Missourians who made their way through Union lines during the month of November. Some of the newcomers were notorious. Guerrilla William C. Quantrill and seventy-six members of his murderous band rode into Fort Smith and announced their intention to spend the winter in the Arkansas Valley. Although Hindman was a strong advocate of what the Confederacy euphemistically termed "partisan rangers," he feared the effect on military discipline if Quantrill's ruffians were permitted to go their own way. He mustered the guerrillas into the army as an independent company of Missouri cavalry and placed them under Marmaduke's authority until such time as they chose to return home. Lieutenant William Gregg assumed leadership of the band after Quantrill became bored and departed for Richmond to press his claim for a colonelcy.[12]

Hindman welcomed new hands, even those stained with blood, because they helped to make up for the absence of many old hands. "Stragglers from the army are to be found in nearly every house throughout the country," he declared. With the Union army apparently on its way back to Missouri, Hindman ordered provost marshals to return to their districts north of the Arkansas River and round up absentees. He also directed the provost marshals to rid the Ozark Plateau of the "deserters, tories, and outlaws" who were terrorizing the populace. This was not quite a return to martial law, but it was not far from it. Hindman had spent the summer restoring order in northern Arkansas. If he had to use the army to prevent that part of the state from sliding back into chaos, he would do so regardless of the wishes of politicians in Richmond and Little Rock.[13]

The name of the Confederate force at Fort Smith was a point of contention. Hindman wanted to call his command the "Army of the West," but that name, like so much else, had been hijacked by Van Dorn and carried across the Mississippi. Moreover, War Department bureaucrats argued, not unreasonably, that to avoid confusion a department and its army should share the same name. They insisted that the military arm of the Trans-Mississippi Department be called the "Trans-Mississippi Army." Holmes sided with Hindman, though he had little hope that the paper shufflers in Richmond could be convinced to change their minds. In mid-November he threw in the towel and told Hindman to call his command the "Trans-Mississippi Army." Hindman balked and suggested an alternative name, the "Army of Missouri," on the grounds that he expected to operate on Missouri soil in the near future. Holmes offered a compromise of sorts. "I cannot call yours the Army of Missouri until it is certain you will go there," he stated. "Whenever you start with a fair prospect of staying I will issue the order, giving you the name, with a God-speed." Mollified, Hindman agreed to use the officially sanctioned name for the time being.[14]

By late November the newly christened Confederate force was beginning to take shape. Lieutenant Taylor observed:

> Until Hindman made his appearance amongst us, the army of northwest Arkansas was a mere *burlesque* of an army. Discipline was wanting among the men and there was a very considerable lack of brain among the officers. Of course such a condition of things was not to be brooked in the face of an enemy, and we *had* to fall back, and be organized and have the chaff sifted away from us as we *fell*. I believe *now* the army is in fair fighting trim, and when the day shall come, if we do not defeat the foe, we shall so cover *his* victory in blood that he shall not rejoice.[15]

It was a prophetic statement.

The Trans-Mississippi Army consisted of four unequal formations: one cavalry division, two infantry divisions, and a catchall reserve division that existed largely on paper. Marmaduke's Division was composed of about 3,100 Arkansas, Missouri, and Texas cavalrymen organized into three brigades of varying size. The four woebegone Texas cavalry regiments that had performed so poorly at White River were dismounted and converted to infantry. The Texans were mortified at having to give up their horses ("It was a bitter pill for them," wrote Marmaduke), but Hindman had little sympathy for men who in his estimation had failed repeatedly to carry out their duties. The troopers that remained were among the most committed soldiers in the army, yet their effectiveness was impaired by a lack of proper arms, equipment, and horses.[16]

Shoup's Division was a force of roughly 5,100 Arkansas infantry, both volunteers and conscripts, organized into two large brigades of roughly equal size. It was led by Colonel Francis A. Shoup, an Indiana native and 1855 graduate of the U.S. Military Academy. Shoup endured four years of humdrum duty in the artillery before resigning to practice law. He moved to Florida and ended up in the Confederate army. Named chief of artillery of the Army of Tennessee after a stellar performance at Shiloh, Shoup followed Hindman to Arkansas. Though he was only twenty-eight years of age, Shoup's military background and organizational ability made him indispensable to the Trans-Mississippi Department. Holmes and Hindman recognized him as a brigadier general long before his promotion was confirmed in Richmond.

Francis A. Shoup in a postwar image (Library of Congress)

Unfortunately, Shoup's northern birth and aloof manner did not gain him any friends in the army. "I do not like General Shoup," Colonel Morgan confided to his wife. "He is a Yankee born and I regard him as a supercilious disagreeable man. Our Brigade despises him. Indeed I know of no one who likes him except General Hindman with whom he is a favorite."[17]

Frost's Division, about 5,800 strong, was composed of a large Missouri infantry brigade and a smaller Arkansas infantry brigade. The commander was Brigadier General Daniel M. Frost, a native of New York, an 1844 graduate of West Point, and a veteran of the Mexican War. Frost had resigned from the army in 1853 and settled in Missouri. Slim, trim, and something of a dandy, he was best known for meekly surrendering the Missouri State Militia to Nathaniel Lyon at Camp Jackson in 1861. His reputation never recovered from that fiasco, though he performed with credit if not distinction at Wilson's Creek and Pea Ridge. Frost was another victim of the xenophobia that gripped the Confederacy. He was regarded with suspicion because of his northern birth and alleged lack of commitment to the southern cause. Frost did not help matters by behaving like a martinet. A fellow Missourian described him as the "most unpopular man in the army; universally despised by all in his command."[18]

Daniel M. Frost (Missouri History Museum)

Roane's Division was the largest but least important formation in the army. Its commanding officer, Brigadier General John S. Roane, was an indolent Arkansas politician so lacking in military ability that even Holmes considered him "useless as a commander." Hindman regarded the division as a reserve at best and a dumping ground for incompetents and malcontents at worst. On paper, Roane's command consisted of 6,700 men organized into two brigades, one of infantry and one of cavalry. The infantry brigade was composed initially of the four Texas regiments banished from Marmaduke's command. Hindman thought so little of them that he made no attempt to replace their shotguns with rifles. "Certainly we are not fit for much," moaned a humiliated Texan. The same might have been said of the entire division. The cavalry brigade encompassed everyone and everything in the Indian Territory. It was an area command rather than an actual military organization. Hindman had little use for the "immense mass of wandering, unorganized, and worthless cavalry" in the Indian Territory and wanted to convert the mounted troops into infantry. He also wanted to place all authority, civil and military, in the hands of his friend, Patrick Cleburne. "With such a man," Hindman promised, "an immensely beneficial change would soon be wrought and it would be permanent." Until his request for Cleburne was acted upon, or until some other solution presented itself, Hindman strove to maintain the illusion that the chaotic array of Confederate units in the Indian Territory represented a viable fighting force.[19]

Indians aside, the Trans-Mississippi Army consisted of about 15,000 men from Arkansas, Missouri, and Texas, though no more than four-fifths of that number were adequately armed and equipped for service in the field. Three of the five highest-ranking officers were West Pointers with seventeen years of combined service in the regular army (Marmaduke, Shoup, and Frost). Three were veterans of the Mexican War (Hindman, Frost, and Roane), and three had served in the Army of Tennessee and fought at Shiloh (Hindman, Marmaduke, and Shoup). By way of contrast, the Army of the Frontier was led by military amateurs. Besides Schofield and Totten, both of whom were in St. Louis, only one Union division commander was a West Point graduate and regular army veteran (Huston) and only one had participated in a major battle (Herron). Whether the Confederate advantage in military education and experience would translate into victory on the battlefield remained to be seen.

Hindman neither sought nor achieved popularity, but as the army took shape along the banks of the Arkansas River he steadily (if grudgingly) gained respect. Colonel Morgan put aside his initial doubts, informing his wife that "I have a growing confidence in General Hindman and feel that he can accomplish as much as any one with his means." Lieutenant Taylor, the chronically unhappy Texas cavalryman, was another convert: "I have great confidence in Hindman. He is a superior man, and every one must receive this impression who comes in contact with him. He issues occasionally some exceedingly stringent orders, and consequently the army generally dislikes him; it is all the fashion to 'cuss' him, but very few seem to doubt his ability." Other officers experienced a similar change of heart, perhaps none more enthusiastically than Colonel Almerine Alexander, commanding officer of one of the dismounted Texas cavalry regiments. If anyone had a grievance it was Alexander, but he was gradually won over by Hindman's drive and determination:

> We have been under the immediate command of Maj. Gen. Hindman for some months, and can cheerfully say to our friends at home, the better we have known him the better we have loved him. He has energy coupled with capacity that fully qualifies him for a leader. All have unlimited confidence in him as a man and a general. He won me on sight.

> So I am (as well as this brigade) a Hindman man. He sees things clearly and quickly, and acts promptly. We will go with him to ——, if he calls.

Not everyone was willing to go quite that far, but Hindman clearly made a positive impression on men hungry for leadership and a sense of purpose.[20]

Morale slowly revived. In early November, after withdrawing into the Arkansas Valley, the Missouri exiles had been in low spirits. Trying to put a brave face on the situation, Surgeon Edwin E. Harris informed his wife that the "prospect of getting to Missouri at present seems very dull, though we hope for the best." By the end of the month, however, many officers and men thought it possible that they might be home in time for Christmas. In a "bully speech" to his regiment, Colonel John B. Clark Jr. announced that it was only a matter of days before the army headed north. "This is what we are ancious to do," commented a soldier in the audience. That same day Samuel Ritchey advised his aunt, who was living in exile in Texas, that she should begin to make preparations to return to Missouri in the spring. "It is believed now that Hindman is on the move."[21]

At this critical juncture events elsewhere nearly derailed Hindman's plans. President Davis urged Holmes to send 10,000 men to Vicksburg at once. Davis wanted to hold the Confederate Gibraltar with soldiers from the Trans-Mississippi Department while Lieutenant General John C. Pemberton concentrated his own forces against those of Major General Ulysses S. Grant in northern Mississippi. Davis assured Holmes that Pemberton would return the borrowed soldiers as soon as they no longer were needed. Holmes found it hard to believe that the "people in Richmond" (as he contemptuously called them) had so little understanding of the desperate state of affairs in the Trans-Mississippi Department. He informed Davis that he was threatened on two fronts and could not possibly transfer nearly half of his command to Vicksburg: "If I leave here there is little doubt the valley of Arkansas will be taken possession of, and with it goes Arkansas and Louisiana." Holmes argued that if any part of the Confederacy was in imminent danger of going under, it was Arkansas, not Mississippi. He refused to move troops across the river unless expressly ordered to do so. "You cannot imagine the anxiety and pain it gives me to be thus idle, but I do not see any help for it," he wrote. Davis was flabbergasted by Holmes's intransigence and backed down.[22]

Standing up to Davis was a trying experience for Holmes. He lost sleep, snapped at his staff, and wallowed in indecision. "I am in great doubt what to do," he lamented to Hindman. Instead of going after the Federals, an overwrought Holmes began to fret that the Federals were coming after him. A reported increase in Union strength at Helena revived fears of an attack on Arkansas Post or Little Rock. "The invasion of Missouri is interdicted," Holmes informed Hindman in late November, "so make your arrangements to give up that darling project."[23]

Hindman ignored Holmes's mercurial outbursts and continued his preparations for a forward movement. "I believe I may clear northwestern Arkansas and the Indian country within ten days," he announced. "Am certain Schofield is ready to run." On 24 November Hindman learned that the Missouri Divisions were moving toward Helena on the Mississippi River. The intelligence report was accurate as far as it went, but it did not include the critical information that Curtis had ordered the Missouri Divisions to reverse course. That same day Hindman also learned that the Kansas Division had not withdrawn in concert with the rest of the Union army. Hindman was intrigued. If the reports were correct, Schofield had departed for points east and Blunt was alone—utterly alone—on the border between Arkansas and the Indian Territory. While Hindman pondered how to take advantage of these promising developments, a bombshell arrived from Marmaduke.[24]

A week after Marmaduke returned from his successful foraging expedition to Cane Hill, the movement that had alarmed Blunt and Schofield and caused Curtis to rush the Missouri Divisions back toward Arkansas, Hindman ordered a repeat performance. On 23–24 November the cavalry and the commissary train plodded up the Line Road to Cane Hill. Back in familiar territory, the Confederates went to work gathering additional food for the famished men and animals in the Arkansas Valley.

Marmaduke took advantage of the pastoral lull to remind Hindman that his division needed to rest and refit. He warned that a "great many of my horses are bare footed and lame" and that the scarcity of iron at Cane Hill made it impossible for his farriers to remedy the situation. If that were not bad enough, his new howitzer carriages were falling apart. "These mountain batteries are badly made and as they are now constructed will not follow cavalry and cannot endure rough service." Ammunition was another headache. His troopers had only about twenty rounds per man and were almost out of percussion caps. If the Federals showed up, Marmaduke feared his men would have to throw bullets at them: "I request that General Hindman will send up *by courier* at the earliest possible moment a package [of caps] for immediate use." Marmaduke also asked for uniforms, shoes, and camp equipment. The only items his horsemen had in abundance at Cane Hill were food and water.[25]

On 24 November a local secessionist informed Marmaduke that he had recently visited Blunt's camp on Flint Creek, twenty-two miles to the northwest, in search of stolen horses. The Arkansan failed to recover his stock but garnered a good deal of useful information about the Federals. He reported that the Kansas Division consisted of 7,000 "well drilled armed and equipped" soldiers, including three regiments of Indians. That same day a Confederate officer, Captain J. C. Stanley, entered the Union camp under a flag of truce to advise Blunt of a problem with some paroled prisoners. Stanley returned to Cane Hill and told Marmaduke that the Union force was about 8,000 strong, the half-dozen cavalry regiments were in "bad condition," and there were no defensive works around the sprawling encampment. Additional information came from a "very intelligent and shrude young lady" who lived nearby and spoke often with Union officers.[26]

These reports convinced Marmaduke that Blunt was vulnerable. That night he reached for pen and paper, not to make another complaint about the state of his command, but to propose to Hindman that the Trans-Mississippi Army cross the Boston Mountains and fall upon the Kansas Division at Flint Creek. "I believe you can capture this force, if you can move secretly and with celerity," Marmaduke declared. "Say you can move eight thousand infantry twenty to twenty-five miles a day. I think with the Cavalry under my command I can keep your movement unknown *at least* till you reach Fayetteville, then by a forced march at night you can be on the enemy at daylight." Marmaduke's enthusiasm grew as his pen scratched across the paper: "General I feel assured that you can bag this party in a short quick fight. Blount and no one else dreams of such a move. It will *surprise* friend and foe, hence the better chance for secrecy and success. . . . What do you say to it?"[27]

What could Hindman say? Here was the opportunity he had been waiting for. He intensified preparations for an advance but realized that it would be a week, perhaps longer, before the army could take the field. In the meantime, there was little Hindman could do except urge Marmaduke to be careful and to protect the commissary train at all costs. Marmaduke assured his anxious commander that he was in no danger at Cane Hill. "All is quiet here," he reported.[28]

7 CANE HILL

MARMADUKE WAS IN FOR A BIG SURPRISE. ON 24 NOVEMBER BLUNT learned that the Confederates had returned to Cane Hill. Instead of assuming a defensive position along Flint Creek, as he had done two weeks earlier, Blunt decided to launch a preemptive attack. "I shall move on Marmaduke tomorrow morning," he informed Curtis. "Hope to destroy him before he can be re-enforced by Hindman." Curtis immediately notified Herron that "General Blunt is about to attack the enemy at Cane Hill" and told him to be prepared to support the Kansas Division "by a prompt movement" should that become necessary. Herron replied that the Missouri Divisions were ready to return to Arkansas at a moment's notice. The rapid exchange demonstrated the critical importance of the telegraph line linking St. Louis, Springfield, and Elkhorn Tavern. It was a small but telling example of the impact of emerging industrial technology on traditional methods of warfare.[1]

In the trans-Mississippi, however, logistics rather than communications dictated the pace and scale of operations, and logistics atop the Ozark Plateau continued to exhibit a preindustrial character. Colonel Thomas Moonlight, Blunt's able chief of staff, stated that despite extensive foraging the Kansas Division "had not quite become a self-sustaining institution." Blunt delayed the start of the operation for forty-eight hours to ensure the safe arrival of a commissary train of two hundred wagons from Fort Scott. The immense train, nearly two miles in length, rolled into camp late on 26 November, much to everyone's relief.[2]

The next morning, Thanksgiving Day, 5,000 men and thirty guns left Flint Creek and headed south on the Line Road. Weer and Cloud led their respective brigades; Salomon and part of his brigade remained behind to guard the trains. The six cavalry regiments, four infantry regiments, and eight batteries were followed by a half-dozen ambulances piled high with ammunition and medical supplies. Each man carried only a blanket, three days' rations, and forty rounds of ammunition. Blunt, as usual, rode at the head of the column in a carriage. The Federals stopped in Cincinnati and consumed a spartan holiday lunch of bacon, hard bread, and coffee. Instead of continuing on to the junction with Cincinnati Road, the usual route to Cane Hill, they turned east on a primitive track that wound across the southern end of Wedington Mountain. Cloud had used this indirect approach against MacDonald three weeks earlier and apparently convinced Blunt of its value. The Union column finally halted for the night on Moore's Creek, one mile west of Rhea's Mill.[3]

Friday, 28 November, was a crisp, clear autumn day. The Federals rolled out of their blankets minus the usual martial clamor. "Marched at six without drum or bugle," noted Sergeant Sherman Bodwell of the Eleventh Kansas. Having learned a lesson at Old Fort Wayne, Blunt made certain every regiment and battery was in column on the road before he gave the order to advance. Moving with as much stealth and celerity as a nineteenth-century army could manage, the Kansas Division passed Rhea's Mill and turned south on Ridge Road. The "obscure and unfrequented" track led directly to Cane Hill, seven miles away.[4]

Cane Hill is a rolling plateau set off from the Springfield Plain by imposing escarpments to the north and east. At the time of the Civil War the plateau was a checkerboard of homesteads, fields, and orchards. The principal settlements, Boonsboro and Newburg (known today as Canehill and Clyde), occupied the winding valley carved by Jordan Creek. Confederate headquarters was located at Kidd's Mill, midway between the two towns. While waiting for Hindman to join him, Marmaduke had learned that the First Arkansas Cavalry was stationed at Elkhorn Tavern. Elimination of the hated "Mountain Feds" would complete Blunt's isolation and allow the Confederates to settle some scores. Marmaduke could not resist the temptation. He casually informed Hindman that "I march with about one thousand men tomorrow night to surprise and capture them." Marmaduke intended to set out after dark on Thanksgiving, but his men had not yet saddled their mounts when a courier galloped up with unwelcome news: a strong force of Union cavalry, infantry, and artillery was moving south on the Line Road in the general direction of Cane Hill. Marmaduke canceled the Elkhorn Tavern operation and ordered the commissary train to withdraw across the mountains on Cove Creek Road.[5]

Since it would take time for the heavily laden wagons to reach Lee Creek, Marmaduke prepared to fight a delaying action. Early on 28 November he placed Joseph O. Shelby's Brigade, a force of 1,200 Missourians, on Cincin-

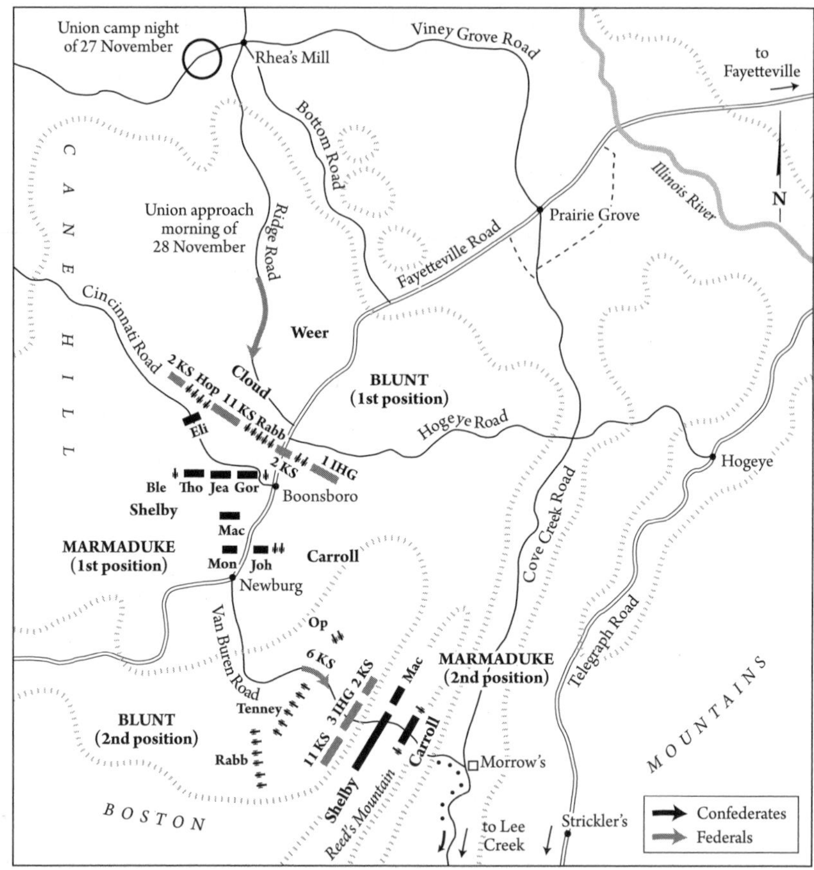

Cane Hill

nati Road northwest of Boonsboro. Shelby's right flank was anchored in the Boonsboro cemetery; his left flank was located on rising ground a half-mile to the west. Lieutenant Colonel B. Frank Gordon's Missouri Cavalry was on the right, Colonel Beal G. Jeans's Missouri Cavalry was in the center, and Colonel Gideon W. Thompson's Missouri Cavalry was on the left. Major Benjamin Elliott's Missouri Cavalry Battalion took up an advanced position while Gregg's lightly armed guerrillas (Shelby referred to them as "Quantrill's famous company") formed a reserve. Captain Joseph Bledsoe's Missouri Battery—a pair of elderly iron 6-pounder guns that had seen service in the Mexican War—provided artillery support.[6]

Marmaduke and Shelby expected the Federals to arrive from the northwest on Cincinnati Road, the most direct route from the Line Road. Neither demonstrated much concern about Fayetteville Road, which approaches

Joseph O. Shelby (Civil War Museum at Wilson's Creek National Battlefield)

from the northeast and follows Jordan Creek. This proved to be a serious oversight because Ridge Road joins Fayetteville Road one mile northeast of Boonsboro. As a result, the Union column reached the junction and turned onto Fayetteville Road without being detected. Blunt climbed out of his carriage, mounted his horse, and ordered Cloud to push forward with his Third Brigade. Cloud promptly moved out with Major James G. Fisk's battalion of the Second Kansas Cavalry and Lieutenant Stover's Second Kansas Cavalry Battery, a force of about three hundred men and two 12-pounder mountain howitzers.[7]

While Cloud advanced, Blunt and Captain John W. Rabb's Second Indiana Battery remained near the junction. Several minutes ticked by but Ridge Road remained empty. Blunt began to fidget. Where was the rest of the Third Brigade? Memories of the botched advance at Old Fort Wayne must have flashed through his mind. A crackle of gunfire in the direction of Boonsboro indicated that Cloud had encountered Confederate pickets. Blunt could wait no longer. He dispatched his most impressively named staff officer, Major Verplanck Van Antwerp, to find out what was the matter and to hurry everyone forward.[8]

Shelby had trouble of his own. When his pickets on Fayetteville Road came scrambling back with Cloud in hot pursuit, he had not completed deploying his forces: "I must confess (though it may reflect somewhat upon myself) that the enemy, by his skillful management, fell upon me sooner than I would have desired." To make matters worse, Fayetteville Road was the one avenue of approach the Confederates had neglected to block. Shelby would be cut off if the Federals reached the junction with Cincinnati Road, and Marmaduke would have fewer than seven hundred men with which to cover the withdrawal of the train. Shelby needed time to establish a defensive position in the Jordan Valley. He rode into the cemetery where Bledsoe was manning one of his antique guns amid a somber thicket of headstones and funerary statuary. He ordered Bledsoe to open fire and keep the enemy at bay as long as possible. It was 10:00 A.M.[9]

Four hundred yards north of the cemetery, Cloud saw the muzzle flash of Bledsoe's gun and ducked as a shell exploded overhead. He directed Stover to wheel his two mountain howitzers up the western slope of the Jordan Valley and open fire. While helping place the guns, Fisk suffered a severe scalp wound from a shell fragment but stayed at his post until ordered to the rear. At the first crash of artillery fire, Blunt ordered Rabb's battery into the fray. Rabb moved down the valley and unlimbered his four 6-pounder James rifles and two 6-pounder guns. ("This battery had no superior on either side in the Civil War," declared a Union officer, "and Captain Rabb in action was all that could be desired.") The Indiana artillerymen were at a slight disadvantage firing uphill, but they blasted the cemetery with shell and case shot. Meanwhile, on the Confederate side, Bledsoe's other gun and a pair of 2-pounder mountain rifles from Captain John C. Shoup's Arkansas Battery joined the fight, evening the odds slightly. Between 10:00 and 11:00 A.M. the fighting north of Boonsboro was limited to an exchange of artillery fire. The only fatality occurred when a solid shot from one of Shoup's small guns killed a driver and two horses in Rabb's battery. The fatal projectile was "about the size and shape of an old-fashioned clock weight," noted a curious Kansas gunner.[10]

Meanwhile, Van Antwerp reached the stalled Union column on Ridge Road and discovered the reason for the delay. The next unit in the line of march behind Fisk's battalion of the Second Kansas Cavalry was the Eleventh Kansas, an infantry regiment. Sandwiched between mounted forces, Colonel Thomas Ewing Jr. had driven his regiment forward at a killing pace all morning. ("Men very tired and falling out fast," a soldier scribbled in his diary.) Ewing finally called a halt in a patch of woods to allow his men to catch their breath. Instead of moving aside and allowing the mounted forces farther back in line to proceed, the winded infantrymen collapsed to the ground in the

Thomas Ewing Jr. (Kansas State Historical Society)

narrow road. Colonel Bassett, leading the remaining two battalions of the Second Kansas Cavalry, asked Ewing to move his men out of the road so his horsemen could advance, but Ewing unaccountably refused. His intransigence brought the Federal column to a halt.[11]

Van Antwerp reached the scene just as the artillery opened fire. "The sound of the guns roused the boys and was received with yells from one end of the column to the other," said one Union soldier. Shouting over the cheers of the troops, Van Antwerp told Bassett that the rest of the Second Kansas Cavalry was needed at the front. He also told Ewing in no uncertain terms to clear the road. Bassett did not wait for Ewing to comply but immediately led his troopers past the prostrate infantrymen. "This was done at a gallop, single file, as the Eleventh filled the road, and it was necessary to pass around them," recalled a cavalryman. The Kansans hurried toward the sound of the guns, followed by Lieutenant Colonel Stephen H. Wattles's First Indian and Captain Henry Hopkins's Kansas Battery (the "Trophy Battery" taken from the Rebels at Old Fort Wayne). Smarting at having been publicly upbraided, Ewing ordered his men to drop their packs and blankets and follow the cavalry at the double-quick.[12]

Cloud placed the First Indian on the left of Fisk's battalion of the Second Kansas Cavalry. Unable to find room in the narrow valley for Hopkins's

Henry Hopkins (Steven L. Warren Collection)

four artillery pieces, Cloud sent the battery to the bluff on the west side of the road. He then dispatched the two remaining battalions of the Second Kansas Cavalry to support Hopkins and secure the Union right flank. When the Eleventh Kansas reached the scene a few minutes later, Cloud placed the regiment in the gap between Rabb's and Hopkins's batteries. Marmaduke watched the steady buildup of Union forces from the cemetery and ordered Shelby to fall back.[13]

The Confederates escaped in the nick of time. The sound of drums and bugles rose above the din of artillery fire, and 1,500 cheering Federals swept down the Jordan Valley. A handful of Confederates attempted to make a stand in the center of Boonsboro but were quickly put to flight. Union artillery fire struck a church and several businesses, but the most serious damage occurred at Cane Hill College, a Presbyterian institution for men. The college buildings were among the largest in town and hard to miss. Shells crashed into the two-story frame structure that served as library and laboratory. "One exploded in the room in which was kept Mathematical, Astronomical, Philosophical, Geographical, etc. etc. instruments," noted a Union soldier. "That one shell destroyed thousands of dollars worth of instruments." The opposing forces passed through Boonsboro so quickly that only minor damage was done to houses and outbuildings.[14]

MacDonald's Missouri Cavalry was deployed in support of Shelby just south of Boonsboro, but two hundred men could do nothing to stem the blue tide and Marmaduke ordered MacDonald to follow Shelby to the rear. MacDonald's departure uncovered Colonel Charles A. Carroll's Brigade, which was located near Kidd's Mill. The brigade boasted a paper strength of 1,700 Arkansans, but on this day it consisted of fewer than 400 men, half of whom were handicapped by broken-down or ill-shod horses. Carroll's own regiment, led by Lieutenant Colonel James A. Johnson, occupied an imposing bluff east of the road; Lieutenant Colonel James C. Monroe's Arkansas Cavalry held lower ground west of the road near the mill. Two 12-pounder mountain howitzers commanded by Lieutenant William M. Hughey were located atop the bluff on Carroll's right.[15]

When the Rebel gunners opened fire, Cloud ordered Hopkins's battery into action. Although the Kansans had not had much time to learn their new trade as artillerymen, they rose to the occasion. Opening fire from the bluff across the valley with three 6-pounder guns and one 12-pounder howitzer, they quickly drove Hughey away. On the way down the hill one of the howitzer carriages fell apart, but Hughey and his gunners managed to retrieve the brass tube. Carroll's Arkansans fired a few "short and ineffectual" volleys from their shotguns, then hurried to the rear after the crippled battery. The departure of Carroll's Brigade marked the end of the first phase of the battle of Cane Hill. As noon approached the opposing forces moved toward Newburg, a half-mile to the south.[16]

Van Buren Road branches off from Fayetteville Road at Newburg and connects with Cove Creek Road at Morrow's, five miles to the southeast. The Confederate commissary train was slowly making its way across the Boston Mountains on this route. In a desperate bid to buy time for the train, Marmaduke assembled his division on a "commanding eminence" east of Newburg and practically invited Blunt to attack. Blunt thought the hill was a "most admirable position for defense" and wanted to concentrate his entire force before launching an assault. Cloud's Third Brigade was disorganized after passing through Boonsboro and struggling across the ravine cut by Jordan Creek west of the road. Weer's Second Brigade, which had deployed behind and to the left of the Third Brigade, was slow to come up because of equally difficult terrain east of the road. Elements of the First Brigade were still in column well to the rear.[17]

A little before one 1:00 P.M. Blunt ordered Rabb to open fire on the Confederate position. Before Rabb could act, Lieutenant Marcus D. Tenney's First Kansas Battery rolled up. Blunt had Tenney unlimber his six 10-pounder

Parrott rifled guns and join in the bombardment. Bledsoe and Shoup did their best to disrupt Federal preparations by banging away "with spirit" from atop the hill, but the Confederate artillery proved ineffectual and Marmaduke concluded that it was time to go. Rabb and Tenney got off only a dozen rounds before the Rebels abandoned the hill and sped away on Van Buren Road. Blunt ordered a general pursuit, and within minutes the narrow road was crowded with men and horses rushing south at breakneck speed.[18]

During the three-mile running fight that followed, the van of the Union column skirmished continuously with the rear of the Confederate column. Blunt was so close to the action that he fired at the Rebels with his Henry rifle. Whether he hit anyone is not known, but some bullets obviously found their targets in the melee. "All along the road, during the pursuit, were scattered dead and wounded men and horses marking spots that had been hotly contested," observed an officer in the Eleventh Kansas.[19]

One mile south of Newburg Van Buren Road turns east and crosses Reed's Mountain, an irregular mass of sandstone that rises four hundred feet above the surrounding terrain. It was 2:00 P.M. and Marmaduke was becoming alarmed at Blunt's tenacity. Unless the Confederates checked the relentless Union pursuit—and checked it soon—they would be pressed against the rear of the train with disastrous results. Marmaduke decided to make a stand on Reed's Mountain. Shelby and MacDonald dismounted and formed a line across the road about a third of the way up the rugged, densely wooded north slope. Carroll established a second line nearer the crest. The second phase of the battle of Cane Hill was about to begin.[20]

The first Federals to reach Reed's Mountain were Blunt, Cloud, Bassett's battalion of the Second Kansas Cavalry, and Phillips's Third Indian. A quick reconnaissance convinced Blunt that "the mountain could be taken in no other way except by storm." The Cherokees dismounted and formed a heavy skirmish line across the road opposite Shelby's center and right. Phillips gave the order to advance, and the Indians surged up the slope whooping and yelling. A Union artilleryman observed that they "advanced from tree to tree, pouring an incessant and galling fire into the foe, and he finally gave back step by step, up the steep and rocky mountain slope." The Second Kansas Cavalry, also dismounted, extended the Union skirmish line to the left and advanced against MacDonald.[21]

Shortly after the advance began, the Eleventh Kansas appeared and formed on the right of the Third Indian. Ewing's men took a few minutes to catch their breath before joining in the attack against Shelby. Ewing reported that his regiment engaged in an "irregular musketry fight with the enemy, who slowly retreated along the hillsides and ravines on both sides of the road." The view from the ranks was somewhat different. Sergeant Bodwell wrote that the Federals plodded up the rocky incline "in close skirmishing order and much confusion" and traded shots with a largely unseen enemy.[22]

Some of that confusion is evident in an account penned by Silas H. Marple, a soldier in the Eleventh Kansas. Ewing called for a volley, and the regiment sprayed the woods directly ahead with buck and ball. Marple wrote: "I supposed, as a matter of course, that the rebels were in full sight, but when I brought up my gun to fire I saw no one to aim at. So I took it down again. In a moment more the Regiment fired their second volley. I looked in vain to see what they were firing at, but could see nothing. I did not like to stand there with a loaded gun, so I shot about the height of a man's breast." Marple was a careful, precise man who noted with more than a hint of disapproval that some of his comrades "loaded and fired as fast as they could and then boasted how often they shot. But I did not see fit to waste my ammunition in that way. I fired my gun about five or six times. I may of shot some Rebel, and I may not. I think the probabilities are against me." Whatever the exact circumstances of the Federal advance up Reed's Mountain, it was no cakewalk. "We went fighting all the way," stated Colonel Moonlight, "for be it said to the credit of the enemy that he contended for every foot of soil."[23]

The Eleventh Kansas was equipped with antique .72-caliber Prussian muskets so cumbersome that the soldiers referred to them as "light artillery," but the Federals also enjoyed an advantage in real artillery. Shells crashed into the Confederate position from fourteen guns and howitzers deployed along Fly Creek. The artillery consisted of Rabb's and Tenney's batteries and Lieutenant Henry H. Opdyke's Ninth Kansas Cavalry Battery. A different kind of artillery support came from four mountain howitzers that advanced up Van Buren Road with the Third Indian. One pair belonged to Stover's battery, the other to Lieutenant Brainerd D. Benedict's Sixth Kansas Cavalry Battery. Whenever the Cherokee advance stalled, the Kansans manhandled the "bull-pups" to the front and blasted the stubborn Missourians with canister.[24]

Confederate resistance weakened under this relentless hammering. Hughey's surviving howitzer was "broken to pieces" by Union artillery and hauled away. Bledsoe ran out of ammunition and withdrew his 6-pounders. Ammunition for carbines and shotguns began to run low as well, and Marmaduke decided to end the unequal contest. Arkansans and Missourians mounted up and retired on Van Buren Road. Ninety minutes after the fight began, a ragged line of Cherokees and Kansans reached the crest and broke out the Stars and Stripes for the benefit of their comrades in the valley below. Thus ended the second and most intense phase of the battle of Cane Hill.[25]

"The resistance of the Rebels was stubborn and determined," Blunt reported. "The storm of lead and iron hail that came down the side of the mountain, both from their small arms and artillery, was terrific; yet most of it went over our heads without doing us much damage." Thick woods, dispersed formations, and poor visibility kept casualties low at Reed's Mountain. Muzzle blasts and shell explosions set the underbrush afire and shrouded the upper part of the mountain in smoke. Thirty minutes after the fight began, soldiers on both sides were reduced to firing at muzzle flashes in the haze. As always in the random chaos of battle, a number of men experienced close calls. Captain Edmund G. Ross of the Eleventh Kansas informed his wife that two men in the regiment had been struck by spent bullets. He added, perhaps somewhat thoughtlessly, that a Confederate artillery round "struck a tree right over my head, and a passing ball scorched my face."[26]

The third and final phase of the battle began when Blunt and Colonel William R. Judson's Sixth Kansas Cavalry surged over the smoky crest of Reed's Mountain in pursuit of the fleeing Rebels. Other Union regiments and batteries followed. A frustrated officer recalled that the sound of battle "was always just ahead, far enough, however, to prevent our participating." Blunt was in his element as the running fight careened down the east slope of the mountain. "All this time Blunt was at the very head of our column, urging on the men, directing their movements, and occasionally 'taking a crack' himself," remarked an officer in the Sixth Kansas Cavalry.[27]

Shortly before 5:00 P.M. the tail of the Confederate column passed through the junction in front of the John Morrow house and turned south on Cove Creek Road. Blunt reached Morrow's a few minutes later and stopped to assess the situation. "It was now near sundown, and darkness must soon put an end to the pursuit," he later explained. "Down the valley, in front of us, the ground appeared adapted to the use of cavalry to good advantage, and I determined to make an effort to capture their artillery, of which they had six pieces." Had Blunt known the true state of the rattletrap Confederate artillery he might not have bothered.[28]

Blunt and Judson galloped after the Confederates with a single battalion of the Sixth Kansas Cavalry, a force of about 250 men led by Lieutenant Colonel Lewis R. Jewell. The Kansans quickly closed the distance and "dashed on to the rear of Carroll's Brigade, cutting and shooting them down with sabers, carbines, and revolvers." Blunt was in the thick of the action and reportedly

William R. Judson (New York State Library, Manuscripts and Special Collections)

shot a Confederate soldier with his pistol at point-blank range. The mass of slashing and shooting horsemen swept south through the deepening twilight. Sergeant Wiley Britton recalled that "the road was almost choked with the fleeing foe then in the utmost confusion." Panic overtook the rear of the Confederate column, and the retreat degenerated into a "regular stampede." Even Carroll acknowledged that his troopers behaved in a "disgraceful" fashion, a rare admission from a Confederate officer. Blunt appeared to be on the verge of capturing not only the Rebel artillery but a good portion of the rear guard as well.[29]

Marmaduke had ridden ahead in the belief that the fight was over, but Carroll realized that the Federals were "pushing the rear with great energy" and had to be stopped. Four miles south of Morrow's the valley broadens into a hollow. Carroll dismounted Johnson's regiment and a battalion of Thompson's regiment, about four hundred men in all, and placed them on a brushy bench running along the east side of the road. He then deployed a battalion of Monroe's regiment across the road a short distance to the south where the hollow narrows.[30]

The Confederate rear guard and the Federal vanguard entered the hollow in a confused mass, unaware of the trap that lay ahead. When the jumble of riders passed in front of the bench, Johnson's Arkansans fired a volley that filled the road with a tangle of fallen men and horses. At least two Confederates and six Federals went down, including Jewell, who suffered a grievous hip injury. Blunt continued to lead a charmed life. A buckshot passed through the crown of his hat, but he escaped injury.[31]

Blunt reported that the Confederates "opened upon us a most destructive fire, which, for the moment, caused my men to recoil and give back, in spite of my own efforts and those of other officers to rally them." The Federals broke off the pursuit and withdrew to the north end of the hollow, about three hundred yards from the ambush site. With the Federals in temporary disarray, Carroll acted swiftly to get his men out of the hollow. He ordered Monroe to make a demonstration while Johnson and Thompson withdrew. Two of Monroe's officers, Major Patrick H. Wheat and Captain John M. Harrell, noticed a Union officer lying in the road. They dismounted and dragged Jewell to the side "where he might not be trodden in a charge of cavalry." With the road clear, Monroe and his eighty-five Arkansans "raised a wild yell" and advanced toward the Kansans.[32]

While all of this was taking place, Cloud reached the hollow with Stover's and Benedict's batteries, a section of Rabb's battery, a battalion of the Third Indian, and, incredibly, a few companies of the Eleventh Kansas. Blunt placed the artillery across the road and prepared to blast the approaching horsemen with canister. At the last moment the Confederates halted and an officer (possibly Monroe himself) appeared between the lines with a flag of truce. The officer proposed that both sides remove their wounded before resuming hostilities. Blunt agreed even though he suspected the real purpose of the truce (which he later termed a "cowardly trick") was to use up the last few minutes of twilight. He was right. By the time the wounded were recovered, the Confederates had disappeared and it was too dark to continue the pursuit. The battle of Cane Hill was over.[33]

Considering the duration of the fight and the number of troops involved, the butcher's bill was remarkably low. Blunt reported eight killed and thirty-six wounded. Among the dead was Jewell, who expired in Newburg on 30 November. "He was brave, perhaps to recklessness," declared a fellow Kansan. "The men speak highly of his courage. So falls another brave officer in defense of the old flag." The Confederates admitted to ten killed and upward of seventy wounded or missing. "A good deal of ammunition used without effect," observed a relieved Union surgeon.[34]

The weary Confederates plodded down Cove Creek Road and reached Lee Creek near midnight. Marmaduke informed Hindman of the day's events in a rambling, disjointed message that revealed his fatigue and anxiety: "I disputed desperately every inch of ground. . . . It has been a hard days work. I think the Federal loss is much heavier than mine. I don't know mine. . . . The Federals may come on to me tonight. I have *no* ammunition for Artillery and small arms." Hindman had been on edge all day as the sound of artillery fire in the Boston Mountains grew louder and more distinct. In midafternoon he ordered his division commanders to be ready "to execute any order which may be given on short notice." After receiving Marmaduke's message Hindman forwarded Lieutenant Colonel R. Phillip Crump's Texas Cavalry, a force of about six hundred men, and a supply of ammunition. He later dispatched several wagonloads of forage for Marmaduke's famished horses, adding rather ungenerously that "it is reducing us to a great strait to furnish it to you."[35]

The next morning Marmaduke fell back to Dripping Springs and penned a second message to Hindman, this one more defiant in tone. "My horses are in a horrid fix, but I am bent upon bagging Blunt," he declared. "I hope to God I may have the pleasure of *pursuing* him *once* to finish him. The rascal was *in* the last charge against me. I think it cured him — at least the pursuit stopped. . . . Blunt's loss is certainly greater than mine and he ought to feel ashamed of himself that he did not do more, in fact use me up." Personal embarrassment aside, Marmaduke had extracted his command from a tight spot and saved the commissary train from capture or destruction. From the Confederate perspective, Cane Hill was a setback rather than a defeat.[36]

The Federals naturally saw things differently. The headquarters journal of Weer's Second Brigade summed up the fight at Cane Hill in four words: "An easily gained victory." Blunt expressed himself in more colorful terms. He informed Curtis that the Rebels were "badly whipped and worse chased." He sent an even more exuberant message to Schofield, announcing that he had attacked Marmaduke and "thrashed him out of his boots and britches and fought him for ten miles over the Boston Mountains in his retreat until night closed the conflict." Curtis passed the good news on to Halleck, then created the District of Western Arkansas and placed Blunt in command, evidence that he expected the Kansas Division to remain in that part of the country for some time. Schofield congratulated Blunt ("The Kansas Division is doing nobly") and provided some personal news ("My health is improving").[37]

Blunt performed well at Cane Hill, despite an unsettling tendency to forget his proper place once the shooting started. Captain Crawford of the Second Kansas Cavalry observed tartly that the battle "began awkwardly, was fought and won gallantly, and ended unfortunately," but others were more generous. A trooper in the Sixth Kansas Cavalry wrote that "Blunt was in the thickest of the fray, and headed the last charge on the enemy in person. He is a gallant soldier." Blunt's second victory in little more than a month confirmed his belief that resolution and boldness were the most effective ways to deal with the Rebels.[38]

During the night of 28 November the Federals dragged themselves back to Cane Hill. Ravenous soldiers ransacked farmsteads along the way in search of food. "The men made the pigs, chickens and sheep fly, which seemed cruel, but they must have something to eat, and there is but little danger of them starving where there is anything getatable," reported a Union officer. The mounted regiments reached the Jordan Valley, but the inexpressibly weary infantrymen of the Eleventh Kansas bivouacked along Van Buren Road. The Kansans had covered thirty-eight miles since dawn, much of it at the double-quick, and were numb with fatigue. "It has indeed been a trying time, although more upon our legs than upon our courage," Captain Ross told his wife. He added, perhaps unnecessarily, that he and his men "were very glad to lie down and sleep without supper, tents, or blankets." The men covered themselves with leaves to stay warm. Ross was barely able to stay with his company during the grueling ordeal: "It seemed at times as though I could not get one foot before the other, but I was determined not to fall behind my company till I dropped down dead, and now I feel very proud of having made the extraordinary effort I did to keep up."[39]

Blunt elected to make Cane Hill his new base of operations. The Second and Third Brigades established camps on Jordan Creek while the First Brigade set up a supply depot at Rhea's Mill. The relationship between Blunt and Salomon had deteriorated steadily since Newtonia. "There is no feeling of friendship" between the two, observed Major Ellithorpe of the First Indian. "General Blunt has the utmost disgust for him and freely expresses that Salomon is a *God Damned Coward*." Salomon did not disguise the fact that he was "very much disgusted with the manner in which the expedition is conducted." It may have been a good thing the two feuding generals were separated by several miles of Ozark countryside.[40]

The Federals quickly settled into their new surroundings. "Our camp is pitched and we again commence to live like human beings," remarked an officer in the First Indian. Now it was Union soldiers who enjoyed the bounty of Cane Hill's fields and orchards and gawked at the panoramas of the Springfield Plain to the north and the Boston Mountains to the south. Sooner or later nearly everyone made his way to Boonsboro to see the sights. "This town is in a very romantic locality," wrote Captain Ross. "The hills on both sides are very high and some of them are occupied by very fine residences, for this country." Another Kansan reported that "all the women that I have seen around here—and there are none but women to be seen—are well dressed and smart looking. They look like a different class of beings from those who live in other localities we have passed through." Ross agreed that Cane Hill society was comparatively "refined and intelligent," but he could not resist telling his wife that the women "pick their teeth and smoke and spit like old tobacco chewers."[41]

The Union occupation of Cane Hill began with an outburst of looting and vandalism that incensed Blunt. "I am determined to suppress such disgraceful conduct," he announced. "There is an excuse for men taking what they need to eat, upon certain occasions, but the cowardly and wanton destruction of household property cannot be tolerated." Blunt ordered officers to make a "thorough search" for pilfered goods. Troopers in the Third Wisconsin Cavalry were found to be in possession of six scholarly books, a flute, and a three-foot-long brass telescope, all obviously purloined from Cane Hill College. The most eclectic collection of stolen goods was given up by the equally eclectic collection of Cherokees, Delawares, Kickapoos, Osages, Quapaws, Senecas, and Shawnees that comprised the Second Indian. They surrendered twenty-six wool hats, five straw hats, four scholarly books, and an "electrical toy."[42]

Cane Hill Female Seminary in Newburg escaped the worst of the vandalism. A Union soldier described the school as a "good frame building with a good private library apparently belonging to the late Principal Reverend Newton Givens of the Cumberland Presbyterian Church." The cloistered atmosphere of the library was spoiled by the presence of a dead Confederate soldier carefully laid out on the carpeted floor. Other Rebel fatalities were scattered from Boonsboro to Cove Creek. Two days after the fight a Confederate burial party arrived and disposed of the corpses.[43]

The Federals kept busy in a variety of ways. An enterprising group of former newspapermen in the Eleventh Kansas commandeered a printing press and set up a short-lived publication they called the *Buck and Ball*. The name referred to the ammunition fired by the regiment's large-bore Prussian muskets. If anyone failed to understand the reference, the masthead also bore the motto "Calibre 72, gives the rebels h—l." Blunt was delighted at the prospect of having his own newspaper and encouraged Captain Ross, the self-appointed editor, to continue publication as long as possible.[44]

Ross took a few minutes out from setting type to explain to his wife what had been accomplished at Cane Hill. "Of one thing I am very glad," he wrote, "that the infamous Quantril, who has made so much trouble on the border of Kansas, is here fighting us, and of course not in Kansas. We drove him with the rebel army over the Boston Mountains . . . so that he will not trouble Kansas any more very soon." Ross thought it likely that Cane Hill marked the end of the campaign. The days were getting shorter and the temperature was dropping. "This part of Arkansas seems to be thoroughly subdued. I hardly think we shall have another battle." Blunt was of the same mind. He advised Curtis that the Confederates "are badly whipped and will probably not venture north of the Boston Mountains again this winter." Both men were in for a rude awakening.[45]

8 RACE TO PRAIRIE GROVE

THE LUNGE FROM FLINT CREEK TO CANE HILL CARRIED BLUNT AND his men thirty miles deeper into the Confederacy. The Kansas Division now was more than one hundred miles south of the Missouri Divisions near Springfield, but only thirty-five miles north of the Trans-Mississippi Army in the Arkansas Valley. Marmaduke realized that the Federals had blundered into a trap. On 29 November he pleaded with Hindman to spring the trap before Blunt saw the danger he was in and pulled back. "I am fully convinced that no force is sufficiently near to give him support in case you attack him," Marmaduke wrote. "I am further convinced you can capture him, but to do so, I think you must use every effort to have *celerity and secrecy*, for neither friend nor foe will anticipate your move. The dash of the men will astound and startle the Federals." Modifying his earlier proposal for an attack on Flint Creek, Marmaduke suggested that the Confederates advance up Cove Creek Road and the Line Road and converge on Cane Hill from two directions. He emphasized that the two columns "must move to the hour and operate urgently together."[1]

Hindman studied Marmaduke's letter and jotted questions in the margins ("Where and what is the strength of the federal force in Arkansas besides Blount's?"), but he needed little convincing. The Federals were almost close enough to touch, and Hindman did not intend to pass up such an extraordinary opportunity. He decided to march on Cane Hill with his "entire effective force" and so informed Holmes. Hindman estimated that he would need two or three days to prepare for an advance and another two or three days to move the army within striking distance of Cane Hill. Recent experience had demonstrated the perils of attempting to do too much too quickly, so Hindman substituted stealth for speed. He informed Marmaduke that "I shall march moderately, not above twelve or fifteen miles a day, if it can be helped, so as not to break the men down before the fight commences." He asked Marmaduke to send a "diagram of all the roads, so far as known to you, leading to the enemy's camp" with additional "memoranda" such as mileage between principal points and descriptions of terrain.[2]

Marmaduke found a civilian "Topographical Engineer" (no mean feat in the sparsely settled country around Dripping Springs) and put him to work. He informed Hindman that "I am having a map made for you which will embrace the country north of the Arkansas River to the Missouri line." Marmaduke was excited at the prospect of bagging Blunt and bombarded army headquarters with suggestions at all hours of the night. This practice provoked a sharp response from Colonel Robert C. Newton, Hindman's chief of staff. "If you don't quit waking me up about two o'clock every morning with your infernal dispatches I will make it a point to reciprocate *in kind*. I have been sparing of your patience and rest for some time." Chastened, Marmaduke sent no more midnight missives to Fort Smith.[3]

On 30 November Hindman and three of his four division commanders (Marmaduke, Shoup, and Roane) met in Van Buren to hammer out the details of the operation. The final plan combined elements of a frontal assault and a double envelopment. It called for a primary thrust against the Union center and a pair of secondary thrusts around each flank. The main body of the Trans-Mississippi Army would advance from Van Buren to Lee Creek on Telegraph Road, then cross the Boston Mountains on Cove Creek Road. At the Morrow house, Hindman and the infantry would turn west on Van Buren Road and move directly toward Cane Hill. Marmaduke and the cavalry, meanwhile, would continue north on Cove Creek Road toward Rhea's Mill. Colonel Douglas H. Cooper and whatever force he could muster would push up the Line Road and join Marmaduke in the Union rear. If everything went as expected, the operation would conclude with the destruction or capture of Blunt's command, including his stores and trains, on 5 or 6 December. With Blunt out of the way, the road to Missouri would be open. The Confederate plan was ambitious but sound. It made effective use of roads and terrain and required only a moderate amount of coordination. Confident of victory, Marmaduke emphasized that "our success depends upon pushing forward. If we go half naked and starved we will whip them. I fear they will scare off."[4]

Hindman did not think Blunt would "scare off," but he shared Marmaduke's conviction that surprise and superior numbers would enable the Confederates to carry the day. His primary concern was the scarcity of ammunition at Fort Smith. There was only enough powder and shot on hand to provide each soldier with forty to sixty rounds of ammunition, barely sufficient for one day of sustained combat. Ammunition for the artillery was in equally short supply. If the Federals stood their ground and put up a fight, the Confederates would have to score a quick and decisive victory. A protracted or inconclusive clash would exhaust the army's meager store of ammunition and spell defeat.[5]

Since most of the Trans-Mississippi Army had moved to the south side of the Arkansas River during November, Hindman assembled a small armada of ferries, flatboats, and light-draft steamboats at Van Buren and Strain's Landing to transfer everyone back to the north side as quickly as possible. Although tents, cooking utensils, and most supply wagons were left behind, it still took nearly three days—one day longer than anticipated—to complete the process. The only serious hitch involved Colonel James R. Shaler's Arkansas Infantry. The Arkansans had turned in their "indifferent rifles and shot guns" to the Ordnance Department a week earlier but had not been issued replacement weapons. Shaler protested that "it would be counted no less than murder to carry his regiment into the fight without arms." Hindman could only agree and reluctantly assigned the "efficient and well drilled regiment" to guard duty at Fort Smith. As luck would have it, that same day 2,000 Enfield rifles arrived in Little Rock "just from England." Hindman was tempted to put the operation on hold until the weapons reached Fort Smith, but when he learned that they would have to travel overland because of low water in the Arkansas, he decided to press on without them.[6]

If the news about the Enfields was not bad enough, Holmes chose this moment to send a pair of disturbing messages. The first was hysterical: "You must save the country if you can. Do so without risk of being destroyed." The second was defeatist: "You must not think of advancing in your present condition. You would lose your army. The enemy will either advance on you or for want of supplies will be obliged to return to Missouri." Hindman realized the time had come to have a chat with his agitated superior. Another trip to Little Rock was out of the question, so on the evening of 1 December Hindman entered the Van Buren telegraph office and initiated what he called a "conversation by telegraph." Holmes hurried to the Little Rock telegraph office, and for the next few hours the two generals exchanged messages in "real time" or something close to it.[7]

Hindman summed up recent developments and outlined his plan to attack the Union force at Cane Hill. "With the infantry and artillery alone I can defeat Blount," he told Holmes. "Using the cavalry on his flanks, I should hope to destroy him." Hindman expressed confidence that his command would prevail in a stand-up fight against Blunt. "If he gives battle I will whip him, and that will help the whole Confederacy. I urge upon you to leave me to my discretion in this matter. I will not trifle with the great interests entrusted to me."

Holmes assured Hindman that "it is perfectly repugnant to my nature to resist enterprise," then proceeded to do exactly that. He emphasized all the terrible things that would follow a Confederate defeat. "If your army is destroyed or demoralized ruin to us will follow," he wailed. "Nothing will justify an advance but to save the Indian Country and Arkansas." In response, Hindman argued that an immediate advance across the Boston Mountains was the only realistic option open to the Confederates. "I really am unable to determine upon any other plan then to push right up at once and try to regain what has been lost." He acknowledged that logistics continued to be the army's achilles heel, but felt certain the commissary could support a brief campaign. "Our subsistence will be beef on foot, meal and salt in wagons. In the last resort, we can live very well on beef and salt alone, driving the beef, and the men taking salt in their pockets." Once across the mountains the Confederates would supply themselves by foraging on the Springfield Plain, just as the Federals were doing.

Hindman believed only three courses of action were open to Blunt, and that all three favored the Confederates. If Blunt stood his ground at Cane Hill, the Confederates would fall on him in overwhelming force from three directions. "We storm the position, Marmaduke and Cooper meantime getting entry in his rear, from the east and west, and attacking him from that direction." If Blunt fell back to Rhea's Mill, the Confederates would pursue and harry. "We follow, take his trains, and attack him in rear." In the unlikely event that Blunt hitched up his skirts and ran, as Schofield had done a few weeks earlier, the Confederates would advance to the Arkansas-Missouri line and pick up where they had left off the previous September.

Holmes was overwhelmed by Hindman's presentation and tried several times to change the subject. At one point he even suggested that the Trans-Mississippi Army abandon northwest Arkansas and reinforce Vicksburg. Hindman lost his temper. "If this is done, all Arkansas is lost," he fired back. "Holding Vicksburg won't save a foot of it. Whenever the enemy gets south of the Boston Mountains, and establishes himself [in the Arkansas Valley], he can press you down to Louisiana or into Texas without difficulty." Holmes backpedaled while Hindman pressed his advantage. "I fully believe I can make the movement," he argued. "Marmaduke is of the opinion that eight thousand, under Blount, is all the federal force south of Cassville, except small parties of jayhawkers." The hour was late and Holmes was tired. Recognizing that he had lost, Holmes acceded to Hindman's wishes and terminated further discussion with a single peevish sentence: "Use your discretion and good luck to you."

Hindman, however, was not quite done. "Marmaduke sends me a woman tonight, arrested as a spy. Circumstances seem very strong against her. What on earth shall I do with her?" The thought of dealing with a female was too much for Holmes. "Do the best you can with her but don't send her here," he snapped. On that abrupt note the "conversation by telegraph" ended. Holmes did his ineffectual best to derail or delay the attack on Blunt, but in the end he permitted his strong-willed subordinate to have his way. The phrase "use your discretion" was hardly a ringing endorsement; from Hindman's perspective, however, it was enough. The operation was on.[8]

Shortly after his telegraphic contest of wills with Holmes, Hindman learned that Union cavalry had crossed the Boston Mountains and overrun Confederate outposts at Lee Creek and Evansville. The Federals carried away seventeen prisoners, including an officer. Alarmed by these bold incursions, Hindman sent Marmaduke back to Lee Creek with instructions to block every road, lane, and footpath across the mountains. The cavalry was to "prevent all communications with the enemy, and to detect any movements he may make." Hindman hoped to seal off his front and prevent Blunt from learning of the Confederate offensive for at least another forty-eight hours. Marmaduke led Shelby's Brigade and MacDonald's Brigade to Lee Creek and secured the junction of Cove Creek Road and Telegraph Road. At the same time he sent Carroll's Brigade (now commanded by Lieutenant Colonel James C. Monroe and hereafter identified as "Monroe's Brigade") to Natural Dam on the Line Road with instructions to rejoin the main column as soon as the infantry reached Lee Creek. Marmaduke did not think the advance on Cane Hill could be kept secret for long and urged Hindman to hurry. "Blunt is vigilant," he warned.[9]

More unsettling news arrived from the Indian Territory. Hindman had ordered Cooper to take the field with all the troops he could raise and advance on the Line Road. Cooper was to "attack the enemy's right and rear, harassing him, and impeding him if he attempts to escape on the Cincinnati or any other road, capturing his trains, if possible, and otherwise crippling him in his effort to get away." Hindman believed Cooper and his men would be eager to avenge their humiliating defeat at Old Fort Wayne, but he soon learned differently. "The force will be very weak and may not accomplish much," Cooper warned. "The Indians are not inclined to venture much *alone*, they need white support." The defeatist tone of Cooper's message convinced Hindman that he could expect little assistance from the Indian Territory. Nevertheless, he believed that the presence of a Confederate force on the Line Road, however small, would distract the Federals and make his task easier. He told Cooper to send whatever troops he could scrape together.[10]

By nightfall on 1 December there were roughly 12,000 Confederate troops bivouacked on the north side of the Arkansas River (another 3,000 remained on the south side, unwell, unarmed, or unorganized). William H. Hoskin noted in his diary that "all are eager to move on to old Missouri as soon as possible," but the infantry and artillery remained in place another day while commissary, quartermaster, and ordnance details distributed food, clothing, and ammunition. On 3 December the infantry and artillery advanced from Van Buren to Dripping Springs, the campsite recently vacated by the cavalry. The day was cloudy and mild, and the Confederates completed the seven-mile march without any difficulty. One soldier remarked that "our forces are in fine spirits." The weather deteriorated the following day, however, as a strong cold front swept across the Ozark Plateau. Although the march from Dripping Springs to Lee Creek was only thirteen miles, it was a trying experience. Driving rain and dropping temperatures made for a miserable day and an even more unpleasant night. Chilled soldiers wrapped themselves in sodden quilts and blankets and huddled around sputtering campfires. After midnight the rain turned into snow. "Camp very disagreeable," grumbled a discomfited Rebel. William Hoskin had more than creature comforts on his mind: "We expect a fight or a run—one or the other soon."[11]

Hindman established his headquarters in Oliver's Store and spent the evening huddled with his staff in a cramped and stuffy "Consultation Room." Sometime after midnight a mud-spattered courier arrived from the telegraph office in Van Buren with a plaintive query from Holmes: "Do your plans still hold?" Hindman's reply, if any, is lost.[12]

BLUNT WAS RECKLESS at times but he was no fool. He realized that his isolated position at Cane Hill practically invited an attack so he kept a close watch on Confederate activity in the Arkansas Valley. By nightfall on 2 December (twelve hours *before* the Rebels marched out of Van Buren), Blunt had accumulated enough information from scouts, spies, and informants to conclude that Hindman was moving, or about to move, in his direction.

That evening a heavily escorted courier left Boonsboro for the telegraph station at Elkhorn Tavern, fifty-six miles to the north. The courier carried three dispatches. The first was for Totten, whom Blunt thought was in command of the Missouri Divisions in Schofield's absence. Blunt informed Totten that the Rebels were advancing on Cane Hill in force. "I desire you to move as much of your force as possible, especially the infantry, to my support, as I do not intend to leave this position without a fight." The second dispatch was for Curtis. It contained a summary of the situation and another declaration of immovability. "I expect an attack tomorrow morning, but shall not abandon my position without a fight. I have requested General Totten to re-enforce me by forced marches on the Fayetteville Road, but I have no knowledge of his present locality, and have got to hunt him up." The third dispatch was for Colonel M. LaRue Harrison at Elkhorn Tavern. Harrison was to take his First Arkansas Cavalry to Fayetteville and hold Telegraph Road open for the Missouri Divisions. The courier reached Pea Ridge around 8:00 A.M. on 3 December, not long after the Confederates set out for Dripping Springs, and handed his dispatches to the telegrapher. Minutes later the wire to Springfield began to hum.[13]

"There was considerable suspense and speculation as to which army would get to us first," wrote a soldier in the First Kansas Battery. Blunt thought it likely the Confederates would win the race, and he prepared the Kansas Division for the fight of its life. On 3 December the Federals struck their tents and marched out to take up defensive positions along the various approaches to Cane Hill. Blunt expected Hindman to advance up Cove Creek Road to Morrow's, then turn west and approach Cane Hill on Van Buren Road. (This was, in fact, precisely what Hindman had in mind.) To counteract this threat, Blunt established a strong cavalry picket at Morrow's and placed Weer's Second Brigade and Cloud's Third Brigade atop Newburg Heights, a line of bluffs overlooking Fly Creek just south of Newburg. Van Buren Road was not the only way to reach Cane Hill, so Blunt looked to his flanks as well. Hogeye Road crossed Cove Creek Road a few miles north of Morrow's. It connected Telegraph Road to the east with Fayetteville Road to the west. The junction of Hogeye Road and Fayetteville Road was located a short distance north of Blunt's headquarters in Boonsboro. To prevent an attack from the east by way of Hogeye Road, Blunt placed elements of Salomon's First Brigade behind a stream a mile and a half east of Fayetteville Road. Later, he reinforced the Hogeye Road position with elements of the Second Brigade. Finally, to check any movement up the Line Road, Blunt established another strong cavalry picket on Evansville Road between Newburg and Dutch Mills. Similar preparations were made around Rhea's Mill.[14]

For the next four mornings, 3–6 December, the Federals followed the same routine. They awoke, broke camp, loaded the wagons, and tramped out to their designated positions. For the first day or two they cleared fields of fire, barricaded roads, and piled up crude breastworks of logs and rocks. After that there was little to do except wait for the Rebels to make an appearance. Bored soldiers played cards and wrote letters or caught up on their sleep. Every afternoon but the last they returned to camp, unpacked, put up their tents, and settled in for another night. The days passed quietly at Cane Hill, but there was quite an uproar at Rhea's Mill on 5 December when a forage train "came in with the teams on a run, and the wildest excitement prevailed." Bugles sounded, drums rolled, and regiments frantically formed lines of battle. It turned out to be a false alarm, but Salomon kept his men on alert for the entire day.[15]

Blunt's refusal to retire in the face of Hindman's advance puzzled his contemporaries. Years later an officer in the First Iowa Cavalry suggested that Blunt remained at Cane Hill because he was a "hearty fighter" who "seemed to think that it was the height of strategy to get himself surrounded by the enemy and fight his way out." In fact, the opposite was true. Blunt was a cavalryman at heart and loved to maneuver in open country. The last thing he wanted was to be surrounded and immobilized by a superior force. Despite repeated declarations of his intention to stand and fight at Cane Hill, Blunt went to great lengths to ensure that the Kansas Division was ready to move—and move rapidly—at a moment's notice. If Hindman approached on Van Buren Road as expected, Blunt was prepared to offer battle on Newburg Heights, where the terrain strongly favored the defense. But if Hindman declined to dash his army against those commanding bluffs and chose another approach, Blunt was prepared to fall back and fight on the Springfield Plain where the superior mobility and firepower of the Kansas Division could be used to good advantage, and where the Confederates would be separated from their base by the Boston Mountains. Blunt's bluster ("I do not intend to leave this position without a fight") was partly a reflection of his pugnacious personality and partly a matter of public relations. He had an image to maintain.[16]

Contemporaries also were mystified by Blunt's failure to block Cove Creek Road. In retrospect, Blunt should have massed his command at the Morrow house, barricaded the road, and held on for dear life, but such extreme measures seemed unnecessary at the time. Blunt went to great lengths to ensure the safety of his logistical arrangements. He assumed, reasonably enough, that Hindman was equally solicitous about the security of his own line of communications. Blunt simply could not believe Hindman would be so foolish as to continue north on Cove Creek Road and expose his lifeline (and his only avenue of retreat) to Union interdiction. Blunt was correct. Hindman

The John Morrow house in a postwar image (John N. Heiskell Collection, University of Arkansas at Little Rock Archives and Special Collections)

intended to turn west on Van Buren Road and keep his connection with the Arkansas Valley safely covered. What neither commander anticipated was a sudden shift in circumstances that caused Hindman to throw caution to the wind and change his approach from Van Buren Road to Cove Creek Road *at the last possible moment.*[17]

The Union force at Morrow's consisted of two battalions of the Second Kansas Cavalry, about four hundred men in all, without artillery support. Blunt told Lieutenant Colonel Bassett to watch for the Confederates on Cove Creek Road, slow their approach as much as possible, then fall back fighting on Van Buren Road to Newburg Heights. In other words, Blunt expected the Kansans to *delay* the Confederate advance, not stop it. On 5 December Bassett sent Captain Crawford and one battalion toward Lee Creek to see what was happening. Several miles down the valley the Kansans encountered a column of Confederate cavalry moving in their direction. "As they advanced, I fell back slowly, trying to determine their numbers," recalled Crawford. "The winding road afforded a good opportunity for this; and as nearly as I could estimate, they had about a thousand men." Crawford's educated guess was close to the mark. The Confederate force was Shelby's Brigade, about 1,200 strong. Skirmishing flared all day as Shelby pushed Crawford up the narrowing valley. When the Rebels stopped for the night, a Union officer reported "camp-fires burning brightly up and down the valley as far as he could see." Bassett informed Blunt that the Rebels were advancing in force on Cove Creek Road and that the head of the enemy column was only four miles south of Morrow's.[18]

Blunt spent much of 5 December on Newburg Heights with Weer and Cloud, but he was back at his headquarters in Boonsboro when Bassett's warning arrived. Blunt informed Herron (whom he had learned was now in command of the Missouri Divisions) of the situation and ordered him to rush his cavalry to Cane Hill. "You will advance your best armed and best mounted Cavalry with as much rapidity as possible, leaving the Infantry and Artillery to follow. I have plenty of subsistence for them so that they need not delay for the commissary train." This order, which undoubtedly seemed like a good idea at the time, would have unfortunate consequences. Blunt concluded his message to Herron with a qualified—and revealing—expression of his determination to stand fast: "I shall not abandon this position without a battle *if they attack me here*." He did not say what he would do if the Rebels turned his position by way of Cove Creek Road, but the fact that his wagons were packed and ready to roll speaks volumes. Around midnight Blunt composed a brief letter to his family. He explained that a "desperate conflict" was imminent and that the Missouri Divisions were on their way. "They are moving by forced marches but I fear will be too late." The letter was uncharacteristically somber, though Blunt closed with a flash of his normal insouciance: "Will telegraph you the result if I come out of the conflict with a whole skin."[19]

At some point during the night it occurred to Blunt that Hindman might be advancing on Telegraph Road as well as Cove Creek Road. If a Confederate force reached Fayetteville, it could turn west and threaten Rhea's Mill or, even worse, continue north on Telegraph Road and plow into Herron. Because Weer and Cloud did not have a regiment to spare, Blunt directed Salomon to send his "best armed cavalry and all howitzers" to the intersection of Bottom Road and Fayetteville Road, three miles northeast of Boonsboro. Once in position, the cavalry was to scout toward Fayetteville and Hogeye and watch for "any flank movement the enemy may attempt to get in my rear." For reasons never explained, Salomon did not carry out this order.[20]

News that the Rebels were close at hand spread like wildfire through the Kansas Division. One casualty of the uproar was the *Buck and Ball*. "On account of the excitement, the paper does not flourish very briskly," noted a member of the editorial staff. Publication was suspended for the duration of the crisis, though more important activities went on without letup. Kidd's Mill and Rhea's Mill continued to churn out 25,000 pounds of flour a day even as the Confederates drew near. The officer in charge of Kidd's Mill, Major Ellithorpe of the First Indian, announced his intention in words that might have come from Blunt himself: "*I shall run the mill until the bullets begin to whistle.*" A few hardheads, most notably Colonel Ewing of the Eleventh Kansas, refused to believe that a battle was imminent. Ewing informed his wife that the rumored Confederate advance was hogwash: "It is reported that Hindman's whole army is coming upon us tomorrow, twenty-thousand strong—all bosh as to the numbers and as to the coming up also." Just about everyone else in the Kansas Division shared Blunt's conviction that the Rebels were on their way, but there was no sense of impending doom. The prevailing mood among Union soldiers was one of quiet confidence. Robert McMahan of Captain Job B. Stockton's Ohio Battery expressed that confidence in his diary: "Let them come. We are ready for them."[21]

ON 5 DECEMBER the Confederates at Lee Creek awoke before dawn, ate a spartan breakfast, and received a few words of encouragement from their commander. While in Van Buren Hindman had composed an address for officers to read to their men at the first suitable opportunity. With the army poised to enter the Boston Mountains, this seemed like an appropriate time. Printed copies of the address were distributed and read by the light of campfires. Believing that self-discipline was the key to success, Hindman enjoined his inexperienced troops to follow five simple rules: not to shoot unless specifically ordered to do so; to take "deliberate aim, as low down as the knee"; to "pick off the enemy's officers, especially the mounted ones"; not to yell "except when you charge the enemy"; and, above all, not to break ranks and plunder the enemy's camps.

The address concluded with a peroration intended to whip the Confederates into a ferocious frame of mind: "Remember that the enemy you engage has no feeling of mercy or kindness toward you. His ranks are made up of Pin Indians, free negroes, Southern tories, Kansas jayhawkers, and hired Dutch cut-throats. These bloody ruffians have invaded your country; stolen and destroyed your property; murdered your neighbors; outraged your women; driven your children from their homes; and defiled the graves of your kindred." Hindman expressed confidence that if everyone followed orders and remembered the five rules the Union army would be defeated, perhaps destroyed: "We can do this; we must do it; our country will be ruined if we fail." After the address was read, the troops formed in column on the muddy road and entered the Boston Mountains.[22]

Shelby's Brigade was in the lead, followed by Frost's Division, Shoup's Division, and a small train. Most of the column swung left on Cove Creek Road and began the long ascent. The primitive road was a severe test for malnourished men and emaciated animals. The difficulties of the steep uphill climb were compounded by Cove Creek. The Confederates splashed in and out of the rain-swollen stream thirty-seven times. Shoes disintegrated, ammunition was soaked, wagons were swept downstream, and equipment was lost. Progress was slowed even more by sustained skirmishing at the head of the column between Shelby's Brigade and Crawford's battalion of the Second Kansas Cavalry. At least Hindman no longer had to worry about maintaining secrecy; the Federals obviously knew he was coming. One of the few bright spots that day was the arrival of Monroe's Brigade. The Arkansans marched from Natural Dam to Lee Creek, then worked their way past the slow-moving infantry and artillery in single file. By nightfall they were in column behind Shelby's Brigade. Meanwhile, a mile or so to the east, MacDonald's Brigade advanced on Telegraph Road and reached Strickler's without being detected. The following day MacDonald turned west on Crossover Road and joined the rest of Marmaduke's Division below Morrow's.

The Confederate offensive was unfolding according to plan, but not according to schedule. The objective for 5 December was Morrow's, fifteen miles north of Lee Creek, but when darkness fell the weary, waterlogged Rebels were still several miles short of that point. Hindman reported that "instead of getting to Morrow's, as I had expected, we went but little farther than halfway, in consequence of some of those apparently unavoidable delays to which troops so ill-provided as ours are liable." The sluggish pace of the advance convinced Hindman to postpone the attack. The new day of reckoning would be Sunday, 7 December.[23]

Hindman's lack of urgency is easily explained. He was unaware that Blunt had called for help *three days earlier* and that Herron was hastening to his relief. Once the offensive began, Hindman husbanded his limited resources and concentrated on the task at hand. The Confederate cavalry was assigned to screen the advance of the infantry and artillery rather than engage in long-range reconnaissance activities. This did not seem unwise at the time because the most recent intelligence placed the Missouri Divisions well to the east of Springfield. As darkness fell on 5 December, Hindman assumed that he still had a "window" of three or four days in which to crush Blunt before reinforcements arrived.

Some Missourians recognized the valley below Morrow's as the place where they had stayed the previous February and March. "Camped on Cove Creek near where we camped last spring just before the Battle of Elk Horn," noted William Bull of Tilden's Missouri Battery. "In the evening the Head Quarters band played 'We are tenting tonight on the old camp ground' which was appropriate and sad considering all that had occurred since we were last here and the certainty of a battle on the morrow when many mens lives would be given to the cause we love so well." Cynics noted that after nine months of strenuous campaigning, the hardluck Missourians were back where they had started. The Confederates huddled around smoldering fires and consumed what little food was available. Several regiments received nothing to eat because their supply wagons failed to arrive. Most soldiers were so tired they fell asleep in their sodden clothes and blankets, while the wind howled down the valley and the temperature dropped to twenty degrees. A few others, too miserable to sleep, watched a lunar eclipse and pondered the value of omens. The celestial phenomenon lasted four hours and was visible across northwest Arkansas.[24]

The next morning, 6 December, the Trans-Mississippi Army resumed its advance up Cove Creek Road. Shelby's Brigade again led the way. The Confederates pushed up the narrowing valley despite the best efforts of the Second Kansas Cavalry to impede their progress. Bassett could not understand why he had been left to delay the Confederates with only two-thirds of his regiment. He did not know that Blunt had ordered Cloud to send the rest of the Second Kansas Cavalry to Morrow's, but the usually reliable Cloud dropped the ball and nothing was done. Two hundred additional troopers and a pair of mountain howitzers may not have made much difference, because Bassett concluded around midmorning that he had done all he could. The Kansans disengaged a little before 11:00 A.M. and withdrew over Reed's Mountain on Van Buren Road. A half-hour later the Confederates took possession of Morrow's.[25]

As Blunt expected, Hindman turned west on Van Buren Road and prepared to seize his next objective, Reed's Mountain. Monroe's relatively fresh Arkansans would lead the attack. Hindman instructed Monroe to "press the enemy vigorously" and gain the summit of the mountain "at all hazards." This was a tall order for four hundred indifferently armed cavalrymen, so Hindman called on Brigadier General Mosby M. Parsons, whose Missouri infantry brigade was next in the line of march, to provide support and "hold the ground which the cavalry might gain." Hindman was surprised by the lack of opposition thus far but suspected that Blunt intended to make a stand on Reed's Mountain.[26]

Blunt had no such intention, at least not initially, but around 3:00 P.M. he changed his mind and ordered Bassett to return to Reed's Mountain and hold it until nightfall. By this time the weary Kansans were watering their horses in Fly Creek at the foot of Newburg Heights, and another hour passed before they made their way back up the mountain. "We dismounted and went up as skirmishers sheltering ourselves as much as possible behind trees and arrived at the top without discovering any enemy," recalled Vincent Osborne. The Federals spread out along the flattish crest and peered down the east side, which already was deep in shadow. They soon spied a line of dismounted Confederate cavalrymen struggling up the slope. "We poured a deadly fire into their ranks and they retreated down the mountain and very fast at that," noted Osborne. By the smallest of margins the Federals retained control of Reed's Mountain.[27]

The blast of musketry and the sight of Monroe's troopers tumbling back down the mountain alarmed Parsons. He formed his brigade into line behind the cavalry and advanced partway up the east slope. "Never was an evolution performed any nicer and prompter," remarked a Missourian. "We were all ready for a fight. No excitement prevailed among us." Monroe welcomed the arrival of reinforcements but insisted on making another try with his own command. The Arkansans regrouped and started back up the mountain. "The firing became heavy and rapid," observed Parsons. The Confederate cavalrymen were armed only with shotguns but gave such a good account of themselves that Bassett believed he was facing a much larger force. Nevertheless, the Federals could not be budged, and Monroe reluctantly asked Parsons for help. Parsons sent Major Lebbeus A. Pindall's Missouri Sharpshooter Battalion into the fray. Bassett in turn called on Blunt for assistance. The Union commander hurried forward a battalion of Ewing's Eleventh Kansas. For the next thirty minutes a "scattering fire" flared along the crest of Reed's Mountain.[28]

The sun had set and daylight was fading fast when Monroe led a "vigorous charge" against the Union center and right. Sergeant Bodwell of the Eleventh Kansas recorded in his diary that the Rebels "charged on us in force, showing colors. Met them with a heavy fire as they were upon us in column. Ordered back down hill under a heavy fire." With darkness coming on and the Rebels moving around his right, Bassett fell back to Newburg Heights. Osborne de-

Looking east from the crest of Reed's Mountain along Van Buren Road (author's collection)

scribed the final moments of the engagement as the Union cavalry and infantry scrambled down the west slope: "The enemy charged to the top of the mountain and halted and poured a shower of buckshot after us but with little effect and occasionally a rifle ball would pass."[29]

Monroe had a different view of events. "The enemy held his position until we were in 10 paces of him, when he broke and fled in confusion," he informed Marmaduke. "I would have pursued him were it not for the nature of the ground, which was so rugged that it was impossible to ride over." Fearing a Union attempt to retake the mountain, the Confederates piled up breastworks of logs and rocks along the crest. "I could hear a gun go off occasionally on the mountain, could see the Reb fires, could hear the sound of their axes all along the mountain as though they intended to fence us in," wrote Thomas Helm of the First Kansas Battery. For the first time in four days the Federals did not return to their camps in the Jordan Valley. Instead, they settled in for a cold, anxious night behind their own breastworks on Newburg Heights.[30]

An Arkansas officer dismissed the clash on Reed's Mountain as nothing more than a "little skirmish with the Feds," but the fighting was serious enough to generate casualty lists on both sides. One trooper was killed and two wounded in the Second Kansas Cavalry, and an unspecified number of men were wounded in the Eleventh Kansas. Monroe's Brigade lost four men killed and a dozen wounded. Losses in Parsons's Brigade, if any, are unknown. "The conduct of Colonel Monroe, who charged at the head of his brigade, and of the officers and men under his command in this affair, was gallant in the extreme," reported Marmaduke. Hindman was equally effusive. He declared that Monroe and his Arkansans had "greatly distinguished themselves" by attacking a superior enemy force "with boldness and vigor, breaking his ranks, and only ceasing to pursue when recalled." The seizure of Reed's Mountain gave the Confederates possession of the only natural obstacle between Morrow's and Newburg Heights. From Hindman's perspective, it was an important tactical victory. But the Federals, too, claimed a victory. They had stalled the Confederate advance at very little cost to themselves. In the morning it would take several hours for Hindman to cross the mountain and deploy for battle—time enough, perhaps, for Herron to arrive.[31]

Parsons's Brigade withdrew from Reed's Mountain after midnight and rejoined Frost's Division along Cove Creek Road, where water was available. It was another cheerless camp for the long-suffering Confederates. A Missouri soldier wrote in his diary that "it was a cold night, and we were very nearly frozen for we were allowed to have but very little fire." Food was another problem. Most of Parsons's soldiers had not eaten since noon of the previous day. Rations finally arrived in the wee hours of the morning. A Missouri soldier recalled how everyone was "delighted with the appearance of our commissary with a lot of crackers, for our craving appetites had been raving and gnawing for hours." The Missourians were less impressed with the next item on the midnight menu: "As we were passing back we came upon our butchers who had ten or fifteen beeves killed, and we were told to send a man for each mess to get some beef, which we did, and dividing this raw beef as we went along, each man put his piece in his haversack, and when he wanted to eat it he had to take it raw with his crackers or do without." The rest of the Trans-Mississippi Army, strung out down the narrow valley for more than a mile, experienced similar hardships.[32]

AFTER THE FIGHTING sputtered out on Reed's Mountain, Blunt returned to his headquarters in Boonsboro. He informed Fort Leavenworth of recent developments:

> The enemy, 25,000 strong, have attempted for three days to force my position here, which I have determined to hold at all hazards until reenforcements can arrive. They attacked yesterday, and again this morning, but were driven back to the mountains. General Herron, with the

> Second and Third Divisions, is making a forced march to re-enforce me. His advance will arrive tonight. You will soon hear of one of the damnedest fights or foot races that has taken place lately.

Blunt was among the most political of political generals, and this message obviously was intended for public consumption in his own District of Kansas. The estimate of enemy strength was ridiculously high and it was the Federals, not the Rebels, who had given ground, but the true significance of the message was its upbeat tone and bluff humor rather than its dubious content. After an anxious forty-eight hours Blunt believed the situation had turned in his favor. An hour later he composed a message to Herron in which he more accurately estimated Hindman's strength at 10,000 men: "Nothing more than picket fighting has occurred during the day, but they are steadily advancing, and will, no doubt, attack in force at daybreak tomorrow morning. You will endeavor to get your command here by that time."[33]

Blunt's mood improved even more as the night wore on. Twenty-four hours earlier he had called on Herron to rush his "best armed and best mounted Cavalry" to Cane Hill. Upon receiving that message, Herron placed Colonel Dudley Wickersham, who had led the successful raid on Yellville, in charge of a "provisional brigade" of 1,600 horsemen and four artillery pieces. The Federals set out from Cross Hollows on the morning of 6 December and reached their destination after a "very fatiguing march" of thirty-five miles in twelve hours. The head of the column clattered into Boonsboro a little after 9:00 P.M., much to Blunt's delight. (Wickersham's march to Cane Hill is discussed in more detail in the next chapter.) Men and animals were exhausted, but Wickersham assured Blunt that his command would be ready for limited duty on the morrow. Wickersham also handed Blunt a letter from Herron. "I will make the best possible marching to you," wrote Herron. "In my opinion, if the enemy presses you in force, it would be advisable to fall back and meet the Second and Third Divisions, so we can make a good fight of it. Keep me advised of any change of location you make; also send me a guide from Fayetteville to Cane Hill." Greatly encouraged, Blunt settled down to get some sleep.[34]

HINDMAN WAS BUSY as well that evening. He established his headquarters in the Morrow house, where he learned that he would be sleeping in the same room (and in the same bed) shared by Price and Van Dorn before the battle of Pea Ridge. After dinner Hindman and his division commanders gathered around the table and reviewed their assignments for the following day. The conference was winding down when an unidentified visitor was ushered into the house. The visitor, whether soldier or civilian is not known, informed the assembled generals that Herron was marching to Blunt's relief with a large force of cavalry, infantry, and artillery, and that he would reach Cane Hill the next day. Hindman was dumbfounded. A glance at Marmaduke's map revealed that the plan to envelop Blunt now was unworkable. If Marmaduke continued north on Cove Creek Road toward Rhea's Mill, he would collide with Herron. Worse, if Shoup and Frost drove toward Cane Hill on Van Buren Road, they would succeed only in pushing Blunt closer to Herron and crushing Marmaduke in the process. Hindman described the altered situation: "It now seemed evident that the plan would simply cause the retirement of Blount upon his re-enforcements, without accepting battle till after the junction should be effected."[35]

A less determined man might have given up and returned to Van Buren, but Hindman refused to concede defeat. The aborted attempt on Fayetteville in late October still rankled, and he had no desire to repeat that demoralizing experience: "To withdraw without fighting at all, would discourage my own troops and so embolden the enemy as to ensure his following me up." Hindman returned to the map and saw a glimmer of hope. "There was a possibility that I might, by adopting a different plan, destroy the re-enforcements and afterward fight the main body upon equal terms," he reasoned. Hindman believed that fortune favored the bold, and he acted accordingly: "I determined to risk an engagement."[36]

The revised plan called for the Trans-Mississippi Army to defeat the two wings of the Army of the Frontier in detail. Instead of turning west on Van Buren Road, the infantry and artillery would follow the cavalry north on Cove Creek Road to the junction with Fayetteville Road at a place called "Prairie Grove," nine miles north of Morrow's. At Prairie Grove the Confederates would turn northeast and assail Herron with overwhelming force. With Herron out of the picture, the Confederates would reverse course and descend on Blunt at Cane Hill.

While fundamentally sound, the revised plan contained several worrisome elements. The Rebels would have to march fast and far if they hoped to intercept Herron and trap Blunt, and thus far they had not exhibited much celerity or endurance. They also would have to fight two battles of uncertain intensity and duration with a limited supply of ammunition. Even more unnerving, they would have to expose their line of communications. Finally, they would have to count on a certain amount of cooperation from the Federals. If Blunt figured out what was happening and fell back to meet Herron, Hindman would be caught between converging enemy forces at Prairie Grove. It was essential that Blunt remain unsuspecting and inert at Cane Hill. Stealth and cunning once again were the order of the day.

A few hours after midnight on 7 December the Trans-Mississippi Army began to stir. An Arkansas soldier recalled that his regiment was awakened "without blast of bugles or beat of drums" and told to form quietly in Cove Creek Road. It was another instance of hurry up and wait. Thousands of shivering soldiers stamped their feet and cursed their officers as the temperature in the narrow valley dropped to sixteen degrees. "The morning very dark, and wretched cold," a Missouri officer scribbled in his diary with numbed fingers. When the advance finally began, the pace was slower than Hindman desired: "The command was not in motion till nearly 4 o'clock, and then the route proved so excessively bad, and the detentions so frequent from the breaking of artillery harness and debility of the battery animals, that the infantry failed to march above 2 miles an hour." Three miles north of Morrow's the road passes over the barely perceptible crest of the Boston Mountains and begins a gentle descent toward the junction at Prairie Grove. As the first hint of dawn appeared in the eastern sky, the pace of the Confederate advance increased. The cavalry trotted ahead and the infantry began to double-quick.[37]

9 OPENING MOVES

ON 1 DECEMBER HERRON ADVISED CURTIS THAT HIS COMMAND WAS fully recovered from the rigors of the fall campaign. "I have been at work getting the [Missouri] Divisions into shape for a prompt and lengthy movement, and would report them ready," he wrote. Herron expected orders to march to Helena or some other point on the Mississippi River, but he did not hesitate when Blunt's call for support reached his headquarters on 3 December. "Will move both divisions entire at noon today, and will make good time to your position," Herron replied. "The distance from here is so great that it may be necessary for you to fall back a short distance, but I will do my best to make that unnecessary." Herron then informed Curtis that he was going to Blunt's support. Curtis gave his blessing and urged Blunt to meet Herron halfway. "You are too far in advance of support and supplies. Had better fall back to meet Herron's re-enforcements that go at your request toward Fayetteville." Curtis scrambled to find additional manpower, but the policy of concentrating Union resources against Vicksburg had drained the Department of the Missouri. There was nothing left for Curtis to do except send Herron a valedictory message: "Have advised Blunt to fall back so as to join your advance. Push forward."[1]

Herron did just that. The Missouri Divisions were on their way six hours after Blunt's telegram arrived. What followed was an epic of human endurance. Between the afternoon of 3 December and the morning of 7 December, a period of three and a half days, the Second and Third Divisions of the Army of the Frontier marched 105 and 120 miles respectively and went directly into battle at Prairie Grove. The actual distance varied from regiment to regiment, but the entire command averaged over thirty miles per day on primitive frontier roads in bitterly cold weather with only brief halts for food and rest. Lieutenant Colonel Joseph D. Barnes of the Twentieth Iowa believed it was the "greatest march made by any troops during the war of the rebellion," and not one of the thousands of participants would have disagreed. Alas, like so many other remarkable episodes of the Civil War west of the Mississippi River, Herron's march has never received the attention it deserves.[2]

The Third Division left Wilson's Creek at 2:00 P.M. on 3 December. As the Federals began their extraordinary march, an officer on Herron's staff experienced conflicting emotions. "I wish you could have seen the Command move out of camp, every one in the best of spirits," Jacob Brewster informed his wife. "The thought struck me, how many of them would never come back." Despite that sobering reflection, Brewster was confident of success: "I feel in good spirits for I believe we have the long wished for chance to do something handsome." The Third Division was the smallest component of the Army of the Frontier, yet it took nearly two hours for the column of cavalry, infantry, and artillery to tramp past Brewster's position. The sight prompted him to add an upbeat postscript: "Our men properly handled will be hard to beat."[3]

During the early stages of the march, few Federals knew what was happening or where they were going. "The whole command [has] left camp for parts unknown," scribbled a mystified diarist in the First Iowa Cavalry. An officer in the Seventh Missouri Cavalry was equally baffled: "There was considerable wonderment as to the route but all believed it was only a change of camp for forage." Word that the Kansas Division was in danger gradually spread through the ranks. On the second day of the march, Edward Smith of the Thirty-seventh Illinois informed his diary that "Blunt has been fighting at Kane Hill. We go to his relief." Captain Chester Barney, Twentieth Iowa, learned that he was bound for Cane Hill from a passing courier who shouted: "If your divisions don't get there pretty soon, Blunt's gone up, sure."[4]

Seven hours and eighteen miles after leaving Wilson Creek, Herron's Third Division halted for the night on Crane Creek. The men dined on hard bread and coffee and slept on the snow-covered ground. "I laid down on the side of a Rocky Hill, my feet to a rousing fire, and without tent or shelter except my blankets took a right good nap," William Orme wrote to his wife. "It froze ice about [a] half inch thick and the frost was very heavy. My little moustache was quite frosty when I got up. I would not have believed I could have slept so well out doors in such a cold night." The next morning, 4 December, the temperature was twenty degrees. The Federals rolled out of their blankets at 4:00 A.M. and resumed the march. "As no tents were now pitched at night our preparations for moving consisted simply in waking up and 'falling in,'" recalled one soldier. After a brutal tramp of twenty-seven miles in fourteen hours, the column finally halted on Flat Creek north of Cassville. "This has been a hard day and one to be remembered by us," wrote Sergeant Benjamin McIntyre of the Nineteenth Iowa. Another diarist in the same regiment, too tired to bother with commas, noted that "our boys are laying along the road side every mile between this point and Springfield entirely disheartened completely exhausted can go no farther." All slept well that night despite the bitter cold.[5]

The thermometer again read twenty degrees when the Third Division formed up an hour before sunrise on 5 December. The Federals passed through Cassville and Keetsville and reached the Arkansas-Missouri line late in the afternoon. An officer in the Seventh Missouri Cavalry wrote that the "fife and drum struck up 'Dixie' and the boys yelled like a pack of wild Indians" when they realized they were back in the Confederacy. The infantry tramped across the Pea Ridge battlefield and camped in Little Sugar Creek Hollow, twenty-two miles from their starting point on Flat Creek. "We have had a long march today and many of my company are so sore and stiff and their feet so severely blistered that they can scarcely walk," commented a soldier in the Nineteenth Iowa. The cavalry continued another nine miles until failing light and falling temperatures compelled them to stop. "We reached Cross Hollows about dark and it was as cold as Greenland," noted Lieutenant Charles W. DeWolf. The grueling twelve-hour march was marred by a terrible accident in Cross Timber Hollow when a runaway wagon crushed one soldier and severely injured two others.[6]

Colonel Huston delayed his departure from McColloch's Spring to wait for the return of several large foraging parties. The Second Division got under way in the predawn hours of 4 December and marched twenty-four miles to McDowell, ten miles north of Cassville. The next day, 5 December, the cavalry covered twenty-six miles and stopped for the night in Big Sugar Creek Hollow, one mile north of the Arkansas-Missouri line and only six miles behind the Third Division. The infantry halted a half-dozen miles farther north near Keetsville. A train of four hundred wagons escorted by several battalions of cavalry brought up the rear. At the close of the second full day of the march, the attenuated Union column stretched twenty-four miles from tip to tail and straddled the Arkansas-Missouri line.[7]

The First Arkansas Cavalry had been stationed at Elkhorn Tavern since the beginning of November, but on 5 December most of the regiment departed for Fayetteville to secure Telegraph Road for the passage of the Missouri Divisions. Responsibility for the vital telegraph station passed to Herron, who stayed the night in the tavern and informed Curtis of his progress.

"Glad to see you are nearing Blunt," replied Curtis. "Be cautious. Hindman is shrewd and active. He will try hard to deceive you by drawing you into [an] ambush." Curtis's advice proved to be prophetic, but caution was the last thing on Herron's mind. He advised Blunt that he expected to arrive at Cane Hill late on 7 December. "I hope to God we will reach you before they get too close, and with our combined forces I do not fear the result," declared Herron. "I am afraid when they hear of re-enforcements coming up they will back down." He need not have worried.[8]

Later that night a courier from Cane Hill picked his way across Pea Ridge in the dim light of the lunar eclipse. Around 2:00 A.M. on 6 December he reached Elkhorn Tavern and delivered Blunt's order for Herron to advance his "best armed and best mounted Cavalry with as much rapidity as possible, leaving the Infantry and Artillery to follow." As noted in the previous chapter, Blunt had written this message nine hours earlier, after learning that the main body of the Rebel army was on Cove Creek Road only four miles below Morrow's.[9]

Once again Herron responded with alacrity. The mounted force in the van at Cross Hollows consisted of two battalions of the Tenth Illinois Cavalry, two battalions of the First Iowa Cavalry, the Eighth Missouri Cavalry, and a battalion of the Second Wisconsin Cavalry—altogether 1,600 men and four pieces of artillery. Herron ordered Colonel Dudley Wickersham, his senior cavalry commander, to lead the entire force to Blunt's relief. Wickersham had the men stuff their pockets and saddlebags with ammunition and rations so they would not be burdened with a train. The long column rode out of Cross Hollows around 9:00 A.M. on 6 December and reached Boonsboro twelve hours later. While Wickersham readied his command, Herron reached back up the column to Big Sugar Creek, in Missouri, where Huston's cavalry was camped. He directed Major Eliphalet Bredett to take two battalions of his Seventh Missouri Cavalry and a battalion of the Sixth Missouri Cavalry and hurry after Wickersham. Bredett's force consisted of about 650 men and a small train.[10]

In retrospect, Herron's decision to send Blunt nearly all of his cavalry, a total of 2,250 men, was a serious error. It deprived Herron of a powerful mounted force capable of scouting ahead and screening his movements as he drew ever closer to the Boston Mountains. At the time, however, no one except Curtis was concerned about the possibility that Hindman might slip past Blunt and waylay Herron. With the cavalry on its way, Herron telegraphed Curtis one last time to apprise him of recent developments:

> The enemy is within fifteen miles of [Blunt], marching on to Cane Hill. I have advised him fully of my location each day, and have advised him to fall back and meet me, should the enemy press him in force. He will make a mistake if he undertakes to fight before we get up. I will have both divisions in Fayetteville during the night. The entire column has marched thirty miles per day since we started. I am doing my best to reach him. Tomorrow will tell the story. May the God of battles be with us.

There was nothing left to say, and Herron took his place at the head of the Third Division. The temperature at Pea Ridge on the morning of 6 December was eighteen degrees. The men were glad to be in motion, if only to ward off the cold.[11]

Despite blistered feet, aching muscles, and frigid conditions, the Federals fairly sped across the rolling landscape between Little Sugar Creek and Fayetteville. At sunset the Third Division halted near Robinson's Crossroads to eat and rest. Union soldiers fell upon nearby farmsteads with surprising vigor considering their physical condition. The men of the Nineteenth Iowa feasted on fowl, pork, mutton, and hard bread, then gathered in a moonlit field to hear a few words from Lieutenant Colonel Samuel McFarland, their popular and well-respected regimental commander. McFarland was an attorney and an accomplished orator who had served as speaker of the house in the Iowa legislature, but on this occasion he kept his remarks brief and to the point. "Boys, we are in probability about to meet the enemy in a short time," he began. "I want you—each one—to remain cool. Do not get excited, take good aim, shoot low." McFarland spoke in a quiet voice, yet his words carried easily in the cold air. The men were much affected by the concise address. One soldier recalled that the colonel "talked in a spirit of devoted patriotism, and they were his last words to us." Before the next sunset McFarland would be dead and the regiment would be shattered.[12]

The Third Division resumed its "toilsome march" down Telegraph Road, but men and animals were so worn out they could not maintain the brisk pace set earlier in the day. "It was a bright moonlight night and the army moved on slowly through the still night," remembered a fifer in the Nineteenth Iowa. The Federals shuffled through Fayetteville in the wee hours of 7 December and finally halted along a stream called Town Branch. After marching more than thirty miles in eighteen hours, the famished soldiers devoured what was left in their haversacks and collapsed. An Iowan recalled that he and his com-

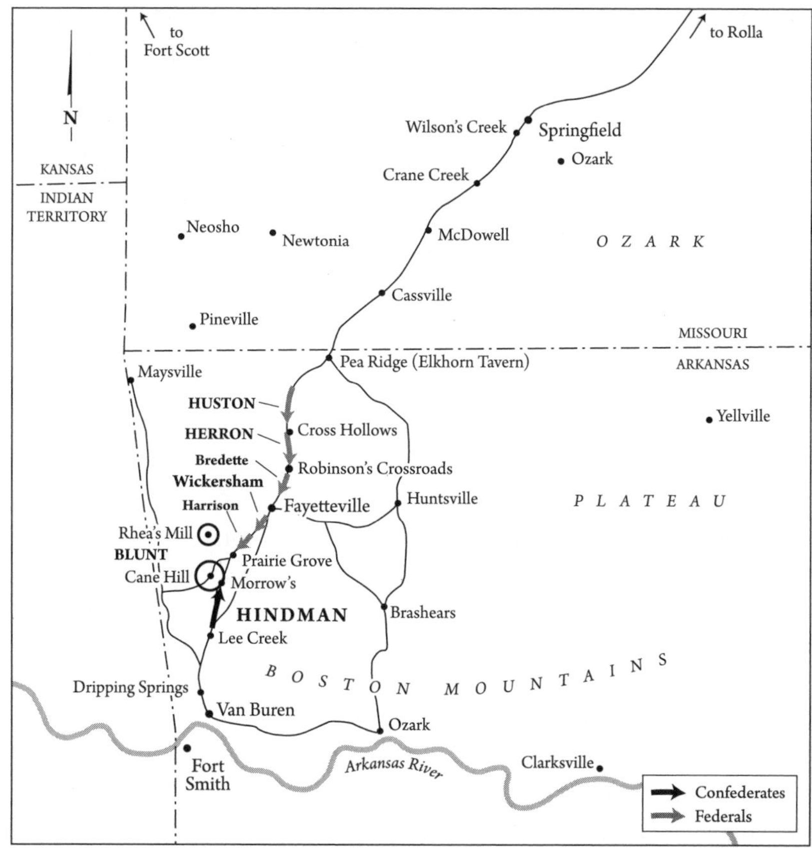

Situation at sunset on 6 December. Herron hurries toward Cane Hill while Hindman crawls over the Boston Mountains.

rades slept next to a cemetery, "little thinking that within three days some of our number would be resting within its gates."[13]

Huston's Second Division set out at dawn on 6 December. The Federals made a "heart-breaking tramp" of thirty miles in ten hours, then dropped to the ground in Cross Hollows. After a brief halt to eat and rest, they staggered to their feet and resumed the seemingly endless trek. "Then came the worse march of all," wrote Henry C. Adams of the Twenty-sixth Indiana. "The men were so sore that they limped and stumbled along in the dark, until the continued exercise produced a better circulation in their almost wornout legs." The Federals covered twenty additional miles during the early morning hours of 7 December and dragged themselves through Fayetteville just as dawn was breaking. They reached Town Branch in time to see Herron's troops set out on the final leg of the march. "Our train was far behind, but by readjustment of individual supplies of rations which we carried, all were supplied scantily." Some soldiers fell asleep while sitting upright and munching crackers or sipping coffee. Adams believed he was "too weary to march another mile," but within a few hours the Second Division would be in motion again.[14]

The Missouri Divisions experienced serious attrition during the latter half of the march. "The men began to fall by the wayside—the road was lined with them," recalled an officer in the Twentieth Wisconsin. The erosion of manpower is illustrated by the experience of the Twentieth Iowa. The regiment set out from Missouri with 27 officers and 615 men but went into the fight at Prairie Grove with only 23 officers and 270 men, an attrition rate of 54 percent. The numbers varied only slightly from regiment to regiment.[15]

Fatigue caused most straggling, though unserviceable footwear was also a factor. Lieutenant Colonel Leake of the Twentieth Iowa described the situation in his regiment: "The men had had no shoes since the first pair issued in Iowa, which were now so worn that many walked with their feet upon the ground. Some boots had been issued at Camp Lyon, but they fitted so badly that the feet became inflamed and blistered, and many took them off and carried them, marching in their bare feet." The Thirty-seventh Illinois experienced similar problems. "I cannot speak of other regiments," stated an Illinois officer, "but I *know* that in my regiment . . . nine-tenths of the men were carrying their shoes and marching in their stocking feet on account of the blisters on their feet." Temperatures ranged from the teens to the forties, and the road surface was a mix of ice, snow, slush, and mud leavened with sharp, flinty rocks. Soldiers in the Nineteenth Iowa and Ninety-fourth Illinois experienced torture of another sort when they carried their packs on the first day of the march. "We arrived at camp near Cassville about sundown, a pretty well used up set of men and there was a good many damnations indulged in and I think if tomorrow comes and knapsacks must be carried there will not be one carried from this camp," snapped an irate Iowan. The next morning the infantrymen defiantly piled their packs along the road and marched away. Colonel Orme, the brigade commander, saw the error of his ways and had the packs placed in wagons.[16]

At 4:00 A.M. on Sunday, 7 December, the soldiers of the Third Division crawled out of their blankets and shivered in the bone-chilling, sixteen-degree cold. As rations were almost exhausted, breakfast consisted largely of coffee and crumbs. Despite the harsh conditions, Herron was in a good mood. For the first time since leaving Wilson's Creek three days earlier, he was confident that his extraordinary effort to reach Blunt would succeed. It was only sixteen miles from Fayetteville to Cane Hill. Unless something unexpected happened, the two wings of the Army of the Frontier would be reunited before sunset. The Union camp was located near the junction of Telegraph Road and Fayetteville Road on the west side of town. The latter ran along the edge of the Springfield Plain and offered travelers impressive vistas of the Boston Mountains. More important, it led directly to the junction with Cove Creek Road at Prairie Grove, nine miles to the southwest.[17]

The Third Division formed up and turned southwest on Fayetteville Road. "We struck out pretty lively" to ward off the piercing cold, recalled an Iowa soldier. Herron's mood grew lighter with every passing mile. "A more beautiful morning or a grander sunrise than that of December 7 I never beheld," he recalled. The sun was barely above the horizon, however, when small arms fire was heard some distance ahead. Herron became uneasy as the popping grew louder and more sustained. The road was supposed to be in Union hands. Who was fighting and who were they fighting with? He directed Major James M. Hubbard to take his two companies of the First Missouri Cavalry, the only mounted force at hand, and investigate. Hubbard and his troopers trotted ahead, guns at the ready. After advancing two miles the Federals halted in amazement. Hundreds of blue-clad horsemen were racing in their direction.[18]

THE LEADING BODY of Union troops hurrying to Blunt's relief was not part of Herron's command. The First Arkansas Cavalry left Elkhorn Tavern on 5 December and reached Fayetteville at noon the following day. Blunt initially wanted Colonel LaRue Harrison and his 485 Arkansans to occupy Fayetteville but later decided that they would be of more use at Cane Hill. He sent Captain Harris S. Greeno, a staff officer, to Fayetteville to advise Harrison of the change in plans. Greeno set up shop on the town square and served as the Union army's traffic director for the next twenty-four hours. Harrison wanted to stay in Fayetteville long enough to shoe and rest his horses, which were in poor condition, but Greeno urged him to push on to Cane Hill at once. Harrison complied, but after only eight miles his horses broke down and he stopped for the night along the wooded banks of the Illinois River. The Union camp was barely a mile from the junction at Prairie Grove, the key to Hindman's plan to defeat Herron and destroy Blunt.[19]

Wickersham's 1,600 troopers reached Fayetteville four hours behind Harrison's hobbled command. Greeno advised Wickersham to "push forward with all possible dispatch" to Cane Hill. Continuing on, Wickersham caught up with the First Arkansas Cavalry an hour or so after sunset. Harrison's men were eating supper when Wickersham's fast-moving column burst out of the darkness and gave everyone a terrific start. Wickersham paused only long enough to water his horses in the Illinois, then hurried on to Boonsboro, which he reached without incident later that night. Whether Harrison and Wickersham conferred is not known.[20]

Bredett's smaller force of 650 horsemen passed through Fayetteville about two hours behind Wickersham. After receiving the familiar plea from Greeno to keep moving, Bredett doggedly pressed on toward Cane Hill despite the exhausted condition of both men and mounts. Three miles beyond Fayetteville, however, he changed his mind and stopped along Farmington Branch, a small creek. "Here we camped till morning," recorded Homer H. Jewett of the Seventh Missouri Cavalry, "the men being fatigued and the Major thinking the exigencies did not demand that he should go ahead." The next day, 7 December, the Sixth and Seventh Missouri Cavalry arose early and set out for Boonsboro. They were accompanied by a company of the Eighth Missouri Cavalry that had become separated from Wickersham's column the previous day. Bredett passed the camp of the First Arkansas Cavalry on the Illinois River an hour before sunrise but did not stop. A scant two miles farther, however, he halted along Muddy Fork to rest and feed his command. The Missourians turned their horses loose in a cornfield, then boiled coffee and butchered hogs for their breakfast. Men huddled around campfires to ward off the biting cold. Jewett recalled that "no one for a moment thought the enemy was near."[21]

The previous evening Colonel Harrison had dispatched Lieutenant James Roseman to inform Blunt that the First Arkansas Cavalry had stopped for the night on the Illinois River but would arrive in Boonsboro early the next morning. Roseman's description of the regiment's "unshod and run-down" horses seems to have convinced Blunt that the Arkansans would be of little use on the front line but might serve effectively in a rear area. Once again Blunt changed Harrison's orders, directing him to proceed to Rhea's Mill to help guard the trains and stores and assist in "running the mill to its utmost extent." (Even with the enemy at the gate, the Federals could not escape the tyranny of logistics.) Roseman left Boonsboro and rejoined the regiment on the Illinois shortly before sunrise on 7 December. He encountered only Union soldiers on Fayetteville Road and informed Harrison that "there was no danger of an attack this side of Cane Hill." Unfortunately for Harrison, the situation changed dramatically in the next forty-five minutes. Harrison intended to continue on Fayetteville Road another four miles, then turn north on Bottom Road and proceed to Rhea's Mill. A few minutes past 7:00 A.M., the First Arkansas Cavalry set out in a column of fours, followed by a train of twenty-one wagons. The Federals splashed across the Illinois River just as the sun rose into view over the Boston Mountains.[22]

UNKNOWN TO BREDETT OR HARRISON, that morning the entire Trans-Mississippi Army (save for Monroe's Brigade on Reed's Mountain) was marching north on Cove Creek Road. An hour before sunrise Marmaduke's Division, a force of 2,000 cavalrymen and six guns, emerged from the confines of the Boston Mountains and debouched onto the Springfield Plain. Marmaduke's objective was the junction at Prairie Grove. His mission was to gain control of Fayetteville Road and keep Blunt and Herron apart until Hindman and the infantry arrived.

The Confederate column halted one and a half miles south of Prairie Grove at a point where Valley Road branched off to the northwest from Cove Creek Road. Valley Road was a little-used track (one Rebel called it a "by-way") that followed the broad valley drained by Muddy Fork and joined Fayetteville Road one mile west of Prairie Grove. Scouts fanned out and located Bredett's camp on Muddy Fork but unaccountably failed to detect Harrison's camp on the Illinois, two miles to the northeast. The Confederates were cold, tired, and hungry, but time was of the essence and Marmaduke opted to attack at once. Shelby's Brigade (with Marmaduke at its head) turned northwest on Valley Road; MacDonald's Brigade continued north on Cove Creek Road toward Prairie Grove. The plan called for the two Confederate columns to converge and crush the unsuspecting Federals on Muddy Fork.[23]

Hindman feared that Blunt would strike the Trans-Mississippi Army in the flank or rear as it moved north to intercept Herron. He had no way of knowing that his turning movement on Cove Creek Road had gone undetected and that it would be midmorning before the Federals at Cane Hill realized what had happened. But while Blunt remained in the dark during these critical hours, his reputation as an alert and aggressive commander served him well. The first thing Marmaduke did upon reaching Fayetteville Road was to dismount most of Shelby's Brigade and form a line facing *southwest* toward Boonsboro. This blocking force consisted of Gordon's Missouri Cavalry, Thompson's Missouri Cavalry, and one 6-pounder gun of Bledsoe's Missouri Battery, or between 700 and 750 of Shelby's 1,200 men. Marmaduke remained with the blocking force to watch for Blunt and wait for Hindman. Shelby led the remainder of his command toward Bredett.[24]

Shelby formed Jeans's Missouri Cavalry, Elliott's Missouri Cavalry Bat-

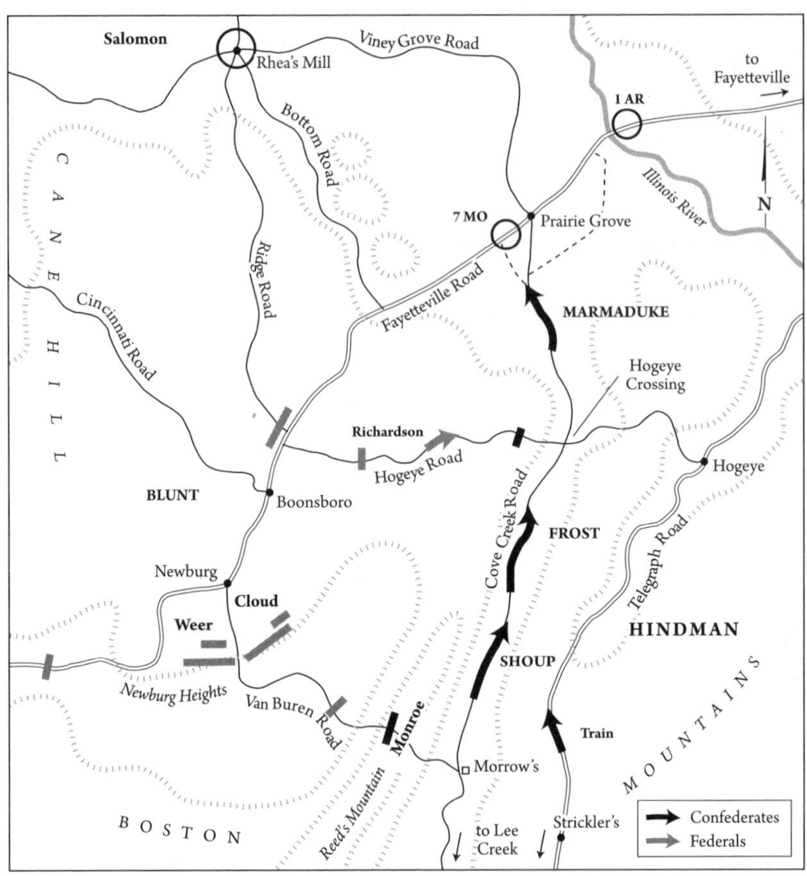

Situation at dawn on 7 December. Marmaduke approaches Prairie Grove with Frost and Shoup close behind.

talion, Gregg's guerrillas, and Bledsoe's remaining 6-pounder gun into three successive lines and advanced toward the unsuspecting Union camp at a walk. Because many of the 450 Confederates were dressed in captured Union uniforms, the Federals may have mistaken them for the First Arkansas Cavalry. As the Rebels drew within hailing distance, a smattering of shots broke out. Shelby gave the order to charge just as the sun appeared over the mountains.[25]

A Confederate officer compared the attack to a "thunderbolt from a clear sky." The cacophony of yells and shrieks and the hail of bullets and buckshot took Bredett and his men completely by surprise. "Some of us were lieing around on the ground catching a few moments sleep while some were hastily cooking a few mouth fulls before we resumed our march," wrote Jewett. Many

Union soldiers were unable to mount their horses, which were grazing with bridles off and girths loosened. Those who did get into the saddle faced other difficulties. "Several attempts were made to form us for a charge, but as the lane was filled with horses and men there was much confusion, and finding it impossible to do so, a retreat was ordered," recalled Sergeant Henry Worthen, Seventh Missouri Cavalry. Bredett was killed after decapitating a Confederate soldier with his saber, and the Union retreat degenerated into a rout. "They never fired a shot at us, being too busy trying to get away," recalled one of Gregg's guerrillas. Captain Milton H. Brawner, who assumed command, was powerless to prevent his men from fleeing "in every direction, quite a number running into the rebel lines, being killed or captured." Those Union soldiers lucky enough to escape raced toward the First Arkansas Cavalry.[26]

MacDonald, meanwhile, had turned northeast on Neighborhood Road, another little-used "by-way." The lane branched off from Cove Creek Road a short distance north of the junction with Valley Road and joined Fayetteville Road near the main ford across the Illinois River. Margaret Mock was up early that frigid morning and watched the Confederate horsemen approach her house in the gray light of dawn. Riding next to MacDonald at the head of the column was Benjamin Pearson, a local minister and farmer. The Rebels halted and "Uncle Ben," as he was known to one and all, asked Mrs. Mock for help. Years later she described her brief conversation with Pearson. "He called at my gate and asked 'if the old time neighborhood road from here to Uncle Billy Crawford's is still used, far as the ford of the creek.' I said you can pass on that." Reassured, the Confederates left Cove Creek Road and passed around the east side of Prairie Grove.[27]

When MacDonald reached Fayetteville Road, he was surprised to find it filled with Union horsemen. The blue-clad troopers belonged to the First Arkansas Cavalry, which until that moment had escaped detection by the Confederates. Spurred on by a fusillade of shots from the direction of Muddy Fork, MacDonald formed most of his command into line in the fields west of Neighborhood Road. Phillip Crump's Texas Cavalry was on the left, Lieutenant Colonel Merritt L. Young's Missouri Cavalry on the right. West's Arkansas Battery remained on the road in reserve. When all was in readiness the 750 Rebels emitted the requisite howls and advanced with carbines, shotguns, and pistols at the ready.[28]

At the sound of "sharp firing" from the direction of Muddy Fork, Harrison had halted the First Arkansas Cavalry and led a company forward to find out what was happening. As luck would have it, the immobile Union regiment straddled the junction with Neighborhood Road. Before Harrison could

M. LaRue Harrison (Shiloh Museum of Ozark History, S-88-183-59)

issue another order, Bredett's panic-stricken troopers stampeded past in "great disorder," followed by Shelby's exultant horsemen. One of the Rebels brandished the national colors of the Seventh Missouri Cavalry. "By this time the pursuing enemy were upon us, bearing our standard and wearing our blue overcoats," declared a loyal Arkansas officer. Things went from bad to worse when MacDonald's command attacked from the south. Assailed in front and flank, the Federals were unable to maneuver because of the press of horses in the narrow road. The Arkansas quartermaster tried to save his wagons but succeeded only in creating a fatal roadblock near the ford. "Our train was only partly turned when we were crowded back over it," reported Harrison. The situation was complicated by the presence of Rebecca Axley Harrison, who had accompanied her husband in the expectation of visiting family and friends in Fayetteville. She escaped, but concern for her safety was a needless distraction at a most inconvenient time.[29]

With so many combatants dressed in blue, the struggle was intense and chaotic. "We had a hand to hand fight that lasted about ten minutes," recalled a Confederate officer. "It was a hot and exciting battle. We were all mixed up, every fellow for himself, all dressed pretty much alike, except the hats were mostly of different style." Harrison reported that "all was confusion" and that he and his officers were barely able "to keep our men from rushing over and killing each other." A disoriented Union trooper remembered that bullets and buckshot "came from all sides." Overwhelmed, the Arkansans joined their Missouri comrades in flight.[30]

The Federals splashed across the Illinois and scrambled up East Bluff. At Walnut Grove Church they encountered Colonel Hubbard and the First Missouri Cavalry, the small force Herron had ordered forward to see what all the shooting was about. Harrison was giddy with relief at the sight of Hubbard's men formed in line in a field across from the church. Harrison and his staff "blocked the road with revolvers in hand, ordering every man shot who attempted to pass us." Results were mixed. "Many went into line with Major Hubbard's men and others struck into the brush and escaped." For a moment it appeared that a degree of order had been restored, but the Arkansans slunk away as larger and larger numbers of Confederates appeared in the distance. A disheartened Harrison wished Hubbard good luck and departed. Despite being outnumbered ten to one, Hubbard remained near the church to cover Harrison's retreat.[31]

The Confederates were disorganized and exhausted by the eight-mile march from Morrow's and the three-mile running fight from Muddy Fork. After struggling up East Bluff they paused to rest their mounts and sort themselves out. Now it was Shelby's turn to blunder. Following the rout of the First Arkansas Cavalry, he had raced back to Muddy Fork and convinced Marmaduke to let him have both of Bledsoe's guns. Shelby hurried after the Federals with the restored battery in tow, oblivious to the fact that the pursuit had petered out during his absence. At Walnut Grove Church he was brought up short by the sight of the First Missouri Cavalry only two hundred yards ahead. Shelby shouted for Bledsoe to unlimber his guns, but Hubbard charged and overran the battery before it could fire a shot. In the press of men and animals around the guns, Hubbard found himself face-to-face with Shelby and demanded his surrender. Shelby complied. The situation was still highly fluid, and MacDonald's Brigade reached the scene before the Federals carried away their prize. Hubbard and a dozen of his troopers were captured in the scuffle around the battery, but the rest of the First Missouri Cavalry got away. The Federals left the road and regrouped near the base of Miller's Mountain. MacDonald attempted to pursue but his horses gave out. By 8:00 A.M. the cavalry fight was over.[32]

Shelby neglected to mention in his report that he had been taken prisoner, but MacDonald's regimental commanders were not so reticent. Young reported with delicious precision that "Colonel Shelby, with two pieces of artillery, was captured by the enemy. The colonel, with his guns, was liberated by our troops." Crump announced that his Texans "had the pleasure of recapturing Colonel Shelby and his battery of light artillery, who had been previously taken by the enemy." Thereafter MacDonald's troopers rarely missed an opportunity to remind Shelby's men who had rescued their commander.[33]

With the Federal horsemen vanquished and several miles of Fayetteville Road in Confederate hands, Shelby and MacDonald retired to gather up the spoils of war. The impoverished Rebels were amazed at their good fortune: "The road was strown with Blankets Overcoats Saddles Sabres Six Shooters and guns of all sorts Knapsacks Haversacks Hats Capts Boots Shoes and all such things." More, much more, was found in the train taken from the First Arkansas Cavalry. "The wagons were loaded with boots, shoes, hats, arms, sugar, coffee, rice, flour, hams, tobacco, cigars, tents and camp equipage," marveled Crump. Harrison's "Mountain Feds," lacking the support of a state government, were poorly equipped and provisioned by Union standards, but the threadbare Confederates lived in a different logistical universe. Young declared that the cornucopia of conquest included "everything that would make a soldier comfortable." The haul included hundreds of carbines and pistols, thousands of rounds of ammunition, and over three hundred horses and mules. Christmas came early in 1862 for Marmaduke's Division.[34]

The Confederates killed, wounded, or captured nearly 300 Federals out of a total force of just over 1,200. With Cane Hill still fresh in his memory, Marmaduke reported with obvious relish that the Federals "were charged and routed wherever found." The debacle cost the Sixth, Seventh, and Eighth Missouri Cavalry 187 casualties: 6 killed, 10 wounded, and 171 captured, a loss of nearly 30 percent. The First Arkansas Cavalry lost 86 men: 4 killed, 4 wounded, and 78 captured, a casualty rate of 18 percent. The hapless Arkansans also lost twenty-one wagons filled with camp equipment, bedding, clothing, and tack, along with all manner of stores and personal items. "Nothing except the ambulances—not even the regimental books, rolls and papers—were rescued," stated a dejected Harrison. The First Missouri Cavalry made only a brief appearance and suffered least: 5 wounded and 13 captured, including Hubbard. Confederate losses probably amounted to fewer than a dozen killed or wounded. The only Rebel casualty mentioned by name was Major Elliott, who was injured when his horse stumbled and fell. By any measure the cavalry fight was an impressive Confederate victory. It must have done wonders for the morale of Marmaduke's long-suffering troopers.[35]

Hindman reached Muddy Fork about the time the cavalry fight sputtered out several miles to the northeast. Anxious to expand the Confederate lodgment on Fayetteville Road and allow the infantry time to arrive, he directed

Marmaduke to find Herron and delay his approach. Marmaduke departed with Gordon's Missouri Cavalry, but Hindman kept Thompson's Missouri Cavalry at Muddy Fork to watch for signs of Union activity in the direction of Boonsboro. Marmaduke crossed the Illinois, conferred with Shelby and MacDonald at Walnut Grove Church, and went in search of Herron. Half a mile past the church he found what he was looking for.[36]

HERRON WAS RIDING at the head of the Third Division about six miles west of Fayetteville when the broken remnants of Bredett's and Harrison's commands streamed past. "The first thing we knew was the advance of our cavalry rushing upon us in the wildest confusion," declared a Union officer. Herron spread his staff and escort company across the road to stop the fleeing cavalrymen. When that failed to have the desired effect, he shot a man out of the saddle. "It was with the very greatest difficulty that we got them checked," Herron informed Curtis, "but after some hard talking, and my finally shooting one cowardly whelp off his horse, they halted." Several witnesses recorded the shooting incident, but none thought Herron's actions inappropriate.[37]

A soldier in the Nineteenth Iowa recalled that many of the fleeing Union cavalrymen were without hats, coats, or weapons and that they "rushed in pell mell haste past us" without stopping. "I never saw such scared men in my life," declared Samuel Baldridge of the Ninety-fourth Illinois. "Shouts of 'hold your hat!' and rude jests were showered on them as they passed by," recalled a soldier in the Nineteenth Iowa, "but failed to check their progress, or even gain their attention." An officer in the same Iowa regiment observed dryly that the spectacle "was not encouraging to raw troops." No sooner had the "white-faced and terror-stricken" rabble thundered past than a woman appeared. She wore a black riding habit and was mounted on a black horse. According to one Iowa soldier the female equestrian, presumably Rebecca Harrison, cried out "Fall back, men! Fall back for your lives, for all is lost!" But another Iowan maintained that Harrison rode along the column waving her scarf and exclaiming "Hurrah for the Union! You are the boys to protect it!" He added that her words "ran through our ranks like electricity" and sparked "cheer upon cheer." Readers may choose whichever version of the truth they prefer.[38]

Drums rolled as the Third Division prepared for action. "Our brigade was at once put into fighting trim, the men throwing off their knapsacks, overcoats, haversacks, and many thoughtlessly their canteens," recalled a man in the Nineteenth Iowa. When all was in readiness the division advanced at the double-quick. "Nearly every one had sore feet from the effects of the hard march, but we all forgot our feet and pushed forward," William Clayton wrote to his parents.[39]

Marmaduke did not expect to find Herron so near. A soldier in the Twentieth Wisconsin stated that the Confederate horsemen approached in column and were "greeted with a volley of Minnie balls, which sent them back much more rapidly than they came forward." The Rebels fell back to Walnut Grove Church and formed a line across the road. The Federals approached at the double-quick, formed a line of their own, and opened fire with artillery. A dozen rounds of shell and case shot convinced Marmaduke that discretion was the better part of valor. The Confederates withdrew in haste a second time.[40]

The Federals followed as fast as they could. Herron recklessly dashed ahead with only his escort company, a section of artillery, and a battalion of infantry. Shortly before 10:00 A.M. he reached East Bluff and gazed across the valley drained by the Illinois River. The sweeping view was dominated by the distant Boston Mountains, but the feature that caught Herron's eye was a steep, forested hill less than a mile away: Prairie Grove.

10 ARTILLERY DUEL

BELOW HERRON'S POSITION ON EAST BLUFF THE ILLINOIS RIVER flows north through a well-defined flood plain incised into the limestone surface of the Ozark Plateau. At the time of the Civil War the narrow plain was covered with a forest of oak, hickory, cedar, poplar, and elm. West of the river is Crawford's Prairie, a broad valley one and a half miles long from east to west and three-quarters of a mile wide from north to south. In 1862 roughly half of the valley floor was still covered with native grasses and used as pasturage; the other half was planted in corn and wheat. Miles of split-rail fences enclosed large rectangular fields that gave the valley floor the appearance of an irregular checkerboard.

The gently rising ground to the north of Crawford's Prairie is Crawford's Hill, then a patchwork of fields and forests, mostly the latter. The imposing elevation to the south that attracted Herron's attention is Prairie Grove or, in the local usage of the time, simply the Grove. Prairie Grove is elliptical in shape and about two miles across from east to west. The flattish crest is 1,260 feet above sea level. The east, south, and west sides of the hill are gradual inclines, but the north side is steeper and cut by a half-dozen ravines of varying size. Early settlers referred to the eroded north slope as the Ridge; later generations would know it as Battle Ridge.

For most of the nineteenth century Prairie Grove was covered with an extension of the hardwood forest that filled the flood plain of the Illinois. A longtime resident wrote that the thicket atop the hill was so dense a "man on horseback could only be seen at intervals." One of the peculiarities of an Ozark forest is that several species of trees retain their desiccated foliage through the winter. Consequently, the woods on and around Prairie Grove provided soldiers in both armies with a measure of concealment even in December.

This was especially convenient for the Confederates, whose somber gray and butternut uniforms closely matched nature's wintry palette.[1]

The most prominent structure in the vicinity was Prairie Grove Cumberland Presbyterian Church. The stout log building, which also served as the local school, was located on the south side of Prairie Grove near the junction of Fayetteville and Cove Creek roads. Close by was the home of Andrew Buchanan, a respected minister and educator and one of the first settlers in northwest Arkansas. "Uncle Buck" had died five years earlier, but his widow still occupied the house. Of the dozens of other homesteads dotting the countryside, eight are of particular interest. Four houses were scattered along the north side of Prairie Grove. On the east was the Archibald Borden home; perched eighty feet above the valley floor atop the steepest part of the Ridge, the two-story yellow house was the most visible structure on the battlefield. The one-story William Morton home, three-quarters of a mile to the west, was more modest, but it had a cellar that would serve as a place of refuge in the storm to come. Midway between the Borden and Morton residences were the Hugh Rogers and William Rogers homes, the former a one-story L-shaped structure, the latter a square two-story building. Both were painted white and located on a natural bench or terrace near the foot of the hill. Two houses occupied opposite ends of Crawford's Prairie, the two-story Josiah Thompson home on Fayetteville Road near the Illinois River and the Samuel Wilson house on Viney Grove Road. The Samuel Crawford house and the Robert West house, about three-quarters of a mile apart, were situated partway up the long slope of Crawford's Hill. The West home sat atop a slight eminence known as West's Knoll, which offered a spectacular view of the valley.

All of the "fine old fashioned farm houses" at Prairie Grove were built of squared logs, though some, like the Borden house, had been improved by the addition of weatherboarding and paint. "Every thing about them [was] as cozy and comfortable as heart could wish," wrote a Kansas soldier. Each homestead typically included an orchard, garden, woodpile, barn, springhouse, smokehouse, chicken coop, corncrib, and assortment of sheds, workshops, and fences. Here and there a few specialized structures could be found. William Morton operated a blacksmith shop on his property, and Hugh Rogers maintained a tiny one-room post office near his residence. A web of secondary roads, farm lanes, and footpaths connected the various homesteads and provided access to all but the most densely wooded parts of the neighborhood.[2]

Although Washington County was only one generation removed from the

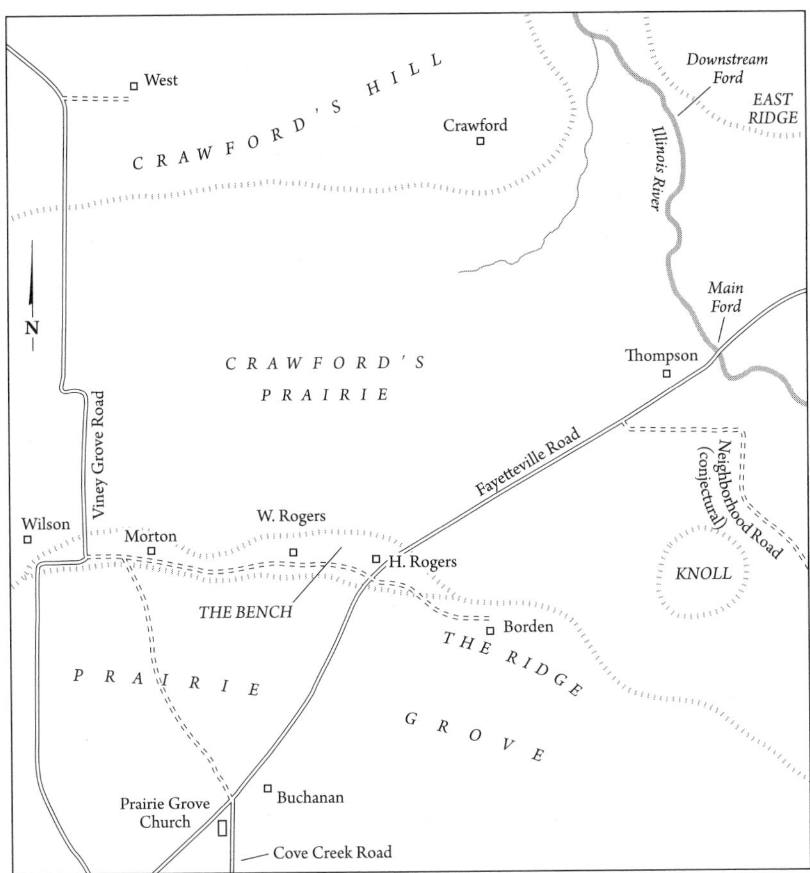

Prairie Grove and vicinity

frontier, evidence of prewar prosperity was everywhere. The sturdy houses, bountiful fields, and rolling landscape reminded many Union soldiers of the Midwest. Located on the southern edge of the Springfield Plain and surrounded on three sides by outliers of the Boston Mountains, Prairie Grove is one of the most attractive places in northwest Arkansas. Men in both armies were struck by the idyllic pastoral setting. Colonel Orme of the Ninety-fourth Illinois informed his wife: "This is a beautiful country—none to excel it—and it has everything in it good." Another Union officer remarked that "if the continent had been searched it would have been impossible to have selected a more beautiful field of battle than that of Prairie Grove."[3]

THE SEVENTH OF DECEMBER dawned clear and cold but with a promise of warming temperatures, a welcome prospect for the Confederate infantry and artillery plodding north on Cove Creek Road. "Sunrise was beautiful to behold," recalled Arkansan Dan P. Thomas. "The suns rays shined through the tree tops with uncommon refulgence." Sunrise also brought the "sharp crack and rattle of firearms" as Marmaduke's cavalry went into action on Fayetteville Road. Hindman immediately picked up the pace. "We were ordered to advance in double quick," recalled Spencer H. Mitchell, a Missouri soldier. "We did so amid cheers and hurrahs." The cheers soon gave way to gasps. A dismounted Texas cavalryman named John C. Williams recalled: "We were put on double quick time until we could stand it no longer, when quick time was resumed until about ten o'clock." Another Arkansan, Cornelius Buckler, told his wife that the pace of the march increased from a walk to a trot. "We then went ahead on a run until ten o'clock in the morning."[4]

For some Confederates the sound of gunfire was cause for concern, not celebration. Several companies of Brooks's Arkansas Infantry were filled with men from western Washington County. "We knew now that the battle was on," wrote Samuel Pittman, "and we knew very near where it would be, right in the midst of our homes, within the hearing of our loved ones. It would be impossible for me to describe our feelings at this point." As the Confederate infantry and artillery neared Prairie Grove, they passed hundreds of captured Union cavalrymen being taken to the rear. They also passed several corpses. All had been stripped of their uniforms and equipment, and several had been trampled into the mud by horses. It was a sobering sight for men unaccustomed to the detritus of battle.[5]

Frost's Division, in the lead, turned northwest on Valley Road and reached Muddy Fork around 8:30 A.M. After conferring with Hindman, Frost placed Parsons's Brigade across Fayetteville Road. Parsons's line of battle, like Shelby's before it, faced southwest toward Boonsboro. Hindman instructed Parsons "to hold this position at any cost, and prevent the enemy, then supposed to be marching on the road from Cane Hill, from forming a junction with his troops moving from Fayetteville." Frost believed he had placed Parsons in a "most eligible position," but Parsons was not satisfied. As soon as Frost departed to look after the rest of the division, Parsons went in search of a better position. He found a place more to his liking closer to the stream and advanced his brigade to that point, apparently without asking or receiving permission from Frost.[6]

It was a measure of Hindman's concern that he used his largest infantry division to block Blunt rather than intercept Herron. For the better part of the day Frost's 6,300 Arkansas, Missouri, and Texas troops remained "in reserve to await the movements of Blunt." Not only did Hindman keep more than half of his army on the sidelines, he squandered precious time. Had Frost continued on toward Fayetteville, he would have encountered Herron several miles beyond Prairie Grove and that much farther from Cane Hill. Herron's immediate command consisted of only the much-reduced Third Division, the smallest formation in the Union army. In all likelihood, Frost would have sent Herron reeling back in disorder. Instead, Hindman diverted Frost to Muddy Fork. As a result, *more than an hour passed* before Shoup's Division, last in the line of march and smaller by half than Frost's command, reached Prairie Grove and turned northeast on Fayetteville Road to confront Herron. During that lost hour Herron advanced from Walnut Grove Church to the Illinois River despite Marmaduke's ineffective delaying tactics. This was the first in a series of questionable command decisions by Hindman and his lieutenants.[7]

During the conference at Morrow's the previous night, Hindman had proposed a bold plan to smash Herron with his entire force, then turn about and deal with Blunt. At some point during the cold, dark march from Morrow's to Prairie Grove, the Confederate commander took counsel of his fears. He decided to hedge his bets by dividing his force, preparing to meet Blunt with the larger of his two divisions, and merely jabbing at Herron with the smaller. In his report Hindman provided a clever but unconvincing explanation of his reasoning. "The interval of time in which I might have attacked Herron was past," he wrote. "Circumstances did not permit me to avail myself of it, for the manifest reason that at the favorable moment the rear of my column could not be where the head of it was." It was Hindman, however, who decided to strike Herron with the *rear* of his column instead of the *head*. Like so many other commanders facing the terrible moment of truth, Hindman lost confidence in his plan and in himself.[8]

A little before 10:00 A.M. the head of Shoup's Division finally passed through the junction at Prairie Grove and turned northeast on Fayetteville Road. Francis Shoup got his first view of Crawford's Prairie from atop the Ridge. It was not an encouraging sight. Marmaduke's horsemen were falling back across the Illinois River and milling around on the valley floor in confusion. Puzzled, Shoup halted his division and rode down the hill to find out what was happening. He learned that Herron was fast approaching and that Marmaduke could do nothing to impede his progress.[9]

Jolted by this unwelcome news, Shoup rejoined his division atop Prairie Grove and considered his options. Should he continue to advance in accordance with Hindman's orders and collide with Herron somewhere east of the Illinois River, possibly in a disadvantageous location? Or should he establish

James F. Fagan (Museum of the Confederacy, Richmond, Va.)

a blocking position on the commanding heights he now occupied and wait for Herron to come to him? Shoup pondered the wisdom of plunging ahead and engaging an enemy force of unknown size on unfamiliar ground with the Illinois at his back. Then he studied the Ridge and discovered it commanded the main ford across the river. Herron would have to cross the Illinois under artillery fire or find another ford. This settled the matter. Shoup decided to remain where he was and hold the high ground. The fate of Arkansas, Missouri, and the Indian Territory would be decided on the wooded heights of Prairie Grove.

Shoup deployed his 3,200 Arkansas infantry to the east of Fayetteville Road. Brigadier General James F. Fagan's Brigade formed a line of battle in the woods facing north. Fagan's left rested near the road; his right ran along the southern boundary of the Borden farm a half-mile to the east. Colonel Dandridge McRae's Brigade formed in reserve behind Fagan's position. Fagan and McRae told their men to get some rest, and hundreds of exhausted soldiers promptly fell asleep on the cold, rocky ground. Too keyed up to follow his own advice, Fagan rode along the Ridge and studied the terrain. "At a glance I was struck with the natural strength of the position and its adaptability to the purpose of defense," he would write.[10]

The Confederates quickly discovered that the position also had a natural

Looking northwest from the site of Blocher's Battery. The 6-pounder points toward the main ford across the Illinois River. The spectacular view of Crawford's Prairie and Crawford's Hill from the Ridge is evident. (author's collection)

weakness. The exceptionally dense tangle of trees, vines, and underbrush atop the hill made it difficult for officers to maneuver their commands or even to understand what was happening. The vegetation also restricted where artillery could be placed. The only suitable clearings on the north side of the hill were well out in front of the infantry. Captain William D. Blocher's Arkansas Battery occupied a commanding position atop the Ridge about two hundred yards east of Fayetteville Road. The three 6-pounder guns and one 12-pounder howitzer were crowded into a narrow lane a short distance west of the Borden house. Captain Henry C. West's Arkansas Battery (now returned to Shoup's command after supporting MacDonald's Brigade earlier in the day) was located on the bench at the foot of the hill. The two 6-pounder guns and two 12-pounder howitzers filled up the small yard of the Hugh Rogers house. The Confederate gunners trained their weapons on the main ford across the Illinois River, three-fourths of a mile to the northeast, and waited for the Federals to come within range.[11]

Marmaduke placed MacDonald's Brigade, a force of about seven hundred Missourians and Texans, on the bench west of the Rogers house to support West's Battery and extend the Confederate left flank west of Fayetteville

Looking northeast from the Borden house toward the main ford across the Illinois River. The west cornfield and the wheatfield occupied the level expanse in the center of the view. East Ridge is in the distance. (author's collection)

Road. Marmaduke then led Shelby's Brigade up the "high and commanding hill" and placed the nine hundred Missourians on the right of Fagan's Brigade. Locating a place for Captain Joseph Bledsoe's Battery was a challenge, but Marmaduke eventually found a site in a cornfield at the foot of the hill two hundred yards east of the Borden house. Like Blocher and West, Bledsoe trained his two 6-pounder guns on the ford a half-mile north of his position. By 11:00 A.M. all of Shoup's Division and most of Marmaduke's Division, a combined force of 4,800 soldiers and ten guns, were in position on the north side of Prairie Grove awaiting Herron.[12]

The Trans-Mississippi Army's small train of fewer than one hundred wagons also was in motion that morning. Hindman wanted to keep Cove Creek Road clear in case it became necessary to make a hasty retreat, so he sent the train to Telegraph Road by way of Crossover Road. The rickety wagons and emaciated teams were accompanied by two companies of cavalry and what Hindman described as "the disabled men of the infantry, of whom there was, unfortunately, a considerable number." Three hundred sick, lame, or exhausted foot soldiers shuffled and limped after the wagons. The doleful caravan halted at Hogeye, six miles southeast of Prairie Grove, to await the outcome of the battle.[13]

Hindman spent most of the morning at Muddy Fork overseeing the deployment of Frost's Division and awaiting word of Blunt's movements. Sometime after 10:00 A.M. he rode up Fayetteville Road to see how Marmaduke and Shoup were faring. At the junction with Cove Creek Road Hindman encountered the rear of Shoup's Division trudging past the church. "It was painful to observe the exhaustion of the men," he reported. "They had marched nearly fifteen miles. None of them had eaten since the preceding day. The rations of all had been insufficient for over thirty days. Many, overcome with fatigue, had been left on the roadside." On the crest of Prairie Grove Hindman was surprised to see the infantry filing off the road and disappearing into the woods. He found Shoup and demanded to know why he was not advancing on Herron as ordered.[14]

Shoup explained that "Marmaduke was falling back before the enemy's infantry, which was advancing, and that he had therefore put his division in position to resist attack." Hindman likely reminded Shoup that he was supposed to make an attack, not resist one, but he did not override the decision to halt. By this time Herron had arrived and a column of Union troops could be seen moving down East Bluff toward the Illinois River. Hindman made a hasty inspection of the ground (he later described the Ridge as an "exceedingly strong" position) and hurried back to the junction. His visit with Shoup was cut short by the sound of artillery fire to the south on Cove Creek Road. Hindman's stomach must have churned as he urged his horse over the crest of Prairie Grove. Could Blunt have arrived so soon?[15]

The crash of Union guns on Cove Creek Road generated considerable alarm and confusion among the Confederates, but it turned out that the attack was merely a wake-up call from the Union force at Cane Hill. As discussed more fully in Chapter 13, when Blunt realized that the Confederates had turned his position, he sent the Sixth Kansas Cavalry in pursuit on Cove Creek Road. The Federals boldly advanced to within a half-mile of Prairie Grove and opened fire with a pair of mountain howitzers. Thirty minutes later they withdrew the way they had come. The noisy demonstration caused no appreciable damage, but it rattled Hindman and reinforced his conviction that Blunt was bold, unpredictable, and dangerous.[16]

Relieved to learn that he would not have to deal with the Kansas Division just yet, Hindman established his headquarters in Prairie Grove Church. While his staff rearranged pews and set up tables, Hindman took a moment to gather his thoughts. Despite stealing a march on Blunt during the night and landing a sharp blow against Herron in the morning, he had fumbled away the tactical initiative and he knew it. In the battle to come the Trans-Mississippi Army would be the anvil, not the hammer. Hindman must have been keenly disappointed by the breakdown of his plans to defeat the Federals in detail, but his natural optimism revived as the sun rose higher in the sky. Prairie Grove was a good place to fight. He might yet achieve a decisive victory by compelling the Federals to dash themselves to pieces against his hilltop bastion.

Shortly after noon Surgeon Keller, the army's medical director, commandeered the church for use as a hospital. Hindman and his staff gathered up their maps and moved to the nearby Buchanan house, but Keller soon claimed that building as well. Evicted a second time, Hindman and company set up shop in an adjacent field. For the rest of the day Hindman remained close to his open-air headquarters and made few visits to the front. Those who knew Hindman well were struck by his uncharacteristically passive behavior at Prairie Grove. Some attributed it to fatigue, but there is another possible explanation. Hindman may have made a conscious decision to avoid meddling in matters best left to his division commanders, all of whom, it should be remembered, were West Pointers with years of experience in the regular army. Whatever the reason, Marmaduke, Shoup, and Frost received only a modest amount of direction from above. The battle was theirs to win or lose.[17]

Confederate officers went from house to house advising everyone to gather up their possessions and flee. Some families had the presence of mind to take food and blankets, whereas others abandoned their homes with only the clothes on their back and a favorite doll or family heirloom. "We hadn't had any breakfast," remembered nine-year-old Caledonia Ann Borden, "we were too excited to be hungry." Caledonia walked alongside her mother while her three younger siblings rode on the back of a pony. By late morning the Bordens and at least a dozen other civilians had gathered at the Morton house, a half-mile west of Fayetteville Road, thankful that the morning clash of arms had been brief but fearful of what the afternoon might bring. If the worse happened, they were prepared to seek shelter in the Morton cellar. Across the valley, the West family remained in their home. Julia West, then fourteen years old, later recalled the fear that gripped everyone in the close-knit community. "Our home being on the north side, we felt we were comparatively safe and our greatest anxiety was for our relatives, neighbors, and friends so we stood out and watched until dark." For the people of Prairie Grove, whatever their political sentiments, the nightmare was only just beginning.[18]

HERRON HAD NO IDEA that the entire Trans-Mississippi Army was in his front. He knew only that a Confederate cavalry force of undetermined size had crossed the Boston Mountains and gained possession of a portion of Fayetteville Road. From his vantage point atop East Bluff, Herron watched Marmaduke's horsemen fall back across Crawford's Prairie. Half of the Rebels halted near a battery at the foot of Prairie Grove; the other half continued up the hill toward a second battery. Seeing no Confederate infantry, Herron concluded, reasonably enough, that Marmaduke was impeding his progress in order to allow Hindman time to overwhelm Blunt.

In the days and weeks after the battle, Herron made misleading statements about what he knew on the morning of 7 December. "It required but a short time to satisfy myself that the rebels were present in largely superior force," he informed Blunt, "and I immediately determined to give them the best fight I could until you could come up with additional forces." Herron told Curtis much the same thing: "I learned the whole force had slipped past Blunt, and was between us, and knew that by opening the fight I could bring [Blunt] up." In other words, Herron asserted in his official correspondence that *he knew from the start* that he faced Hindman and that he went into battle in order to compel Blunt to come to his aid.[19]

The truth is somewhat different. When Herron reached East Bluff, he believed the only Confederate force in his path was Marmaduke's cavalry. Over the next five hours he tried repeatedly to open the road to Cane Hill by dislodging what he supposed was a relatively small blocking force. It was midafternoon before Herron finally understood that he was engaged with most or all of Hindman's army and that his only hope of salvation, ironically, lay with Blunt. Embarrassed at having misread the tactical situation, Herron claimed forever after that he went into battle at Prairie Grove to alert Blunt to his plight. This manifestly was not the case.

Herron was under orders to get to Cane Hill as quickly as possible, and that is precisely what he attempted to do. The only question in his mind at 10:00 A.M. on that Sunday morning was how to push the Rebels out of the way. Herron had earned a general's star at Pea Ridge by leading from the front, and his performance at Prairie Grove was no less impressive. "I crossed the [Illinois River] with one of my staff to reconnoiter, keeping every one else out of sight, and, after getting a view of the ground and surrounding country, determined at once to attack." Or so Herron stated in his report. In fact, he was uncertain how to proceed. He later told Curtis that the Confederate position on Prairie Grove was the "strongest one I had ever seen."[20]

Perplexed, Herron made his way back to the main ford across the Illinois River, where he encountered a section of Lieutenant Joseph Foust's Battery E, First Missouri Light Artillery. The two guns were commanded by Lieutenant Cyrus L. Edwards. The arrival of artillery gave Herron an idea. A few minutes later, Edwards and his guns splashed across the Illinois and raced down Fayetteville Road at breakneck speed. After barreling past the Thompson house, the little cavalcade careened through a narrow gate on the right side of the road and halted in an expanse of shoulder-high prairie grass. The Union gunners unlimbered and opened fire on Blocher's Battery, eight hundred yards to the south atop the Ridge. The purpose of this maneuver was to "feel" the Confederate position by provoking the Rebels into shooting back and revealing the location and strength of their batteries. Fagan observed the unfolding drama from the Ridge: "They came up boldly and confidently and opened a brisk fire upon our position. The fire was responded to by Captain Blocher with great accuracy and admirable effect." Shoup watched the exchange with keen professional interest and later complimented Blocher on his "excellent" performance, rare praise from the former artillery commander of the Army of Tennessee. Henry West could barely see the Union guns because of the tall grass and fired only a few rounds.[21]

Unknown to the Confederates, one of the distant blue-clad figures near the Union guns was the commander of the Missouri Divisions. Displaying more courage than judgment, Herron accompanied Edwards to observe for himself the effectiveness of the Confederate batteries. The gaggle of horsemen drew the attention of Blocher's gunners, and Herron found himself in an uncomfortable situation. He wrote that he and his staff "made a very narrow escape here as we were standing by the side of our pieces when they directed the fire of all their guns on us. For about ten minutes the solid shot and shell flew thick, several passing within a foot of me." Surgeon Milton B. Cochrane of the First Iowa Cavalry, who had even less reason than Herron to be present, reported that a shell burst only twenty feet above his head. Thirty to forty rounds were fired during the exchange, though neither side suffered any significant damage. "I withdrew my pieces," Herron reported, "satisfied we couldn't cross at that place." Edwards took his guns back to the cover of the woods along the Illinois while the jubilant Confederates erupted into cheers that could be heard across the valley. The celebration irritated Sergeant Charles D. Thompson of the Ninety-fourth Illinois, which had just arrived on the scene. Thompson complained to his father: "You ought to have heard the rebs yell for they thought they had done a big thing in getting our guns to withdraw."[22]

For the next hour Herron supervised the deployment of the Third Division while his staff searched for another way across the Illinois. The infantry shuffled down East Bluff to the stream, careful to stay under the cover of the trees as much as possible. After wading across the frigid waist-deep water, the long-suffering soldiers went into line on either side of the road behind the west bank of the stream. The bank was four to six feet high and provided protection against artillery fire. From left to right, the Union formation consisted of the Ninety-fourth Illinois, Nineteenth Iowa, and Twentieth Wisconsin. Tired, hungry, and wet, the Federals collapsed in heaps on the cold, damp ground. Most fell asleep or dropped into a kind of stupor. The rest of the artillery rattled down the bluff but remained in column east of the Illinois. By 11:30 A.M. the Third Division was in place. Nothing more could be done until the Second Division arrived.[23]

Huston and his men were enjoying a well-deserved rest near Fayetteville when they heard the boom of Herron's artillery at Walnut Grove Church. "Our Division immediately fell in and with many a yell of exultation at the thot of at last getting a crack at the wily devils whom we had been pursuing all the autumn marched on with a light and boyant step towards the scene of action," wrote an Illinois officer. For the next three hours the soldiers of the Second Division tried to ignore their aching muscles and empty stomachs as they hurried toward the sound of the guns. Near Walnut Grove Church they came across a Unionist family. "Three buxom blooming lasses, real country beauties dressed with taste and seeming care in striped homespun flannel" were standing in front of their modest home, recalled an Iowa soldier. "As we passed them they had various expressions of encouragement for us which I will give in their own language as it fell from as pretty lips as ever made sunshine in an Arkansas cabin. 'Go in, boys, give them h-ll!' 'You are the boys who can whip all the G-d d—md Secesh in Arkansas!' 'I'll bet on you fellers!'" Responding with cheers and choice comments of their own, the weary Federals marched on with just a bit more spring in their step. Much to Herron's relief, the head of the Second Division reached East Bluff a little before noon.[24]

Huston's arrival coincided with the discovery of a second ford across the Illinois. The downstream ford was a half-mile north of the Fayetteville Road crossing. It was out of sight of Confederate observers and, even more important, was out of range of Confederate guns. Herron intended to slip a battery across the downstream ford and open fire on the Ridge from an unexpected direction. With the enemy distracted, the other Union batteries would rush over the main ford and join the fight. As soon as the Rebel guns were silenced, the infantry would advance and gain possession of the hill. Having witnessed the crushing power of massed Union artillery at Pea Ridge nine months earlier, Herron hoped for a repeat performance at Prairie Grove.[25]

Herron explained the situation to Huston and directed him to cut a road to the downstream ford. Hundreds of Illinois and Iowa soldiers cleared a narrow lane through a "thick growth of young wood" in less than an hour. Huston selected Captain David Murphy's Battery F, First Missouri Light Artillery, for the honor of leading the attack. The well-drilled company was equipped with four 3-inch Ordnance rifles and two 6-pounder James rifles. Murphy negotiated the downstream ford without mishap; however, once on the west side of the Illinois, he and Huston could not agree whether to place the battery on Crawford's Prairie or Crawford's Hill. Following a "brief consultation" they decided to do both. Lieutenant James Marr led three guns to the elevated northeast corner of the valley floor, while Lieutenant John L. Matthaei took the other three guns up the slope in search of a higher firing position. Matthaei found a place to his liking four hundred yards northwest of Marr's position. Huston's three infantry regiments followed Murphy across the downstream ford and went into line behind the shelter of the bank. From left to right, the formation was composed of the Twentieth Iowa (behind Marr), Twenty-sixth Indiana, and Thirty-seventh Illinois (behind Matthaei). Shortly after 1:00 P.M. the Second Division was in position.[26]

The Confederates remained inactive while the Federals perfected their arrangements. Several hours after the initial exchange of artillery fire, Shoup's curiosity (or impatience) got the better of him and he ordered Blocher to stir things up. What Blocher thought of that order was not recorded, but around 1:30 P.M. he dutifully fired a howitzer in the general direction of the Union army. The shell arced high over Crawford's Prairie and fell harmlessly into the woods along the Illinois without exploding.[27]

Murphy responded to Blocher's shot as if it were a signal to commence firing. One after another of Battery F's six guns roared into action and shattered the midday calm. The Missouri gunners quickly found the range and smothered Blocher's position with a barrage of well-placed projectiles. Murphy "fired his guns with the precision of a sharpshooter," marveled Herron, who had crossed the downstream ford to join Huston and watch the Missouri artillerymen at work. Herron liked the unobstructed view from Crawford's

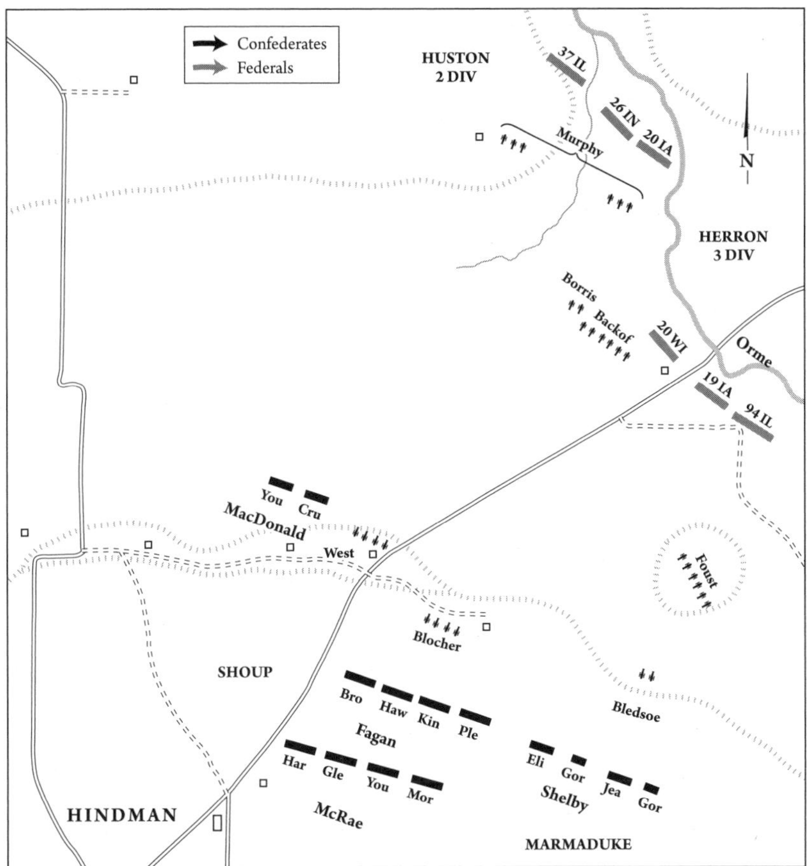

Shoup and Marmaduke deploy on the Ridge. Herron crosses the Illinois River and deploys on Crawford's Prairie.

Hill so much that he established his command post near the Crawford house, one hundred yards west of Matthaei's position.[28]

The Confederates took a long time to pinpoint the location of Murphy's guns and even longer to find the range, which proved to be near the effective limit of their 6-pounders. The fumbling response to Murphy's challenge convinced Herron that the time had come to send the rest of his artillery into action. He ordered the three batteries east of the Illinois to advance. The Federal artillerymen had been briefed on where to go and what to do. They crossed the main ford and emerged from the woods at a dead run, just as Edwards had done three hours earlier.[29]

West's Battery opened fire as soon as the Union column came into view.

The Confederate gunners could not have asked for an easier target because Fayetteville Road led directly toward their position, but not one of their rounds found its mark. Lieutenant Foust, in the lead with Battery E, First Missouri Light Artillery, advanced into the teeth of what he described as a "terrible fire," though not a man or an animal in his company suffered a scratch. Foust turned sharply left and raced to the top of a prominent knoll in the sprawling Borden wheatfield. The knoll, which is almost as high in elevation as the Ridge, dominates the southeast corner of Crawford's Prairie. Possession of the rounded hill gave the Federals a superb artillery platform. The Missourians unlimbered their four 10-pounder Parrots and two 3-inch Ordnance rifles and went to work. Captain Frank Backof's Battery L, First Missouri Light Artillery, followed Foust across the Illinois but turned into the Thompson pasture where Edwards had dueled briefly with the Rebels earlier in the day. Backof quickly put his four 6-pounder James rifles and two 12-pounder howitzers into action. Lieutenant Herman Borris and his section of Battery A, Second Illinois Light Artillery, followed Backof into the pasture. The Illinoisans unlimbered their 6-pounder gun and 12-pounder howitzer on Backof's right and joined in the fight.[30]

Herron now had all twenty of his artillery pieces in action: four 10-pounder Parrots, six 3-inch Ordnance rifles, six 6-pounder James rifles, one 6-pounder gun, and three 12-pounder howitzers. Shoup and Marmaduke together could muster only ten pieces: six 6-pounder guns and four 12-pounder howitzers. (The odds tilted even more in Herron's favor when Blocher withdrew a 6-pounder gun after a friction primer broke off in the vent.) The quantitative and qualitative edge enjoyed by Union artillerymen was substantial. "The enemy greatly outnumbered us and outranked us in the character of cannon, having the most improved rifle guns, and handled them with remarkable skill," observed a Confederate officer. He might have added that the Federals had ammunition to burn and the Confederates did not.[31]

Some of Hindman's artillerymen boasted of creating "havoc" among the Union batteries, but exactly the opposite was true. While Herron's cannoneers went about their business with deadly efficiency, Confederate shooting was erratic, uncoordinated, and inaccurate, a puzzling state of affairs considering Shoup's reputation as a crack artillerist. The very randomness of Rebel fire posed a hazard to the unwary, as Colonel Orme discovered when he rode into Borden's wheatfield to gain a better view of the proceedings. "About the second or third round a cannon ball or shell passed so close to my side as to knock off my hat and throw me from my saddle," he informed his wife. "The boys thought I was struck."[32]

Few Union soldiers witnessed Orme's close encounter in the wheatfield. Most huddled behind the bank to avoid Confederate overshots, which were plentiful. William H. Jaques of the Nineteenth Iowa lay on his back and watched the "balls and shells screaming and whistling through the air and tree tops close by," though none "bursted near us." A short distance downstream, an officer in the Twentieth Wisconsin was fascinated by the sight and sound of Confederate projectiles "exploding over our heads and tearing through the treetops." When he checked to see how his company reacted to being under fire for the first time, he discovered to his amazement that nearly everyone was asleep: "The men's clothes, soaked in wading the creek, which was waist deep, froze to them, but still they slept as if they would never wake, while the shells burst over their unheeding heads."[33]

The situation was much the same on the Union right. Captain Chester Barney of the Twentieth Iowa watched Confederate rounds "doing great execution among the tree tops on either side of us" with a certain morbid fascination. Nearby, worn-out soldiers slept undisturbed by the appalling racket. "So completely were the men exhausted that I saw them sleeping quietly around, paying no heed to the fierce missiles," reported Lieutenant Colonel John C. Black of the Thirty-seventh Illinois. The men catching forty winks had the right idea. Confederate artillery fire at Prairie Grove, what little there was of it, was largely sound and fury. "They did us but little damage," concluded Captain Edwin B. Messer, Thirty-seventh Illinois.[34]

Foust's Battery E had a canine mascot named "Old Bull" who ran himself ragged chasing Confederate projectiles as they bounced and rolled along the ground. Many shells failed to explode because of defective fuses, but it seemed unlikely Old Bull would survive the day unless he saw the error of his ways. The wiry mongrel's chances improved around 2:00 P.M., when Hindman returned to the Ridge and told Shoup and Marmaduke to stop wasting ammunition. Captain West reported that "I had been engaged but a short time when General Shoup in person ordered me to cease firing." Similar instructions soon reached Blocher and Bledsoe, and all nine Confederate guns fell silent.[35]

For the next thirty minutes or so Herron's artillerymen had it all their own way. "Nothing makes a man shoot so coolly as not being shot at in return," observed a Confederate officer, "and from the necessary silence of Hindman's artillery, the Federal batteries were as undisturbed as if practicing at a target." West and Bledsoe withdrew after losing a half-dozen men and an equal number of horses. Blocher stubbornly kept his guns in place, but he and his men sought shelter in the woods to the rear. "The scene at this point of the engagement was magnificent," declared a Union officer. "The roar of [twenty] pieces of artillery, the shrieking and explosion of shells filled the air. Great commotion was soon visible in the ranks of the enemy, where their batteries were posted, and in the open spots in the line of woods." Union gunners hammered the wooded crown of Prairie Grove on the not unreasonable assumption that the Rebels visible in the "open spots" represented only a fraction of the troops hidden in the trees. The Federals methodically "walked" their shots back and forth along the top of the hill between the Borden house and Fayetteville Road. Foust's six guns were particularly effective because they enfiladed the Confederate formation. "In artillery we were superior to them and our firing was the prettiest *I ever saw*," declared an officer in the Thirty-seventh Illinois.[36]

The Confederates were of the same mind. Colonel McRae, a survivor of the furious Union bombardment at Pea Ridge, thought the "terrible storm of shot and shell" at Prairie Grove was the most destructive fire he had ever experienced. "Such shelling and artillery firing I have never heard or known," he told his wife. "If the Federal fire at Cane Hill had been admirable, here it was perfect and unsurpassable," remarked a member of Shelby's Brigade. Projectiles plowed into the ground and threw up fountains of rock and dirt or smashed into trees and sent splinters flying in every direction. Other rounds exploded in the air and showered fragments of hot metal on defenseless men and animals below.[37]

The bombardment was a terrifying experience for the men in the ranks, most of whom were new to combat. Alexander Cameron of Crump's Texas Cavalry wrote: "Of all the shelling that ever had been done, men that had been in battle before said this was the most severe. The Cannon Balls and Bomb Shells was as thick as hail seemingly." A soldier in Morgan's Arkansas Infantry could not stop shaking: "I was feeling as though an old fashioned ague had full control of my body and limbs, for my body was so uncontrollable as to try to keep double time to the shaking of my legs." When the bombardment finally ended, most Confederates were surprised to discover that they had survived without suffering serious injury. "I did not get a man [in my company] hurt at all," marveled Captain Thomas D. Thomson of Grinsted's Arkansas Infantry, "but the way the shot and shell rained down on us it looked like we could not escape as well as we did."[38]

Union troopers captured during the morning cavalry fight were gathered in a field near Prairie Grove Church. "It was a beautiful scene as we lay on the ground (over 200 of us) while the balls were tearing through the trees around us and the shells were bursting in mid air," recalled Homer Jewett of the

Seventh Missouri Cavalry. As the bombardment progressed, however, Union projectiles fell deeper and deeper in the Confederate rear, and the Federals feared they would become victims of their own artillery. Whenever an errant shell came too close, prisoners and guards alike scrambled to their feet as if by mutual consent and dashed to another location.[39]

Herron was immensely pleased with the effectiveness of the Union cannonade. "The firing on our side was elegant, both for rapidity and accuracy, and excelled any thing I had ever witnessed." It appeared to be Pea Ridge all over again. With the enemy guns dispersed or silenced, Herron concluded it was time to send the infantry forward and gain possession of the hill.[40]

CURTIS AROSE EARLY on 7 December and went to his office near the St. Louis waterfront. He paced the floor for hours awaiting some word from Arkansas, but the telegraph remained silent. Around midday he scribbled a message to Blunt that revealed his state of mind: "Have been very anxious. Hope you have been re-enforced. Herron is a true man. Success to you." By the time the message reached the telegraph operator at Elkhorn Tavern, a pillar of smoke was rising over Prairie Grove.[41]

11 HERRON STORMS THE RIDGE

THE MISSOURI DIVISIONS WERE A SHAMBLES AFTER THE ATTRITION and detachments of the past few days. Herron might have fared better had he bypassed the existing organization and consolidated his depleted infantry force into two ad hoc brigades of three regiments apiece. Instead, he kept his six understrength regiments spread among four brigade commanders. Herron further complicated matters by retaining personal control of the Third Division despite his larger responsibilities, a decision that left the division without firm direction. Although a resolute and inspiring leader, Herron had never commanded anything larger than a regiment in battle. His lack of experience was evident at Prairie Grove.

Herron also was hindered by a problem not entirely of his own making. Nineteenth-century commanders relied heavily on cavalry to provide tactical intelligence, but Herron had sent nearly all of his horsemen to Blunt the previous day. What little information he had about enemy dispositions came from personal observations made under less-than-favorable circumstances. Thus handicapped, Herron underestimated not only the strength but also the length of the Confederate formation. After studying Prairie Grove for several hours from various positions, he concluded that the Borden house marked the approximate right flank of the Confederate line. In fact, the house was located near the center.

Confident that he could drive Marmaduke off the hill by rolling up his right, Herron made the fateful decision to send his infantry forward. The Third Division, on the left, would make the assault; the Second Division, on the right, would provide support as necessary. Forty-five minutes after the bombardment began, the 1,460 men of the Twentieth Wisconsin, Nineteenth Iowa, and Ninety-fourth Illinois emerged from the woods along the Illinois

River, wheeled left, and joined Lieutenant Foust's battery in the Borden wheatfield south of Fayetteville Road.[1]

Southern farmers of that day usually left their corn standing after the harvest, and Archibald Borden was no exception. His two cornfields were filled with withered stalks tall and thick enough to hide a line of infantry. Shortly before the Third Division moved forward, Confederate skirmishers from Fagan's and Shelby's brigades took advantage of this cover and advanced from the foot of the hill to the fences bordering the south and west sides of the wheatfield. They opened fire on Foust's battery in the expectation that the unsupported artillerymen would retire to a safer spot. Much to their surprise, the Federals lowered their sights and fired back with canister. This was more than the Rebels had bargained for, and they beat a hasty retreat into the shelter of the cornstalks. As soon as Foust resumed his bombardment of the Ridge, however, the Confederates cautiously made their way back to the fences.[2]

The Third Division entered the wheatfield and drove away the persistent Rebels. First to arrive was Colonel William W. Orme's Second Brigade. Orme was a handsome and well-respected attorney from Bloomington, Illinois, without a shred of military experience. Like so many amateur soldiers he was brave, earnest, and naive. "I want to try my hand in a battle," he had confided to his wife six weeks earlier. "I do like a good fight. There is something in it that seems to thrill and charm me." Now Orme had his wish.[3]

Orme's command consisted of the Ninety-fourth Illinois and Nineteenth Iowa. He sent three companies of the Nineteenth Iowa under the command of Lieutenant Richard Root to clear the west cornfield of Fagan's skirmishers. When the Iowans approached the fence separating the two fields, they were met by a flurry of musketry. "We lay low for bullets flew thick around us and we seemed to be fair targets for their sharp shooters," wrote a Union soldier. Assisted by repeated blasts of canister from Foust's battery, Root and his 150 men drove the Arkansans out of the west cornfield and up the hill. The rest of the Nineteenth Iowa lay down on the stubble at the foot of the knoll and watched Foust's men at their work. The choreographed movements of the crews, the crash of the guns, and the billows of smoke provided a noisy but satisfying diversion.[4]

Orme assigned his own Ninety-fourth Illinois the task of dealing with Shelby's skirmishers in the east cornfield. The regiment was under the command of Lieutenant Colonel John McNulta, a successful Bloomington cigar maker with a talent for war. McNulta led the Ninety-fourth Illinois at the

William W. Orme (McLean County Historical Society)

double-quick toward the fence separating the wheatfield and the cornfield. "We all started towards them hallowing a little, not much though," recalled William H. Horine. The 520 Illinoisans were armed with a mix of American, British, and Austrian rifles. Two hundred yards from the fence they halted and fired a volley. "After the first fire every man loaded and fired as fast as he could," remembered Joseph B. Weaver. "The first round or two I felt like dodging a little but after firing several times I didn't think anything more about it," wrote another Illinois soldier. "I loaded and fired as deliberately as if I was shooting hogs." Outnumbered and outgunned, the Confederate cavalrymen fell back through the cornstalks and the Federals took possession of the contested fence.[5]

Ten minutes later the Confederates regrouped behind the fence bordering the south side of the east cornfield and fired blindly at the Federals through several acres of cornstalks. The Ninety-fourth Illinois answered, and the volume of fire increased to the point where an observer might have thought a small battle was in progress. A Union soldier wrote that "for some time a heavy fire was kept up on both sides," but distance, smoke, and cornstalks kept casualties low. McNulta rode back and forth "encouraging his men, and giving them directions how to fire." Herron did not have enough cavalry to cover his flanks, and McNulta was anxious about the large gap on his left be-

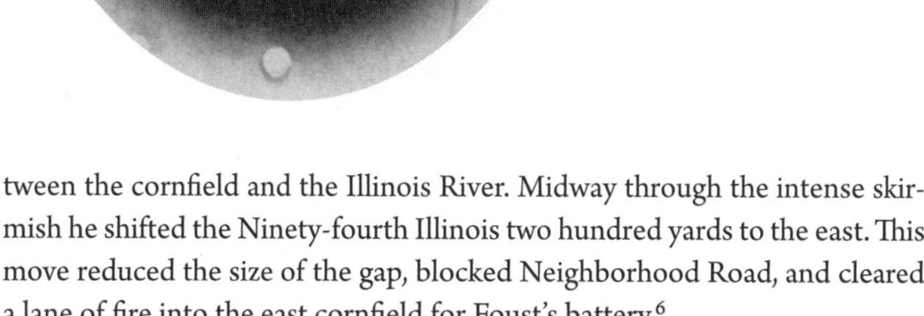

John McNulta (Roger D. Hunt Collection, U.S. Army Military History Institute)

tween the cornfield and the Illinois River. Midway through the intense skirmish he shifted the Ninety-fourth Illinois two hundred yards to the east. This move reduced the size of the gap, blocked Neighborhood Road, and cleared a lane of fire into the east cornfield for Foust's battery.[6]

While all of this was taking place, Lieutenant Colonel Henry G. Bertram's First Brigade entered the wheatfield on Orme's right. A native of Prussia, Bertram had sailed around the world as a merchant seaman and fought in the Mexican War on behalf of his adopted country. His "brigade" consisted of a single regiment, his own Twentieth Wisconsin, which he placed in a swale two hundred yards northwest of the knoll. The Third Division was ready for action, but at this critical moment it experienced a breakdown in leadership and communication at both the division and brigade levels. Herron may have conferred with Bertram and Orme and explained what he wanted them to do, but there is no evidence of it. Nor is there any evidence that Bertram and Orme got together on their own and agreed on a course of action. Instead, a little past 2:30 P.M., Bertram set out to capture Blocher's Battery, which was visible on the brow of the hill six hundred yards in front of his position. "I immediately ordered the Twentieth Wisconsin to charge the battery," he stated in his report. A few minutes later Orme directed the Nineteenth Iowa to "support" the Twentieth Wisconsin. The Iowans advanced without a specific

Henry Bertram
(Library of Congress)

objective and with only the vaguest of orders. Bertram, meanwhile, pressed ahead on his own.[7]

Shoup and Marmaduke had formed their line along the top of Prairie Grove to take advantage of the concealment offered by the woods. In military parlance, the Confederates occupied the "natural" crest rather than the "military" crest of the hill. In this instance, the military crest was the relatively open brow of the hill, that is, the Ridge. Defenders located on the military crest of Prairie Grove could sweep the slope and the valley floor below their position with gunfire and break up attacking formations. Defenders located farther back on the natural crest could not because attackers would be hidden from view—and protected from fire—in the "visual shadow" below the Ridge. Only after attackers ascended the slope and reached the brow of the hill would they come into view of defenders. For defenders, the first indication that attackers were approaching would be the sight of regimental flags appearing over the foreshortened horizon created by the Ridge. The Federals were relieved to discover that they were sheltered from Confederate fire during most of their approach. But if Shoup's and Marmaduke's soldiers could not see the Federals until they topped the Ridge, the reverse was also true. Herron's men had no clear idea of what awaited them atop Prairie Grove.

Union artillery fire slackened as the Twentieth Wisconsin and Nineteenth

Iowa advanced across Crawford's Prairie in the bright winter sunlight. "These regiments marched across the valley as coolly as on parade," remarked an admiring soldier in the Second Division. The handful of Confederates who could see what was happening had much the same impression. "They came up with a boldness and an assurance that argued a certain belief of easy success," observed Fagan from his vantage point on the Ridge. Another Arkansas officer noted that the Federals approached "in fine order, and assailed our brigade violently, apparently confident of an easy victory." The Union attack may have looked impressive but it was doomed from the start.[8]

Bertram's Twentieth Wisconsin was a new regiment entering combat for the first time. Few of the 440 officers and men knew what to expect, but many were filled with dread at the prospect of storming the smoke-wreathed hill. "I can distinctly remember how scared I was at the time we made our charge," one soldier wrote a quarter-century after the battle. The Twentieth Wisconsin had numerous German and Scandinavian immigrants in its ranks and, like most Civil War regiments, a smattering of underage boys as well. One such "tadpole" was William M. O'Neil. The fourteen-year-old had the dubious distinction of being the youngest combatant in either army at Prairie Grove.[9]

The nominal commander of the Twentieth Wisconsin was Major Henry A. Starr, a modestly successful printer from Milwaukee blessed with courage and common sense. Moving forward at the double-quick, Starr's men swept across the wheatfield and into the open woods below the Borden house. At the foot of the hill they fired a pair of volleys to drive away any lurking Confederate skirmishers, then surged forward with a shout. The Federals slung their .69 Harpers Ferry muskets over their shoulders and scrambled up the steep incline on all fours. Captain Edward Miller recalled that "the whole slope was covered with underbrush and we advanced with great difficulty, but we struggled on in as good order as possible and soon stood before the rebel battery." Nearing the top, the gasping Federals discovered that Blocher's Battery was close enough to touch. "We came out nearly at the crest," recalled an officer, "and there was a newly-built rail fence, and there, a few feet off, so that we were looking into their muzzles, were the guns, and near by the horses standing quietly attached to the caissons." The Wisconsin soldiers braced for a blast of canister, but the Confederate guns remained silent.[10]

When Blocher saw Union infantry advancing across the valley floor in his direction, he sought permission from Shoup to resume firing. Several minutes passed without any reply during which time the Federals slipped into the visual shadow below the Ridge and disappeared from sight. Because the three Confederate guns were located on the military crest of the hill, it would have

The Twentieth Wisconsin surged up this slope to reach Blocher's Battery. The ground was covered with stumps and brush at the time of the battle. (author's collection)

been a small matter for Blocher to walk forward a few steps and peer down the steep slope. Incredibly, he did nothing. Moments later Blocher got the shock of his life when the Twentieth Wisconsin suddenly appeared in front of his position. The blue-clad infantrymen were "unseen by me until within twenty yards of my battery," Blocher admitted. Both sides were astonished to find the enemy so near, but the Federals recovered first. They unslung their weapons and fired a volley that mowed down two dozen Arkansas artillerymen and scattered the rest, including Blocher. The hail of buck and ball also killed most of the battery's horses.[11]

Starr bellowed "Forward!" and the Twentieth Wisconsin dashed toward the Rebel guns. "We rushed over a rail fence and *the battery was ours,*" wrote Captain Miller. "What a shout of exultation arose!" Color Sergeant Lindsey E. Teal climbed onto one of the guns and exuberantly waved the Stars and Stripes. The "whole command was wild with excitement," noted a Wisconsin soldier. "We thought we could clear up the whole business at once," recalled another. A quick check revealed that not a man in the regiment had been hurt. Buoyed by the bloodless capture of the battery, Bertram instructed Starr to resume the advance. The Federals re-formed and continued forward. Fifty yards beyond the silent guns, the left wing of the Twentieth Wisconsin encountered a wall of trees and vines and the right wing dipped into a deep ravine choked with brush. Starr struggled to maintain control as the Union line twisted into an awkward curved shape. At that moment Fagan's Brigade emerged from the woods and opened fire.[12]

SHOUP WAS ALARMED by the sight of Union infantry advancing across Crawford's Prairie, but he could not tell where the blow would fall because the Federals were "almost entirely concealed by the high weeds of the prairie and standing corn." Shoup decided to strengthen both flanks and hope for the best. He ordered MacDonald to abandon his untenable position on the bench at the foot of the hill and redeploy atop the Ridge on Shelby's right, then told McRae to move three of his four regiments to Fagan's left. The 1,200 men of Lieutenant Colonel Robert A. Hart's Arkansas Infantry, Lieutenant Colonel John E. Glenn's Arkansas Infantry, and Lieutenant Colonel Charles L. Young's Arkansas Infantry formed a line across Fayetteville Road. Their arrival drew the attention of Union artillery, and within minutes Colonel Young was struck in the head and killed by a shell fragment. A Union soldier who had been taken prisoner during the morning cavalry fight saw Young's lifeless body being carried to the rear. He noted that the officer's face was covered with blood.[13]

McRae's fourth regiment, Colonel Asa S. Morgan's Arkansas Infantry, fell victim to confusing orders and failed to get into the fight. Shoup detached Morgan from McRae's Brigade and sent him to support Fagan's right. The four hundred Arkansans plowed through the thicket atop the hill and reached their assigned position near the Borden orchard only to learn that Shoup now wanted them to rejoin the rest of McRae's command on Fagan's left. The men faced about and returned to their starting point on Fayetteville Road. Shoup then informed Morgan that, because of a change in the tactical situation, he should take his regiment back to the orchard. Disgusted, Morgan reversed course a second time. The Arkansans were still thrashing around in the woods when Herron's first attack ended.[14]

Fagan, like Shoup, found it difficult to determine the strength and direction of the Union assault. Distance, smoke, and the "high weeds of the prairie" (not to mention cornstalks) masked the advancing blue lines even before they entered the visual shadow and disappeared from view. In his report Fagan made the revealing statement that he did not discover the "full extent" of the Union attack until Herron's infantry was "near the summit upon which my line of battle was formed." At that point Fagan frantically called on his troops to push the Federals off the hill before they gained a lodgment.[15]

Fagan's Brigade, from left to right, consisted of Colonel William H. Brooks's Arkansas Infantry, Colonel Alexander T. Hawthorn's Arkansas Infantry (which included Major Robert E. Chew's Arkansas Sharpshooter Battalion), Colonel James P. King's Arkansas Infantry, and Colonel Joseph C. Pleasants's Arkansas Infantry. For four hours these 1,600 troops had endured the brunt of the Union bombardment. Now their moment had come. Brooks and Hawthorn were separated by a deep ravine but maintained a tenuous contact as they unknowingly advanced toward the Twentieth Wisconsin. Meanwhile, King and Pleasants groped through the woods in the direction of the Nineteenth Iowa.[16]

Brooks and Hawthorn were effectively blind; neither knew who or what lay ahead. "The ground in my front was covered by an almost impenetrable thicket," wrote Hawthorn. "So great was the difficulty in getting forward through the thick undergrowth, that I asked and obtained permission to advance by the right of companies, rather than *in line*." In other words, each company advanced in single file. Suddenly the Confederates heard a blast of musketry and encountered a stampede of panic-stricken artillerymen. Only then did Hawthorn realize that he was approaching Blocher's Battery and that something was seriously wrong. He re-formed his regiment into line, no easy task given the circumstances. "A moment after halting I heard loud cheering just ahead of me; but I could not tell who it was that cheered, nor why they cheered." The cheers came from the Twentieth Wisconsin, still invisible through the wall of brown foliage. "I could see nothing ahead of me more than forty yards," explained Hawthorn. The Arkansans resumed their difficult advance. Moments later they reached the brow of the hill and emerged into an open woodland. Directly ahead was a line of blue uniforms.[17]

Federals and Confederates opened fire simultaneously. "For a few moments the fight was terrific," wrote an Arkansas officer, "and rapid and deadly volleys were exchanged." The two formations met at an angle; the distance between the opposing lines ranged from thirty feet to sixty yards. Hawthorn's right flank was located roughly opposite Bertram's left, but Brooks's center and left extended far beyond the Union right. Brooks wheeled right until his regiment faced roughly east. His Arkansans advanced to the edge of the ravine and unleashed a "murderous fire" on the Federals below, "killing and wounding many." The Confederate onslaught brought Bertram's advance to a halt. For several minutes the lines swayed back and forth. Hawthorn feared the stalemate would allow the Federals to carry off the captured battery. "I dashed to the front and called on my brave '*Conscripts*' to charge and retake the guns. They responded with an Arkansas '*yell*' that rang out loud and clear

William H. Brooks (Prairie Grove Battlefield State Park)

above the roar of battle." The weight of Hawthorn's attack forced back the left wing of the Twentieth Wisconsin and brought the Confederates to within a few yards of the contested battery. Dozens of men fell dead or mortally wounded in the struggle for the guns, including Major Chew of the Sharpshooter Battalion. Hawthorn's second in command, Lieutenant Colonel Cadwallader L. Polk, escaped death by the narrowest of margins when a bullet struck him in the face and lodged against an artery in his neck. The wound appeared fatal and Shoup listed Polk among the dead in his report, but Surgeon Keller extracted the bullet a week later and Polk lived another fifty-nine years.[18]

The Twentieth Wisconsin struggled to hold its position—half in and half out of the ravine—against a force twice its size. "Here we stood and fired up the slope, and a hail of bullets answered, smiting our line, and then the men lay down and fired as they had been taught to do," remembered a Wisconsin officer. The range was short and the volume of fire was extraordinary, especially in the ravine. "The bullets flew as thick as hail, and the boys fell thick and fast all round me," wrote Henry E. Thompson. Three Wisconsin color-bearers were shot down in quick succession before Captain John McDermott picked up the regimental flag. For a few moments McDermott led a charmed life waving the flag with one hand and his sword with the other, then he, too, was killed. Two other Wisconsin officers were killed and eleven wounded. Among the latter was Bertram. He was thrown to the ground when his horse was shot, then struck in the leg by a spent bullet. Dazed by the fall and the blow, Bertram limped down the hill using his sword as a crutch. Command of the "brigade" passed to Starr, whose "gallant behavior" drew praise from Bertram and everyone else.[19]

The Confederates steadily gained the upper hand. A Wisconsin officer wrote that the "line in the ravine began to thin out" as "wounded men dragged themselves back out of the fire, and occasionally an unhurt man arose and made a dash for the rear." The end came when Brooks's regiment gained control of the mouth of the ravine and opened a "most tremendous cross fire." It was "impossible to make headway against such a storm of bullets and the whole right wing gave way," stated another Union officer. At about the same time the left wing finally collapsed under pressure from Hawthorn's regiment. The situation was hopeless and Starr ordered a retreat. "Some good angel must have leant me their wings for I have never been able to say how I reached the bottom of the hill or whether I went over or under the twelve rail fence," recalled Sergeant Joseph P. Rundle. Amid the chaos some Federals had the presence of mind to open a gap in the fence and push a pair of Blocher's caissons off the hill. The two-wheel vehicles careened down the slope and came to rest in the west cornfield. Sheltered under the brow of the hill, Starr re-formed the survivors and led them back to the wheatfield.[20]

The fight for possession of the Ridge was far from over. Coming up behind and to the left of the Twentieth Wisconsin was Lieutenant Colonel Samuel McFarland's Nineteenth Iowa, another untried regiment in its first battle. The 350 Iowans hurried up the relatively easy incline east of the Borden house at the double-quick, stopping once or twice to fire volleys at Rebel skirmishers using buildings, fences, and woodpiles as cover. McFarland halted the regiment near the northeast corner of the large orchard behind the house. The drifting smoke made it difficult to see what lay ahead. McFarland was uncertain whether to continue on his present course or change direction and assist Bertram, who by the sound of it was engaged in a desperate fight a short distance to the right. He apparently decided he could best support the Twentieth Wisconsin by driving deeper into what he mistakenly believed was the Confederate rear. The Nineteenth Iowa resumed its advance through the orchard.[21]

King and Pleasants had reached the opposite side of the Borden orchard only minutes earlier. King's larger regiment, on the left, crowded up to the fence bordering the west side of the orchard. The right wing of the regi-

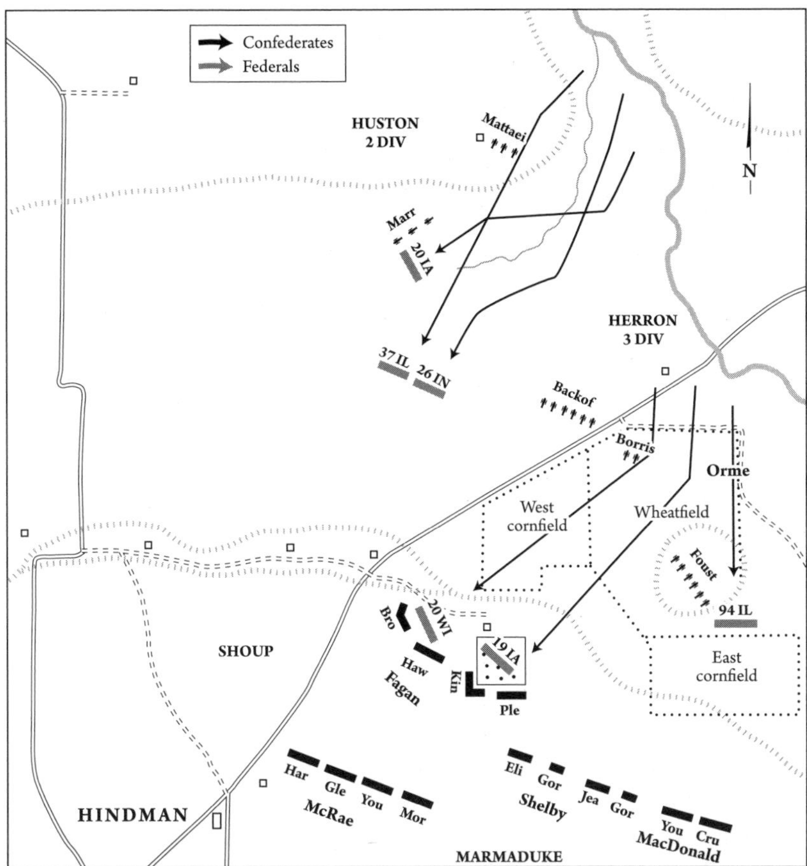

The Twentieth Wisconsin and Nineteenth Iowa assault the Ridge.

ment ran out of fence and wrapped around the southwest corner. Pleasants's smaller regiment occupied the rest of the fence bordering the south side of the orchard. Neither Confederate commander was happy about the ninety-degree angle in their formation, but neither could devise a better arrangement. A tremendous explosion of musketry indicated that Brooks and Hawthorn had engaged the enemy a short distance to the left, but Fagan was nowhere to be found and King and Pleasants were uncertain whether to hold their position or march to the support of their comrades. The decision was taken out of their hands when the Nineteenth Iowa came into view.

Halfway through the orchard McFarland ordered the Nineteenth Iowa to halt and fire a volley. The 750 Arkansans hugged the ground as bullets smashed into fence rails and skittered through the trees. McFarland ordered a second volley. This time the Confederates responded. "At length we ceased

The Nineteenth Iowa ascended the slope in the foreground and passed to the left, or rear, of the Borden house. A short time later the Twenty-sixth Indiana traversed this same ground from right to left. (author's collection)

firing and the rebels all at once rose out of their hiding place and began to fire at us," stated William Clayton. Pleasants's Arkansans stood up and fired a volley at point-blank range. The south fence exploded in flame and a hail of bullets shredded the center and left of the Nineteenth Iowa. McFarland, who had spoken so eloquently to his men alongside Telegraph Road only eighteen hours earlier, was struck in the chest and killed instantly. His horse was shot as well, and animal and rider crumpled to the ground. A moment later King's regiment arose and blasted the Federal center and right. A stunned Iowan wrote that the Rebels "raised up on three sides of us" and "poured an incessant fire into our ranks. They were on one side of the fence and we were on the other."[22]

For the next few minutes the Borden orchard was the scene of one of the most intense firefights of the Civil War west of the Mississippi River. The crossfire of bullets, balls, and buckshot was accompanied by a cacophony of shrieks and yells of every description. "It was a perfect slaughter pen into which we were led," wrote Clayton. Another Iowa soldier stated that "no pen can trace the words that could describe the scene that followed." Both wings of the Union regiment bent back under the "murderous fire" from the angled Confederate formation.[23]

Command of the Nineteenth Iowa passed to Major Daniel Kent, who later stated that "officers and men behaved nobly and fought desperately, as if the fate of the battle depended on them alone." If anything, the inexperienced Iowans stood their ground too long. Clayton was convinced that "had we remained in the orchard but a few minutes longer we would all have been killed, wounded or taken prisoners." Kent reached the same conclusion and ordered a retreat. Some Federals broke and ran, but most withdrew from the orchard in reasonably good order. "Balls fell like hail on all sides of me," recalled Clayton. "How I ever got out safely as I did I cannot tell." A spent bullet struck him in the side but failed to penetrate his overcoat. ("It made a blue spot though," he told his parents.) William Jaques escaped unharmed, though "many a poor fellow did I see reel and fall as I came across that fatal orchard. The air was alive with the shower of lead, and the balls passed thick and fast through our midst." Lieutenant William S. Brooks did not get the word to fall back and his company stood its ground for several minutes, exchanging fire with hundreds of Arkansas Rebels only yards away. Despite being wounded in the leg, Brooks picked up the bullet-riddled regimental banner and carried it to safety. The corpses of the three previous color-bearers remained in the orchard. The Iowans fell back to the shelter of the Borden house and its outbuildings.[24]

Confederate accounts corroborate the horror of the fight in the orchard. "We were all laying down and the Federals came up in fifty steps of us when our colonel ordered us to rise and fire," wrote Columbus H. Gray of Pleasants's regiment. When the Iowans gave way, Pleasants urged his men to follow and finish up the victory. Three hundred exultant Arkansans surged forward. "We cleared the fence and [charged] across the orchard, firing and yelling like savages, the boys tumbling here and there," remembered William J. Wright. "We were on the move all the time, firing and loading as we went."[25]

Gray and his brother, Sergeant James Addison Gray, hurried forward with their disorganized company. "When we was ordered to charge we all broke [ranks] and Ad got ahead," wrote Columbus to his parents. "He runn up in ten steps of the Enemy before they hit him. They fired and runn. When I got to him I stoped [and] squatted down by him and I said 'Oh my brother whare are you hurt' but he could not speeke to me. I saw that he was brething his last. It almost run me distracted. I did not know what to do. I knew I could not do him any good by staying there with him so I jumped up and runn on with the company." King's 450 men poured into the orchard in the wake of Pleasants's regiment, adding to the congestion and confusion and providing more targets for the Iowans clustered around the Borden house.[26]

Among the dozens of Rebels who fell in the orchard was Colonel Pleasants. A bullet broke his leg, but he stayed on his horse until the animal was shot out from under him. In excruciating pain, the forty-seven-year-old Virginia native was dragged clear of his horse and propped up against a tree. When Captain Henry C. Pleasants attempted to carry his father to the rear, the older man would have none of it. He stated that "his place was with the regiment" and that "he would take care of himself." Others offered to move Pleasants to the opposite side of the tree so he would be protected from enemy fire. "No," he said, "my boys fight so well I must see them through this charge." When the fighting ended, Colonel Pleasants insisted that all other wounded members of the regiment be removed before he allowed himself to be taken to the rear. At the hospital he refused to let surgeons dress his wound until everyone else had been looked after. Pleasants's selfless behavior may have contributed to his death ten days later. Command of the regiment passed to Lieutenant Colonel John A. Geoghegan, who found himself on foot after his own horse was shot.[27]

The Confederates soon drove the Federals from the Borden house. One of the fatalities in the hopeless struggle to maintain a Union foothold on the Ridge was Sergeant Major Charles B. Buckingham, of the Nineteenth Iowa, who fell near the house trying to rally his comrades. At the foot of the hill Major Kent re-formed the "broken disordered mass" of soldiers and led them back to the wheatfield. Richard Root's three companies of skirmishers remained in the west cornfield during the attack and suffered only a handful of casualties. Nevertheless, the regiment was a shambles.[28]

When the Twentieth Wisconsin and Nineteenth Iowa went forward, Union artillerymen ceased firing so as not to endanger their own troops. Captain Backof and Lieutenant Borris took advantage of the lull to move closer to Fayetteville Road, possibly in the expectation that they would soon be called upon to pursue a beaten foe. The two batteries advanced about three hundred yards. Backof placed his four rifled guns and two howitzers on a slightly elevated terrace across the road from the west cornfield. Borris needed less space for his mismatched gun and howitzer; he found a suitable spot in the northwest corner of the wheatfield. Meanwhile, Foust and his six rifled guns maintained their position on the knoll. When Fagan's troops appeared on the brow of the Ridge, the Federal cannoneers loaded their weapons with canister and waited for the dazed and wounded survivors of the failed attack to get out of the way. Several anxious minutes passed before the last of the Wisconsin and Iowa infantrymen reached safety behind the artillery line.[29]

James Fagan was not an officer who led from the front. He often drifted to the rear during engagements, and on this occasion his instinct for self-preservation cost him control of his brigade. Fagan did not want his men to follow the Federals down the hill, but the sight of hundreds of blue-clad soldiers fleeing in disorder apparently convinced many Confederates that a crushing victory was within their grasp. One or two of the Arkansas regiments set out in pursuit and the others followed. "Immense hordes came out of the woods on our left and spread upon the field, looking from a distance like a nest of ants," reported a flabbergasted Union officer. "Our infantry seemed a mere handful in comparison to this multitude." Any lingering illusions Herron may have harbored about the size and composition of the Confederate force at Prairie Grove disappeared at that moment.[30]

It seemed to many in the Missouri Divisions that the "multitude" pouring down the hill would sweep everything before it, but the Union artillerymen on the valley floor were determined to prevent that from happening. Salvo after salvo of canister from fourteen guns—tens of thousands of iron balls—tore through the Confederate ranks and knocked men down in clumps. The Ninety-fourth Illinois and remnants of the Twentieth Wisconsin and Nineteenth Iowa added their fire to the defense of the wheatfield. Some Arkansans wavered and turned back as the carnage mounted, but others pressed ahead seemingly heedless of the storm raging all around them.

A Union officer wrote that the Rebels approached "under a withering fire of grape and canister from all our guns, and the infantry fire of the Third Division, to within fifty yards of our batteries before they broke and retreated in great disorder, receiving as they ran a terrible fire, which strewed the ground with their dead clear up to the brow of the hill." The batteries "fired canister into them with such deadly effect as to cause them first to pause in their career, then lie down, and finally hastily to retreat," noted another officer. It was over in less than fifteen minutes. The Rebels streamed back up the hill and disappeared into the trees. Left behind in the wheatfield and the two cornfields were more than one hundred broken bodies clad in butternut and gray. The Federals raised a defiant cheer.[31]

The Confederate counterattack failed because of the brutal efficiency of the Union artillery. The nineteenth century was an age of bombast, but the Federals who served the fourteen guns on the valley floor never made much over their role in the fight. Foust, for example, reported only that the Rebels charged and he "forced them back with canister." Herron showed no such reticence. In both official and private correspondence he showered praise on the intrepid gunners. "Never was there more real courage and pluck displayed, and more downright hard fighting done, than at this moment" by Foust, Backof, and Borris, he declared.[32]

For reasons known only to himself, Shoup claimed that he ordered the botched counterattack: "I first directed an effort be made to capture [Herron's] batteries but seeing that my command had, in pressing forward and from the confirmation of the ground, become somewhat commingled, I deemed it imprudent to attempt to gap the wide space in front, to which we would be exposed, and ordered the line to retire from the immediate effect of the artillery, to rectify the alignment." Shoup, of course, had nothing whatever to do with the spontaneous and leaderless affair. Moreover, his bizarre assertion that the Confederates returned to the Ridge in order to "rectify" their "alignment" illustrates the surreal nature of much of his official correspondence. Fagan did not mention the counterattack at all in his report, a truly amazing omission considering that his brigade *was* the attacking force. He may have been so far in the rear that he never realized a counterattack had taken place.[33]

HERRON DESCRIBED HIS ATTACK and the ensuing Confederate counterattack in six words: "The fighting was desperate beyond description." Sadly, so was the cost. A distraught Union chaplain wrote that the walking wounded "were in a great perspiration, and the dust and powder had blackened their faces, and many were all bloody. Some had their faces partly shot away, others with an eye hanging out, and some others part of the face. Many had arms and legs broken and were dragging themselves along, and all looked ghastly and wild." The more seriously wounded, both Union and Confederate, lay where they had fallen.[34]

"From the time our first man fell in our terrible charge, until we withdrew, was not more than *fifteen minutes* and we lost fifty killed and 150 wounded—*nearly half of the command!*" So wrote an anguished officer in the Twentieth Wisconsin. Those figures were very close to the mark. The regiment began the day with 440 men and lost 217: 50 killed, 154 wounded, and 13 missing, a 49 percent casualty rate. Most of the Union losses occurred in the ravine, where buckshot and bullets flew from all points of the compass and multiple wounds were common. "My clothes are full of bullet holes," Henry Thompson informed his parents. "There is one through the sleeve of my overcoat, one through my pants below the knee, four through my cap, one through the collar into my neck (that was a buckshot but it is not a dangerous wound), and one through my cartridge box." Thompson was fortunate, amazingly so. Not so George M. Rickeman, whose body was found in the ravine with eight bullet wounds. Three-fourths of the men in Lieutenant Nathan Cole's company were casualties. Himself dangerously wounded, Cole was distraught at the terrible loss: "My brave boys are all cut to pieces. They fought like devils." Starr marveled at his own survival. "I never expected to pass through so hot a fire without a scratch, but a providential hand was over me," he confided to his father. "All the time a hail storm of bullets was playing around my head." After a moment's reflection he added: "Our men behaved like veterans, they can't be beat, neither can Colonel Bertram." One of the "men" of whom Starr spoke so highly was William O'Neil. The fourteen-year-old escaped without a scratch.[35]

The Nineteenth Iowa was wrecked. "It was as brave a fight as men ever made, but here it did not avail," declared a soldier. "They performed deeds of valor almost incredible, and shed their blood in torrents, but it was all useless." The Nineteenth Iowa went up the hill with fewer than 350 men and lost 193 (45 killed, 145 wounded, and 3 missing) for an appalling casualty rate of 55 percent, the highest regimental loss recorded on either side at Prairie Grove. Four officers were killed, 5 were wounded, and 1 was captured. In one company, 34 of 56 men were killed or seriously wounded. Most of the carnage took place in the Borden orchard. A Union soldier later counted twenty-two bullet holes in the trunk of an apple tree only six inches in diameter.[36]

By contrast, the Ninety-fourth Illinois emerged practically unscathed. Regimental casualties for the entire battle were one killed, thirty-one wounded, and two missing. On the other hand, *every company* in the Twentieth Wisconsin and Nineteenth Iowa that went up the hill suffered higher losses. It became an article of faith in the Third Division that Orme deliberately kept his former regiment out of the fight to minimize casualties and enhance his political prospects after the war. "The 94th remained in the background," snapped a soldier in the devastated Nineteenth Iowa. "If they had followed perhaps the fortunes of this day would have been different and we might have remained possessors of what we took from the foe." In retrospect, however, it seems unlikely that the presence of another Union regiment would have altered the outcome of the attack except to increase the butcher's bill. Orme always maintained that his decision to hold the officers and men of the Ninety-fourth Illinois in reserve was correct. He stated in his report that the "safety of our left wing depended in a great measure upon their efforts."[37]

"Our loss during this fighting was heavy, but theirs was awful," wrote Herron. Perhaps. The number of killed and wounded Confederates in Fagan's Brigade at this stage of the battle, while certainly heavy, will never be known because for the Arkansans the fight was not yet over. The Second Division was poised to enter the struggle, and once again the focal point of the Union attack was the Borden house.[38]

FIGHT FOR THE BORDEN HOUSE

SURVIVORS OF THE CONFEDERATE COUNTERATTACK STRUGGLED TO regroup atop the Ridge amid renewed Union artillery fire. Fagan's four Arkansas regiments formed a new, more compact line centered on the Borden house. Brooks and Hawthorn, on the left, crowded into the space between the house and the ravine. King and Pleasants, on the right, reoccupied the fences bordering the west and south sides of the orchard but shifted closer to the house. By 3:30 P.M. Fagan's Brigade, considerably battered and reduced to fewer than 1,300 men, was packed into an L-shaped line between the ravine and the southwest corner of the orchard. This opened two gaps in the overall Confederate formation: one between Fagan's left and McRae's right and another between Fagan's right and Shelby's left. Each gap was about two hundred yards wide.

Thirty minutes earlier Herron had ordered Colonel Huston to lead his Second Division forward in support of the Third Division. After lying on the cold ground for hours, many officers and men experienced a "feeling of positive relief" when ordered to stand up and fall in. Huston did not hesitate to reorganize his command to fit the circumstances. He formed two of his three infantry regiments, the Twenty-sixth Indiana and Thirty-seventh Illinois, into an improvised brigade under his personal command and led them forward. The 850 men marched southwest across Crawford's Prairie and halted about two hundred yards north of Fayetteville Road. Huston kept his third infantry regiment, the Twentieth Iowa, in reserve near the foot of Crawford's Hill.[1]

Because the Second Division started fifteen minutes after the Third Division and had more ground to cover, Huston was just completing his transit of Crawford's Prairie when Bertram and Orme launched their ill-fated assault on the Ridge. Huston and his men watched the Twentieth Wisconsin and Nineteenth Iowa "moving steadily and gallantly forward to the foot of the hill, and carrying their banners proudly up and over its crest, till they were lost to our view in the woods." A swelling roar of musketry was followed by the discouraging sight of the two regiments reeling back in disorder. "The whole woods was one continuous flash of fire," observed a horrified Indiana officer. Some in the Second Division wondered loudly why they were not ordered forward to assist their comrades. "You should have heard our boys chafing at being held back!" remarked an officer in the Thirty-seventh Illinois. Huston was unmoved by these entreaties. His orders were to support the Third Division and nothing more.[2]

Everything changed when Fagan's troops poured down the hill. When Backof's and Borris's batteries seemed in danger of being overrun, Huston advanced his two regiments to the fence running along the north side of Fayetteville Road. To his surprise, the Confederates were repulsed before anyone in the Twenty-sixth Indiana and Thirty-seventh Illinois fired a shot. As the Rebels streamed back up the hill in obvious confusion, Huston decided to follow. He later explained that the Twentieth Wisconsin and Nineteenth Iowa had "fallen back so far, and were so badly cut up that it was necessary to give them time to reform," but it is unlikely Huston would have ordered a second assault without a reasonable expectation of success. He may have believed he could overwhelm the Confederates before they recovered from the drubbing they had received on the valley floor.[3]

The 450 inexperienced officers and men in Colonel John G. Clark's Twenty-sixth Indiana were understandably nervous after witnessing the repulse of the Third Division. "We could realize somewhat the work we had to do, for we had just seen some of it," recalled one Hoosier. The Thirty-seventh Illinois was the only veteran infantry regiment in Herron's command. The four hundred Illinoisans had made a name for themselves at Pea Ridge; Lieutenant Colonel John C. Black still carried his right arm in a sling as a painful reminder of that desperate fight. The regiment's two flank companies were armed with five-shot Colt revolving rifles, the only repeating weapons in either army at Prairie Grove.[4]

The Federals dismantled the fences along both sides of the road and hurried across the west cornfield at the double-quick, the Twenty-sixth Indiana on the left and the Thirty-seventh Illinois on the right. "We were in splendid order," recalled an Indiana officer. "I never saw the 26th in our drills do better; we went with closed ranks and in a straight line." For the second time the Confederates watched a Federal line of battle approach behind the "terrific fire of their admirably handled and destructive artillery." Huston halted the two regiments at the foot of the hill and accompanied several companies of

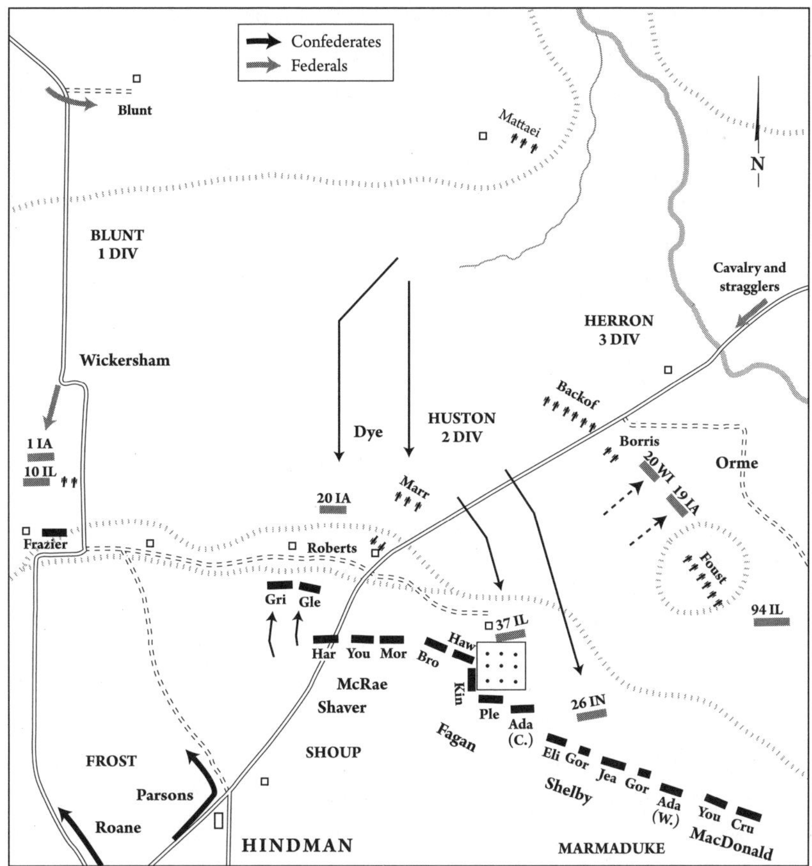

The Twenty-sixth Indiana and Thirty-seventh Illinois assault the Ridge. Dye extends the fight to the west. Blunt arrives.

skirmishers up the slope to get an idea of what lay ahead. The appearance of a mounted officer triggered a fusillade of bullets from Arkansas skirmishers who had reoccupied the Borden house and outbuildings, but Huston escaped injury. "It was a wonder to me that he was not shot," marveled a soldier in the Twenty-sixth Indiana.[5]

Huston returned to his proper place in the rear of the formation and resumed the advance. Years later an Illinois officer remembered how the two regiments "with colors flying and drums beating, ascended the hill at a left oblique, pressing forward up the hill eagerly and fiercely, driving the oncoming Confederates before them." Hundreds of soldiers from both armies had passed over the same ground minutes earlier, and the hillside was littered with corpses, cripples, and discarded weapons and clothing. It was a dreadful sight. Huston's men, half of whom had never set foot on a battlefield before, stepped gingerly over the dead and wounded.[6]

John Clark, only twenty-six years old, was a Virginia native and Indiana businessman. He had no military education or experience to speak of, but he was brave and popular with his men. The Twenty-sixth Indiana passed around the east side of the Borden house and entered the woods east of the orchard. Two hundred yards inside the smoky thicket Union skirmishers encountered a large force of Confederates. "The undergrowth was so thick that in our advance we did not see the rebels until we were almost right onto them," recalled one Indiana soldier. Another Hoosier noticed that the Confederates "could hardly be distinguished from the leaves; their butternut clothes being exactly the same color." The skirmishers fired on the camouflaged Rebels, then fell back and rejoined their regiment. Rifles at the ready, the entire Twenty-sixth Indiana pressed forward in line of battle. If Clark noticed that he had become separated from the Thirty-seventh Illinois and was about to engage the enemy on his own, he gave no sign of it.[7]

The dimly seen Confederate force in the woods was Shelby's Brigade. The Missourians had spent most of the day huddled in a shallow ravine that began south of the Borden orchard and ran down the east side of Prairie Grove to the Illinois River. They had suffered only a handful of casualties from the Union bombardment and had played no role in the repulse of the Third Division. Stiff and cold after hours of inactivity, the dismounted cavalrymen scrambled to their feet as the Twenty-sixth Indiana approached. The Confederate formation, from left to right, was composed of Elliott's Missouri Cavalry Battalion (with Quantrill's band, led by William Gregg), half of Gordon's Missouri Cavalry, Jeans's Missouri Cavalry, and the other half of Gordon's command. Although fewer than seven hundred of Shelby's nine hundred troopers were on the firing line (the remainder were in the rear with the horses), the Confederates still enjoyed a substantial numerical advantage. "It looked as though the woods were literally full of them in our front," an Indiana officer recalled. The opposing forces fired at nearly the same instant when about one hundred yards apart. A storm of bullets and buckshot filled the air with leaves, bark, twigs, and billows of smoke. Most soldiers sought cover behind trees and logs after the initial exchange, but some in the Twenty-sixth Indiana continued to push forward until they were within fifty or sixty yards of the Confederate line.[8]

WHEN SHOUP SAW HUSTON approaching the Ridge, he appealed to Hindman for help. Hindman detached Colonel Robert G. Shaver's Brigade from

Frost's Division and rushed it to Shoup. This was a significant development, because it marked the first time Hindman shifted a substantial portion of his army from one front to the other. He obviously felt that it was safe to do so. The afternoon was waning and still there was no sign of the Kansas Division. Puzzled by Blunt's failure to make an appearance, Hindman belatedly turned his attention to Herron.[9]

Hindman instructed Shaver to hasten toward the sound of "heavy firing" and support "our troops engaged with the enemy in that quarter." Shaver responded with alacrity. His 1,050 men had spent the day waiting for Blunt and dodging occasional overshots from Herron's batteries. Now they hurried toward the Ridge in three columns. Shaver accompanied Captain Westly Roberts's Missouri Battery over the crest of Prairie Grove on Fayetteville Road. The battery consisted of two 12-pounder James rifles and two 6-pounder guns. The rifled guns had been captured at Lone Jack in August and were the only such weapons in Hindman's army. By this time the Union batteries had shifted their fire away from the Borden house to avoid endangering Huston's men. The result was a heavy fall of shot and shell on the road. "The approach to the front was under terrific artillery fire from the enemy, their balls and shells plowing the ground before and all around us," wrote Lieutenant Samuel T. Ruffner. "Cannoneers dismounted from the limber boxes and ran alongside the gun carriages and drivers ducked their heads as they urged the horses at a gallop." After conferring with Shoup, Shaver sent Roberts down the hill to the Hugh Rogers house, the position recently vacated by West's Battery, with instructions to engage the Union artillery.[10]

Roberts did as instructed, but his exposed position drew an immediate barrage of "well-directed shots" from three of the four Union batteries. The Federals "exploded a shell in our midst before we could jerk a lanyard, wounding two men and two horses," recalled Ruffner. The Missourians persevered and sent a dozen rifled rounds shrieking toward Backof's and Borris's batteries, but the hail of Union shells and case shot was relentless. "I was nocked off my horse by a piece of a shell," Roberts recalled, "but [it] only stuned me for a short period of time. I soon came to my fete." Even in his wobbly condition Roberts recognized that the situation was untenable. He ordered the guns limbered up and returned to the brow of the hill, probably hoping that the additional elevation would improve the battery's chances of survival, but the volume of Federal fire was simply overwhelming. A badly rattled Roberts told his men to save themselves. The artillerymen abandoned their guns and teams in the road and fled into the woods.[11]

Colonel Hiram L. Grinsted's Arkansas Infantry arrived on the Ridge a few minutes behind Roberts's Battery. Shaver placed the 230 Arkansans on the left of McRae's Brigade and extended the Confederate line west of Fayetteville Road to a point above the William Rogers house. Shaver instructed his other two regiments to "move as rapidly as possible in the direction of the heaviest firing and support such commands in that quarter as might be in greatest need." The "direction of the heaviest firing" meant the area around the Borden house on the east side of the road. More than half of Shaver's Arkansas Infantry had been left behind in Fort Smith because of a lack of arms. Fewer than 150 men were present at Prairie Grove, and they were commanded by Lieutenant Colonel William C. Adams. When Adams received the order to redeploy, he took the most direct route to the front. Using a compass as a guide, he and his battalion plowed through the thicket and miraculously emerged behind Shelby's right, exactly where they were needed. The 370 men of Colonel Charles W. Adams's Arkansas Infantry did not fare as well. They, too, chose a direct route to the front but lost their way in the "very thick growth of scrub oak and other small undergrowth" and drifted into the large ravine behind Fagan's left. It required the combined efforts of Shoup, Fagan, and a half-dozen staff officers to extract Adams from the ravine and place his regiment in the gap between Fagan's right and Shelby's left. The Arkansans occupied the fence bordering the south side of the orchard, the position occupied by Pleasants's regiment a short time earlier when it first engaged the Nineteenth Iowa.[12]

Shoup urged Charles Adams to get into the fight at once, but Adams kept his men in place until they were, in his estimation, "perfectly cool." This was one of several indications that Adams's regiment was unsteady. Meanwhile, the firefight between the Twenty-sixth Indiana and Shelby's Brigade raged on only a short distance to Adams's right. The right wing of the Federal regiment was visible through the drifting smoke when Adams finally ordered his men to fire. The Arkansans steadied their large-caliber muskets on the fence rails and loosed a "truly terrific" volley of buck and ball. "Their fire was a most deadly one," Adams asserted, "and I can say with truth that the enemy fell in heaps of slain." The Arkansans inflicted less damage than Adams claimed, but their belated appearance marked the beginning of the end of Huston's attack.[13]

Encouraged by the arrival of reinforcements on both flanks, Shelby ordered his brigade forward. Twelve hundred Rebels, a mix of dismounted Missouri cavalry and Arkansas infantry, surged "like an avalanche" toward the Twenty-sixth Indiana. The "intensely hot" Confederate assault bent back the right wing of the Union regiment. "Oh then it was when it took nerve, but, alas for us, we soon found we could not stay there under such a murderous fire and live," wrote Captain Courtland E. Whitsit. The Union officer lost his hat but kept his feet when a spent bullet bounced off his head. (The blow "stunned me a little," he told his parents.) Whitsit experienced a far heavier blow when he lost sight of his younger brother. "I remembered that I had last seen him in the thickest of the fight; then I thought of mother." Whitsit later discovered that Lieutenant John A. Whitsit had left his place in line to carry the severely wounded regimental adjutant to the rear.[14]

A bullet ripped away Clark's sword belt and three others passed through his coat, but the Indiana colonel displayed "remarkable coolness and deliberation" for a man in his first fight. Recognizing that the situation was hopeless, Clark ordered a retreat. The Confederates followed, "firing volley after volley without intermission." Captain Robert F. Braden described the harrowing retreat as the Federals emerged from the woods and sprinted down the open slope. "As we came off the field the bullets were flying seemingly as thick as hail and nearly every one was struck either in his person or clothing (I was one of three in my company who did not receive a mark of a bullet)." Clark gathered as many survivors as he could in the sheltered area at the foot of the hill and led them back to the north side of Fayetteville Road. Other Indiana soldiers milled around in "considerable disorder" on Crawford's Prairie or slipped away to the cover of the woods along the Illinois.[15]

JOHN BLACK LEFT Wabash College when the war broke out and volunteered for military service. His impressive performance at Pea Ridge and his enviable political connections (Abraham Lincoln was a close family friend) resulted in a meteoric rise in rank. At the tender age of twenty-three he was lieutenant colonel of the Thirty-seventh Illinois. Mounted on a black horse and wrapped in a dark blue cloak lined in scarlet, the handsome young officer personified the Victorian ideal of an officer and a gentleman. Even enlisted men noted for their ironclad cynicism fell under his spell. One admiring soldier remarked that Black's shoulder-length hair "gave him rather a peculiarly grand appearance."[16]

Black rode back and forth shouting commands and offering encouragement as the Thirty-seventh Illinois advanced on the right of the Twenty-sixth Indiana. "It was now our turn to go up and charge the terrible hill," wrote an officer. When the regiment reached the Borden house, Black allowed his men to break ranks and re-form on the other side. The process took longer than expected—possibly some Arkansas holdouts still occupied the cluster of buildings—and a gap opened between the two Union regiments that never

John C. Black (Vermillion County Museum, Danville, Ill.)

closed. The Thirty-seventh Illinois resumed its advance but proceeded only a short distance into the orchard before Black called a halt. He never explained why he stopped, although the sight of hundreds of dead and wounded, both friend and foe, sprawled among the ravaged fruit trees was the likely reason.[17]

The fight in the thicket east of the orchard now reached its climax, and the Twenty-sixth Indiana stampeded to the rear, followed by hundreds of cheering Rebels. Black ordered the Thirty-seventh Illinois back to the fence bordering the north side of the orchard, the place where the Nineteenth Iowa had made a brief stand before fleeing down the hill. Now alone on the Ridge, anxious Illinois officers and men peered through the drifting smoke toward the Confederate position. Several minutes passed, then commands rang out and Fagan's troops stood up.

The Confederates "rose like a wall before us," recalled the colonel's younger brother, Captain William P. Black. It was apparent to everyone that the Thirty-seventh Illinois was hopelessly outnumbered. "The enemy were in immense force immediately in my front," Colonel Black stated, "advancing and firing rapidly as they came." The Federals responded with a volley, and a deafening exchange of musket and revolving rifle fire erupted at point-blank range. "We let them have all that we had but it did not faize them," wrote an

Illinois soldier. Casualties in the closely packed Rebel ranks were heavy, but Colonel Black observed with a mix of horror and fascination that the barrage of bullets "did not seem to check them at all in their advance." Confederate fire was equally intense. "The leaden hail came in one continuous stream of fire, not unlike a severe hail storm," recalled another Union officer. Nearly every account described the continuous "whizzing and hissing" of bullets. One of those bullets smashed the upper bone in Black's unwounded left arm, but the grievously wounded colonel remained in the saddle and on the Ridge.[18]

Among the Confederate regiments jostling for position in the crowded orchard was Charles Adams's Arkansas Infantry. Adams stated that his men encountered "extremely heavy fire" from the Thirty-seventh Illinois. The storm of lead threw the Arkansans "into the greatest consternation and confusion, few or none of them having ever before that day been under fire." Most dropped their weapons and fled. Fewer than a hundred officers and men, most of them veterans of Wilson's Creek, remained on the field. One who stayed was Acting Color Sergeant John Howerton, who continued to wave the regimental flag while every other member of the color guard was shot down around him. Adams was so impressed that he reported Howerton's display of "cool unflinching courage and bravery" to Hindman. Among those who departed was George T. Maddox. The soldier next to Maddox was struck in the foot just as the regiment went to pieces. As Maddox turned to flee, the wounded man called out: "George, for God's sake don't leave me!" Maddox picked up his comrade and staggered out of the orchard. He recalled that "as I went with him on my back it looked as if a million balls were playing around us." The two Arkansans made their way to the Buchanan house, a mile in the rear, where they found dozens of other wounded men, most of them lying on the ground untended. The scene convinced Maddox that he could do more good at the makeshift hospital than on the firing line. He spent the rest of the day as a volunteer medical orderly. Meanwhile, back on the Ridge, Adams and what remained of his command drifted eastward and eventually fell in with MacDonald's Brigade.[19]

The disintegration of Charles Adams's regiment had little effect on the tactical situation around the Borden house. The Confederates crowded around both flanks of the Thirty-seventh Illinois and regained possession of Blocher's abandoned artillery pieces. Colonel Black feared the guns would be turned on his men and ordered a withdrawal. "In a moment more it would have been hand to hand combat but just then orders were given for us to retreat," recorded Alcander O. Morse. The Federals did not tarry when they received the order to fall back. "I was not long in getting to the foot of the hill with my company," Captain Black admitted. Two officers and a half-dozen men on the Union left were taken prisoner, but nearly everyone else made it to the foot of the hill. The dash to safety across the valley floor was a harrowing experience as the Rebels massed on the brow of the Ridge and fired down on the fleeing Federals. "Balls whistled thick and fast by my ears, and rattled upon the cornstalks and blades like hail upon the dead leaves of autumn," wrote William D. McCord. The Confederate view of the fight around the Borden house was best expressed by Hawthorn, who declared that his men "charged with such fury that the enemy broke and fled in the utmost disorder, leaving the ground literally covered with their dead."[20]

Huston watched in dismay as the Twenty-sixth Indiana was "thrown into confusion, broke, and retreated down the hill." After being carried some distance into the west cornfield by the fleeing troops, he started back up the hill to withdraw the Thirty-seventh Illinois, unaware that John Black already had ordered a retreat. "I discovered that they also had broken, and were rushing down the hill in some confusion. I tried to rally them but without success." Huston encountered Black below the Borden house. "Great God, Colonel Black, can't you do something to stop this." Black was in obvious distress: "Colonel, my arm is broken all to pieces, and I cannot hold my horse." Huston immediately changed his tone: "Colonel, go at once to the rear if you are wounded." He directed an aide to take the reins of Black's horse and lead the grievously injured officer to safety, then assisted the remaining officers in getting the regiment off the field in reasonably good order. The Thirty-seventh Illinois, like the Twenty-sixth Indiana, retreated to its starting point on the north side of Fayetteville Road.[21]

The unsuccessful assault cost Huston 275 of the 850 troops engaged, a third of his improvised brigade. An officer in the Twenty-sixth Indiana wrote that "our numbers are sadly diminished by this affair," and the official casualty list bears him out. The regiment lost 25 killed, 175 wounded, and 1 missing, a grim casualty rate of 45 percent. Captain Whitsit discovered that 36 of 57 men in his company had been killed or wounded. Shocked by the calamity that had befallen his command, Clark took what comfort he could in the way his soldiers had handled themselves: "The conduct of the regiment was all I could expect under the circumstances, and I cheerfully attest to the bravery and good conduct of both officers and men." Nevertheless, the fact remained that the Twenty-sixth Indiana was wrecked.[22]

Losses in the Thirty-seventh Illinois were less severe: 8 killed, 58 wounded, and 8 captured for a casualty rate of 18 percent, by far the lightest toll suffered by any of the four Union infantry regiments that stormed the Ridge. One Illinois officer reported only a single man wounded in his company. Although the regiment's escape seemed miraculous, it was Colonel Black's decision to back out of the orchard—not divine intervention—that probably saved the Thirty-seventh Illinois from destruction.[23]

The second Union attack was, in the words of one officer, a "heroic, terrific, desperate charge, with few equals and no superiors." It also was another costly failure. Herron acknowledged as much in his report. "It was a repetition of the first charge," he wrote, "the enemy again driven back, and we, in turn, compelled to abandon the position by force of numbers." Huston was acclaimed as the "hero of the day" because he "rode into the thickest of the fight, urging and by his example, animating his men," though many other officers and men in the Second Division also performed admirably. On the Union side, the problem was not an absence of courage. The problem was numbers. Herron simply lacked the strength to push Hindman off the hill.[24]

THE CONFEDERATES RESPONDED with another counterattack. They "came down like a cloud into the valley in pursuit," wrote Captain William Black of the Thirty-seventh Illinois. "We had the rebels now, just where we had always wanted them, on level clear ground, and we felt now was an hour of vengeance." The 1,800 Confederate attackers outnumbered the 1,250 to 1,300 Union defenders by a substantial margin, but the sketchy line of blue-clad infantry was bolstered by fourteen guns on the valley floor and three more on the slope beyond. (The three remaining Union guns were employed elsewhere, as we shall see.) "Every time that we drove them down the hill, their batteries would open furiously upon us, throwing solid shot, shell, canister and grape," complained Hawthorn. He did not exaggerate. Union artillerymen fired "volley after volley of shell" into the Confederates as they descended the slope. When the Rebels reached the valley floor, the gunners switched to canister. Men fell in heaps but the ragged lines came on.[25]

Fagan's Brigade hurried across the west cornfield toward Backof's and Borris's batteries. Brooks apparently failed to notice that his regiment was passing directly across the front of the Thirty-seventh Illinois, which was partially concealed by cornstalks, tall grass, and the dismantled fences running along both sides of the road. When the Confederates trotted past at the double-quick, intent on reaching the roaring batteries as quickly as possible, the Federal infantry "rose as one man" and fired a volley that ripped through Brooks's ranks like a "great scythe of death." The Rebels were staggered by the unexpected blow. A Union officer observed that they "stopped as if amazed." The Illinoisans fired a second volley, and Brooks's regiment reeled back in the wildest disorder. "Our men put a volley into them that made them git to the brush as fast as they could" was how an exuberant David Ash described the moment. Hawthorn halted to lend support but succeeded only in exposing his own regiment to the deadly enfilade fire. Soon more Rebels were streaming to the rear across the trampled cornfield. "Our revolving rifles kept playing and one and another fell, and one and another fled back to the cover of the wooded hill," wrote Black. Encouraged by these developments, Clark and the Twenty-sixth Indiana joined the fight. The Federals cheered and yelled in derision as the Rebels ran for their lives. When some actually started out in pursuit, Huston called them back, saying, "Boys, I cannot allow you to go up there again."[26]

King and Geoghegan continued toward the Union batteries, seemingly unaware of the disaster that had befallen the left wing of Fagan's Brigade. Backof and Borris fired their last few rounds of canister at the approaching Confederates, then limbered up and fell back to the Thompson pasture, the place where they had opened the bombardment two hours earlier. The departure of eight guns created a gap in the center of the Union line, but the ravaged Arkansas regiments were without direction or support. They also were under fire from Matthaei's half of Murphy's battery on Crawford's Hill. King saw no point in going any farther and ordered everyone back to the Ridge. The ebbing Confederate tide left a fresh deposit of mangled bodies in the west cornfield. "The enemy were checked," Murphy observed with satisfaction.[27]

Meanwhile, Shelby's dismounted cavalry regiments descended the hill east of the Borden house and hurried across the wheatfield toward the knoll. The Missourians made a "great effort" to capture Foust's guns but were stopped in their tracks by a storm of canister that littered the field with additional bodies. Shelby ordered an immediate withdrawal. Foust, his ammunition now exhausted, held his ground until the Rebels were gone, then abandoned the knoll and joined Backof and Borris on the Thompson farm. Despite heavy losses among their horses (eight animals killed and eleven wounded), the Missouri artillerymen brought away all of their guns and five of their six caissons.[28]

The Confederates were not quite done. About the time Shelby's counterattack faltered, MacDonald carried out a weak demonstration against the Ninety-fourth Illinois on the Union left. His Missouri and Texas troopers descended the slope and entered the east cornfield, where they came under sustained fire from the Ninety-fourth Illinois. The Rebels promptly faced about and returned to the Ridge. MacDonald reported that his advance "succeeded in compelling the enemy to fall back rapidly," but, in fact, it had no effect whatever on Union dispositions. McNulta dismissed the brief affair with a single sentence: "We again opened fire upon them, when they again withdrew." A short time later the Ninety-fourth Illinois retired to Fayetteville Road "under immediate orders from General Herron" and rejoined the rest of the Third Division. McNulta led a squad to the knoll and recovered the caisson that Faust had left behind.[29]

At the height of the counterattack, Herron left his command post on Crawford's Hill and rode along the wavering Union line, calling on officers and men to stand by their colors and throw the Rebels back. He had another close call when a round from Roberts's Missouri Battery decapitated the horse immediately behind his own and wounded its rider. "I can assure you it was hot work," he told Curtis. Herron helped Orme, Bertram, and Huston establish a new line along Fayetteville Road. The Thirty-seventh Illinois and Twenty-sixth Indiana remained in place across from the west cornfield while the Twentieth Wisconsin and Ninety-fourth Illinois re-formed north of the wheatfield. The devastated Nineteenth Iowa withdrew across the Illinois River. While the infantry redeployed, the artillery refilled their ammunition chests in anticipation of the next round.[30]

By this time Herron's train had reached Fayetteville. A portion of the train escort, accompanied by reorganized elements of the cavalry regiments routed in the morning engagement, hurried toward the sound of the guns at Prairie Grove. Because it was too late for the Union horsemen to engage in reconnaissance or screening activities, Herron used them to support the artillery and extend his flanks. Lieutenant Charles W. DeWolf and about one hundred men of the Seventh Missouri Cavalry splashed across the Illinois and dismounted near Backof's battery. "I moved onto the field and all the splendors and horrors of a battlefield lay before me," wrote DeWolf. "Immediately in front of me I could see the rebel lines, but only from their fire and yells, they being undercover of thick underbrush. Our brave boys were in front of them in the open field and the Regiments looked very few and painfully small to engage the heavy fire and superior number opposed to them." DeWolf was struck by the extraordinary scene ("I was spellbound for a moment"), but he did not stay long. He had been ill for several days and felt so weak that he led his horse back toward the river. At that moment a Confederate shell shrieked overhead. The shot "passed so close that both the horse and myself involuntarily squatted down," wrote DeWolf. "It struck in advance of us with a short thud. I think if I had been mounted it would have struck me." Unable to go any farther, DeWolf lay down in the grass alongside Fayetteville Road and watched walking wounded, stretcher bearers, and ambulances "passing in a steady stream" to the rear. Eventually he joined the dolorous current and left the field.[31]

The second Confederate counterattack was over by 4:00 P.M. The Rebels succeeded, at substantial cost to themselves, in pushing back the center and left of the Union line, but they failed to inflict any additional damage on Herron's infantry or capture any of his guns. The second counterattack, like the first, was notable for an absence of leadership above the regimental level. Of the four division and brigade commanders involved (Shoup, Marmaduke, Fagan, and Shelby), only Shelby appears to have accompanied his men at least partway down the hill. Shoup never strayed from his command post on Fayetteville Road. Marmaduke's whereabouts between 2:00 and 6:00 P.M. are largely a mystery, but he seems not to have been with his division. Brooks reported that he was the "senior officer immediately present" on Crawford's Prairie during the counterattack, which places Fagan somewhere back on the Ridge and helps to explain the progressive fragmentation of his brigade as the counterattack unfolded.[32]

Confederate commanders, once again, seemed unwilling to acknowledge that a counterattack had taken place. Shoup included very little about the event in his report even though half of his division was involved. Marmaduke reported nothing at all—not a word—despite the participation of three-fourths of his division. Much of what Fagan penned is incorrect or obviously secondhand. Only Shelby provided a recognizable if typically exaggerated account. It was all very strange.

The paucity, opacity, and unreliability of Confederate accounts make it difficult to reconstruct events. The dismal quality of Confederate record keeping, combined with an apparent tendency in some commands to undercount losses, makes it equally difficult to determine the human toll. Nevertheless, it is clear that Fagan's Brigade bore the brunt of the fight against Herron's command. In the seesaw struggle the four Arkansas infantry regiments and accompanying battery lost close to 40 percent of their collective strength: 614 men killed, wounded, and missing. Perhaps one-tenth of that number were victims of the unrelenting Union bombardment, but the rest fell in the vicious firefights on the Ridge and the suicidal assaults against the Union artillery line. Although Fagan did not venture onto Crawford's Prairie, he acknowledged that "many of my men were killed and wounded" there. Not all Confederate commanders were as forthcoming. The Missouri cavaliers (Marmaduke, Shelby, and MacDonald) neglected to broach the unpleasant subject of casualties in their colorfully written reports.[33]

William M. Dye (New York State Library, Manuscripts and Special Collections)

WHILE TWO OF Huston's infantry regiments stormed the Ridge, the third entered the fight on its own some distance to the west. Colonel William M. Dye was an 1853 graduate of the U.S. Military Academy (Schofield was a classmate) who had attained the rank of captain in the regular army. Dye led the Second Brigade in the Second Division, but after Huston marched away with the Thirty-seventh Illinois he found himself in command of only a single regiment, his own Twentieth Iowa. Dye was miffed by what he regarded as a slight. Like Henry Bertram in the Third Division, he maintained the fiction that he was still a "brigade" commander. The officer in actual command of the Twentieth Iowa was Lieutenant Colonel Joseph B. Leake, a New Jersey native, Ohio University graduate, and Iowa attorney and legislator. A man of many talents, the thirty-four-year-old Leake also proved to be a capable amateur soldier. Dye and Leake worked well together, but the Twentieth Iowa was the smallest regiment in Herron's command. The 290 officers and men hardly needed two commanding officers.[34]

Desperate to get into the fight, Dye ignored Huston's orders to remain in reserve. He commandeered Marr's half of Murphy's battery and personally led it across Crawford's Prairie in the wake of Huston's advance. When the Twenty-sixth Indiana and Thirty-seventh Illinois advanced to the road following the repulse of the Third Division, Dye placed Marr's three guns in an expanse of prairie grass two hundred yards behind the right flank of the Thirty-seventh Illinois and about twice that distance north of the Hugh Rogers house. Dye intended only to secure Huston's exposed right flank, but his unauthorized maneuver alarmed the Confederates and extended the arena of conflict to the west.[35]

After Huston led his command toward the Borden house, Dye called on Leake to support Marr. The Twentieth Iowa hurried across Crawford's Prairie at the double-quick. Officers and men formed a line behind the fence bordering the south side of the Hugh Rogers cornfield, fifty yards north of Marr's position, and watched grimly as Huston's attack unfolded. "The crack of rifles and crash of musketry in that part of the field soon became terrible and the hill was almost hid in smoke," reported Captain Ellsworth N. Bates. The Iowans did not stay long in the cornfield. Noticing an ominous increase in Confederate activity west of Fayetteville Road, Dye ordered Leake to "check a movement of the enemy on our right flank." The Twentieth Iowa dashed westward to the fence bordering the north side of the Robert West wheatfield.[36]

By this time Huston's attack was under way and Shoup's attention was focused on his right. As a result, the three Confederate regimental commanders west of the road were left to their own devices. Grinsted, Glenn, and Hart advanced skirmishers to the bench at the foot of the hill, and Grinsted and Glenn eventually followed with their entire regiments. This was the activity that alarmed Dye. The Rogers homesteads provided the Rebels with plenty of cover. From the shelter of houses, outbuildings, woodpiles, and fences they opened a "steady galling fire" on the Twentieth Iowa four hundred yards to the north. A Union officer observed bullets "striking the rails in our front, and falling among our men as they lay behind the fence." The exchange of fire ended abruptly when Marr advanced his three guns to within two hundred yards of the Hugh Rogers house and opened fire with canister. The barrage of iron balls "was so severe that the position was found to be entirely untenable," stated McRae. The Arkansans "fell back in some confusion" and Dye ordered Leake to advance.[37]

The Iowans stood up, fired a volley, and charged with a shout. Major William G. Thompson wrote that the regiment dashed "through the field into the woods through a perfect hail storm of bullets." The Federals halted at the foot of the hill—whether they crossed the bench is unclear—and "fired a few vollies to feel of the enemy and got a fair response." Leake did not attempt to ascend the Ridge. Instead, he slowly fell back and reformed alongside Marr, whose guns continued to pound the Confederates at point-blank range. Dye reported that his Iowans charged "in gallant style" and "retired with the order of old soldiers." Coming from an officer in the regular army, there was no higher compliment. The Iowans were just as pleased with their unflappable commander. One soldier wrote that Dye "smoked his old pipe alongside of the battery, as if nothing exciting was going on."[38]

By this time the second Confederate counterattack had ended, and Herron noticed Dye's unauthorized presence on Crawford's Prairie for the first time. He realized at once that Marr was too far in advance of the rest of the army and ordered him back to Crawford's Hill. For the rest of the day Murphy's six rifled guns were in action together. Murphy wrote: "It was truly a gratifying sight to witness the magnificent practice of my officers and men." With the other Union batteries busy setting up in new positions and refilling empty ammunition chests, the regular crash of Murphy's cannons measured the passing minutes like a metronome. Marr's departure left the Twentieth Iowa alone in the center of Crawford's Prairie, about four hundred yards west of the rest of Huston's command. Rebel skirmishers crept back down the hill and resumed harassing the Federals. Leake advanced two companies "to pick off some of the butternuts that were constantly showing their heads." The result was a "lively" but inconclusive skirmish.[39]

It was late afternoon, and the officers and men of the Missouri Divisions were physically and emotionally drained. "So far as we were concerned, the fight had now ceased, and we had got the worst of it," wrote a soldier in the Ninety-fourth Illinois. Colonel Orme felt much the same way. "About 4 o'clock I thought things looked blue," he confessed to his wife. "Everything, nearly, pointed to a defeat of our forces," wrote another discouraged officer. Even Herron conceded that the game was up. He no longer talked of pushing the Rebels aside and succoring Blunt. Instead, he urged everyone to "hold out till night." Darkness, however, was still ninety minutes away.[40]

For some time Dye had been watching an unidentified cavalry force maneuvering and skirmishing on the valley floor a half-mile west of his position. The horsemen were dressed in blue but that meant little on the frontier. Fearing the worst, Dye told Leake to change front from south to west and establish a skirmish line across the valley. Minutes later an unidentified battery appeared on West's Knoll and began "blazing away like fury." Shells dropped dangerously close to Leake's skirmishers. Herron studied the distant battery from his elevated position on Crawford's Hill. "It seemed to be the enemy's guns, and our case looked tough," he later told a friend. Unable to endure the suspense, Herron set out with a single staff officer to discover whether the newcomers were friend or foe. Halfway up the valley Herron encountered a small party of Union officers coming the other way. They saluted and announced that the Kansas Division was on the field.[41]

Blunt had arrived.

BLUNT SAVES THE DAY

WHILE THE MAIN BODY OF THE TRANS-MISSISSIPPI ARMY HURRIED north on Cove Creek Road to intercept Herron, James Monroe and his small Arkansas cavalry brigade maintained a lonely vigil atop Reed's Mountain. Hindman's revised plan called for Monroe to "threaten and press the enemy vigorously" in order to keep Blunt's attention focused on Van Buren Road. It was a tall order for four hundred cavalrymen, but the Arkansans did their best. They prepared crude breastworks along the crest of the mountain and kept campfires burning all night. At dawn on 7 December they moved down the west slope and formed a dismounted line of battle in the woods near the foot of the mountain. While the rising sun illuminated long lines of Union troops on Newburg Heights, the much smaller Confederate formation remained hidden in shadow.[1]

Blunt spent the night at his headquarters in Boonsboro. He believed that a "general engagement must take place next day" and wanted nothing left to chance. Weer's Second Brigade and Cloud's Third Brigade occupied Newburg Heights and blocked Van Buren Road. Wickersham's improvised cavalry brigade and part of Salomon's First Brigade watched Hogeye Road. The rest of Salomon's command stood guard over the stores and trains at Rhea's Mill.[2]

No Union troops were posted on Cove Creek Road, but around 5:00 A.M. on 7 December Blunt finally acted to rectify that oversight. He ordered Colonel John M. Richardson to proceed to the intersection of Hogeye Road and Cove Creek Road and see what, if anything, was happening. The intersection, known as "Hogeye Crossing," was located five miles east of Boonsboro and about the same distance north of Morrow's house. Why Blunt suddenly decided to investigate possible Confederate activity on Cove Creek Road is not known, but he told Richardson that if he found the Rebels marching north he was "to resist their advance to the last extremity, and notify me promptly of their movements." When Richardson pointed out that his two companies of the Fourteenth Missouri State Militia Cavalry included fewer than one hundred men, Blunt added Captain Theodore Conkey's company of the Third Wisconsin Cavalry. Dawn was breaking by the time Richardson and his ad hoc battalion of about 150 troopers clattered out of Boonsboro and headed east on Hogeye Road.[3]

Unknown to Blunt and Richardson, another Union scouting party was on its way to Hogeye Crossing. Following a tedious night march from Rhea's Mill, Colonel Edward Lynde's Ninth Kansas Cavalry reached its assigned position near Boonsboro a little before daybreak. As Lynde was unfamiliar with the country, he directed Captain Charles F. Coleman to take his company and probe eastward on Hogeye Road. A short distance west of Hogeye Crossing Coleman encountered a Confederate cavalry force and fell back. He met Richardson coming the other way and warned him that enemy horsemen were on Hogeye Road. Exactly what Coleman said has been lost, but Richardson got the impression that the Rebels were moving west toward Boonsboro. Richardson "immediately dispatched" a courier to alert Blunt and placed his own command (now reinforced by Coleman's company) in a "strong position" behind Blair Creek. When the Confederates failed to make an appearance, Richardson sent Captain Stephen Julian of his regiment to find out what was going on. Julian, described as a "prompt and efficient officer," slipped past the stationary Confederate horsemen on Hogeye Road and reached a hill overlooking Cove Creek Road. Julian hastened back to Blair Creek and told Richardson that Cove Creek Road was filled with a seemingly endless column of Rebels. "That fact I immediately reported to General Blunt," noted Richardson. A second courier galloped away with the alarming news that the Rebels were not moving west as previously reported; instead, they were marching north in great force toward Prairie Grove.[4]

Richardson had discovered Hindman's turning movement, but this critical piece of information failed to make its way up the Union chain of command in a timely fashion. Although the two couriers reached Blunt's headquarters in Boonsboro without incident and delivered their messages, Blunt and his staff had departed for Newburg Heights some time earlier. The messages lay on a table, unnoticed and unread, for nearly two hours before someone thought to forward them to the Union commander.

Blissfully unaware of developments on Cove Creek Road, Blunt joined Weer and Cloud shortly after 7:00 A.M. His arrival on Newburg Heights coincided with Marmaduke's attack on the unsuspecting Union cavalry at Prairie Grove, six miles to the northeast. Blunt, of course, knew nothing of this because the rattle of small arms fire was muffled by distance and terrain. The only potentially troubling bit of information was a report, now several hours old, that Union pickets could hear the "heavy rumbling of artillery and tread of cavalry" in the direction of Morrow's on the far side of Reed's Mountain. Blunt was not concerned because he assumed Hindman was making preparations for an attack. When the sun rose over the Boston Mountains, Blunt still believed that the Confederates were present in "considerable force" on Van Buren Road and that the battle to come would take place on Newburg Heights.[5]

The first rays of sunlight painted the forested slopes of the Boston Mountains in shades of gold but failed to dispel the tension or the bone-chilling cold. "We waited anxiously for the enemy to appear," wrote a Kansas cavalryman on Newburg Heights, but the Confederates remained out of sight. Soldiers bundled in overcoats and wrapped in blankets stamped their feet and cursed the Rebels for their lack of consideration. Blunt rode back and forth, chatting and joking with officers and enlisted men in his bluff manner. He exuded confidence and repeatedly declared that the Kansas Division would "pound hell out of 'em this time."[6]

After an hour of inactivity on the part of the Confederates, Blunt's patience began to wear thin. He ordered his skirmishers to fall back in an attempt to draw the Rebels out into the open. This was the moment Monroe had dreaded. He waited as long as he dared, then moved his small brigade out of the shadow of Reed's Mountain and into the sunlight. Three hundred Confederates (the rest remained on the mountain with the horses) advanced a few hundred yards and engaged in a desultory exchange of fire with Union skirmishers. "It seemed that they did not want to fight but was hard up for amusement," observed a Kansas soldier. Puzzlement spread through the ranks of the Kansas Division. Where was the rest of Hindman's army?[7]

At long last Blunt realized that the force in his front was a diversion and that the Confederate main body had passed around his left flank during the night. Perhaps Blunt wondered what had become of Richardson, whom he had sent to Hogeye Crossing to watch for precisely this sort of thing, but his immediate concern was the safety of the Missouri Divisions. Grabbing paper and pencil he scribbled a warning to Herron: "I am engaging the enemy in front and am fearful of a flank movement by the Cove Creek and Fayetteville road. I am sending all my transportation to Rheas Mill. You will direct yours there also. Your infantry and artillery will advance on the road directly to this place." Had the message reached its destination, Herron would have learned that Hindman was moving in his direction, but fate intervened in the form of Confederate cavalry. Two heavily escorted couriers set out from Newburg Heights around 9:00 A.M., but both returned within the hour to report that all roads leading to Fayetteville were blocked. "Neither of these dispatches reached [Herron]," lamented Blunt, "the messengers being cut off by Marmaduke's advance." Herron thus remained unaware of the altered tactical situation.[8]

The belated discovery of Hindman's turning movement released Blunt from his self-imposed confinement at Cane Hill. If Herron could not come to him, he would go to Herron. After a hasty conference with his staff and a quick look at whatever maps were available, Blunt put the Kansas Division in motion. He ordered the Third Indian to escort the wagons to Rhea's Mill by way of Ridge Road, the shortest and safest route, and told everyone else to prepare "to move rapidly in the direction of Fayetteville and form a junction with General Herron." Blunt believed that if he acted quickly, he just might be able to shoulder Marmaduke's cavalry aside and reach Herron before Hindman did.[9]

Events now proceeded with a rush. Richardson's messages finally reached Newburg Heights and confirmed that Hindman had given Blunt the slip. Additional confirmation, if such was needed, came a little past 10:00 A.M. when the "dull heavy booming of cannon" was heard in the direction of Fayetteville. A Kansas artilleryman listened with a practiced ear and noted that the "discharge of the pieces could not be distinguished, but the bursting of the shells could be heard much plainer, which showed that the shells were bursting high in the air." Blunt did not know that the distant cannonade was the artillery exchange triggered by Herron's dash across the Illinois with Lieutenant Edwards's section of Foust's Battery E, but he knew what it meant: Hindman and Herron had collided.[10]

Blunt was disappointed, but only for a moment, for he realized that he had been presented with a once-in-a-lifetime opportunity to achieve a victory of Napoleonic proportions. Hindman had played directly into his hands. The Confederates were squarely between two converging Union forces. If the Kansas Division marched northeast on Fayetteville Road, it would strike the Trans-Mississippi Army in the flank or rear while the latter was engaged with the Missouri Divisions. Hindman, of course, was keenly aware of the threat Blunt posed to his attenuated column. At that very moment he was deploying half of his strength at Muddy Fork to block Fayetteville Road and keep Blunt at bay.

The Kansas Division began to move as soon as the last wagon turned on Ridge Road. "In a few moments there was inexplicable confusion," recalled a Kansas cavalry officer. "Infantry filled [Fayetteville Road] in spite of all command to the contrary, cavalry rushed in, knocking them right and left in a frightful manner, and the artillery in turn overrode both and beat its way through. There was a tumult of voices, in which oaths and execrations predominated, but no attempt at military order in the horde of armed men who swarmed through the woods down that mountainside." Even allowing for literary license on the part of the soldier who penned that overwrought account, the situation in the Jordan Valley must have been disorderly, if not downright chaotic, as dozens of regiments and batteries streamed down from the hills and forced their way onto the narrow, winding road.[11]

The chaos intensified as the column passed through Boonsboro. Disabled wagons, broken harnesses, piles of corn, and anything else that could not be moved was put to the torch, and columns of smoke rose into the air. The editorial staff of the *Buck and Ball* gathered up the half-finished newspaper (only the front page had been printed) and threw it into the Eleventh Kansas headquarters wagon for safekeeping, but they were forced to abandon the bulky tray set with type for the back page. A block or two from the print shop, surgeons and medical orderlies struggled to evacuate the sick and wounded from what was grandly termed the "General Hospital." Despite the last-minute assistance of the Second Kansas Cavalry at the rear of the column, some patients could not be moved and were left behind under the care of a surgeon.[12]

Blunt later wrote that "Hindman and myself were moving by parallel roads, my advance opposite his rear." Another Union officer remarked that the contending "armies were only about five miles apart and running parallel." The Confederates had both the lead and the inside track, so the Federals had to hurry. "We would double quick for half a mile, then walk another half mile," wrote Lieutenant Henry E. Palmer of the Eleventh Kansas. "Men in the ranks cried out that they could not travel so fast." The pace was relentless but straggling was almost nonexistent. Everyone seemed to understand that the decisive moment of the campaign was at hand.[13]

Desperate to slow or distract Hindman, Blunt sent Colonel Judson's battalion of the Sixth Kansas Cavalry and the Sixth Kansas Cavalry Battery to "attack and harass" the rear of the Confederate column. Judson hurried east on Hogeye Road and joined forces with Richardson, who seems to have been forgotten in the rush to evacuate Cane Hill. Now nearly four hundred strong, the Federals turned north at Hogeye Crossing and followed the trail

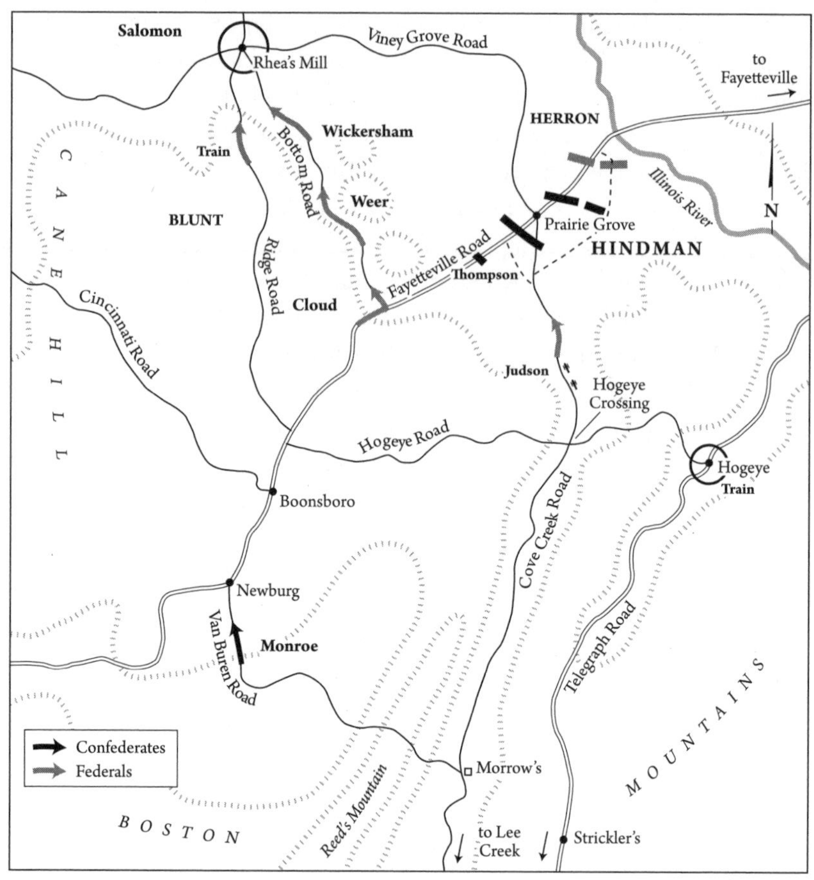

Blunt's march from Cane Hill to Prairie Grove

of the Trans-Mississippi Army up Cove Creek Road. They closed to within a half-mile of Prairie Grove Church before being detected, whereupon Judson ordered Lieutenant Brainard D. Benedict to open fire with his pair of mountain howitzers. Although the bombardment did little damage (Benedict had nothing in particular to aim at), it threw the Confederates into temporary confusion. Hindman acted swiftly and decisively to confront the Federals. Sergeant Wiley Britton and his comrades in the Sixth Kansas Cavalry watched anxiously as "large masses" of Confederate soldiers moved in their direction, but Judson had no intention of getting into a hopeless fight. After thirty minutes Benedict ceased firing and the Federals withdrew to Boonsboro and, eventually, Rhea's Mill. One can only wonder what would have happened had Blunt followed Hindman up Cove Creek Road with his entire force.[14]

Blunt stopped in Boonsboro to supervise the evacuation of his headquarters and deal with other administrative matters. While there, he informed Salomon by courier that Hindman and Herron were engaged near Fayetteville and that he was on his way to assist Herron. ("I go to his relief," were Blunt's exact words.) As always, Blunt was anxious about the safety of his logistical arrangements. He urged Salomon to be on guard against Marmaduke's cavalry and, if attacked, to defend the stores and trains at Rhea's Mill "to the last extremity."[15]

While Blunt was writing to Salomon, his plan to overtake Hindman fell apart. The first formation in the Union line of march on Fayetteville Road was Wickersham's improvised brigade of Illinois, Iowa, Missouri, and Wisconsin cavalrymen on loan from Herron. Blunt expected Wickersham to "proceed directly" toward Fayetteville, but Wickersham believed he was supposed to reinforce Salomon. Two miles past Ridge Road, Wickersham turned north on Bottom Road and hurried toward Rhea's Mill as rapidly as the poor condition of his horses would permit. The rest of the Kansas Division followed. Blunt did not realize anything was amiss until he left Boonsboro and discovered his command heading in the wrong direction. Blunt was so exasperated he considered setting out after Hindman with only the Third Brigade, which was last in the line of march and had not yet reached Bottom Road. Coming to his senses, he realized that his only realistic course of action was to get to the head of the Union column as quickly as possible and steer it in the proper direction.[16]

As Blunt hurried past the long line of cavalry, infantry, and artillery hastening north on Bottom Road, he must have wondered what else could go wrong. He did not yet apprehend that Wickersham's blunder was a blessing in disguise. The detour to Rhea's Mill took the Kansas Division around the strong Confederate blocking force at Muddy Fork and brought it within a few miles of Herron's beleaguered command. The mistaken turn actually enabled Blunt to make contact with Herron by the fastest route available.[17]

The Federals reached Rhea's Mill shortly before 1:00 P.M. "We returned to the Mill at a double quick but no enemy were there and our train was yet all safe," wrote an Ohio artilleryman. The column halted a short distance east of the hamlet on a "beautiful undulating and cultivated prairie dotted by fine farms and patches of woods." Winded soldiers broke ranks and sprawled in the tall grass. Some found the strength to brew coffee while others promptly fell asleep despite the bright midday sun. It was strangely quiet. The artillery fire that had caused so much excitement a few hours earlier had died away. Rumors spread that Herron had fled.[18]

Rhea's Mill in the 1890s (Bob's Studio, Fayetteville, Ark.)

Blunt arrived in quite a lather twenty minutes later and demanded to know why Wickersham had ignored his orders to march toward Fayetteville. Wickersham must have had a good explanation because Blunt let the matter drop. Wickersham was just as anxious as Blunt to "open communication and effect a junction" with Herron, but Bottom Road was clogged with traffic and he had to find an alternate route. Wickersham decided to head east on Viney Grove Road after learning that it joined Fayetteville Road at Prairie Grove, six miles to the southeast. Neither he nor anyone else at Rhea's Mill realized that Viney Grove Road led directly to the scene of confrontation between Hindman and Herron. Around 1:30 P.M. Wickersham and his troopers departed at a walk. It was the best their worn-out mounts could do.[19]

The Union cavalry had barely passed out of sight when the quiet of the afternoon was shattered by the "roar of cannon towards Fayetteville." This was the beginning of the prolonged bombardment that silenced Hindman's batteries and paved the way for Herron's infantry assaults. An Ohio artilleryman judged the fire to be "quite brisk and hot." A rising pillar of smoke soon marked the spot where the artillery was at work, but Blunt resisted the temptation to rush off half-cocked. His men and animals needed rest and he needed information. So he waited impatiently for his scouts to inform him about the lay of the land, the location of the contending forces, and, if possible, the point where his arrival on the field would do the most good.[20]

In time a small group of riders returned to the rise where Blunt and his staff were gathered. Reverend Francis Springer, chaplain of the Tenth Illinois Cavalry, watched as a "lank, sharp-featured, sandy-complexioned youth, dressed in butternut and wrapped in an old blue army coat," dismounted and began a "close conversation" with Blunt. The "youth" was Captain William S. Tough, Blunt's celebrated chief of scouts, who was all of twenty-two years old. "While the general listened and asked questions, he plied his pocketknife most industriously on stick after stick that he cut from the lowly sumac that had grown on the spot," noted Springer. "Interrogating, listening, and whittling sticks and occasionally pointing with his hand in a southerly direction were signs of an earnest spirit in the general during the twenty or thirty minutes of his interview." When Tough finished, Blunt asked for writing materials. "With a piece of paper on his knee, and pencil in hand, the general wrote a few words" and returned the paper to a staff officer. The officer made copies and handed them to other officers and orderlies who mounted their horses and hurried away.[21]

The orders called for the First Brigade to remain at Rhea's Mill and for the Second and Third Brigades to "march immediately to reinforce General Herron" or, as one officer put it, to "go where they are fighting, and go quickly." Drums rolled as men struggled to their feet and dressed ranks. At first the Federals proceeded in column, each regiment and battery turning east on Viney Grove Road, but to the thousands of troops stacked up on Bottom Road the prairie offered an inviting alternative.[22]

No one recorded exactly what happened, but most likely an impatient commander—someone like Colonel Ewing of the Eleventh Kansas—ordered his troops to make their own way to the battlefield cross-country. Other commanders followed suit. When Colonel Bassett of the Second Kansas Cavalry saw what was happening, he pulled his regiment out of the dissolving line of march. "It became necessary for me to pass through the fields, throwing down fences for that purpose, and through the tangled undergrowth, without the benefit of roads or paths," he reported. Although Blunt did not initiate the unorthodox maneuver, he quickly recognized its advantages and urged everyone to join in. "Tell the --- ---- fool to turn to the right and come on," he bellowed when a regimental commander failed to demonstrate sufficient initiative. The soldiers loved it. "When we heard the old man the boys raised a yell and felt safe," wrote a Kansas officer. "The profanity sounded sublime."[23]

By 2:30 P.M. the Federals were in motion. "The prairie was now alive with men, rushing in four or five parallel columns toward the wooded hill where a cloud of smoke hung and we heard the sound of battle. Incredible as it may seem, the infantry kept well up with the cavalry." The soldiers in the Eleventh Kansas had demonstrated their extraordinary powers of endurance at Cane Hill ten days earlier. Now they rose to the occasion a second time. Ewing's troops trotted forward at the double-quick as if their lives depended on it: "They were leaning to the front as though a great wind was sweeping them down, and their trail was strewn with blankets and overcoats they had thrown away." Inevitably a degree of competitiveness seeped into the proceedings. "Then followed such a race as I never saw before," marveled an officer in the Thirteenth Kansas. "The 13th, 11th, and 10th [Kansas] infantry ran side and side, stretching away for the scene of conflict like race horses . . . with terrific yells." The yells soon died away, but the pace flagged only slightly. Colonel Moonlight, Blunt's chief of staff, described the infantry "marching through fields by the right flank four regiments deep, each vying with the other who would reach the scene of coming strife first." Even the staff officer who maintained the staid headquarters journal of the Second Brigade was caught up in the excitement. "The march was over fences and through brush on the double quick," he wrote, "men exhibiting the greatest enthusiasm under the sound of the enemys guns."[24]

A few miles ahead of the swarming blue mass, Wickersham realized that Viney Grove Road was taking his command directly toward the ominous pillar of smoke. The road passed over the crest of Crawford's Hill, three-fourths of a mile northwest of the West house, and there the Federals stopped to behold an extraordinary panorama. The "whole field was in plain view as we arrived," wrote an astonished Iowa trooper. After doing his share of gawking, Wickersham remembered to inform Blunt that he had found both Herron and Hindman. Then he led his brigade down the hill.[25]

Captain William H. Frazier's company of Young's Missouri Cavalry, a part of MacDonald's Brigade, was resting in the woods on the west side of Viney Grove Road when a column of Union cavalry appeared out of nowhere. Startled, the Confederates fired an ineffectual volley and fell back in some disorder. They finally halted on the Samuel Wilson farm a half-mile to the south where they were reinforced by a company from Crump's Texas Cavalry. The rest of MacDonald's Brigade was holding the extreme right of the Confederate line more than a mile to the east, so Frazier was on his own. He ordered his men to dismount and take cover behind the Wilson house and outbuildings. Then he informed Hindman that a large Union cavalry force was threatening Shoup's left.[26]

Wickersham pursued Frazier as fast as the condition of his horses would permit, and a "lively skirmish" erupted on the Wilson farm. As Colonel James O. Gower's First Iowa Cavalry, in the lead, was armed only with pistols, Wickersham called on his own Tenth Illinois Cavalry, commanded by Lieutenant Colonel James Stuart, to drive the Rebels away. The Illinois regiment was equipped with carbines and a battery of four 2-pounder Woodruff guns. Two of the guns closed to within one hundred yards of the Confederate position and came under a "terrible fire" that wounded two artillerymen. One gun was immobilized when its team was killed, but Lieutenant James M. Simeral and twenty troopers of the First Iowa Cavalry dashed forward on foot and dragged it to safety. Moments later all four Woodruffs opened fire with canister. Frazier's men kept their heads down but refused to budge.[27]

Frustrated by his inability to dislodge the Confederates, Wickersham fell back about two hundred yards and arrayed his 1,600 men in line along the north edge of the expansive Wilson wheatfield. A Union officer explained that the purpose of this demonstration was to "gain time by making as great a *show* as possible" and thereby compel the Confederates to "move slowly and cautiously forward." Wickersham obviously believed that the Rebels would react strongly to his presence on Viney Grove Road, yet Frazier and his men were content to stay put and pop away at the distant Federals with their carbines. Wickersham may have been exhausted by the rigors of the previous thirty-six hours. He displayed none of his usual aggressiveness at Prairie Grove and made no effort to "open communication and effect a junction" with Herron. Indeed, Wickersham might have remained immobilized on the Wilson farm for the rest of the afternoon had not Blunt arrived and stirred things up.[28]

Blunt claimed to be the "first man of the First Division on the field," and apparently he was. Accompanied only by his staff and escort company, he reached the West house about 3:15 P.M. Located atop a slight rise four hundred yards east of Viney Grove Road, the house offered an unsurpassed view of the battlefield. The panoramic vista included all of Crawford's Hill and Crawford's Prairie, the Illinois Valley, Prairie Grove, and, in the distance, the Boston Mountains. The only part of the field not visible from the West house was the Confederate rear on the south slope of Prairie Grove. Blunt studied the scene for several minutes. He probably did not see Huston's attack come to grief around the Borden house, but he definitely witnessed the ensuing Confederate counterattack and the subsequent withdrawal of Herron's forces to the north side of Fayetteville Road.[29]

Blunt could not tell whether Wickersham had made contact with Herron, so he took matters into his own hand. He had his headquarters flag unfurled in front of the West house and directed the recently arrived Second Kansas

Cavalry Battery to fire a few shells in Herron's direction, taking care to avoid the tiny blue figures on the valley floor. Finally, Blunt dispatched a group of staff officers to find Herron and tell him that the Kansas Division had come at last. It was this party that Herron encountered midway between the Crawford and West farms a short time later.

News that help had arrived spread like wildfire through the dispirited ranks of the Missouri Divisions. "It was hailed with loud cheers all down our lines you may be assured," wrote an officer in the Twenty-sixth Indiana. Another Hoosier recalled how "every man that had life enough gave a yell that made the rebel yell sound like a baby's cry in comparison." Herron shared the general feeling of relief, reporting that a "new spirit was infused in my command, now almost worn out by the severe work, and they went at it again with increased vigor." The reference to "increased vigor" was an exaggeration, to say the least. By this time the soldiers in the Missouri Divisions were dead on their feet and more than willing to let their comrades in the Kansas Division pick up the slack.[30]

Blunt always believed that his timely arrival at Prairie Grove saved Herron from destruction. "I did not get there a minute too soon as they were preparing to overwhelm him by surrounding him," he wrote shortly after the battle. Several years later Blunt again asserted that he had reached Herron "just as Hindman was making his dispositions to crush him with an overwhelming force." Blunt was not alone in thinking that he had frustrated Hindman's grand design. Many in Herron's command were of the same mind. Sergeant McIntyre of the Nineteenth Iowa, for example, was persuaded that the Kansas Division had appeared "at the very nick of time to turn the wavering fortune of the day." The widespread Federal conviction that Hindman was about to advance and sweep Herron off the field was understandable but incorrect. The increase in Confederate activity on the Ridge west of Fayetteville Road undoubtedly appeared threatening, but it was a response to the movements of Huston's Second Division and was entirely defensive in nature.[31]

By this time several Union batteries were stacked up on Viney Grove Road awaiting instructions. It was a moment made for Blunt. He rushed back to the road and personally led the artillery down to Crawford's Prairie. Bugler William P. Allen of the First Iowa Cavalry watched the cavalcade descend the hill and careen onto the valley floor: "The rapidity and precision with which the Union batteries, coming up on the run under General Blunt's personal direction, swung into position and got down to business, was as interesting as it was novel to us cavalry men, who had been theretofore accustomed only to the desultory fighting of horsemen." The batteries rolled to a halt and deployed on an east-west line about two hundred yards north of the Morton house.[32]

While the gunners readied their weapons, Blunt recklessly continued on to the east, "passing a long distance in front of the enemy, nearly up to Herron's command," to learn as much as he could about the terrain and enemy dispositions. The Confederates paid little attention to the gaggle of horsemen, and Blunt completed his "hasty reconnaissance" without incident. He returned to the artillery line determined to attack as soon as his infantry arrived.[33]

14 CHANGE OF FRONT

THE WELL-DEFINED BROW THAT GIVES THE RIDGE ITS NAME DOES not continue west of Fayetteville Road. The only significant natural feature on that part of Prairie Grove is the prominent bench at the foot of the hill. The Rogers and Morton homesteads were located on the bench, and years of industry had produced a more or less continuous strip of cleared yards, outbuildings, fences, gardens, orchards, and woodlots between Fayetteville and Viney Grove roads. The slope above the bench was thickly wooded save for a rectangular clearing south of the Morton house. A lane ran east-west along the bench between the two roads; another passed north-south over the crest of the hill and connected the Morton house with the church. The lay of the land had tactical implications. The absence of a brow, for example, favored defenders because there was no visual shadow to shelter attackers, but it also exposed defenders to direct artillery fire from Crawford's Prairie.

Hindman had watched and waited for some sign of Blunt's approach on Fayetteville Road since midmorning, but the road remained empty except for occasional sightings of Union cavalry. The brief stir created by Judson's hit-and-run bombardment had long since died away, and the thousands of Rebels arrayed along the south and west sides of Prairie Grove were bored and restless. Shortly before noon "dense columns of smoke" appeared over Cane Hill, a possible indication that Blunt was burning stores in preparation for a rapid movement, but in what direction? Hours passed and still there was no sign of the Kansas Division. Hindman was perplexed. It seemed as though Blunt was marching away from Prairie Grove, not toward it.[1]

Hindman would have been dumbfounded had he known that between 11:00 A.M. and 2:00 P.M. the Kansas Division passed within two miles of the Trans-Mississippi Army without being detected. How this could have happened is difficult to understand, but happen it did. Earlier that day Hindman had sent Thompson's Missouri Cavalry toward Cane Hill to discover, if possible, what Blunt was doing. The Missourians advanced cautiously on Fayetteville Road. Near the junction with Bottom Road, less than two miles from their starting point on Muddy Fork, they engaged in a "sharp little fight" with a company of the Ninth Kansas Cavalry. The Kansans proved obstinate despite their inferior numbers. After thirty minutes of bloodless skirmishing, Thompson broke off the engagement and returned to Muddy Fork.[2]

Thompson commanded the only Confederate cavalry force of any size on the west side of Prairie Grove, but he demonstrated little initiative. In fact, Thompson and his vaunted Missouri horsemen must have spent the afternoon napping, as they failed to see or hear the Kansas Division when it approached on Fayetteville Road and turned north on Bottom Road. (Once on Bottom Road, the Federals were screened by a series of wooded hills and were effectively out of sight of the Confederates.) Because of Thompson's inexplicable failure, Hindman had no inkling that Blunt was moving around Prairie Grove by way of Rhea's Mill. The similarity with the Confederate turning movement on Cove Creek Road earlier in the day is striking. Within the space of twelve hours each commander stole a march on the other.

Around 2:45 P.M. a courier from Captain Frazier, the officer in charge of the Confederate cavalry picket on Viney Grove Road, galloped up to Prairie Grove Church and informed Hindman that a column of Union horsemen was approaching from the northwest. Hindman was not particularly concerned. He made no changes in his dispositions except to order MacDonald, on the Confederate right, to reinforce Frazier. MacDonald detached Young's Missouri Cavalry, but by the time the regiment reached Viney Grove Road after a roundabout and unhurried journey, the situation had changed dramatically. Shortly after 3:00 P.M. Frazier sent a second courier to Confederate headquarters with the alarming information that the Union cavalry was followed by what appeared to be an artillery train. Hindman was jolted by the news. Artillery meant infantry and infantry meant Blunt. He ordered Frost to abandon the Muddy Fork position and "move without delay" to Shoup's support.[3]

Frost promptly initiated a "speedy change of front to rear." He directed Parsons to rush his oversized brigade to the north side of the hill and form on Shaver's left. The Missourians scrambled to their feet amid shouts and drum rolls and hurried toward Prairie Grove Church. At the junction Parsons paused to confer with Hindman, then turned north on the lane that led to the Morton house. As luck would have it, the Missourians struggled over the crest of the hill just as Huston's attack reached its noisy climax around the Borden

Mosby M. Parsons (Civil War Museum at Wilson's Creek National Battlefield)

house. Parsons could not see a thing because of the foliage, but the "crack of thousands of guns" caused him considerable alarm. Assuming that Huston's attack was the reason why he had been sent to Shoup's support, he stopped where he was—probably 250 to 300 hundred yards behind Shaver's left—and prepared for a fight.[4]

Parsons had no formal military education, but he had seen action in Mexico and Missouri and was one of the most experienced senior officers in the Trans-Mississippi Army. He sent his 2,900 infantry into the woods on either side of the lane. The Missourians eventually established an unwieldy line three-fourths of a mile in length. Colonel Josiah H. Caldwell's Missouri Infantry was posted on the left near Viney Grove Road. Then came Colonel Dewitt C. Hunter's Missouri Infantry, Lieutenant Colonel Willis M. Ponder's Missouri Infantry, and Colonel Alexander E. Steen's Missouri Infantry. A fifth regiment, Lieutenant Colonel Charles S. Mitchell's Missouri Infantry, formed in reserve slightly to the rear. At Hindman's direction, the 130 men in Major Lebbeus A. Pindall's Missouri Sharpshooter Battalion remained near the church for the better part of an hour but rejoined Parsons shortly before the close of the battle. Captain Charles B. Tilden's Missouri Battery also remained near the church. Frost reported that the guns "could not be brought into action in consequence of the thick wood and underbrush which covered the field." It was a familiar story.[5]

Frost next instructed Roane to form his command on Parsons's left. Initially Roane's Brigade was composed of only the dismounted Texas cavalry regiments, but the last-minute addition of Colonel John B. Clark's Missouri Infantry provided a significant boost in both firepower and morale. Not knowing what else to do with Roane's makeshift brigade, Hindman had attached it to Frost's Division. Roane had only the vaguest notion where Parsons's left was located, so he led his 1,990 men north on Viney Grove Road and placed them in the "verge of the timber" (by which he meant the edge of the woods) south of the Wilson farm. Although the exact arrangement by regiment is unknown, Colonel Almerine M. Alexander's Texas Cavalry, Lieutenant Colonel George W. Guess's Texas Cavalry, and Major Robert D. Stone's Texas Cavalry were on the left, while Colonel Thomas C. Bass's Texas Cavalry and Clark's Missouri Infantry were on the right. Roane's arrival allowed Frazier's two companies of Missouri and Texas cavalry to abandon their precarious hold on the Wilson house and fall back for a well-deserved rest. Sometime later Young's Missouri Cavalry arrived after its circuitous march from the Confederate right. Still later Thompson's Missouri Cavalry abandoned its fruitless vigil at Muddy Fork and joined the swelling Confederate mounted force on Viney Grove Road. Toward sunset, Hindman moved these mounted units around to Roane's left and extended the Confederate line into the woods along Muddy Fork.[6]

Roane was not much of a soldier and his brigade was the least effective in the army, so Hindman rode to Viney Grove Road to make certain that Roane understood what was expected of him. He informed Roane that a powerful Union force was in his front, or soon would be, and that he was "to hold them in check at all hazards." Hindman's talk must have had the desired effect because Roane had his best day of the war. While Union shells exploded close overhead, Roane rode along his line, joking with officers and men and encouraging everyone to do their duty. A Texan recalled that the portly Arkansas politician stopped in front of his regiment and said that "he was proud of us, to see us look so cool, calm and determined." Satisfied that his command was steady, Roane rode forward and found two or three small clearings along the road suitable for artillery. He placed Captain John G. Reid's Arkansas Battery (two 6-pounder guns) and Captain John C. Shoup's Arkansas Battery (three or more 2-pounder guns) in the clearings, then asked Hindman for additional firepower. In response, Hindman dispatched one section of West's

Arkansas Battery (two 6-pounder guns). Although the guns had little effect on the course of the battle, they produced enough noise and smoke to create the impression that the Confederate left was held by a more substantial force than was actually the case.[7]

By 4:15 P.M. the Confederate line of battle on the north side of Prairie Grove was complete. It was slightly over two miles in length and had a shallow crescent shape because it followed the elliptical contour of the hill. Nineteen infantry regiments and battalions held the center, while ten cavalry and dismounted cavalry regiments and battalions secured the flanks. A handful of guns bolstered the left but nearly all of the artillery was in reserve near the church, unable to go into action because of the dense woods that covered the high ground. Hindman had committed his entire force except for a few scattered companies of infantry and cavalry. There was nothing more he could do. What happened next was up to the Federals.[8]

BLUNT'S INFANTRY FLOWED down the long slope of Crawford's Hill and moved into place alongside the batteries on Crawford's Prairie. The regiments arrived in no particular order, and it took some time to sort them out. Cloud's Third Brigade, or most of it, deployed on the left; Weer's Second Brigade, on the right. Wickersham's ad hoc cavalry brigade remained in place west of Viney Grove Road and became the far right. From left to right, the Union formation consisted of the First Indian, Kansas (Trophy) Battery (three 6-pounder guns, one 12-pounder howitzer), the left wing of the Eleventh Kansas, Second Indiana Battery (four 6-pounder James rifles, two 6-pounder guns), the right wing of the Eleventh Kansas, Thirteenth Kansas, Second Kansas Cavalry, Tenth Kansas, First Kansas Battery (six 10-pounder Parrotts), one company of the Third Indian, two battalions of the First Iowa Cavalry, one battalion of the Third Wisconsin Cavalry, Tenth Illinois Cavalry and Battery (four 2-pounder Woodruff guns), Eighth Missouri Cavalry, and one battalion of the Second Wisconsin Cavalry. Allowing for attrition during the exhausting dash from Rhea's Mill, Blunt probably had a little over 4,000 men on the field, though that number steadily increased as stragglers and additional regiments arrived.

Acting once again on his own authority, Colonel Dye offered Blunt the services of the Twentieth Iowa: "I immediately sent General Blunt word, as we were near him, and there appeared at the time nothing else to do, that the Twentieth [Iowa] would move in conjunction with his forces." Blunt accepted Dye's offer and asked him to align his 270 troops on the left of the First Indian. An officer in the Indian regiment watched the Twentieth Iowa draw

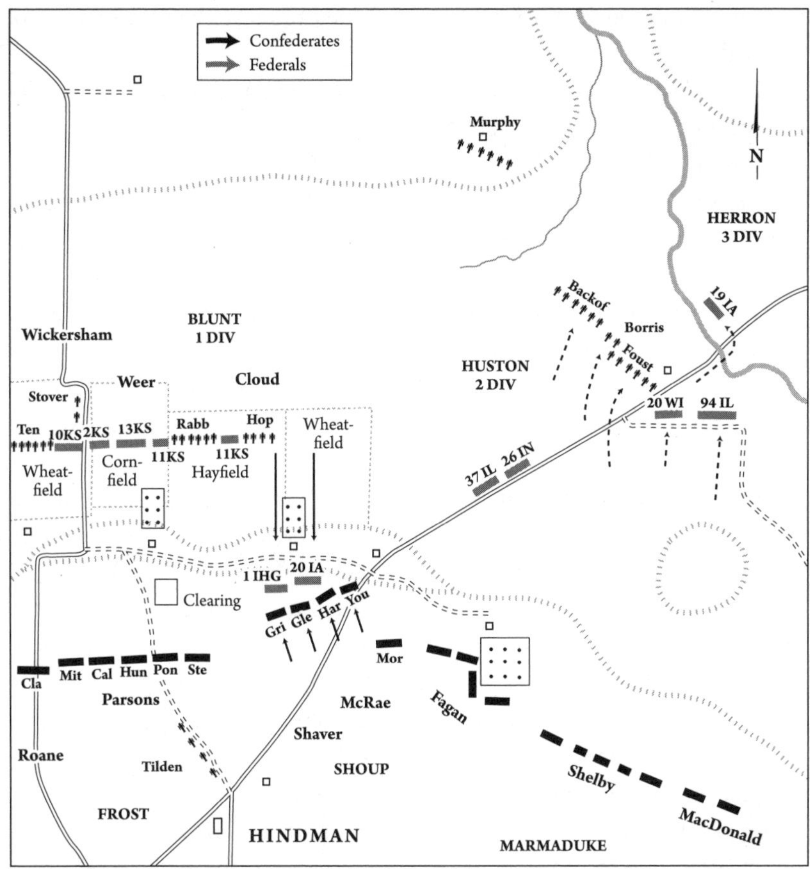

Herron withdraws while Blunt deploys on Crawford's Prairie.
Frost changes front to meet Blunt.

up alongside and realized what it meant. "We had formed the junction with General Herron and nothing now remained to be done but to fight."[9]

The second and final phase of the battle of Prairie Grove began a little before 4:00 P.M., when the three Union batteries on the Morton and Wilson farms roared to life. The sixteen guns poured a "terrible and destructive fire" on the Confederate position west of Fayetteville Road in preparation for an infantry assault. Spencer Mitchell of Mitchell's Missouri Infantry wrote that "furious cannon shells, canister, and grape shot came flying all around us." One projectile narrowly missed Mitchell and crashed into the earth, "throwing the soil sky high and ploughing up the ground with a fury undescribable for one hundred yards when it struck the root of a large oak." Confederate soldiers who had passed a relatively quiet day near Muddy Fork now hugged the ground or crouched behind trees and tried to make themselves as small as possible.[10]

Blunt placed Colonel William Weer, his senior brigade commander present, in charge of the assault. No photograph of Weer is known to exist, but another officer described him as a "bold, bluff, brave man" with a "big head, bushy whiskers, and well knit form," who had the "endurance of a mule and the heart of a lion." Weer was a prominent Kansas attorney and a promising amateur soldier. An admirer called him a person of "exceptional brain power." Unfortunately, Weer also was an alcoholic. Six months earlier he had gone on such a bender that his subordinates removed him from command of the expedition into the Indian Territory. When sober, however, Weer was just the sort of man to lead an attack against a heavily defended hill. At least Blunt thought so.[11]

To have a reasonable chance of driving the Confederates off the hill, or even holding them at bay, Blunt concluded that he would have to attack with his entire available force, that is, he must hit the Rebels with everything he had. At the last moment, however, he decided to keep the left wing of the Eleventh Kansas in place on Crawford's Prairie between the Kansas (Trophy) Battery and the Second Indiana Battery. Blunt's concern for the safety of his artillery was commendable, but his meddling created a gap nearly three hundred yards wide in the Union line, divided the attacking force into two unequal formations, and made it impossible for Weer to exercise effective command. Having sabotaged his own plan of attack, Blunt turned to Weer and directed him to proceed. Shortly after 4:00 P.M. the artillery fell silent and the six infantry and dismounted cavalry regiments advanced.[12]

The smaller of the two Union formations, on the left, was composed of about 520 men in the First Indian and Twentieth Iowa. When Lieutenant Colonel Stephen H. Wattles received the order to advance, he promptly ordered his First Indian forward. Wattles's 250 Creeks and Seminoles knew nothing of close order drill and trotted across the Morton hayfield in a loose formation that resembled a heavy skirmish line. They crossed the bench west of the William Rogers house and plunged into the tangle of vegetation that covered the slope. Halfway up the hill, the Federals spotted a line of Confederate troops thrashing through the woods in their direction. They were about to open fire on the approaching Rebels when they were struck by a shower of bullets, not from the front, but from the rear. In the hurry and confusion, the left wing of the First Indian had drifted across the front of the Twentieth Iowa.[13]

When Wattles ordered the First Indian forward, Lieutenant Colonel Leake quickly followed suit with the Twentieth Iowa. The 270 officers and men of the

Joseph B. Leake (Roger D. Hunt Collection, U.S. Army Military History Institute)

Twentieth Iowa hurried across the West wheatfield at the double-quick, only a few steps behind the Creeks and Seminoles on their right. Leake and Major William G. Thompson advanced on horseback "as cool and self-possessed as [on] an ordinary battalion drill." The Iowans passed through the William Rogers orchard and obliqued around the east side of the house. Leake called a halt on the bench and sent two companies to clear Confederate skirmishers out of the house and outbuildings. The remainder of the regiment loosed volley after volley into the woods "as rapidly as the men were able to load and fire." Now several minutes behind the First Indian, the Iowans resumed their advance. In the dense woods they became disorganized and disoriented, and several companies on the right nervously opened fire at dimly seen figures in their front. Leake ordered his men to stop shooting, fearful that they might be firing on the First Indian. "We were ordered to halt and cease firing," wrote Lieutenant William Steel, "which was done with much reluctance."[14]

Leake was right to be cautious. The shadowy figures ahead of the Twentieth Iowa were indeed members of the First Indian. The burst of fire caused few if any casualties among the Indians, but it triggered a "five-minute panic." The Creeks and Seminoles fell back to the bench in their disorderly fashion. As the Indians streamed around his right flank, Leake noticed many were "gesticulating violently and pointing toward the direction whence they came."

Believing they were trying to warn him of approaching danger, he rode to his left where the woods were slightly more open. When Leake peered through the foliage, he understood what the Indians were trying to tell him. "I saw directly in front of us a mass of troops moving down upon us," he reported.[15]

The Confederate force plowing through the thicket was an ad hoc "brigade" composed of the four Arkansas regiments located west of Fayetteville Road. Three of the regiments belonged to McRae's Brigade, but the fourth, Grinsted's Arkansas Infantry, was part of Shaver's Brigade. Grinsted held the left flank of the Confederate line. When the Federals started up the hill, he called on Shaver for support, but Shaver had no one to send because his four regiments had been parceled out along the line. Grinsted then sought assistance from McRae, only to discover that McRae was nowhere to be found. At this point Shaver stepped forward and persuaded the Arkansas commanders to cooperate, but he declined to assume command. In fact, he faded into the foliage and disappeared without a word. Why Shaver departed, where he went, and who, if anyone, he left in charge are unknowns.[16]

All that can be stated with certainty about this puzzling affair is that it produced the first *organized* Confederate counterattack of the day. From left to right, the formation consisted of Grinsted's, Glenn's, Hart's, and Young's Arkansas regiments, about 1,300 men in all. The Rebels emitted a chorus of shrieks and howls as they started down the slope. An officer in the Twentieth Iowa remarked offhandedly that the Confederate attack was "prefaced as usual by a yell," but otherwise took no notice of the caterwauling. The banshee wail of charging Confederates had lost much of its power to intimidate by this stage of the war.[17]

The Confederates advanced in a northwesterly direction, and their ragged line overlapped the left flank of the Twentieth Iowa. Outflanked and outnumbered nearly five to one, the Iowans "recoiled" from a volley of musketry and fell back in disorder. During the chaotic retreat, Leake rode through the storm of lead shouting orders and encouragement. He survived the ordeal without a scratch and won the admiration of his soldiers, one of whom declared that Leake was "as brave a man as ever rode at the head of a regiment." Dye watched anxiously from the wheatfield as "overwhelming numbers" of Rebels poured down the slope. He ordered Leake "to retire gradually and take a covered position under the hill," but Leake was ahead of him. "Finding the enemy in full force moving down upon us," wrote Leake, "we fell back fighting to the fence at the foot of the hill, from which we continued firing, the Rebels swarming through the orchard after us." Wattles and the First Indian quickly followed suit.[18]

The drop-off from the bench to the valley floor served as a natural rampart for the embattled Federals, who re-formed and fired through the fence rails at the pursuing Arkansans. The Confederates made several attempts to cross the orchard but were beaten back each time. Grinsted claimed that his troops inflicted "considerable slaughter" on the Federals (a considerable exaggeration), though he admitted they could not be dislodged. With matters at an impasse, the Arkansans reoccupied the Rogers house and sought shelter behind the outbuildings and fences.[19]

The Federals were in a tight spot. They were running out of ammunition and could not stay where they were much longer, but neither could they retreat across the valley floor without suffering potentially heavy losses. Cloud had been little more than a spectator to this point; however, with Weer busy on another part of the field, he ordered Hopkins and Rabb to open fire on the Rebels. Officers shouted for the infantry to get down while the artillerymen traversed their guns and howitzers to the left. The range was so short that the sounds of muzzle blasts and exploding shells were nearly simultaneous. The barrage was a frightening experience for the Federals, who lay flat on the cold ground while artillery rounds screamed close overhead, but it was far worse for the Confederates. The rain of metal fragments from exploding shells and case shot "made sad havoc among them," observed Lieutenant Steel of the Twentieth Iowa. The Arkansans abandoned the bench in droves and hurried back up the hill, where the woods provided at least the illusion of protection. "From this terrible artillery fire the Rebels recoiled along their whole line, taking up positions further back in the timber," wrote another Iowa officer. Thus ended the third Confederate counterattack. Like the others, it pushed the Federals off the hill in short order. Unlike the others, it stopped short of the valley floor and resulted in only modest Rebel losses.[20]

Wattles withdrew the First Indian, and Dye ordered Leake to remove the Twentieth Iowa. The order "was obeyed with more or less haste by the whole right and center in about the same time," recalled an Iowa soldier, but two companies on the left were involved in a firefight with Rebels in the Rogers house and were slower to leave. The delay nearly proved fatal for Major Thompson. "The balls were going and coming so fast and thick, and my whole attention was on the enemy who were not twenty yards from us," he informed his wife. "At last I heard some of the boys say 'for God's sake Major get off your horse' or you will be killed, for they [are] shooting at [you] out of the house." Thompson stayed in the saddle and suffered the consequences. "One of the cowardly curs raised [a second-story] window and took good aim, and I was hit that time." The bullet struck Thompson in the hip and exited near his groin but failed to shake his composure: "I quietly rode to Colonel Dye and told him of it." Dye assigned an orderly to escort Thompson to a field hospital. While this little drama played out, the First Indian and Twentieth Iowa took up new positions to the left and rear of Hopkins's battery. The two regiments supported the artillery for the rest of the battle.[21]

The First Indian officially lost two killed and four wounded in the abbreviated attack, a remarkably low casualty rate of only 2 percent, but the Creeks and Seminoles rarely reported minor injuries so the number of wounded may have been somewhat higher. Losses in the Twentieth Iowa were more serious. The regiment absorbed the brunt of the Confederate counterattack and suffered accordingly. During the course of the battle nine soldiers were killed and forty-nine wounded, an overall casualty rate of 11 percent. How many of those fifty-eight men fell in the skirmishing on the valley floor before Blunt's arrival and how many were lost in the push up the hill cannot be determined. From his hospital bed, Major Thompson wrote to his wife that the regiment had performed handsomely: "Our boys fought nobly, every man of them done their duty." His description of his troops applied equally well to himself.[22]

Confederate losses are less certain. Grinsted reported twenty casualties (two killed, nine wounded, and nine missing) but added that a "number of others were slightly wounded." Another account, however, lists twenty-six casualties. Hart reported two killed and twelve wounded in his command. Casualty figures for Young's and Glenn's regiments apparently do not exist. Grinsted submitted a wildly egocentric report in which he claimed that he, not Shaver, organized the counterattack. He also asserted that his regiment led the way down the slope, charged repeatedly through the Rogers orchard, and fell back only after being abandoned by the other Arkansas units. If Grinsted's claims are true, it defies belief that his command could have experienced a casualty rate of less than 9 percent. Unfortunately, Grinsted's highly suspect report is the only surviving official Confederate account of the third counterattack.[23]

Firing sputtered out along the foot of the hill as Federals and Confederates withdrew to their original positions. All eyes now turned a short distance to the west, where the final clash of the day was under way near the Morton house.

15 CONFEDERATE SUNSET

THE ATTACKING FORCE ON THE RIGHT OF THE UNION LINE WAS COMposed of 1,350 infantry and dismounted cavalry from Weer's Second Brigade and Cloud's Third Brigade. It consisted of Colonel Thomas Ewing's wing of the Eleventh Kansas on the left and Colonel Thomas M. Bowen's Thirteenth Kansas, two battalions of Bassett's Second Kansas Cavalry, Major Henry H. Williams's Tenth Kansas, and Lieutenant William Gallaher's company of the Third Indian on the right. Weer gave the order to advance, and the Federals hurried across the Morton cornfield and Wilson wheatfield at the double-quick. No one mentioned plowing through cornstalks, so William Morton may not have followed the same agricultural practices as his neighbors.

Most of the attacking force advanced straight ahead, but the Eleventh Kansas obliqued to the left in order to pass around the east side of the Morton house. This opened a gap between Ewing's regiment and the Thirteenth Kansas. Bowen had his hands full getting his troops across a ravine and failed to notice what was happening on his left, but Bassett alertly detached two companies of his Second Kansas Cavalry to close the gap. Ewing, however, was more concerned about the larger opening between his command and Wattles's First Indian, three hundred yards to the east near the William Rogers house. When the two companies of dismounted troopers arrived, led by the redoubtable Samuel Crawford, Ewing placed them on his left.[1]

Weer called a brief halt atop the bench, allowing his men to catch their breath. The pause also permitted Blunt to catch up. Instead of remaining in the rear as befitted an army commander, Blunt followed close behind the advancing line. He did so, explained a staff officer, "to observe as far as was practicable what was going on, and to direct any movement that might be necessary." In truth, Blunt simply could not stay away from a fight. He established

Thomas M. Bowen (Kansas State Historical Society)

a command post in Morton's yard and signaled Weer to carry on. Weer threw out a screen of skirmishers — Kansans on the left and center, Cherokees on the right — and resumed the advance. Many Federals were struck by the "half stooped characteristic movements of the Indians as they advanced stealthaly from tree to tree as though they were trying to slip up on some game." When the line of battle followed the skirmishers into the woods, a soldier in the Thirteenth Kansas noticed everyone in his regiment "crouching close to the ground" in emulation of the Cherokees. There were no cheers, no huzzahs. The Federals advanced in silence.[2]

Parsons, like Shaver, did not wait for the Federals to come to him but led his 2,900 troops straight down the hill. The converging forces beat their way through the trees and underbrush, neither side able to see more than a few steps ahead, and collided with little warning despite the best efforts of the skirmishers. Only yards from the Eleventh Kansas, a phalanx of gray-clad Missourians emerged from the foliage and leveled their rifles. Ewing barely had time to bellow "Down!" before the Rebels fired. The Kansans sprawled in all directions as a storm of bullets passed over their heads, then clambered to their feet and fired a volley in return. Similar scenes of shock and surprise took place all along the lines. Within minutes every one of Weer's and Parsons's regiments was engaged, and the hillside above the Morton house

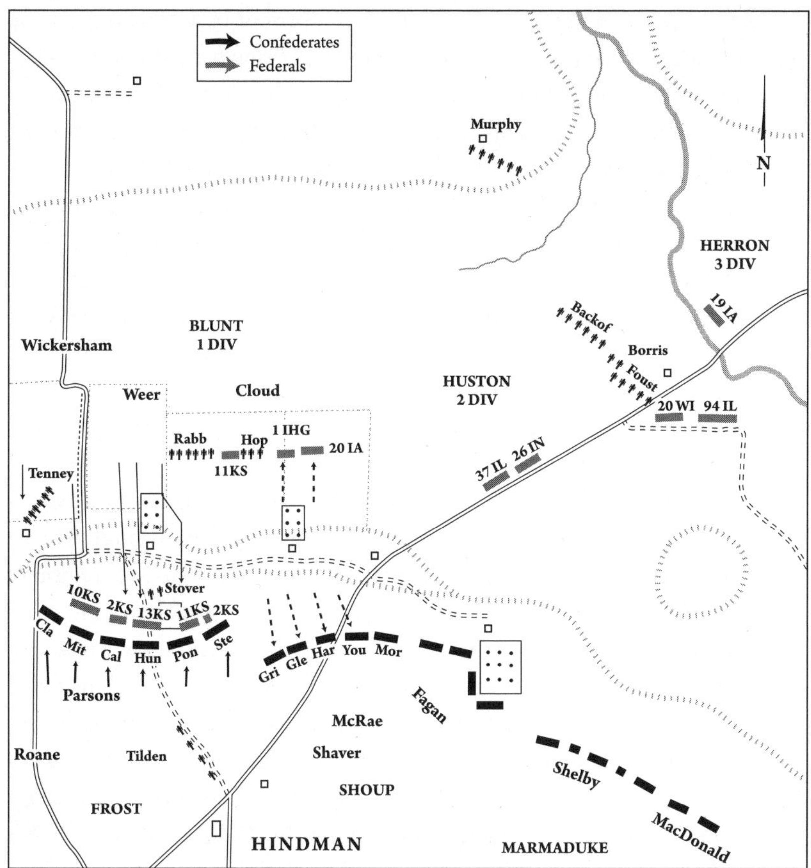

Weer assaults the hill but is repulsed by Parsons.

erupted in flames and smoke. A Union artilleryman on the valley floor wrote that the "firing commenced and increased so rapidly that I had no doubt but what they had struck the Rebs in full force."[3]

Fighting "raged furiously, and without a moment's cessation, along our entire front," reported Blunt. A Union soldier stated that the "fire was incessant, and the balls literally rained upon our boys." Another described a stream of "leaden hail that was simply awful." Following the initial exchange of volleys, the instinct for self-preservation won out and everyone sought cover. Vincent Osborne recalled his comrades in the Second Kansas Cavalry "sheltering themselves as much as possible behind trees" while keeping up a "brisk fire" on the Rebels only a few paces away. "We did not fire by volleys but each man fired when he saw some enemy to shoot at and the enemy fired in the same manner." A soldier in the Eleventh Kansas wrote that the "firing of small arms was almost incessant, a perfect storm of bullets falling around our men, who lay flat on the ground, loading and firing from this position."[4]

The Confederates also went to ground. A soldier in Colonel Caldwell's regiment noted that he and his comrades "lay down upon our knees to avoid the showers of balls that came flying in death-like fury through the trees." The regimental color-bearer, Edward Depp, persisted in waving his flag. The motion drew a shower of bullets that missed Depp but killed another member of the color guard. (The unfortunate soldier "fell and expired without a groan.") Everyone in the vicinity shouted at Depp to lower the flag, and he finally did so. The firefight was no less intense farther to the left, where Mitchell's regiment was located. "I lay down behind a bush about the size of my arm," wrote Spencer Mitchell. "That bush saved my life several times for several bullets struck it right before my head."[5]

Parsons judged the fire to be "more terrible than any I had before experienced during the present war." When he received an erroneous report that the Federals were moving around his left flank, he rushed Mitchell's regiment in that direction. Support for the supposedly threatened flank also came from an unexpected source. Roane sent John Clark's Missouri Infantry, his largest and best-armed regiment, toward the "very heavy firing" to his right front. Clark formed on Mitchell's left, west of Viney Grove Road. Parsons feared for his right flank as well and implored Hindman "to send me up my battalion of sharpshooters." A short time later Pindall's Missouri Sharpshooter Battalion arrived and deployed in the ravine on Steen's right. The accession of Clark's regiment and Pindall's battalion extended Parsons's line in both directions and increased his strength to 3,550 men. The Confederates now had a numerical advantage of nearly three to one.[6]

When Blunt sent his infantry forward, Herron ordered his batteries to resume pounding Confederate positions east of Fayetteville Road. The weary artillerymen responded as best they could, doubtless spurred on by the sights and sounds of Blunt's batteries furiously blazing away at the Rebels on the opposite side of the road. "I commenced firing again, and kept it up until I ran short of ammunition," reported Lieutenant Borris. Herron hoped the renewed rain of shells would pin Shoup and Marmaduke in place and prevent them from moving against the Kansas Division. The Thirty-seventh Illinois and Twenty-sixth Indiana did their part by peppering the woods along both sides of the road with rifle fire. By 4:30 P.M. more than forty guns and thousands of muskets were in action.[7]

"I have not the power of description sufficient to tell you of the grand magnificent sight presented when all our batteries opened, and our whole line for

John B. Clark Jr. (Civil War Museum at Wilson's Creek National Battlefield)

more than a mile in length commenced [firing]," wrote an Iowa officer. The noise was deafening, indescribable. "The cannon roared like thunder while the clash of the small arms was dreadful," penned Christian Keller, a trooper in the Eighth Missouri Cavalry. Soldiers in both armies used the word "roar" to describe the experience. "They talk of the *rattle* of musketry but the sound was one continuous *roar*," remarked an Iowa man. Another Iowan wrote of a "steady roar like a waterfall, or train of cars, that lasted until dark." One Kansas cavalryman noticed that the "roar of artillery and musketry was so heavy that single shots were altogether undistinguishable," whereas another thought the "roar of small arms was such as almost to drown the roar of the cannon." A man in the Eleventh Kansas expressed his belief that "such a roar of musketry and cannon was never heard before on this side of the Mississippi River." He added that veterans of Wilson's Creek and Pea Ridge said those battles "were not to be compared to this one of Prairie Grove." Confederates expressed themselves in similar fashion. "The roar of artillery and musketry beat anything I ever heard, and I have been in several battles," observed Major Thomas H. Murray of Mitchell's regiment.[8]

Participants ransacked their vocabulary to capture the actual sounds of battle. "Cannon balls went shizzing and cutting through the tree tops over our heads, while musket and Minnie balls came cutting, tearing, and hissing among the trees around us," wrote a Missouri Rebel. Some admitted defeat. "I am pretty sure the English dictionary does not contain words that could give but a faint idea of the infernal noise now raised," remarked a Union officer. He concluded that the artillery and musketry "all together made a fuss worthy [of] anything that could be kicked up in Pandemonium."[9]

Watching from afar, a soldier in the Nineteenth Iowa commented that whereas the fight "had raged before with fury it was now terrific and until dark the battle raged with all its terror and with scarce a moments cessation." Weer was slow to realize that he was engaged with a Confederate force much larger than his own and continued to urge his men forward. Captain Eathan A. Pinnell, a Missouri Confederate, was impressed by the tenacity of his opponents. "They made one attack after another with great courage and determination; when driven back at one point, they would rally and try some other." The opposing lines swung back and forth, but the distances gained and lost were measured in yards. The angle of the slope saved many Federals from injury or death because the Confederates frequently overshot their targets. A Union soldier recalled how his company lay on the ground "with a heavy infantry fire whistling over our heads." Ireneus Myers of the Eleventh Kansas was more explicit: "When I think of the time we were engaged and the way the balls flew around us, it looks almost like a merricle that we were not cut to pieces. All that saved us was laying flat on the ground and they shot over us."[10]

The terrified civilians in the Morton cellar undoubtedly prayed for a "merricle" of their own as the battle swirled around their stony sanctuary. They huddled together, numb with fear and cold, while the house above them shook with every concussion. Nancy Morton was the heroine of the hour. She made repeated forays into the house to bring food and blankets to those trapped below. On the opposite side of the valley, the West family watched in horror as the tide of battle engulfed the place where so many of their relatives and neighbors had taken refuge. The clamor of battle extended far beyond the immediate precincts of Prairie Grove. Waves of sound rolled across the Springfield Plain to Fayetteville, ten miles to the northeast, and rattled windows and nerves. The noise even reached the Arkansas Valley, forty miles away on the opposite side of the Boston Mountains, where soldiers and citizens in Van Buren and Fort Smith turned their faces to the north. It was a Sabbath like no one in northwest Arkansas had ever experienced.[11]

Parsons decided the time had come to break the stalemate. "My brave soldiers," he bellowed, "these cut-throats stand between you and your outraged homes. Cut them down and stamp them into the earth! Give them

Rear view of the Morton house showing the steep drop-off from the bench to the valley floor. The Eleventh Kansas advanced around the left of the house, then fell back and made a brief stand in the orchard, which is visible to the right in this 1911 image. (John N. Heiskell Collection, University of Arkansas at Little Rock Archives and Special Collections)

cold steel! *Charge bayonet!*" The Missourians responded with a "wild cheer" and surged down the slope. Weer watched helplessly as thousands of Confederates "arose in the timber with loud yells, surrounding us on all sides, and charged." The Federals gave ground, slowly at first, then with increasing speed as the Confederate line overlapped both flanks of the smaller Union formation. "I think the Rebels was about to over power us," wrote Lieutenant Alfred C. Pierce, Eleventh Kansas. The Kansas Division was in trouble.[12]

At this critical moment Blunt called for the Second Kansas Cavalry Battery. Lieutenant Elias Stover rushed up the lane and placed his two mountain howitzers in the clearing above the Morton house. "The bullets came thick and fast," noted an anxious observer, and the artillerymen "scarcely fired a shot before four of their horses were wounded." The clearing was a dangerous place, but it provided a perfect field of fire for the stubby "bullpups" (or "bitch pups" as some Kansans called them). The howitzers finally crashed into action and blasted the oncoming Confederates with canister. The hail of iron balls "silenced the musketry of the Rebels" and drove them back into the woods, but Stover warned Blunt that his supply of ammunition was limited and he could not stay long. Blunt turned to the First Kansas Battery. Lieutenant Marcus Tenney sent two Parrott guns to the Morton house, where they went into action alongside the little howitzers.[13]

Parsons called up Tilden's Missouri Battery in response, but there was no place for the guns to deploy on the Confederate part of the wooded hillside. The frustrated artillerymen moved from place to place in search of a suitable clearing, all the while under a rain of bullets, balls, and buckshot. "Every shot that was fired at the infantry passed uncomfortably close to us," wrote Sergeant William Bull. "The cannoneers and drivers were permitted to dismount and shield themselves as much as possible behind the carriages and horses which were led, but the officers and sergeants had to remain mounted and set a good example to the men by *appearing* to be indifferent to danger. I don't know how it was with the others but I found it very difficult to avoid *ducking* when the balls seemed to come very close to my head." Tilden and his men eventually followed the infantry down to the foot of the hill, but by then it was too dark to see.[14]

The presence of Union artillery in the Morton clearing stalled but did not stop the Confederate counterattack. Stover ran out of canister and switched to shell and case shot. When that was gone he withdrew. Tenney followed soon afterward. Blunt watched the artillery roll away and instructed Weer to fall back. The Federals west of the Morton clearing got to their feet and hurried down the slope with the Confederates in hot pursuit. The "air was thick with bullets," but they re-formed behind the fences at the foot of the hill. Near the Morton house the drop-off from the bench to the valley floor is unusually deep. The natural rampart afforded welcome protection for the Eleventh Kansas and Thirteenth Kansas. Farther west, however, the drop-off is so shallow that it provided only minimal cover for the Second Kansas Cavalry, Tenth Kansas, and Third Indian. Nevertheless, Weer gave it as his opinion that the terrain saved his command from "annihilation."[15]

The Federals east of the clearing waited almost too long to fall back. The Eleventh Kansas and the two companies of the Second Kansas Cavalry were on the verge of being surrounded by "overwhelming numbers" of Missourians when the order to withdraw finally arrived. Troops and troopers dashed madly down the slope with a "tremendious force" of Confederates close behind. "Almost all the killed and wounded in our Company was hurt while we were falling back," wrote Ireneus Myers. "The nearest I came [to] being hurt was a ball through my coat. I consider myself lucky in getting off." Ewing attempted to form a new line in the lane in front of the Morton house but found that the "enemy was too close upon us to render such formation practicable or the position tenable." In other words, everyone ignored his commands to halt. “I was afraid we would never rally and that we would fall an easy prey to the Rebels,” remembered Silas Marple. The Kansans poured down the drop-off and finally stopped in what Ewing called the “orchard lane,” a narrow space between two parallel fences bordering the north side of the Morton orchard. The right flank of the Eleventh Kansas was one hundred yards or more behind the left flank of the Thirteenth Kansas, but there was no time to make adjustments. The Federals stacked up fence rails and prepared to receive the Rebels.[16]

Parsons’s exultant Missourians swept down the hill. “Rising from our knees we started [after them] and a continual rattle of small arms filled the air, as we kept up a running fire as we advanced,” wrote a solder in Caldwell’s Missouri Infantry. Victory seemed at hand. But as soon as the Confederates reached the bench, they came under renewed fire from the supposedly vanquished Union infantry. An officer in the Thirteenth Kansas wrote that his troops steadied their weapons on the fence rails and “delivered their fire with the deliberation of men attending a turkey hunt.” Union artillery filled the air above the bench with explosions and fragments of metal. “I never enjoyed sweeter music than the shrill screeching of the shells that [the Second Indiana Battery] sent about ten feet over our heads among the Rebels,” wrote a grateful Kansan. Soldiers in gray and butternut dropped by the dozens. Parsons realized that he could go back or he could go forward, but the one thing he could not do was stay where he was.[17]

Weer, too, was in a predicament. Now that both forces had emerged from the woods, the Confederates could see just how short the Union line actually was. Mitchell and Clark, on Parsons’s left, overlapped the right flank of the Tenth Kansas by a wide margin. (By this time Gallaher’s company of the Third Indian was back in line with the Tenth Kansas, so the troops on the far right actually were Cherokees.) Firing volley after volley the Confederates advanced to within 150 yards of the Union position. Major Williams attempted to meet the threat by changing front, but the “leaden rain” forced his Kansans and Indians to return to the shelter of the shallow drop-off. Williams believed it was “almost a miracle that the regiment was not annihilated,” but salvation actually came in the form of the First Kansas Battery. Blunt anticipated the move against Weer’s right and ordered Tenney to move his battery into the Wilson wheatfield on the west side of Viney Grove Road. With Crawford’s Prairie shrouded in smoke, neither Mitchell nor Clark noticed the six Union guns moving in their direction. Tenney placed his battery in a perfect position to enfilade the advancing Rebel line. The first salvo of canister staggered the Missourians; the second sent them reeling backward. Blunt sat his horse a

Henry H. Williams (Kansas State Historical Society)

short distance behind Tenney's guns and watched the brief, bloody affair with grim satisfaction.[18]

Weer's right was safe, at least for the moment, but his left was in imminent danger. Alexander Steen and Willis Ponder pushed into the Morton orchard and exploited the gap between the Eleventh and Thirteenth Kansas. Weer ordered a second withdrawal, and the Federals bolted for the artillery line on Crawford's Prairie. "Then our trouble began," recalled Lieutenant William J. May of the Thirteenth Kansas. "We had been well sheltered by the [drop-off] but as soon as we rose to our feet and started to retire we became a target on three sides for the rebels." May later counted six bullet holes in his uniform. Descriptions of the Union withdrawal varied. Major Williams insisted that his Tenth Kansas retired in "good style," whereas Lieutenant Horace Moore of the Second Kansas Cavalry recalled that "our line crumbled like clay" and we "went back through that cornfield at a very lively pace." Union artillery ceased fire while the shaken infantry and dismounted cavalry re-formed their original line on the valley floor. The Confederates took advantage of the lull. They "followed in vast crowds to the fence and into the field."[19]

The situation looked grim but Blunt was still full of fight. Although his attack had failed, his soldiers had performed well against a force several times larger than their own. Blunt reported that Weer "behaved throughout with great gallantry, leading his men into the thickest of the fight"; he was equally generous in his praise of other officers. For his part, Weer believed the men in ranks deserved "great credit" for the "pertinacity with which they clung to their position or rallied when broken." The fact remained, however, that the Kansas Division had suffered a serious repulse. Whether that would lead to a serious defeat remained to be seen. The battle was not quite over, and Blunt, Weer, and Cloud rode along the Union line offering words of praise and encouragement.[20]

It now was about 5:00 P.M. on a short winter day. The sun had disappeared behind the Boston Mountains fifteen minutes earlier, and the entire field was in deepening shadow. The Confederates were out of time. Unless they landed an immediate and decisive blow, they would have to return to Fort Smith. Hindman was in the rear; Frost was nowhere to be found. The outcome of the battle—the fate of the trans-Mississippi—was in the hands of a Confederate brigade commander. Parsons watched the helter-skelter Union withdrawal from the Morton house and made his decision. "I rode to Colonel Steen and remarked to him that the contest must be closed and that I had determined to charge the enemy with the bayonet."[21]

Parsons had not witnessed the earlier Confederate counterattacks against Herron's divisions. He underestimated the steadfastness of the Federal artillerymen and the effectiveness of their weapons on the level surface of Crawford's Prairie. He also underestimated the resiliency of the Federal infantry. Finally, he may have underestimated (or, more likely, refused to acknowledge) the power of his own emotions. Like every Missourian in the Confederate army, Parsons desperately wanted to liberate his home state and avoid spending another dreary winter in exile. If that meant risking everything on one last charge, so be it. The Federals appeared to be on the ropes. It was time to finish them off.

Both wings of the long, disjointed Confederate line had swung forward and inward while attempting to envelop the Union position at the foot of the hill. In the rush to get under way before darkness cloaked the field, Parsons chose not to waste time realigning his command. Steen and Ponder on the right, and Mitchell and Clark on the left, simply stepped off in the direction they were facing. As the two wings advanced across the valley floor on a shallow converging course, they passed diagonally across the center of the Confederate line and blocked Josiah Caldwell's and Dewitt Hunter's regiments. One of Caldwell's soldiers stated that his company took only a few steps forward before "our officers called us back and prevented us from going on to try to capture the enemies cannon as we were expecting to do." This traffic

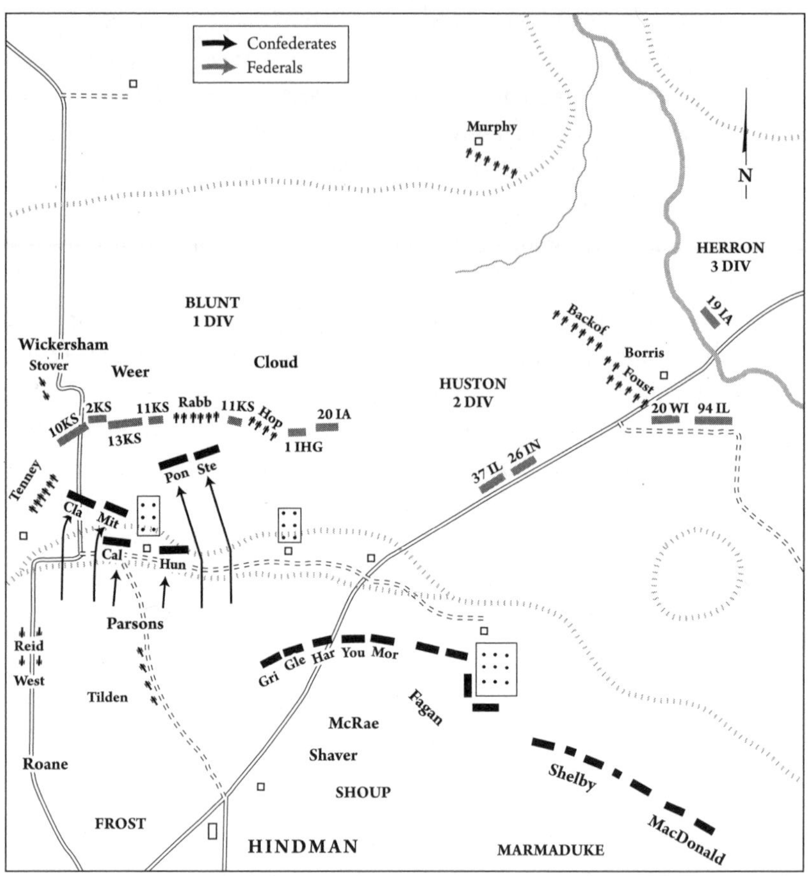

The final Confederate counterattack

jam kept Parsons's two largest regiments out of the final stage of the counterattack. Parsons had provided more effective leadership at Prairie Grove than any other Confederate officer, but at the critical moment, when the outcome of the battle hung in the balance, he was unable to bring the full power of his reinforced brigade to bear on the Federals.[22]

Alexander Steen was a native Missourian who had served with distinction in Mexico and had been commissioned directly into the regular army not once, but twice. He had seen action at Wilson's Creek and Lexington, and his well-drilled regiment was among the best in the Trans-Mississippi Army. When Steen received Parsons's order to advance, he rode out in front of his regiment and pointed his sword toward the Union line. "Remember that yonder is the way to your homes," he shouted. The Missourians responded with "wild ringing shouts" and surged forward. The fourth and last Confederate counterattack was under way. Four regiments clad in gray and butternut hurried across the Wilson and Morton farms at the double-quick, officers and men alike cheering for Missouri. Some Federals were impressed, some were not. "They came on with a yell" was all a laconic Kansan had to say. Blunt's batteries fell silent for a moment as the gunners prepared to repel an infantry assault, and the high-pitched Rebel wails could be heard all the way to the Illinois River.[23]

"It was then pandemonium broke loose," wrote a Kansas soldier. Parsons's men were barely one hundred yards from Blunt's line when the Union artillery roared back to life with a tremendous rolling crash. The ground shook and a visible shock wave roiled the smoky air as all sixteen Union guns went off within seconds of one another. Clark and Mitchell, on the Confederate left, were savaged a second time by the First Kansas Battery. A Missourian wrote that Tenney and his men fired their "infernal contents of grape and canister shot right into the midst of our regiment." Moments later the Tenth and Thirteenth Kansas entered the fray. "The minnie balls of fifteen hundred muskets came whizzing around us. The sky was fairly darkened by the bullets, and for awhile the noise of musketry silenced that of the artillery." Overwhelmed by the storm of iron and lead, the two Confederate regiments turned and disappeared into the gloom. Half of Parsons's attacking force was out of the fight.[24]

Steen and Ponder, on the Confederate right, paused halfway across the hayfield and fired a volley toward the Second Indiana Battery. "I answered with canister," Rabb reported. "For fifteen minutes my men stood firm, firing their pieces with terrible precision, making [in]roads in the ranks of the enemy, which were quickly filled by fresh men from the rear." A soldier in the Eleventh Kansas, his fingers jammed in his ears, watched in morbid fascination as the Indiana gunners "sent the grape and shell at them at a most furious rate, and literally mowed them down." To an Iowa trooper, Rabb's battery "appeared to be in one constant sheet of flame, so rapid were the discharges." Hopkins's Kansas Battery joined in from the left and enfiladed the Confederate lines with "well-directed and rapid discharges of spherical case and canister." The Rebel formations disintegrated, but here and there groups of men continued to stumble forward. Cloud directed Rabb and Hopkins to retire by prolonges, and they did so, firing all the while. The Eleventh Kansas kept pace with the artillery, the men slowly walking backward with their faces turned toward the enemy.[25]

After each salvo of canister and volley of buck and ball, the Missourians "staggered back like drunken men, then rallied and pushed on again." The

Federals could not help but admire the courage displayed by their adversaries. Even Blunt acknowledged that the Confederates exhibited "boldness and determination" in the final moments of the battle. But there was only so much men could take. Steen was struck in the forehead and killed instantly. Lieutenant Colonel William C. Chappel, his second in command, went down minutes later. The surviving Missourians turned and fled "in the utmost disorder, leaving the field strewed with dead and wounded." By this time, observed a Kansan, "it was already so dark that the fire could be seen streaming from the guns at every discharge." A burning haystack at the south end of the hayfield provided enough illumination for Rabb's battery to send a few last rounds of canister after the fleeing Rebels. The final Confederate effort to win the day had failed.[26]

As the remnants of Steen's and Ponder's regiments streamed back across the hayfield, the Confederate infantry near the foot of the hill opened a belated harassing fire on the Federals. Hundreds of muzzle blasts flared in the darkness from Viney Grove Road to the Morton house. "It reminded me of seeing a post-oak ridge on fire," wrote a Missouri soldier. At the same time the handful of guns on Viney Grove Road resumed firing on the Kansas Division. The First Kansas Battery responded with a half-dozen well-aimed shots that scattered the Confederate gunners and silenced their guns. "I could see the Rebs faces by the light of our shells that exploded in their midst," recalled a Kansas artilleryman. As the light failed the firing slackened "until there were only a few fiery arches in the gathering darkness, then these ceased and the silence was painful." Thus ended the battle of Prairie Grove.[27]

THE FIGHTING AROUND the Morton house cost Blunt 190 soldiers, or 14 percent of Weer's attacking force. Hardest hit was the Tenth Kansas, which lost 69 men (6 killed and 63 wounded), a casualty rate of 18 percent. In the Thirteenth Kansas 56 men were lost (8 killed, 43 wounded, and 5 missing), a 15 percent casualty rate. The Eleventh Kansas lost 38 men (7 killed and 31 wounded). Nearly all of the losses occurred in Ewing's wing, which experienced a 12 percent casualty rate. The numbers seem low considering how close the Eleventh Kansas came to disaster, not once but twice, but Ewing had an explanation: "My command suffered less than might have been expected, owing to our position being at all times lower than that of the enemy, who generally overshot." Ewing and his men also benefited from the protection afforded by the drop-off at the foot of the hill. In the Second Kansas Cavalry, 4 troopers were killed and 20 wounded, a 7 percent casualty rate. Among the dead was Captain Avra P. Russell, the highest-ranking officer in the Kansas Division lost at Prairie Grove. One soldier in the Third Indian was killed and another wounded.[28]

The Union artillery also experienced losses in the final moments of the counterattack. The Second Indiana Battery was engulfed in the hottest part of the fight on the valley floor and took a beating. Rabb wrote that the "carriages of the battery bear marks of the storm of bullets and buckshot poured upon us." He reported two men wounded, four horses killed, and twelve horses wounded. Tenney listed one dead and ten wounded in the First Kansas Battery, but a postwar history listed two dead in addition to the wounded. None of the men or animals in Hopkins's Kansas Battery received a scratch.[29]

The Union cavalry regiments west of Viney Grove Road were essentially inactive after Blunt and the infantry arrived, and their losses were correspondingly low. "We fired but few shots and not one Second Wisconsin man was hurt," reported a trooper in that regiment. The Third Wisconsin Cavalry also emerged unscathed despite being within easy reach of Roane's artillery. "Two Confederate cannon were firing at us all afternoon, and every shell went over our heads," recalled Addison B. Myers. One trooper in the First Iowa Cavalry was wounded during the initial skirmish on the Wilson farm, but the Hawkeyes suffered no other casualties despite moving across the road to the Morton cornfield just before the Confederate counterattack. The skirmish also left two men wounded in the Tenth Illinois Cavalry. After the fighting sputtered out, Blunt ordered Wickersham to fall back a mile or two and watch for "any flank movement of the enemy" toward Rhea's Mill. Blunt kept an eye on his line of communications to the very end.[30]

CONFEDERATE COMMANDERS, true to form, all but ignored the last and largest counterattack of the day in their official correspondence. Frost did not include one word about it in his report even though three-fifths of his division was involved. Parsons provided a brief account of the struggle on the hill (which his Missourians won) but failed to mention the final assault on the valley floor (which his Missourians most decidedly did not win). If Mitchell, Steen, Hunter, Ponder, Caldwell, Pindall, or Clark submitted reports, they have not survived. For the record, reports exist from only *two* of the fifteen Missouri regiments, battalions, and batteries at Prairie Grove (Young's Missouri Cavalry and Roberts's Missouri Battery). The small number raises suspicions that Missouri division and brigade commanders either lacked basic administrative skills or acted in concert to put forward a sanitized version of events. For purposes of comparison, *seven* reports exist from the fifteen Arkansas units in the battle.[31]

The reported number of Confederate casualties in the final stage of the battle was low—one is tempted to say *unbelievably* low—considering the horrific carnage described by soldiers in both armies. Parsons claimed an overall loss of 435 men (45 killed, 341 wounded, and 49 missing) out of roughly 3,550 engaged, a casualty rate of only 12 percent. (The 39 percent casualty rate in Fagan's Brigade was more than three times as heavy.) Reported losses by regiment in Parsons's Brigade are even more perplexing, because there is only a modest distinction (and sometimes no distinction at all) between regiments that sat out the final counterattack and regiments that literally charged up to the cannon's mouth. According to a variety of sources, including unofficial tallies published in Missouri newspapers, Steen's Regiment lost 96 men (17 percent); Ponder's Regiment, 72 men (14 percent); Caldwell's Regiment, 48 men (7 percent); Hunter's Regiment, 51 men (7 percent); Mitchell's Regiment, 20 men (5 percent); Clark's Regiment, 26 men (5 percent); and Pindall's Battalion, 3 men (2 percent). Roane reported seven Arkansas and Texas soldiers struck down by Union artillery.[32]

Whatever the actual cost in blood, five hours of desperate fighting had produced a stalemate. Hindman's bold gambit had failed. The best he could hope for now was an opportunity to retire with army and honor intact.

16 RETREAT

ALEXANDER CAMERON, A TROOPER IN CRUMP'S TEXAS CAVALRY, thought the day had gone well. "It was the full calculation of all that I saw that night after the battle that we had whiped them and that we would renew the battle next morning if they were there." The actual situation was more complicated. Although the Confederates defended their hilltop position against repeated Union assaults, they failed to achieve any of their larger objectives. In fact, by bringing the widely separated wings of the Army of the Frontier together at Prairie Grove, the Confederates strengthened the Union military presence in northwest Arkansas to such a degree that a Rebel advance into southwest Missouri no longer was possible.[1]

When the sun set on 7 December so did Hindman's dream of a resurgent trans-Mississippi Confederacy, but it would not do to make such a damaging admission in public. Hindman reported that "at dark the battle closed, leaving us masters of every foot of the ground on which it was fought," but he knew perfectly well that possession of Prairie Grove meant nothing. After the fighting ended, Hindman conferred with his staff and division commanders and ordered a withdrawal. He explained that his command was short of food and ammunition, which was true, and that it was outnumbered, which was not. He also remarked, rather oddly, that his "battery animals were literally dying of starvation, and could not be foraged in the presence of a superior force of the enemy." Had Hindman been more forthright, he would have added that his attempt to defeat the Federals in detail had failed, albeit by the slimmest of margins, and that there was no reason for the logistically challenged Trans-Mississippi Army to remain north of the Boston Mountains.[2]

Members of the rank and file rarely think in strategic terms, and Hindman's soldiers found the order to withdraw unfathomable. "With mortification, we were compelled by our General to leave the field so gallantly won," wrote an unhappy Arkansan. When the withdrawal began, many Confederates believed they were changing positions to prepare for a second day of battle. "We had not the least idea of retreating," recalled one Rebel, "but around midnight we were roused up with orders to march, but only expected an advance instead of a retreat. Starting off, we soon discovered to our surprise that we were actually retreating." A perplexed Captain Ethan Pinnell informed his diary that "we held the battlefield until midnight, when General Hindman ordered a retreat, for what reasons I am unable to tell, though I suppose *he* deemed them sufficient." A few sentences later Pinnell's exasperation showed through: "We have whipped the foe, whipped him badly . . . but Hindman says retreat, and off we go for Van Buren." Missourians like Pinnell were particularly devastated. A Texan observed that a few days earlier the Missouri troops in Frost's Division were "rejoicing to think that they had some prospect of geting back to their own State but when they were ordered back they seemed considerably down in the mouth." Some Confederates agreed with Hindman's decision to depart. "Had we remained one day longer we would have nearly starved," declared a Texas officer. "On the day of the battle I had five corn dodgers and two crackers in my haversack, and I was better off than nine-tenths of the men."[3]

The exodus began before midnight. Shoup's and Frost's infantry and artillery quietly pulled back from their positions atop the hill and departed on Cove Creek Road. Exhausted men and emaciated animals trudged south until dawn, rested for several hours at Morrow's, then continued across the mountains. The small Confederate train at Hogeye fell back on Telegraph Road and rejoined the main body at Lee Creek. The first stage of the withdrawal took the better part of two days. "Men much fatigued and the command mutch scattered," scribbled a Missouri officer. He might have added that men and animals were consumed with hunger. "Every tree that had horses tied to them had the bark knawed off," wrote a Union cavalryman who followed the Rebel column. "Grape vines two and three inches in diameter were knawed clear off." The circumstances reminded some of an earlier Confederate fiasco. Colonel McRae informed his wife that "I have been over the mountain again and have been Van Dorning of it," a caustic reference to the disastrous retreat after Pea Ridge. "I never in my life have been so sleepy," McRae confessed. "Could not ride a horse as I would fall off and would go to sleep while walking along." At least McRae had a horse.[4]

Some Confederates suffered more than others. Artillerymen wrapped blankets around the wheels of their vehicles to muffle the sound of cannons, caissons, and limbers rumbling over the stony ground. "We willingly gave up our blankets for this purpose," remembered William Bull of Gorham's Missouri Battery, "believing it was the intention to move silently and take a position near the enemy and resume the fight in the morning." A few hours later the artillerymen learned they were returning to Fort Smith. Then came the awful realization that the iron-rimmed wheels and flinty rocks had reduced their blankets to shreds. The Missourians endured the next three nights without shelter or cover. Their ordeal may have been for naught because the forest that covered Prairie Grove probably did more to mask the noise of the withdrawal than threadbare blankets. Even so, Union pickets on Crawford's Prairie heard "sounds like artillery moving but in what direction we could not tell." The Federals assumed Hindman was repositioning his guns for a second day of battle and did not inform their superiors.[5]

Marmaduke's cavalry stayed on the field to screen the withdrawal and to collect as many discarded weapons as possible. The number of Confederate horsemen increased by four hundred when Monroe's Brigade arrived around 9:00 P.M. After spending the previous night on Reed's Mountain, the Arkansans had moved "slowly and cautiously" up the Jordan Valley in the wake of the Kansas Division. They encountered no resistance and occupied Boonsboro without incident. Monroe held the town until sunset, then proceeded to Prairie Grove on Fayetteville Road. Hindman asked Monroe if he had any information about Cooper's command. Monroe did not, but Hindman later learned that Watie and a pickup force of six hundred men (mostly Cherokees and Choctaws) had reached Evansville on 6 December. After milling around on the Line Road for forty-eight hours, the Indians departed. The third prong of the Confederate offensive had failed to materialize.[6]

Some Confederates delayed their departure from Prairie Grove for personal reasons. Columbus Gray returned to the Borden orchard, where the body of his brother James lay amid the shattered fruit trees. "Just at night I went to him. Oh my god he looked so pale and bad and there was a teare in one of his eyes. I through my armes around him and hallowed to some of the boys to come and help me carry him off of the field and they would not come to me . . . so I laid him on his back and straitened him out and had to leave him." Gray begged his parents to help salve his loss: "You must write to me often for I do feel mity sad and lonesome." Sergeant Samuel P. Pittman was another man on a mission. After the shooting stopped, he slipped away and visited his family home on the east side of Prairie Grove. When he returned he found that his regiment had departed: "It was midnight, and up from the orchard came cries and groans, and men calling for water." Pittman carried three canteens that he had just filled from his own well. He spent the next hour moving from form to form in the orchard, giving a drink to all who begged for help. His canteens empty, Pittman set out after his comrades with a heavy heart.[7]

Other Confederates performed missions of mercy in a more organized fashion. As soon as the shooting stopped, soldiers slipped out of the ranks and made their way down the slope in search of missing comrades. Ambulances and stretcher bearers appeared a little later. An easterly breeze dissipated the smoky haze, and the full moon, only two days past its prime, washed the field in a milky light. A Union soldier on picket duty wrote that "great commotion was observed among the rebels, whose ambulances could be seen constantly moving from point to point among the timber on the hill." The horror of death or serious injury at Prairie Grove was magnified by the presence of feral hogs. Ozark farmers allowed their swine to forage in the woods, and by the time of the Civil War the countryside was swarming with thousands of "razorbacks." Rebels from Arkansas and Missouri were aware of the danger posed by these powerful and voracious creatures. They gathered seriously wounded men into groups for mutual protection and placed revolvers in the hands of those who seemed most likely to remain alert or at least conscious. The Confederates also dragged corpses into piles and surrounded them with fence rails to ward off the hogs. Not immediately understanding the reason for the enclosed heaps of bloody bodies, mystified Union soldiers dubbed them "slaughter pens."[8]

A few kind-hearted Rebels went out of their way to comfort their adversaries. George C. Miller, Twentieth Iowa, fell on the slope above the William Rogers house. During the night two Arkansas soldiers gave him water and carried him to the top of the hill, where they built a small fire to provide heat and light. Miller survived but never learned the names of his benefactors. Captain Samuel E. Payne of the Nineteenth Iowa had a similar experience in the Borden orchard. Additional acts of kindness certainly occurred, but not everyone was moved by the plight of the wounded. Some Rebels scrounged the field for anything of value. They stripped dead and wounded soldiers of coats, shirts, pants, socks, shoes, and equipment; sliced buttons off blood-soaked clothes; removed wedding rings (sometimes cutting off fingers in the process); and turned out pockets and packs in search of money, watches, knives, lockets, spectacles, and other valuables.[9]

The Confederate effort waned as the night wore on and the Trans-Mississippi Army departed. A Texas cavalryman named George A. Watford was on picket duty near Viney Grove Road. He was surrounded by the "continual moans of the wounded, which ranged from the slightest expression of pain to that expressing the greatest agony. About 2 o'clock all became quiet, as suffering had become too much for human endurance and many had given up the struggle for life, or had frozen, as the night was very cold." The temperature fell to eighteen degrees by morning. How many perished from exposure will never be known.[10]

For the Confederates, it was the second consecutive night without adequate food or sleep and the withdrawal proceeded at a snail's pace. Hindman grew anxious as the hours passed and dawn approached. If Blunt launched a vigorous pursuit at first light, he might overtake the rear of the retreating column before it reached the safety of the Boston Mountains. Hindman decided to gain additional time by reaching an understanding with Blunt. Around 3:00 A.M. Marmaduke cautiously approached Herron's position on Fayetteville Road and told his bugler to sound the call for a parley. The unfamiliar notes caused quite a stir on the Union side of the field. "We were all up at once," wrote Colonel Orme. When it seemed safe to proceed, Marmaduke entered the lines of the Thirty-seventh Illinois with a white flag and demanded to meet with Blunt. When asked the purpose of his visit, Marmaduke replied flippantly that he wanted to know if the Federals "were going to surrender." The ill-advised remark generated a heated response. After everyone cooled down, Marmaduke was blindfolded and taken to the Crawford house. There he proposed to Herron that the army commanders hold a "personal interview" to arrange a truce. Intrigued, Herron forwarded Marmaduke's proposal to Blunt at the West house. Blunt agreed to a meeting "without delay" and Marmaduke departed. The Union response was just what Hindman had hoped for.[11]

The "personal interview" took place in the Hugh Rogers house between 9:00 and 10:00 A.M. on 8 December. Hindman, Marmaduke, and a handful of staff officers represented the Confederate side. The Union delegation included Blunt, Herron, several staff officers, and a gaggle of "curiosity seekers." A Union officer observed that Hindman was "courtly and affable, diminutive in size, has brown curly hair and spare features and shows ability and daring." Widely circulated secondhand accounts claimed that Blunt and Hindman traded insults and nearly came to blows, but in fact everyone behaved in a civil manner and the meeting was quite businesslike. Following a round of introductions, Hindman proposed a truce of thirty-six hours to care for the wounded (and, of course, allow his army to withdraw unmolested). Blunt replied that six hours would be adequate. Hindman agreed to the shorter truce with the understanding that it would begin after the meeting ended. (This meant that the truce would expire just before sunset, too late for the

Federals to mount an effective pursuit.) The conversation then turned to practical matters such as succoring the wounded, burying the dead, exchanging and paroling prisoners, protecting medical personnel, and policing the truce. The final order of business was the selection of a suitable name for the battle. Blunt and Hindman quickly agreed on "Prairie Grove." No other Civil War engagement was christened by mutual agreement of the opposing commanders.[12]

Blunt later professed to be incensed by Hindman's duplicity in proposing a truce to cover the withdrawal of his army. "Had I discovered that his force had already gone and [was] in the mountains beyond my reach, I would not have given him ten minutes." Years afterward he still expressed outrage that the "sacredness of a truce had been prostituted, and proved to be a trick of the high-toned chivalry to get their defeated army out of further danger." But both Blunt and Herron told Curtis they could see the Confederates had withdrawn during their ride to the Rogers house. No unwounded Rebels were in sight save ambulance drivers and stretcher bearers. Blocher's guns had vanished and the shattered, blackened forest atop the hill was empty. "On meeting [Hindman]," reported Blunt, "I soon became satisfied that no other force was there, except his staff and escort and a party to take care of the wounded." Hindman's ruse was "perfectly transparent," wrote an officer on Herron's staff, but the "etiquette of war" required everyone to pretend that nothing untoward was happening. Hindman was anxious to be gone, and Blunt was just as anxious to have him gone. To put it a bit more elegantly, when it became clear that Hindman was willing to leave Blunt in undisputed possession of the field in return for a clean getaway, Blunt was agreeable. The indignation over Hindman's supposed "prostitution" of a "sacred" truce was manufactured for public consumption after the fact. Political spin was in play long before the twentieth century.[13]

The "personal interview" ended with Hindman satisfied that he had secured the safe withdrawal of his army. Marmaduke gathered up his cavalry and hurried after the infantry and artillery. Hindman stopped briefly at the church to explain the terms of the truce to the surgeons, then departed with his staff and escort company. He was among the last Confederates to leave Prairie Grove. By noon the battlefield was in Union hands.

Few of the Rebels slogging south on Cove Creek Road had much interest in the posturing of generals. Most were happy to have passed through the "dreadful, awful, bloody, bloody battle" without serious injury. Colonel Hawthorn could not account for his good fortune: "I never dismounted during the entire engagement, and yet strange to say, though I was in the hottest fire . . . I never received a single scratch, nor was my horse touched by a single bullet. My battle flag was literally riddled with bullets." The nineteenth century was a religious age, and many soldiers believed they were alive only because of divine intervention. Arkansan Dan Thomas confided to his wife that when the shooting started, "I felt as though I would be protected. I did not know what to do but when we went to fighting I put my trust in the Saviour and went ahead." Phillip Smith felt the same way. "I was not mutch excited," he told his wife, "for I trusted to my God for my life and he spared it." Still another Arkansan, James Edmondson, was content to be counted among the living, whatever the reason: "The first thing that I thought of when the battle opened was my family, and that was on my mind when it ended." Survivors also shared a newfound respect for their opponents. "One thing I do know the Feds fought well," wrote a trooper in Crump's Texas Cavalry.[14]

It took two days for the Trans-Mississippi Army to march from Lee Creek to Van Buren. There was little pomp and less ceremony when the weary men and animals shuffled through town on 11 December and established temporary camps along the north side of the Arkansas River. Captain Pinnell marked the occasion in his diary: "I got here last evening completely exhausted by hard marches, day and night, without rations or sleep, my feet badly blistered." An Arkansas soldier admitted to his wife: "I am in very low spirits lower than I ever was. I dont have any hope of the Confederacy gaining her independence by fighting." The entire command was gripped by despondency. "All discouraged," wrote a dejected Missouri officer.[15]

Public criticism of Confederate generalship at Prairie Grove was muted because of the widespread desire, then and later, to portray the battle as a heroic fight against overwhelming odds. Nevertheless, a good deal of frustration was vented in private correspondence. Hindman had made no secret of his intention to take the Federals by surprise, but things had turned out rather differently. "We got there just as General [Herron's] whole force from Missouri got up," Colonel McRae told his wife. "So if anybody was surprised it was our side." Colonel Hawthorn believed that Hindman opened with a "most splendid and masterly" turning movement, but thereafter allowed the initiative to slip from his fingers. "We did not pursue our advantage with sufficient rapidity," Hawthorn wrote. "We ought to have thrown our whole force upon one part [of the Union army] and destroyed it, before the other could come to its relief; instead of which, we halted, fronted to all points of the compass . . . and waited for the enemy to come to us." An unidentified officer on Hindman's staff offered a possible explanation for the passivity that puzzled Hawthorn. Hindman, the officer wrote, was "always distrustful of his own skill in handling troops in the field, because he had not been bred a soldier." He believed this was the reason Hindman was reluctant to impose his will on Marmaduke, Shoup, and Frost despite repeated instances of "hesitation and confusion" on their part. Hindman, however, never blamed anyone but himself for what happened at Prairie Grove.[16]

Determined to dispel the malaise afflicting his command, Hindman issued a stirring address in which he praised volunteers and conscripts alike for standing firm against repeated assaults by a powerful "abolition army." He closed with a simple but heartfelt expression of appreciation to all who had done their duty: "I am proud of you and thank you." The next day Hindman went a step further and announced his intention to recognize members of the rank and file for acts of heroism. He ordered commanders of every regiment, battalion, and battery to nominate one soldier "whose conduct was preeminently brave" at Prairie Grove. Division commanders were instructed to evaluate the nominations from their respective commands and select the three most deserving soldiers for special recognition. In an age before medals and citations were commonplace, it was an innovative attempt to reward dedication and devotion.[17]

Other Confederates also attempted to put the best possible face on the abortive campaign. A Missourian argued that Prairie Grove "deserves classification as a *failure* and not as a *disaster* by any means," while an Arkansas soldier believed the battle demonstrated "that the 'Arkansas conscript' will not only fight, but is a hero equal to any of antiquity." A Texan agreed. "Our army will fight like tigers," he wrote. "They fought desperately enough at Prairie Grove. The enemy did not gain an inch during the whole battle." Another Missourian seconded that notion. "Never did men fight with more courage and determination than the southern boys on the bloody field of Prairie Grove." Such comments, while understandable, could not disguise the fact that the objective of the campaign was to eliminate Blunt and open the road to Missouri, not defend an obscure hill in northwest Arkansas. Realization that the Confederate cause had suffered a major setback slowly sank in. In the immediate aftermath of the battle the editor of the *Little Rock True Democrat* was surprisingly upbeat, but a few weeks later he wrote that "matters wear a gloomy aspect" because the campaign had been a "disastrous" failure.[18]

Hindman knew that he had fumbled away an extraordinary opportunity. His troubled state of mind is reflected in a second "conversation by telegraph" with Theophilus Holmes on 12 December. "I am very proud of my troops," Hindman began, but "not satisfied with myself. I did not press the enemy as vigorously as I ought. The tremendous responsibility made me timid." Holmes assured Hindman that the decision to withdraw was correct. Had the Confederates remained at Prairie Grove a second day and suffered a serious reverse, "all would have been lost."

The discussion turned to the wisdom of keeping the Trans-Mississippi Army at Fort Smith. Holmes did not think such a large force could be sustained indefinitely on the frontier. He also feared that Blunt might attempt to cross the Boston Mountains below Fort Smith and cut Hindman off. Holmes wanted Hindman to retire closer to Little Rock. Hindman desired to stay where he was and have another go at Missouri in the spring. A polite contest of wills ensued. "I don't wish to contend," Hindman telegraphed, but "I fear you do not understand the merits of this position [Fort Smith]. It may not be necessary to retire at all." Holmes usually gave in to Hindman, but on this occasion he stood his ground. "I deeply regret differing with you because I have the highest appreciation of your strengths but any mishap and the Trans-Mississippi Department is gone. I hope you will think with me in this." Sensing, perhaps, that Holmes would not be moved, Hindman agreed to evacuate Fort Smith. A few moments later he lapsed into a somber and introspective mood: "I feel so completely dissatisfied about my failure to destroy the enemy's force that I think seriously of quitting the service. I believe I am only useful in organizing and providing. I don't know enough to handle an army in the field." Holmes advised Hindman to "forget the past if it is painful and be yourself." On that enigmatic note the "conversation" ended.[19]

Holmes was so disturbed by Hindman's tone that he decided to visit Fort Smith and see the situation for himself. He arrived on 18 December after a tedious journey up the Arkansas on a light-draft transport. The next day he reviewed the army. The officers and men of Shoup's and Frost's divisions cleaned their uniforms and weapons and assembled on Mazzard Prairie. The weather was sunny and mild, and a Missouri soldier thought the army made a good showing "considering the condition of the troops." He noted that "some are barefooted, others are necked." Holmes impressed everyone with his equestrian skills: "It was surprising to us to see General Holmes as old as he was to ride horse back and urge the animal along at full speed as he passed by in front of the different regiments."[20]

The martial array could not disguise the magnitude of the logistical crisis gripping Hindman's command. The Confederates had experienced shortages of one kind or another for months, but an unexpected drop in the Arkansas River in mid-December halted most river traffic and brought the army to the brink of disaster. Stocks of food dwindled alarmingly. "We had very little before the battle to eat and now for weeks afterwards there was less to eat than ever," recalled a Missouri soldier. "We were starving." An Arkansan remembered that "corn bread mixed with part of the bran, corn meal bran coffee, and a very limited supply of exceedingly poor beef was our only diet." Hindman estimated that he had 47,000 mouths to feed: 30,000 soldiers, civilian employees, refugees, and "destitute Indians," and 17,000 horses and mules. Chronic malnourishment contributed to the epidemics that swept through the camps. Measles, mumps, pneumonia, dysentery, chronic diarrhea, and a host of "camp fevers" felled thousands. "Men taking sick rapidly," wrote a Missouri officer. "The prospects for this Army look gloomy in the extreme." Holmes was appalled. He told a friend that "I have never seen such ruinous losses by disease."[21]

Holmes ordered Hindman to move the army immediately to Lewisburg (present-day Morrilton), midway between Clarksville and Little Rock, where the river was still navigable. The game was up and Hindman knew it. "We are about to starve here," he informed a subordinate, "and will be compelled to retire." Faced with what was essentially an administrative task, Hindman snapped out of his depression and went to work with his usual brusque efficiency. He ordered department heads and division commanders to prepare for a general evacuation "*as rapidly as possible,*" but to do so "without confusion, and in perfect secresy, even from your subordinates." The campaign to recover Missouri was over; the campaign to save the Trans-Mississippi Army was beginning.[22]

Hindman calculated that it would take a week to prepare the army for a change of base, but he was uncertain whether his meager store of food would last even half that long. A providential rise in the Arkansas allowed Holmes to depart and gave Hindman hope that some of the stranded transports could reach Fort Smith before it was too late. "It is of the very first importance that you use extraordinary energy in the matter," he informed the commanding officer at Clarksville. "Our all depends upon our getting the very largest possible supplies of corn on this rise. It is our only hope—much depends upon you." Hindman closed with a sentence that revealed his desperation: "For God's sake move heaven and earth to send us every grain that can be gotten here." To Hindman's inexpressible relief, a half-dozen steamboats worked their way past shoals and sandbars and reached Fort Smith just in time to avert a calamity.[23]

All the while morale continued to plummet among the troops. "I cant hear from you at all," wrote a despondent Arkansas soldier to his wife. "Some times I give up all hopes of ever seeing or hearing from home any more." More and more men slipped away, sometimes in groups numbering in the dozens. Americus Helms of Alexander's Texas Cavalry confided to his spouse that a "good many gathered their guns and clothes and left for Texas" just before Christmas. He noted that forty-five of the deserters were from his regiment, five from his company. Arkansas conscripts continued to flee in large numbers. A disgusted Missouri surgeon observed: "In some instances [Arkansas] Regiments have been reduced to mere Companies by desertion and the mountains north of us are literally full of them." Hindman warned Captain Caleb Dorsey, commanding an outpost in the Boston Mountains, that several bands of deserters were heading in his direction. "Look out for them!" exclaimed Hindman. "They must be stopped at all hazards." Dorsey replied that "it will take more men than I have to catch all of those that have deserted."[24]

Ozark residents were not the only Arkansans ready to throw in the towel. Phillip Smith, a conscript from the lowlands of east Arkansas, informed his wife that "this army will not hold me mutch longer under the treatment I am giting at the present, giting no Shoes no Money nor only half enough to eat." A week later Smith had determined to desert despite the obvious danger: "If I am not treated Better and paid I am comeing [home] at the Risk of my Life for I will Dy hear if I stay hear and get the treatment I do." The army seemed on the verge of disintegration.[25]

Hindman sympathized with his long-suffering soldiers even as he took draconian steps to maintain discipline. He ordered the deaths of several deserters, mostly Texans, but the executions failed to have the desired effect. Hindman blamed the erosion of morale in the army on "starvation, lack of clothing, and withholding of pay," but Holmes thought the problem was more fundamental: "The desertions are caused by privations and—I am grieved to say—the demoralization of the people." Holmes believed the "growing disaffection to the war" was due to a combination of factors, notably the drought, the unbroken string of military reverses since Wilson's Creek, and Davis's wrong-headed decision to rescind martial law in Arkansas. On that last point Holmes and Hindman were in complete agreement.[26]

The Trans-Mississippi Army began moving down the south side of the Arkansas River the day after Christmas. Hindman was uneasy about leaving his Indian allies in the lurch, despite their lackluster performance. "There will be nothing left to them except to abandon their country entirely or go over to the enemy," he warned Holmes. "No supplies of subsistence or forage, no white troops to strengthen them, nothing to fall back on. What is to be done respecting them?" Holmes had no answer but approved Hindman's decision to maintain a nominal Confederate military presence on the border:

one regiment of Texas cavalry and one brigade of Arkansas infantry. Several hundred commissary and quartermaster troops also stayed in Fort Smith and Van Buren to transfer food, clothing, and equipment to the flotilla of transports that had recently arrived. The vessels were to accompany the marching column downstream.[27]

By 28 December some of the transports were fully loaded, or nearly so; others were still taking on stores. There was no sense of urgency. The Federals had been quiet since the bloodbath at Prairie Grove, and no one seriously expected them to make an appearance in the Arkansas Valley.

17 AFTERMATH

AFTER THE FIGHTING ENDED ON 7 DECEMBER, THE FEDERALS WITHdrew into the woods north and east of Crawford's Prairie. Many soldiers had discarded their overcoats, blankets, and packs during the dash to the battlefield and had little protection against the bitter cold. "We suffered terribly during the night," wrote an Illinois infantryman. "We packed as close as we could." Blunt and Herron prohibited fires, but the cold was so severe that their orders were widely ignored. By midnight the Union side of the field was dotted with hundreds of blazes, large and small. Practically everyone in blue believed the battle would resume as soon as it was light enough to see. "I cannot imagine how this struggle may terminate," Benjamin McIntyre scribbled in his diary. "Tomorrow morning we shall renew it and what I pen tonight may be my last."[1]

It was not only the plunging temperature that kept men awake. A heartrending chorus of screams, wails, and moans went on for hours. "The voices of the wounded, from every direction, were heard pleading for help or full of despairing agony," recalled Captain William Black of the Thirty-seventh Illinois. An Indiana soldier testified: "To hear the crys and screams of the wounded soldiers was enough to chill the blood of the most hard hearted man." As the night wore on, individual cries softened into a "long low wail or moan." The dismal sound carried for miles. Men covered their ears to muffle the noise. "Not one living rational soul who survived that night at Prairie Grove, Arkansas, will ever forget it to his dying day," wrote an anguished Kansas soldier.[2]

Blunt established his headquarters in the West house. Teenaged Julia West remembered the Union commander "sleeping in mother's baby crib with his feet hanging over. During the night when dispatches came he would rise up, read it, write answers or give orders. Men stood and sat around all night with their guns in their hands talking about the fight." She recalled that "all available beds and bedding was used for the wounded except one bed they left for mother and the children but very few of us slept anyway." A little after midnight Blunt decided to concentrate the army's immense collection of wagons and teams in a single defensible location. He ordered Salomon to move the division and commissary trains at Rhea's Mill to Fayetteville (where Herron's trains were located), then hurry to the battlefield with the reserve ammunition wagons and "all the stragglers that you may find." As a result of these roundabout movements, it was late morning before the First Brigade reached Prairie Grove with thousands of fresh (and not so fresh) troops.[3]

When dawn came on 8 December, the officers and men of the Army of the Frontier—cold, hungry, tired, and fatalistic—trudged back to Crawford's Prairie and prepared to renew the fight. They formed a mile-long line of battle on the valley floor and waited, shivering and stamping their feet, for orders that seemed slow in coming. Hardly anyone knew that Blunt and Herron were meeting with Hindman in the small white house at the foot of the hill. Soon after the meeting ended, word spread along the Union line that there would be no more fighting. "At about 12 oclock the news came that the day was ours," wrote a Wisconsin soldier in his diary. Some Federals were struck dumb with amazement; other fell to their knees in relief. "We formed to storm the batteries again and do or die," recalled a soldier in the Nineteenth Iowa, "but thank God they were not there." Then came the celebration as thousands of men found their voices. "Such cheering, I reckon, you never heard," wrote an Illinois soldier. Captain Whitsit of the Twenty-sixth Indiana was overcome with emotion: "I was compelled to give way to my feelings, and a flood of tears came to my relief." Lieutenant Colonel Leake marked the moment in a more prosaic fashion by distributing newly arrived stores of hardtack and whiskey. An officer in the Twentieth Iowa recalled that the food and drink disappeared "in an *unusually* short time."[4]

Hindman was gone, but Blunt remained on the battlefield to deal with the dead and wounded and demonstrate in accepted nineteenth-century fashion that he was the victor. His decision to forego even the pretense of a pursuit was influenced by the frazzled condition of the Missouri Divisions. "Our men were all so footsore and weary from heavy marches and want of rest that we could not follow them," admitted an Illinois officer. Blunt hastened to inform Curtis that the Army of the Frontier had engaged in a "hard fought and bloody battle" and won a "complete victory." He gave "great credit" to Herron for his rapid march to Prairie Grove and his "gallantry upon the field." Herron announced the victory in his own fashion. He advised the Union commander in Springfield that "we have given Hindman and company a damned sound thrashing, and that they have indefinitely postponed their Missouri trip." Shortly after noon these and other dispatches were on their way to the telegraph station at Elkhorn Tavern.[5]

Curtis had been on edge for days, and his reaction to the news from northwest Arkansas can easily be imagined. He congratulated Blunt and Herron and expressed his thanks to the "officers and soldiers of the Army of the Frontier for the victory that will carry despair into the hearts of our foes and gladness to the friends of liberty throughout our country." Curtis passed the good news on to Halleck with a recommendation that Blunt and Herron "deserve special commendation for their gallantry." He had received a second star after Pea Ridge and believed the victors of Prairie Grove deserved no less. Curtis maintained an upbeat tone in his public pronouncements and official correspondence, but privately he commiserated with Herron over the heavy losses in the Missouri Divisions. "Due credit is given to you and Blunt both, although you had the long, hard day's work."[6]

Not everyone was in a celebratory mood. Curtis told Herron that Schofield was "deeply mortified at not being in the fight." In fact, Schofield was seething with envy and frustration. He recognized at once that the victory at Prairie Grove meant promotions for Blunt and Herron but not for him. Rank amateurs who had been his subordinates would soon be his superiors. Schofield was so upset at the unfairness of it all that he could not bring himself to communicate directly with Blunt or Herron. Instead, he penned a formal note to Curtis in which he stiffly congratulated the "able generals" of the Army of the Frontier: "While regretting my (to me) unfortunate absence, it affords me great satisfaction to know that my noble little army has, under the gallant Blunt and Herron, added another and greater proof of its high qualities in the hard-fought battle and brilliant victory."[7]

As soon as that missive was on its way, Schofield wrote to Major General John A. McClernand in Illinois and asked for a job. "I am very desirous of joining you in the Mississippi expedition," Schofield wrote, "provided I can have in it a command not less than that I now hold." This was not Schofield's first attempt to leave the trans-Mississippi. Three weeks earlier he had complained to Halleck about being forced to serve under Curtis, whom he described as a usurper and the "cause of all my troubles." In the letter Schofield once again portrayed himself as a martyr: "I, the only officer who has tried to do anything in this department, am tied down and condemned to almost obscurity." Schofield pleaded for a transfer east of the Mississippi, where greater opportunities for recognition and promotion beckoned. "I have broken myself down in the service—and all for nothing," he whined. "I beg of you relieve me from this miserable condition." Now, in the aftermath of Prairie Grove, Schofield contacted Halleck a second time and renewed his request for a transfer. Halleck, who regarded Schofield as a fellow intellectual, promised to do what he could.[8]

Meanwhile, the dreadful consequences of a Civil War battle unfolded at Prairie Grove. In the early hours of 8 December, Union stretcher bearers crossed the trampled fields and entered the shattered woods in the wake of the withdrawing Confederates. Moonlight illuminated a macabre landscape. "Father, it was an awful scene," wrote James C. Dungan, Nineteenth Iowa. "Your blood would chill if you could have walked over the field with me that night [and seen] the ghastly distorted faces gazing up into the cold sky." Thousands of additional Federals followed later in the day, some to search for friends and comrades, some merely to gawk. Lieutenant Colonel Gad Bryan of the First Iowa Cavalry described the horrific scene to his wife:

> It is a fearful sight to see, after one has cooled off, when the blood is no longer up to battle heat, and take a look at your own work. Dead men and horses, friends and foes, broken gun carriages, and arms all in one promiscuous heap. Men mangled in every conceivable manner. Some with heads torn off, some shot clear in two, some with legs off. Blood on the ground, blood on the fences, and blood on the trees. I saw trees bloody higher than you could reach, and there was a leg of one of the enemy hanging up in a tree top thirty feet high.

An Indiana soldier said as much in fewer words: "It was the awfulest sight I ever saw in all my life."[9]

Hogs feasted on dozens of corpses during the night despite Confederate efforts to protect the dead. The Federals found body after body "torn and mutilated in a most terrible manner" by scavenging swine. A Seventh Missouri Cavalry trooper discovered the remains of Captain William McKee, killed in the morning cavalry fight. The officer had been "stript of his cloths all but his shirt and the hogs eat half of his face off." Other corpses had abdomens ripped open and intestines pulled out. Union soldiers found a few hogs still at work and shot them on the spot.[10]

Disposal of the dead was a laborious and unpleasant undertaking, though the cold temperatures retarded decomposition and minimized the nauseating smell that enveloped other Civil War battlefields. Three days after the fight, the officers and men of the Twentieth Iowa gave their departed comrades a military funeral. "They were all put into coffins and carried at the head of the Regiment," wrote William H. Boyce. "They were buried in a nice spot—a large white oak stands in the center where they were buried. After the chaplain had made a prayer and made a fine remark they were put into the graves. Company G fired three volleys and we went back to camp. I could tell the spot twenty years from now if I should ever come down here again." Few other Union regiments opted for coffins, but all prepared individual markers. Members of the Seventh Missouri Cavalry made "rude head and foot boards, cutting the name, Company, and Regiment, with their knives." They placed their dead in trenches "as close as they could lay with their clothes on and blankets wrapped around them."[11]

The Confederates displayed less reverence toward their dead. A Kansan was shocked by the "calloused indifference" of the Rebel burial details. Hindman's men tossed the bodies of their comrades into shallow trenches "with about the same consideration that sacks of potatoes would have received, and when one layer had been completed another was placed on top of the first, and then, sometimes after their coats had been wrapped over them and sometimes without, the clay and gravel was shoveled on and the job was complete." He added that afterward "we saw many feet protruding from the ground." If that were not bad enough, the Confederate details departed with many of their fallen comrades still above ground. An Iowan complained that the Rebels "seem disposed to leave all their dirty work to us." Four days passed before all the corpses were interred.[12]

Neither army was adequately prepared to deal with the carnage produced by a Civil War battle. Curtis suggested that the wounded be removed to Springfield, where a well-established hospital already existed, but Herron recoiled at the thought of jolting broken, mangled men along Telegraph Road for days on end. "I do not think our wounded could be carried back with safety to themselves," he replied. Herron believed casualties could be "very comfortably fixed at Fayetteville in good houses." He asked Curtis to send medicines, instruments, bandages, linen, blankets, hospital clothes, bedpans, and everything necessary to equip a proper hospital. Blunt appealed directly to the Western Sanitary Commission in St. Louis, a private charitable organization similar to the Red Cross, to "forward without delay supplies for the hospitals." The Western Sanitary Commission had prepositioned a "Flying Hospital" (two wagons packed with medical stores) in Springfield in anticipation of a battle, but the danger from guerrillas was so great that the wagons were compelled to wait for the next supply train before attempting to reach Fayetteville. More than a week passed before the precious cargo arrived, but it was welcome nonetheless. The Western Sanitary Commission stores were a "perfect godsend," exclaimed a Union surgeon. "Enough cannot be said of an institution which performs such deeds."[13]

Fayetteville was rapidly transformed into "one vast hospital." Churches, public buildings, and houses were filled with wounded soldiers. Regrettably, the medical director of the Army of the Frontier, Surgeon George H. Hubbard, was criminally lax or incompetent, or both. He failed to ensure that the army was equipped with adequate medical stores when it took the field, and he neglected to establish or enforce minimal standards for care of the wounded. A shocked William Baxter, a local minister and educator, found the straw-covered floors of the Fayetteville Female Seminary "so thickly covered with mangled and bleeding men that it was difficult to thread my way among them." Reverend Baxter encountered a similar scene in his own church. Conditions in private homes were little better. Sixty-five men were crowded into one house with only two medical orderlies to dress their wounds and tend to their needs. "For the first week the hospitals were in a miserable condition as the supplies were scant, and the rooms crowded, and the stench, to one unaccustomed to it, unbearable," declared a wounded Indiana officer. Nutrition was another problem. Medical orderly George W. Williams wrote that the "poore fellows" under his care had a "hard time for they cant get eney thing to eat that is very palatable to a sick man. We have plenty of hard crackers and coffee and fresh beef but we have poore cooks. There has been a good many died and there is several that will dy yet." Each morning the bodies of men who had died during the night were laid out on sidewalks for the "dead cart."[14]

Not all of the hapless men crowded into the hospital wards were victims of bullets and shell fragments. Reuben Norton of the Twentieth Wisconsin survived the slaughter in the ravine without a scratch only to come down with measles the next day. He died a week later in Fayetteville. The disease spread rapidly, and the surgeons soon had a full-blown epidemic on their hands. The outbreak produced hundreds of new patients, including large numbers of civilians, and conditions in the overcrowded hospitals deteriorated even further.[15]

While official complaints about Hubbard made their way up the chain of command to St. Louis, unofficial appeals for help appeared in newspapers across the Midwest. Dozens of volunteers toting bags and boxes packed with medical supplies set out for northwest Arkansas. The journey was slow, arduous, and not a little dangerous. Dr. William Fithian, stepfather of the Black brothers in the Thirty-seventh Illinois, left Bloomington, Illinois, as soon as he learned of the battle but did not reach Fayetteville until Christmas Eve, nearly two weeks later. (Nine months earlier Fithian had made an almost identical trip to assist the wounded at Pea Ridge. He was one of the true heroes of the war in the West.) Fithian was appalled by conditions in the hospitals and infuriated to learn that additional shipments of medical stores from St. Louis were being delayed by bureaucratic snafus and the ever-present threat of guerrillas. As he told his wife: "More than three weeks since the Prairie Grove battle and not yet here!! Just think of it. With what a snail's pace they come to our brave noble wounded defenders who still suffer in the same blood stained and clotted garments they fought and bled in on the battlefield of Prairie Grove." Fithian worked twelve-hour shifts and took some comfort in the knowledge that his elder stepson would not lose his arm. Surgeon Benoni O. Reynolds of the Third Wisconsin Cavalry chose to resection rather than amputate John Black's shattered bones, a daring procedure for that time and place. Black kept his arm and went on to a long and distinguished career in the law.[16]

On 23 December Surgeon Ira Russell arrived from St. Louis and assumed direction of what was now called the "General Hospital of the District of Western Arkansas." Shocked by the "horrible mismanagement" evident at every turn, Russell shoved Hubbard aside and made wholesale changes. He ordered abandoned buildings demolished and the scrap lumber converted into bedsteads for every patient. He instituted new, stringent standards of sanitation and hygiene. Finally, he instructed Surgeon Seymour D. Carpenter to "scour the town, and surrounding country, and to confiscate everything in the way of bedding, plates and knives and forks, that could possibly be spared by any family." Carpenter (who described himself as a "predatory agent") had few qualms about impressing bedclothes and housewares from the predominantly secessionist population, and went about his business with ruthless efficiency. Dr. Fithian approved wholeheartedly. He noted that the local secessionists "are very bitter and vindictive and would rejoice in an opportunity to cut our throats, sick or well."[17]

Conditions improved dramatically. "The hospitals have been fitted up in a style I thought impossible so far from where anything could be procured and the men are now comfortably situated," noted Captain Robert Braden, Twenty-sixth Indiana. "Now everything is clean—the floors are scrubbed and the walls whitewashed three times a week." It had not been easy. Establishing and overseeing a large military hospital on the frontier was a "most herculean task," reported Russell. "Almost everything had to be created, and all kinds of expedients resorted to, in order to make the poor fellows even passably comfortable."[18]

Confederate wounded endured far greater trials. “Every house in the neighborhood for miles around [Prairie Grove] was turned into a hospital, the dead, dying and wounded covering the floor of every room,” wrote Captain Edmond Ross, Eleventh Kansas. “Their moaning is heart-rending, and what is still worse, not a mouthful of provisions has been left behind by the rebel commanders.” The day after the battle Chester Barney of the Twentieth Iowa visited the Buchanan house and watched Confederate surgeons “busily engaged dressing wounds and amputating limbs.” The severed arms and legs “were thrown out the back door, and I observed a number of hogs feeding on them.”[19]

In accordance with the terms of the truce, the Federals transported Hindman’s wounded to Boonsboro. Nearly every building in town was filled with broken humanity. Confederate surgeons and orderlies were overwhelmed, and some of the latter abandoned their posts and their charges. Visiting wounded Rebels a week after the battle, a Union soldier was shocked to discover that “many of their wounds have not yet been dressed.” Blunt reported that the Confederates were “entirely destitute of a morsel to eat and [had] scarcely any Hospital supplies. I have got at least eight hundred of them to care for, and shall do it to the best of my ability. The poor devils feel very grateful, as well as astonished at the kind treatment they receive.” An Illinois soldier wrote that “all unkind feelings vanish as one looks upon those poor suffering men. It is true they brought it on themselves. Still it is hard to see them suffer so.” The situation improved after Hindman established a shuttle service on the Line Road. Every week or so a convoy of ambulances brought medical stores from Van Buren and returned with wounded soldiers deemed able to travel.[20]

While burying the dead and succoring the wounded, the Federals had an opportunity to examine Confederate weapons and equipment. Nearly everyone was struck by the prevalence of modern, European-made firearms in the Rebel infantry regiments. Captain Edwin B. Messer, Thirty-seventh Illinois, wrote that the Arkansas troops who fell around the Borden house were “well armed and equipped, many of them with the best Enfield Rifles and entirely new equipments of the latest style, and furnished with the best cartridges bearing the stamp of the English manufacturer.” He also noted that they were “well and warmly clothed” with heavy woolen socks, though their shoes were of poor quality. Messer concluded that the “only thing they appeared to lack was good rations.” Lieutenant Charles E. Stevens of the Twentieth Wisconsin thought the Confederate infantry were about as well armed and equipped as their Federal counterparts, but he was struck by the poor physical condition of the Rebels themselves: "They were literally skin and bones." Lieutenant DeWolf of the Seventh Missouri Cavalry also commented on the "sallow cadaverous" appearance of Confederate soldiers, living and dead. "Our men look fresh and healthy while theirs look thin and yellow." With few exceptions, Rebel haversacks were found to contain only corn bread, parched corn, or raw ears of corn. DeWolf surmised that "their bad and unnatural food has something to do with their sallow skins."[21]

The Federals agreed to a man that their malnourished opponents had put up a tremendous fight. Hindman's troops "fought with desperate bravery, and disputed every inch of ground with great stubbornness," wrote William D. McCord, Thirty-seventh Illinois. Another Union soldier felt the Rebels "fought through the day like devils incarnate, and as if resolved on victory or death." He believed they displayed "bravery worthy of a better cause." Writing home after the battle, Ransom S. Phillips of the Ninety-fourth Illinois had some advice for his younger brother: "Cyrus when you hear any one say that the Rebbels will not fight, you tell them for me that is a mistake."[22]

Union soldiers also were unanimous in their conviction that they had survived an extraordinary experience. A Kansan who fought in all three major battles atop the Ozark Plateau—Wilson's Creek, Pea Ridge, and Prairie Grove—thought the "severest of all" was Prairie Grove. "Pea Ridge was a chicken fight compared to it." In like manner, Illinois soldier Samuel Baldridge considered Prairie Grove to be the "severest battle I was in during the three years I was in the army." Dozens of letters, diaries, and memoirs include similar remarks. "I have had a great longing to see a battle as you are aware," Colonel Orme confessed to his wife. "Now I have had my curiosity gratified."[23]

The severity of the fight was reflected in the casualty list. The Army of the Frontier officially lost 1,251 men at Prairie Grove: 175 killed, 813 wounded, and 263 missing, mostly captured. The attrition in Herron's ranks during the three-day march and the helter-skelter arrival of Blunt's command make it difficult to estimate how many Federals reached the field before the fighting ended. The best guess is that between 7,500 and 8,000 Union troops took part in the battle in some fashion. If so, the Federals experienced a 16 percent casualty rate. The Trans-Mississippi Army probably had about 11,500 men at Prairie Grove and officially lost 1,483: 204 killed, 872 wounded, and 407 missing, nearly all of them deserters. Circumstantial evidence suggests that these numbers may be low, but assuming for the moment that they are reasonably accurate, the Confederates experienced a 13 percent casualty rate. If the hundreds of Arkansans who deserted (and, in many cases, switched sides) in the days immediately following the battle are figured in, Confederate losses rise appreciably. Whatever the exact numbers, the cost in pain and suffering was beyond measure. As many as one-fourth of the wounded of both armies perished for lack of proper care in the days and weeks after the battle. "Terrific fight and terrible loss," recorded a laconic Kansas soldier in his diary. A more loquacious Kansas officer wrote that "for the forces engaged, there was no more stubborn fight and no greater casualties in any battle of the war than at Prairie Grove, Arkansas."[24]

The landscape was another casualty of the battle. An Iowan observed that "for the space of a mile there is scarce a tree or even a bush but bears upon it the marks of a ball. Large trees have been cut entirely off, limbs torn from the trunks, and many huge trees split and splintered as if struck by a thunderbolt while bushes and underbrush seems to have been cut and clipped to pieces by small shot." The soldier thought the shattered landscapes of Wilson's Creek and Pea Ridge paled in comparison to the devastation at Prairie Grove. "The trees are more cut up than they are at Pea Ridge," agreed another Iowan. "If you could see it you would wonder how a man escaped as nearly every sapling bears the marks of bullets." Thousands of artillery projectiles and hundreds of thousands of bullets and balls had splintered fences and shredded vegetation almost as far as the eye could see.[25]

Many Federals shared with their Confederate counterparts the same sense of wonder that they had come out alive. A Wisconsin soldier named David B. Arthur scribbled a hasty note to his wife on the morning of 7 December: "We are just going into battle, but I am going into it in the fear of God. I trust that He will spare me to return home again, but if it [is] Gods will that I should fall, I fall trusting in Him and you must try to meet me in heaven." Arthur survived. Another Wisconsin soldier, Benjamin Sanborn, expressed a similar sentiment to his spouse: "I never had so much faith in prayer as I have had lately. I have thought a thousand times since the battle how the bullets whistled around me so near that I could feel them and how my companions were shot down by my side and I was spared. I always think it was the prayers that have been offered up by you and other friends that saved me. I cannot imagine what else could have done it." William Orme put his faith in a personal talisman. He told his wife that "even in the heat of battle I thought of you." Other Federals pondered the mystery of human behavior. Reflecting on the events of the day, an Indiana officer marveled at the number of heroic acts "performed by those no one imagined would have any heroism about them."[26]

A Civil War battle cast a long shadow, and men learned not to count their blessings too quickly. A month before Prairie Grove, an officer in the Twentieth Wisconsin wrote his sister: “You ask me if I don’t feel *squeamish* sometimes at the idea of a battle. I havent yet. I don’t know what I may feel when I get into it [but] I hope I may execute my part in the great drama with an honest heart and steady hand.” Lieutenant George W. Root did just that. He went up the hill and into the ravine with his company. There he was shot in the mouth and lost several teeth and part of his tongue. From his hospital bed in Fayetteville Root informed his sister that the wound was healing and that he would soon be home on leave. Root returned to Ripon only to die in his bed, surrounded by his family, on 3 February. The cause of death was a lingering infection.[27]

The occupants of the Morton cellar emerged shaken but unharmed an hour or so after the final shots were fired on 7 December. House and yard were filled with dead and wounded, but, incredibly, the Borden pony was unharmed and still hitched to a rail in front of the house. Mrs. Borden placed her three youngest children on the frazzled animal and set out for the Mock farm south of town. Most of the women and older children stayed to comfort the legions of wounded. “Such pitiful wails and cries that came from those poor men,” recalled Nancy Morton. “We made them tea from herbs and did all we could for their comfort.” Caledonia Ann Borden was only nine years old. “It sure was scary and pitiful,” she remembered.[28]

No civilians were killed or injured during the battle, but everyone who lived on or near the battlefield suffered grievous material losses. In addition to the damage caused by artillery and musketry, soldiers destroyed buildings and fences, stole or vandalized personal possessions, fouled wells, trampled fields and gardens, confiscated horses and mules, and generally did everything possible to make the region uninhabitable. Some of the damage was incidental but most was deliberate. On the day after the battle Union soldiers unaccountably burned the Borden, Thompson, and William Rogers houses. Caledonia Ann Borden wrote:

> Our beautiful two-story house that was painted light yellow with green trim, the home that we all loved so much, had been burned to the ground after the Yankees plundered the inside. . . . We never got a thing out of our home, not even a change of clothes. They killed and ate our cattle, hogs, sheep and chickens and used what we had stored in the cellar. . . . All of the kinfolks and neighbors gave us food, clothing and some bedding and household goods that they could spare, to help us get started again.

Decades later she was still bitter: "Well we lived over it but I don't have any love for a Yankee."[29]

Hundreds of civilians hastened to Prairie Grove to learn the fate of friends and family members. Brooks's Arkansas Infantry was composed in part of Washington County residents, both conscripts and volunteers, and several other Arkansas regiments also included northwest Arkansas soldiers. Wives, mothers, and sisters fanned out, and it was not long before a "continuous wail" of grief rose from the Ridge and the fields below. One woman found the bodies of her husband and two brothers near the ravine where Brooks's command had engaged the Twentieth Wisconsin. She let out a "wild unearthly shriek," fell to the ground, and embraced each corpse. Then she stood and cried out: "Oh it was them God-damned federals that killed you, I wish they were in hell!" An Indiana soldier wrote: "So intense was her *grief* and *rage* that we could plainly hear her shrieks and cries" from the opposite side of the valley. "I turned away heartsick," wrote a Union officer, "wondering how many hundreds of homes were made desolate by this one battle."[30]

During the process of policing the battlefield, the Federals turned up copies of Hindman's address to his troops. The incendiary document caused a sensation. "What a dirty dog the fellow must be," exclaimed a Union officer, "to indulge in such low blackguardism as this!" The address was widely reprinted in midwestern newspapers and denounced as a "masterpiece of scoundrelism." Blunt sent a copy of the "notorious document" to Curtis. Writing to Hindman a day or two later, he observed sarcastically: "Your instructions to your soldiers to pick off my officers smacks very strongly of chivalry." Had Blunt known of the address before he met with Hindman on 8 December, the two generals might well have come to blows.[31]

Blunt and Herron were popular commanders, but many in the Army of the Frontier were dissatisfied with their performance at Prairie Grove. "There was much quiet criticism in the army of the way in which this campaign has been conducted," according to Lieutenant Horace Moore, Second Kansas Cavalry. Some Federals were mystified by Blunt's refusal to meet Herron halfway or his failure to block Cove Creek Road. Others took Herron to task for attacking in driblets. Still others criticized the ham-handed tactics displayed on the field by both commanders. "There were no braver men than Generals Blunt and Herron," wrote an Indiana soldier, "but it seemed to many then, that while the battle was desperately and bravely fought, it was not well planned." Silas Marple, Eleventh Kansas, expressed the widespread conviction that the "victory of Prairie Grove did not result from superior generalship but from the obstinacy of our soldiers and the superiority of our artillery." As to who deserved credit for saving the day, an officer in the First Arkansas Cavalry thought the relief was mutual: "*Herron saved Blunt and Blunt saved Herron.*"[32]

However ill-managed the battle may have been at the tactical level, it was a resounding strategic victory. A major Confederate effort to reassert control over northwest Arkansas, the Indian Territory, and part of Missouri had been turned back. "The stake played for in this battle was an important one," explained Blunt. "Had our little army been defeated, there was nothing in our rear to have checked their progress." Instead of marching to the banks of the Missouri River, the Confederates were compelled to retire into the Arkansas Valley. The verdict of Pea Ridge was confirmed. An Iowa officer aptly summed up Prairie Grove as a "powerfully stunning blow, from which the western portion of the so-called Southern Confederacy never recovered." Colonel Cloud went even further. He thought the battle was the "most decisive of the war upon this side of the Mississippi River." It was a civilian, however, who said it best. Prairie Grove, wrote the editor of the *Bloomington Daily Pantagraph*, was the "deathblow to rebel hopes in Arkansas." The battle brought to a close a season of Confederate strategic counteroffensives. In Maryland, Kentucky, Mississippi, and, finally, Arkansas, Confederate attempts to repel Union incursions and recover lost territory began with high hopes and impressive gains but ultimately ended in military and political disasters.[33]

The three divisions of the Army of the Frontier were together for barely a week during the entire four-month campaign. On 9 December the army once again devolved into its component parts. The Kansas Division returned to Rhea's Mill where Blunt set up housekeeping in a "fine rebel mansion," a two-story home with tasteful furnishings and a cooperative but secessionist mistress. The Missouri Divisions remained on the battlefield. Herron moved into the battered but conveniently located Hugh Rogers house. For the next three weeks the Federals were relatively inactive. "Dull dull dull—laying around in camp with little or nothing to do," grumbled an Iowa soldier. Trains arrived regularly from Fort Scott and Springfield, but the logistical situation, fragile even in the best of times, steadily deteriorated. After five months of continuous effort vehicles and draft animals were breaking down at an alarming rate. Herron warned Curtis that "there will be trouble" unless he received another one hundred wagons and teams to maintain his fraying line of communications. Blunt had similar problems. The bountiful farms around Prairie Grove provided foodstuffs of every description, but within a few weeks the countryside was exhausted. "We find everything in the line of provisions very scarce," reported a Wisconsin soldier. Leaving women and children with empty larders in the midst of winter made many Federals uncomfortable, but others were more pragmatic. "Cant help it," explained an Iowan, "we must have rations and when Uncle Sam wont furnish them somebody in Arkansas must do it."[34]

The Federals spread out to facilitate foraging. Elements of the Kansas Division returned to Boonsboro. The town had been spared serious damage during the previous occupation (28 November–7 December) because of Blunt's insistence that Union soldiers behave themselves, but this time Blunt stayed at Rhea's Mill and some of his men ransacked stores and homes with impunity. Cane Hill College was vandalized and its impressive library was ruined. "Thousands of volumes have been destroyed by our troops," wrote Silas Marple, Eleventh Kansas. "It made me feel bad to see large, handsome bound books comitted to the fire or trampled in the mud. . . . It was a wanton destruction of property to destroy such things, and criminal in our officers to allow it." On a more positive note, the editorial staff of the *Buck and Ball* resumed work and published the first issue of the newspaper on 15 December. It proved immensely popular not only with the men of the Kansas Division, for whom it was intended, but also with the rest of the army. Avid readers poured through four pages of dense (and slightly blurry) print to learn what they had done.[35]

In mid-December the weather turned unseasonably mild and daytime temperatures soared into the seventies. "Lovelier weather never was seen in Iowa in June," enthused an officer on Herron's staff. A soldier in the First Indian noticed that the "pleasant sunshine and the pure clear air has been a magic tonic upon the whole army." The balmy conditions induced a military version of spring cleaning. Thousands of men commenced to wash and brush their clothes, air out bedrolls and blankets, and generally tidy up the sprawling and not very sanitary camps. Campaigning took on an almost festive air and morale rebounded. A Wisconsin soldier declared: "I never was in a country I like better than this, were it nearer the *world* and not devastated by war."[36]

The twenty-fifth of December was cool and damp, but most messes came up with something special. An Ohio artilleryman at Rhea's Mill enjoyed "extra chicken fixens" for Christmas dinner, while a particularly fortunate Missouri officer waded through a "splendid" holiday repast of "Roast turkey nicely stuffed and baked, Onions, Potatoes, Oysters, Apple (green) sauce and pie, Cake, Biscuit, and Coffee." Some Federals celebrated the holiday in style. Blunt held a "*merry Christmas dance*" in his Rhea's Mill mansion. He advised Herron to "bring partners if you can get them, either *volunteers* or *conscripts,* but come any way, whether you get partners or not. I will try and have a *surplus on hand*." Herron attended, but whether he found suitable female companionship is not known. At the other end of the social scale, more than a hundred refugee slaves, many of them attired in borrowed or cast-off Union uniforms, enjoyed a "grand ball" in a house near Prairie Grove. Christmas at Elkhorn Tavern was marred when a firearm accidentally discharged and killed Lieutenant Nathaniel J. Baily of the Seventh Missouri State Militia Cavalry.[37]

In accordance with the terms of the truce, the Confederates returned captured Union soldiers to Boonsboro on 20 December. The handover went smoothly with the men being exchanged or paroled based on circumstances. Once back in friendly hands, the Federals angrily accused their captors of stealing clothing and valuables, including cash, watches, and wedding rings. Meanwhile, the process of switching sides continued. "On the night of the battle many conscripts came into our lines," wrote a soldier in the Thirty-seventh Illinois. The trickle of unhappy Arkansans soon became a stream. "Conscripts are coming over by tens, twenties and fifties," reported an Illinois officer a few days later. One evening an Arkansas captain and his entire infantry company approached a Union outpost near Prairie Grove and turned themselves in. Nearly all of the deserters brought along their arms and accouterments. Some wanted to join Union regiments, others wanted only to go home. Blunt tried to accommodate everyone.[38]

As the days passed, the Army of the Frontier gradually regained its fighting trim. Blunt and Herron waited for Schofield to return and for Curtis to decide on a new course of action, but mostly they waited to see what Hindman would do next.

18 RAID ON VAN BUREN

ON 23 DECEMBER CURTIS INFORMED BLUNT THAT SCHOFIELD WAS ON his way back to Arkansas to resume command of the army. He also passed along a rumor that Holmes was reinforcing Hindman. "Be on the alert," Curtis advised. "Do not venture too far at present." Blunt did not put much stock in the rumor because his own sources of information indicated that Hindman was preparing to evacuate Fort Smith and join Holmes near Little Rock. The next day Schofield chimed in from Waynesville, twenty-five miles southwest of Rolla. He repeated the warning about Confederate reinforcements and urged Blunt to exercise caution. "Keep your divisions in close supporting distance, and fall back if necessary. Do not risk a battle where you are unless very sure of success."[1]

The message from Schofield was a breach of military protocol, and Blunt expressed his annoyance to Curtis: "I have been somewhat surprised at receiving telegrams from General Schofield, now *en route* from Saint Louis, giving directions relative to the movements of this army. I am in command of the Army of the Frontier, and until General Schofield arrives and assumes command by general orders, I shall direct its movements." Curtis, too, was irritated by Schofield's interference and told him to confer with Blunt and "ascertain all the facts" before deciding on future movements of the army. Schofield assumed the familiar mantle of martyrdom and accused Curtis of undermining his authority.[2]

With Schofield coming and Hindman going, Blunt decided to take one last swing at the Confederates. During the Christmas party at Rhea's Mill he and Herron agreed on a plan for a dash into the Arkansas Valley. The following day Blunt informed Curtis that he intended to "move upon Van Buren with all of my best troops, leaving my transportation this side of the mountains." The plan was simple and opportunistic. The Federals would rush across the Boston Mountains, overwhelm any Rebels they encountered on the north side of the Arkansas, "then, if the river could be crossed, attack those on the south side." Curtis was agreeable. Two weeks earlier he had urged Blunt to press Hindman and "scare him over the river." Now, with the Confederates about to give up Fort Smith, a strong push seemed just the thing to hurry them on their way.[3]

The Union camps at Rhea's Mill and Prairie Grove buzzed with activity. "Secresy was everything so that up to the hour of starting, except the Generals and Staffs, no one knew where the party was going to," explained an officer. "We left our camps with tents pitched and wagon trains just as they have been since the battle here, taking with us only the ambulances and one wagon to each Regiment to carry provisions." Men deemed too ill or weak to endure the rigors of a strenuous march remained behind to guard the camps and trains. Everyone else prepared to head out into the unknown.[4]

The twenty-seventh of December dawned clear and cold. A Kansas cavalryman noticed that "the puddles in the road are covered with thin sheets of ice. The three or four inches of snow that fell a few days ago, have not quite disappeared, and as all the little depressions in the road are filled with water or slush, the outlook for the infantry and artillery is not very cheerful." Nothing could be done about road conditions, however, and the 8,000 men and thirty guns of the Union expeditionary force got under way as soon as it was light enough to see. It was not long before the Federals realized they were heading south. "The words Van Buren and Fort Smith were whispered along our long lines of cavalry and infantry," remembered a Wisconsin soldier. "You should have seen the animated faces of the boys when the truth flashed upon them that they were about to do something again."[5]

Blunt and Herron followed different routes across the Boston Mountains. The Kansas Division marched from Rhea's Mill to the John Morrow house by way of Cane Hill. At Morrow's the column turned south on Cove Creek Road. The Federals splashed in and out of the icy water thirty-seven times, just as the Confederates had done three weeks earlier on their way to and from Prairie Grove. Each crossing was deeper and more difficult than the one before. A trooper in the Ninth Kansas Cavalry noted that the recent precipitation had swelled the creek into a sizable stream forty yards wide "and at no ford less in depth than up to the bellies of the horses. In making one crossing the infantry had to hold their guns at arm's length above their heads, with their cartridge belts slung over them, the water being up to their armpits. As the current is very swift, some of the soldiers were swept off their feet and came near drowning." After marching twenty-six miles in sixteen hours, the

Federals halted just short of the junction with Telegraph Road at Lee Creek. Weary soldiers kindled smoky fires to dry sodden clothes and blankets.[6]

The Missouri Divisions were hampered more by mud than water on their march from Prairie Grove to Hogeye, but the situation changed after they turned south on Telegraph Road. Unlike Cove Creek Road, which winds through the Boston Mountains at the bottom of a gorge, Telegraph Road follows a ridge over the top of the range. An Iowa soldier remarked that the view was "most magnificent but you dare not look at it, because your next step may be off a rock three feet high." In the early afternoon Herron called a halt at Strickler's, the highest point on Telegraph Road at 1,560 feet above sea level. The march resumed at sunset, but it was nearly midnight when the column finally ground to a halt three miles from Lee Creek and the junction with Cove Creek Road. Everyone was tired, sore, and irritable after the grueling twenty-four-mile tramp. A disgruntled officer in the Seventh Missouri Cavalry complained that the "night was very cold and the boys doubled up to keep warm."[7]

The next morning, 28 December, the Federals were up early. The moon had set and it was pitch dark. "I could not distinguish the color of my gray horse sitting on him," recalled a trooper in the Sixth Kansas Cavalry. Blunt and Cloud led the Second, Sixth, and Ninth Kansas Cavalry and two battalions of the Third Wisconsin Cavalry across Lee Creek. One of the Federals noted that the "sun was just visible over the eastern hills" when the column of horsemen clattered past Oliver's Store. Herron's men also were up early, but they lost several hours getting across Lee Creek. With fast-flowing water covering the ford, the Federals improvised an equine shuttle service. "One cavalry man would lead two or three horses, on *each* of which two or three of the infantry would scramble," recalled a soldier in the Nineteenth Iowa. This was slow going and the troops eventually threw together a rickety footbridge of tree trunks and fence rails. Herron left Huston in charge of the infantry and hurried after Blunt with the First Iowa Cavalry, the First, Sixth, and Eighth Missouri Cavalry, a battalion of the Seventh Missouri Cavalry, and a battalion of the Second Wisconsin Cavalry. The Union cavalry force consisted of about 3,000 men and mounts.[8]

Two miles south of Oliver's Store the Federals encountered Confederate pickets. The pickets fired a few shots and fled. Blunt ordered Cloud to follow and not to stop until he reached the Arkansas River, fifteen miles to the south. "The bugle sounded the gallop and on ward we rushed," wrote a trooper in the Third Wisconsin Cavalry. Crump's Texas Cavalry was camped eight miles away at Dripping Springs. When Crump heard sporadic gunfire in the direction of Lee Creek, he started up Telegraph Road with two companies to find out what was happening. The Texans advanced only three miles before colliding with two companies of the Second Kansas Cavalry led by Captain Amaziah Moore. The Federals "immediately formed in line and fired a volley into the enemy, then drawing pistols, charged at full speed." Surprised, the Texans turned and fled.[9]

Crump raced back to Dripping Springs firing his pistol and shouting at the top of his lungs. "Every man to his arms, the Feds are right on to us," he bellowed as he galloped into the Confederate camp. Astonished Rebels gathered their belongings and saddled their mounts. Some formed a line in a field north of the springs to confront the Federals; others established a second line farther south to cover the escape of the regimental train. Cloud deployed a battalion of the Second Kansas Cavalry opposite the first Rebel position and directed Stover to blast the Texans with his two mountain howitzers. The cannoneers unlimbered their guns and discharged a half-dozen rounds. When the "bullpups" ceased firing the Kansans "moved straight forward at a steady trot, every man with pistol in hand," recalled a Kansan. The Federals closed to within one hundred yards, then charged with a shout. The Texans "made a good fight for a few minutes and then fled," reported a Kansas trooper. "The howitzers broke their lines and they became demoralized." The second Confederate formation gave way shortly afterward. The rapid collapse of Crump's Texans caused Moonlight to quip: "We soon *crumpled him* up, giving his regiment no time to look after anything but their dear selves."[10]

The Federals swept through the Confederate camp in search of plunder. "The tents were still standing," observed a Union horseman. "The meat for their dinner lay upon logs, where they were slicing it up for the stew kettles. Pistols hung in tents, and other arms, shot-guns, rifles, sabers, huge bowies, etc., strewed the ground. Hundreds of saddles were scattered about. The corn meal, just mixed for baking, sat beside the fires. Everything betokened the most hurried and frightened retreat." The captured wagons turned out to be part of the train lost by the First Arkansas Cavalry at Prairie Grove. Much of what the Texans managed to carry away was discarded during their flight to Van Buren. The Federals described a road littered with dead and wounded men and "every thing that pertains to a soldiers outfit."[11]

Blunt described the seven-mile pursuit from Dripping Springs to Van Buren as a "brisk running fight," but for most of that distance the Texans made only slight resistance. "They commenced a hasty retreat and we hurried them considerably," recalled William Gulick of the First Iowa Cavalry. "Never stoped a gallop except to use the cannon. I never saw such skedaddleing in

Van Buren in 1867. The Union cavalry charged (and the infantry later paraded) down Main Street to the distant tree line, which marks the north bank of the Arkansas River. (Arkansas History Commission)

my life." Another Union horseman remembered the surprise on the faces of the inhabitants as the blue-clad column thundered down Telegraph Road. "The citizens came out of their houses as we passed by, some to cheer, some to curse, and the women to cry." Conscious of being deep in hostile territory, Blunt sent companies down every side road and farm lane to protect the flanks of the attenuated Union column, which soon stretched more than a dozen miles from teeth to tail as the cavalry pulled away from the infantry.[12]

The Texans turned and confronted their pursuers on a steep hill immediately north of Van Buren. Rowland S. Mantor of the Second Kansas Cavalry described the clash at Logtown: "When within about one hundred yards of them they opened fire upon us and for a few moments the bullets whizzed past us like hail stones. The Colonel [Cloud] remarked that he never was in a place where the bullets flew so thick for a short time as here." Unable to endure the fire from Stover's battery or withstand the "impetuous charge" of the rest of the Second Kansas Cavalry, the Texans abandoned their remaining wagons and disappeared over the hill. "Their train, every hoof and wheel, many horses, all their baggage and many prisoners were captured," exulted a Missouri cavalryman.[13]

The Federals followed to the crest of the hill, which rises four hundred feet above the Arkansas River and is known, appropriately, as "Mount Vista."

Cloud halted to get his bearings and enjoy a spectacular panorama of the Arkansas Valley. "We suddenly saw the town of Van Buren lying below us," wrote an Iowa officer. "We could see the whole place at a glance, a portion of the flying Rebels even running through the town, but what interested us the most were four steamboats just starting out." The halt allowed Blunt and Herron to catch up. The three officers studied the scene for a few moments, then resumed the pursuit. The Union cavalry careened downhill and entered the town. "You ought to have seen us go through Van Buren," recounted an elated trooper in the Second Kansas Cavalry. "Went down Main Street waving our hats and hurrahing for the old flag." Citizens heading home from Sunday services watched in amazement. "Our appearance was a perfect surprise to everybody," declared a Union officer. The only Confederates in residence were convalescents and commissary and quartermaster troops who offered no resistance. They were quickly rounded up and paroled.[14]

At the waterfront the whooping and cheering Union cavalrymen beheld a scene of frantic activity. One steamboat, its fires banked, was tied up along the wharf, but three others were churning downstream trailing clouds of smoke. The transports were loaded with food and stores for Hindman's army, and all would have been on their way had the Federals arrived a day or even a few hours later. Now, in a desperate attempt to escape, the crews of the fleeing vessels were dumping tons of precious cargo overboard. Captain Henry J. Stierlin of the First Missouri Cavalry noticed that "the whole Arkansas River, as far as could be seen, was but one floating mass of corn."[15]

Blunt and Cloud set out in pursuit. The river was low and the sternwheelers were confined to a narrow, winding channel. Two miles below Van Buren the Second Kansas Cavalry caught up with the hindmost vessel. The Federals peppered the *Frederick Notrebe* with their carbines, and the crew waved bedsheets in token of surrender. Blunt clambered aboard and asked the captain how much he would charge for a ride back to Van Buren. The bullet-riddled transport soon was on its way upstream with a high-ranking prize crew. An hour later a Union horseman on the Van Buren waterfront watched as the *Frederick Notrebe* approached "ringing her bell, in good steamboat style, with General Blunt on the hurricane deck as Captain."[16]

Cloud continued after the other two transports. The *Key West* soon ran aground and surrendered, but the *Rose Douglas* reached Strain's Landing, six miles below Van Buren, before admitting defeat. "She was hailed and ordered to land which she did," noted a laconic Kansas trooper. Cloud returned to Van Buren aboard the *Rose Douglas* while the Union cavalry kept pace on shore. During the chase the Federals surprised and captured three ammunition wagons heading east and twenty-seven wagons heading west with supplies for the Confederate wounded at Cane Hill. Vincent Osborne of the Second Kansas Cavalry was unimpressed with what passed for transportation in the Trans-Mississippi Army. "The wagons were old and worn out and the mules looked as if they were strangers to corn or any other kind of food." Meanwhile, Herron occupied the Van Buren waterfront and seized the immobilized steamboat *Violet* and a small horse-powered ferry.[17]

By early afternoon the *Frederick Notrebe* was tied up alongside the *Violet*, and the *Key West* and *Rose Douglas* were working their way upstream. The raid appeared to be a complete success and the Federals relaxed. Blunt and Herron enjoyed lunch in a waterfront hotel, then strolled around the business district. A few blocks from the river they passed the Crawford County Courthouse where a large Confederate flag was flying. Blunt had the symbol of rebellion taken down and replaced with a more congenial banner. A brief ceremony was held to raise the national colors, and Blunt informed Curtis that the "Stars and Stripes now wave in triumph over Van Buren." Returning to the waterfront, Blunt and Herron walked along the levee that protected the town. Both men wanted to press on to Fort Smith (the four captured transports gave the Federals control of the Arkansas River above and below Van Buren), but they hesitated to launch an amphibious operation without precise knowledge of Hindman's whereabouts. While they were deep in conversation, the levee exploded.[18]

BLUNT AND HERRON were a day late. Hindman had said his good-byes and joined the Confederate exodus while the Federals were crossing the Boston Mountains. Rather than travel to Lewisburg in relative comfort aboard a transport, Hindman chose to accompany Frost's Division down the south side of the Arkansas. He was twelve or fifteen miles from Fort Smith when he learned that a Union cavalry force had stormed into Van Buren. Fearful that the Federals intended to disrupt his withdrawal, Hindman ordered Frost to reverse course and place infantry and artillery at every crossing point on the river above Strain's Landing. The troops were to keep the Federals on the north side of the Arkansas or, if that proved impossible, delay a crossing as long as possible. He instructed the commandant at Fort Smith to remove everything of military value and to destroy the post if it seemed about to fall into enemy hands.[19]

Shaver's Brigade deployed in the woods and cornfields on the south side of the Arkansas opposite Van Buren. Shaver studied the waterfront but could not detect any signs of an impending crossing. The Federals seemed to be milling around the town in an aimless fashion, almost as if they were on holiday. Shaver decided to stir things up. Around 2:00 P.M. he advanced a section of West's Arkansas Battery to the bank of the river a short distance below the ferry landing. An officer in the First Iowa Cavalry was just dozing off on the porch of a store in Van Buren when "all at once *boom, boom* went the cannon, and it only required us to look over the river to see the smoke from where the shells came." The initial salvo from West's mountain howitzers nearly decapitated the Army of the Frontier. One shell arced across the river and buried itself in the levee only a few yards from the spot where Blunt and Herron were planning their next move. The two generals were startled but unhurt by the explosion. Blunt dusted himself off and "coolly remarked that he would give them Hell in a moment." Herron also appeared unfazed, though he later admitted to Curtis that "General Blunt and myself made a narrow escape."[20]

Blunt ordered everyone to mount up and fall back. The order caused "much rejoicing" among the Van Buren citizenry, but the Union cavalry withdrew no farther than the top of Mount Vista. For the next two hours the Federals observed the desultory bombardment of the town as if it were a sporting event. West fired more than one hundred shells into steamboats, mercantile establishments, and, occasionally, houses. An officer in the First Missouri Cavalry remarked that he had witnessed Confederate gunners in action before but this was the "first time I saw them hit something."[21]

Thirty minutes after the bombardment began, a courier reached the column of Union infantry and artillery on Telegraph Road and handed Huston an urgent summons for a battery of long-range guns. Huston rushed all five batteries to Blunt's relief. The infantry crowded to the sides of the road and shouted encouragement as the horses and artillery vehicles rumbled past. Around 4:00 P.M. Tenney's First Kansas Battery reached the top of Mount Vista and went into action. The Kansans sent shell after shell shrieking toward the Confederate artillery on the opposite bank, much to the delight of the Union horsemen who cheered every round. Other batteries joined in as they arrived, some firing from atop the bluff alongside Tenney, others from the waterfront and business district.[22]

Many rounds overshot the Rebel howitzers and exploded close to Shaler's Arkansas Infantry, the regiment that had missed the fight at Prairie Grove because of a lack of arms. The Arkansans were armed now but it did them little good. "This was the first artillery fire that our regiment was ever under before and we all began to turn white behind the ears," recalled Silas Turnbo. "As we lay flat on the ground and heard the booming of the cannon and the whistling of the shots we tried to scratch a hole in the ground deep enough

Mount Vista looms over the Arkansas River in this postwar image. The levee where Blunt and Herron nearly came to grief is visible to the right. A steam-powered ferry has replaced the earlier model. (University of Arkansas at Little Rock Archives and Special Collections)

to hide in." The storm of metal also rattled Shaver, who thought the Union force in Van Buren consisted only of cavalry. "Boys this is no place for us!" Shaver announced. The Arkansans agreed with their commander and beat a hasty retreat. Union gunners failed to detect the Confederate withdrawal and continued to shiver trees and shred cornstalks on the south bank until sunset.[23]

Herron described the bombardment of Van Buren as the "greatest outrage perpetrated since the war commenced." Federal sources reported up to six townspeople killed and injured, but the figures do not agree and the number of civilian casualties, if any, remains elusive. Public opinion is easier to gauge. A Union soldier wrote that residents were "very indignant at their rebel friends for firing on the town," and there is no reason to doubt his assessment.[24]

After sending the artillery forward, Huston ordered the infantry regiments on Telegraph Road to quicken their pace. "Marched fast and with hardly any rest, the men falling out much," noted a soldier in the Eleventh Kansas. "Reached Van Buren a little before sunset in time to see the last of the enemys shot fired over the river upon the town." The grueling sprint took a toll. Jacob Haas stated that he and his comrades in the Ninth Wisconsin were "so tired that we could hardly walk or stand and many fell down by the way side but by and by they trundled after us." By 7:00 P.M. the last of the winded infantry regiments had settled into camps on the outskirts of town. Van Buren was firmly in Union hands.[25]

Darkness did not bring an end to the sparring. While in pursuit of the *Rose Douglas* earlier in the day, Cloud had spotted a Confederate camp on the south side of the Arkansas near Strain's Landing. An hour after sunset he returned with a battalion of the Second Kansas Cavalry and the First Kansas Battery. After hallooing across the river and striking up a conversation with a party of Rebels, Cloud directed Tenney to open fire. "It was a beautiful sight," a Union cavalryman told his parents. "The moon shining brightly, the Arkansas still and pleasant flowing along at our feet, the Rebel camp in full view, and the shells from our guns flying like burning meteors through the air and bursting in a thousand pieces in their midst. You should have been there to have enjoyed the scene." Cloud returned to Van Buren, satisfied that he had roughed up the Rebels, but Confederate accounts tell a somewhat different story. A Missouri officer remarked that the Federals "threw some thirty or forty shells into our old camp from the opposite side of the river, but there were none there to return or receive the salute." The men Cloud engaged in conversation belonged to a battalion of Hunter's Missouri Infantry and a section of Tilden's Missouri Battery that had arrived at Strain's Landing shortly after sunset as part of Frost's redeployment. Under strict orders not to waste ammunition, the Confederates withdrew when Tenney opened fire and observed the bombardment from a safe distance.[26]

Hindman's order to evacuate and, if necessary, destroy the post at Fort Smith was carried out with more enthusiasm and less judgment than he intended. When Confederate commissary and quartermaster troops heard artillery fire in the direction of Van Buren, they panicked and set wharves and warehouses ablaze. Not satisfied with burning down the Fort Smith waterfront (and nearly incinerating the business district in the process), they also torched two fully loaded steamboats, the *Arkansas* and the *Era*. No precise accounting of the loss at Fort Smith was ever made, but the flames consumed thousands of bushels of grain along with the irreplaceable transports. With nothing left to protect at Fort Smith, Hindman recalled Frost and resumed the downriver movement.[27]

Hundreds of Federals congregated along the Van Buren waterfront after dark to watch the pyrotechnics at Strain's Landing and the pillars of fire at Fort Smith, but others prowled the unlit streets in search of spoils. "Men were at work all last night with dark lanterns and candles in shops and stores all over town," observed Sergeant McMahan, the Ohio artilleryman. McMahan was inside a warehouse when a familiar stocky figure burst through the door. "Blunt made his appearance revolver in hand and drove us all out!!!! Such dropping of goods and skedaddling!!" Blunt could not be everywhere, however, and most of the Federals engaged in after-hours provisioning went about their business undisturbed. A trooper in the First Iowa Cavalry informed his sister that "all the stores and shops in town were ransacked" and that he had picked up a nicely bound copy of John Bunyan's *Pilgrim's Progress*. Most Van Buren businesses were looted during the two-day occupation, but only a handful of homes suffered damage.[28]

Blunt arranged a parade on 29 December to impress the locals with his strength. Lieutenant DeWolf of the Seventh Missouri Cavalry described the scene as the Federals marched down Main Street: "About eleven o'clock the whole army came in with banners waving and music and as the boys passed the flag staff where the *Glorious old flag* was fluttering the cheers went up loud and lusty." A soldier at the head of the column recalled that "orders were passed along the line to brace up, cease smoking and talking, and present a soldierly appearance. As we looked back (when the officers were not watching) it was a grand sight to see." The martial array impressed even those who had grown cynical in the service. "Oh, but you ought to have seen us file into the town of Van Buren," wrote Captain Payne of the Thirty-seventh Illinois. "It was grand and fully repaid us the toils of the trip."[29]

Blunt and Herron stood on the wooden sidewalk in front of the courthouse and received the salute of every regiment and battery. DeWolf studied the two generals in their moment of triumph. "I had a good opportunity to notice Gen. Blunt and was struck by the honest, fearless look of his face. He is short and heavy with a large mustache. His name is characteristic of the man, *Blunt*." DeWolf seemed less certain how to characterize the stylish man with bushy sideburns standing next to Blunt. "Gen. Herron looks younger, slimmer and more dandified, but we like him notwithstanding."[30]

Civilians also turned out to see the "Lincolnites." One group of spectators could not contain their enthusiasm at the sight of Federal troops pouring into town. "The colored people seemed to enjoy it hugely," observed an Iowa officer. Van Buren was the first town occupied by the Army of the Frontier where the "peculiar institution" was undisturbed, but the slaves clearly understood what the arrival of Union soldiers meant. "It was a gala day for them—a regular fourth of July," observed Sergeant McIntyre of the Nineteenth Iowa. "The colored population had arrayed themselves in their Sundays best and now stood in rows along the pavements on either side of the streets seeming mute spectators to our entrance into their city and I must acknowledge I never before saw as neat and nicely dressed ebony beauties as I have met here today." Following the parade the Federals found themselves surrounded by dark, smiling faces. Benjamin Sanborn of the Twentieth Wisconsin asked a man "if he knew that they could all be free after New Year's if they had a mind to be. He said yes, and he guessed they all had a mind to be."[31]

Blunt gave everyone the rest of the day off. The Federals bathed in the river, enjoyed home-cooked meals at reasonable prices, strolled (or limped) about town, and recorded their impressions. "A place much larger than I thought, and quite well built," observed a Kansan. A Missouri soldier agreed: "The town has a smart business look and its main street is very handsome." Many Federals remarked on the high prices and limited selection in the stores. One officer was struck by the drabness of Confederate life eighteen months after the start of the war: "The ladies now hunt up their oldest dresses, and make them do even for Sunday attire. Butternut colors are the prevailing colors in Dixie."[32]

A group of Union soldiers poking around the Van Buren telegraph office discovered a complete file of military messages sent and received during the previous two months. This was an intelligence coup of the first magnitude. The telegrams revealed much about the Confederate side of the war in Arkansas and the Indian Territory. "The tale of destitution in [Hindman's] army is pitiable," marveled a Union officer after leafing through the file. Herron was delighted by the find and informed Curtis that a "large number of telegrams in Hindman's hand writing were taken and brought away." He promised to send the telegrams and a "splendid rebel flag" to St. Louis as trophies of the raid.[33]

Later that afternoon Blunt, Herron, Huston, and fourteen troopers of the First Missouri Cavalry rode the ferry across the Arkansas. The gaggle of officers milled around on the south bank for a while, then returned to Van Buren. The only purpose of the foolhardy excursion seems to have been to allow Blunt and company to claim that they were the first Union officers to set foot on the Confederate side of the river, or what one member of the party termed the "interior of Dixie." The pall of smoke hanging over Fort Smith and reports from Confederate stragglers and deserters confirmed that there was no one left to fight and nothing left to destroy on the south side. Blunt issued orders for the Army of the Frontier to return to Rhea's Mill and Prairie Grove.[34]

Around sunset on 29 December Herron departed with the infantry, artillery, and a train of fifty captured or confiscated wagons loaded with ammunition, corn, sugar, and bedding. (The bedding came from the steamboats and was intended for the hospitals in Fayetteville.) A herd of four hundred to five hundred horses, mules, and cattle followed the train. North of Dripping Springs Herron encountered the Army of the Frontier's long-absent commander. After reaching Fayetteville and learning that the raid was in progress, Schofield rode nonstop across the mountains on Telegraph Road in a vain attempt to halt the operation or, failing that, take part in it. His hopes were dashed on both counts. Schofield's disappointment deepened when he noticed that his return was met with indifference, even hostility, by the men in the ranks. "Not a cheer greeted him or a cap was raised as he passed us," recalled a man in the Nineteenth Iowa. An Illinois soldier remarked that Schofield "was one day after the fair and cannot claim even a share of the glory." Exhausted by his ride and discouraged by his reception, Schofield fell in with Herron and bedded down for the night in Oliver's Store.[35]

Blunt remained in Van Buren to oversee the final act in the drama. Soon after Herron's departure he ordered the transports and the ferry set afire. By 10:00 P.M. all five vessels were "wrapped in flames," and a reddish glow illuminated both banks of the Arkansas. The fires burned through mooring lines and the doomed vessels drifted downstream, their bells tolling mournfully. It was a melancholy sight, and the crowd of soldiers and civilians watched in silence. A warehouse on the waterfront was next to go. It burned with such intensity that the crowd formed bucket brigades to prevent the flames from spreading to the business district. The Federals estimated that they destroyed 20,000 bushels of corn and tons of other stores in addition to the vessels.[36]

Blunt led the cavalry out of Van Buren the next morning, 30 December. Men, women, and children carrying all their possessions thronged Main Street and Telegraph Road. A trooper in the Ninth Kansas Cavalry described the joyful if chaotic scene. "The negroes are flocking from every direction and falling in with the column. All along the road as we march they are standing, grinning from ear to ear, and waiting as they have been all the morning for the train to come along so that they may throw their bundle on some wagon and trudge along on foot with hundreds of others who are following us out." Reverend Uriah Eberhart, chaplain of the Twentieth Iowa, spoke with numerous refugees and discovered that "they seem as happy as they could be. They all declare themselves free under the presidents proclamation." Although no one bothered to count heads, upward of five hundred people (some accounts say as many as a thousand) accompanied the Federals in search of a better life. "The Army of the Frontier is a unit for liberty or rather emancipation," a Union medical orderly wrote to his family in New England. "If you want to see abolitionists just come out here. The genuine article ain't in Massachusetts."[37]

Blunt caught up with Schofield and Herron at Lee Creek. Schofield declined to assume command (whether out of courtesy or pique is impossible to say) until the operation was complete, so Blunt remained in charge for two more days. He decided to spare the Kansas Division another encounter with Cove Creek and sent everyone back across the mountains on Telegraph Road. The steep ascent from Lee Creek to Strickler's was a trial for man and beast alike, and a particularly rugged half-mile stretch called the "Devil's Staircase" nearly brought the column to a standstill. An officer described the unusual formation as a "succession of stone steps almost as regular as a staircase in a house. We came down it in the night but going back by daylight I was astonished when I saw the place we had passed over." It required twelve horses and fifty men to haul each wagon and artillery vehicle up the exposed strata.[38]

The weather turned cold during the night and a dusting of snow fell the next day, but most of the expeditionary force completed the journey by nightfall on 31 December. The operation ended tragically when a branch snagged the rifle of a soldier in the Ninety-fourth Illinois. The weapon discharged and killed Captain Joseph P. Orme, brother of the brigade commander. The regiment was in sight of its camp when the accident occurred.[39]

The human cost of the raid was small. Two Union soldiers died and a half-dozen others suffered serious wounds or injuries. Blunt reported "quite a number of the enemy" killed during the running fight on Telegraph Road but did not mention a precise figure. Other Union soldiers told of seeing dead and wounded Rebels at various times and places. A reasonable guess is that the Federals killed a dozen Confederates, wounded perhaps twice that number, and captured and paroled several hundred more.[40]

On New Year's Day Herron congratulated the officers and men of the Missouri Divisions for their heroic efforts. "We have bearded the tricky rebel, General Hindman, in his den," he declared. "We claim the country to the Arkansas River." The occasion was marked by music, singing, and cheering for the Emancipation Proclamation. "The day of our nations redemption, and the turning point of the war in our favor, I hope and believe," wrote a soldier in the Eleventh Kansas. For most Federals the holiday celebration was muted due to fatigue and involuntary temperance. A Missouri officer observed that the day "passed away very quietly there being no liquor in our camp for the men to jollify in."[41]

An Illinois officer believed the Van Buren raid was the "greatest achievement of the war in this part of the country. We have penetrated the fastness of the Boston Mountains, and, with our whole army, crossed them in one night, an achievement that will make us historically famous." A cynical Kansan was closer to the mark when he reported that "another dash has been made by our gallant Army of the Frontier, which, as I suppose, will soon be forgotten, like all other efforts for the success of the 'Flag of the Country' made by this far-off Western army." Despite cynicism, aching muscles, and sore feet, morale rose to new heights. "We have just returned to camp from one of the most successful and brilliant expeditions of the war," crowed a trooper in the First Iowa Cavalry. "There is nothing left for us to do here. Hindman's army is *played out*. This country is eat out of everything. We are all in good health and spirits, ready for any thing. We have just heard that Burnside is badly whipped at Fredericksburg. *Let the Army of the Frontier go to Virginia*."[42]

The architects of the raid on Van Buren were the toast of the army. "It was a splendid success, and characteristic of the bold officers who undertook it," declared a Union officer. Curtis could not have agreed more. The victory at Prairie Grove had been eclipsed by a string of recent disasters east of the Mississippi River, and a cloud of gloom hung over headquarters in St. Louis. "The only redeeming affair is the daring dash of Blunt and Herron on Van Buren," Curtis wrote to a colleague. "It was a signal success." Curtis congratulated both generals for yet "another gallant achievement which deserves the gratitude of your country." The prevailing sentiment in the ranks was best expressed by an Iowan who announced that "Blunt and Herron are the idols of the Army of the Frontier." Even the Confederates acknowledged their accomplishments. In a gloomy editorial the *Little Rock True Democrat* conceded that Blunt and Herron were "energetic men, hard fighters and full of dash. They have done immense mischief in Arkansas."[43]

19 EPILOGUE

THE VAN BUREN RAID MARKED THE END OF THE PRAIRIE GROVE campaign. Shaken by the ease with which the Federals had crossed the Boston Mountains, Holmes ordered Hindman to move the Trans-Mississippi Army to Little Rock. Hindman offered no objections. During the first two weeks of 1863 the Confederates slowly made their way down the Arkansas Valley. The 180-mile march was a miserable experience, more damaging and demoralizing than the withdrawal from Prairie Grove. Winter returned with a vengeance, pelting men and animals with ice, snow, and freezing rain. Horses and mules died by the hundreds; men straggled or deserted in numbers too great to count. Abandoned wagons and discarded arms and equipment marked the passage of the army. "The retreat from northwestern Arkansas was a most disastrous affair," acknowledged Holmes. "Out of 12,000, not more than 6,000 effectives arrived here." A Missouri surgeon wrote: "Our army is reduced most deplorably and unless some other means are used, or other commanders appointed, the boasted army that was to invade Missouri will soon be scattered, broken and helpless (it is almost so now) and numbered with the 'eternal past.'" His fears were realized a few weeks later when Hindman's command was merged with Confederate forces in central Arkansas and lost its identity as a separate military organization.[1]

While these developments were unfolding, stunning news arrived from eastern Arkansas. A massive Union amphibious force, repulsed in its initial attempt to take Vicksburg by storm, had turned around and pushed fifty miles up the Arkansas River. On 10–11 January the Federals struck Arkansas Post, the only fortified position on the river below Little Rock. Fort Hindman was lost along with its 4,800 defenders and large quantities of arms, ammunition, and supplies. Low water was the only thing that prevented the Federals from continuing upriver and taking Little Rock. The disasters of Prairie Grove and Arkansas Post, occurring barely five weeks apart, effectively knocked Confederate Arkansas out of the war. When the editor of the *Chicago Tribune* learned of the latest Union triumph, he observed that "Arkansas seems fatal to the rebels, for in every fight upon her soil they have been terribly beaten."[2]

The Arkansas Post debacle was the last straw for Hindman. Exhausted and exasperated, he requested a transfer back to the Army of Tennessee. When Holmes predictably refused the request, Hindman appealed directly to General Braxton Bragg. "Matters have not prospered here since General Holmes came," he informed Bragg. "I am satisfied they will never prosper while he commands." Hindman assured Bragg of his willingness to serve in any capacity so long as he did not deprive a deserving officer of his proper command. "What I most desire is to escape from this grave of ambition, energy, and system." Hindman urged Bragg to be discreet. "The personal relations between General Holmes and myself are not unkind, and I have no wish to injure him, though he has about destroyed me." Hindman's request was approved by President Davis as part of a personnel shuffle at the upper levels of the Trans-Mississippi Department. Davis finally recognized that Holmes was not up to the job and appointed Lieutenant General Edmund Kirby Smith in his place. Demoted to command of the District of Arkansas, Holmes was relieved after a botched attack on Helena in July 1863. Union forces captured Little Rock two months later.[3]

In March 1863 Hindman reviewed the Trans-Mississippi Army—*his* army—for the last time. It was his final official act in Arkansas. Many soldiers noticed that their diminutive commander "seemed very much affected as we were passing in review. He sat on his horse with his cap off and he was too full [of emotion] to speak." Arkansas's most accomplished orator published his farewell remarks in a Little Rock newspaper. No sooner was Hindman on his way than his detractors emerged from the shadows. In response, outraged Confederate officers published a letter denouncing those who spread "misrepresentation and calumny" about their former commander in an attempt "to blacken his reputation." The officers declared that "if this army has failed to accomplish the results that were anticipated, the cause of the failure we believe is not to be found in the incapacity of Gen. Hindman." Enlisted men expressed their feelings about Hindman in simpler terms. "I am really sorry that he is now going to leave us," wrote a Missourian. "He is really a better man than we have taken him to be."[4]

Hindman commanded a division in the Army of Tennessee until injured by a fall from his horse in the summer of 1864. He joined the exodus to

Mexico when the Confederacy collapsed, but returned to Helena two years later and plunged into the free-for-all that was Reconstruction politics in Arkansas. Denied a presidential pardon and unable to vote or hold office, Hindman nonetheless toured the state advocating the formation of a conservative biracial coalition to oppose radical policies. In 1868 he was murdered in front of his wife and children while sitting in his living room. The killers were widely assumed to be in the hire of the Republican Party, but no one was ever brought to trial. Hindman was buried in Helena near the grave of his friend, Patrick Cleburne, who had died at Franklin four years earlier. Hindman's eldest son, Biscoe, attended the U.S. Military Academy and served as national commander of the United Sons of Confederate Veterans. Biscoe prospered in Chicago real estate and left $100,000 toward a memorial for his father at Prairie Grove Battlefield State Park. The result of his bequest is Hindman Hall, which has served as park headquarters and a visitor center for half a century. It is the only building on a Civil War battlefield dedicated to the memory of a Confederate general.[5]

Schofield resumed command of the Army of the Frontier on New Year's Day, 1863, and began a methodical withdrawal from northwest Arkansas. The operation proceeded without incident save for occasional brushes with guerrillas. Word that the Federals were leaving, this time for good, sparked a final Unionist exodus. "Refugees from Arkansas pass through almost every day on their way north," wrote an Iowa soldier stationed near the state line. "They look pitiable indeed, with their skeleton teams, ragged clothes, and pallid, restless children." Those who chose to stay, mostly though not entirely secessionists, were no better off. "Heaven have mercy on the women in Arkansas," remarked a Kansan on his way home. "When we pass by, they look out from the door and windows with faces the picture of despair." In the trans-Mississippi, "hard war" was not a strategic innovation. It was a fact of life. By the end of February 1863 the Kansas and Missouri Divisions were back in their respective states of origin. The Army of the Frontier never again operated as a whole. It was officially dissolved six months later and passed into history.[6]

Schofield should have been pleased with the successful outcome of the campaign he had initiated, but that was not the case. He was enraged by the praise heaped on Blunt and Herron and immediately set about cutting the competition down to size. Schofield began with a remarkable letter to Curtis in which he asserted that the "operations of the army, since I left it, have been a series of blunders, from which it narrowly escaped disaster where it should have met with complete success." He claimed that Blunt and Herron "were badly beaten in detail" at Prairie Grove and "owed their escape to a false report of my arrival with re-enforcements."[7]

The letter was vintage Schofield, a mix of insinuations, half truths, and lies. It also was the opening salvo in what became quite literally a lifelong campaign—an obsession, really—to blacken the reputations of Curtis, Blunt, and Herron and downplay their achievements. In the short run, Schofield failed. Blunt and Herron were promoted to major general with Curtis's support. But in the long run Schofield's poison pen, political skills, and professional connections proved effective. He succeeded Curtis as commander of the Department of the Missouri in 1863. The following year he finally managed to finagle a transfer to the east side of the Mississippi. Schofield served without distinction in Georgia, Tennessee, and North Carolina in the closing months of the war, but successfully ingratiated himself with Ulysses S. Grant and William T. Sherman. With their patronage he rose rapidly in rank and eventually became commanding general of the postwar army. Toward the end of his life, Schofield produced a self-serving autobiography in which he described how he saved the Union despite being surrounded by knaves and incompetents. He died in 1906. Schofield Barracks in Hawaii is named for him.[8]

Unlike Schofield, Curtis was happy with the way things turned out. The Confederate threat to Union control of Missouri was nullified, perhaps permanently, and Rebel forces in Arkansas and the Indian Territory had taken a beating. Curtis was not given to self-promotion, but on this occasion he let himself go. "My success in my department has been so far extraordinary," he confided to his older brother. It was Missouri politics, not Confederate armies, that proved his undoing. Curtis was a Republican and an abolitionist. His efforts to punish secessionists and protect freedmen brought him into conflict with Schofield, Halleck, and Missouri governor Hamilton R. Gamble—all conservative, proslavery Democrats. Frustrated beyond reason by the political bickering in St. Louis, Lincoln removed Curtis from command of the Department of the Missouri. After successfully defending himself against trumped-up corruption charges brought by his political enemies, Curtis assumed command of the reconstituted Department of Kansas in time to smash Sterling Price's Raid at Westport, Missouri. He finished the war as commander of the Department of the Northwest and died in 1866 while on an inspection tour of the Union Pacific Railroad.[9]

Blunt returned to Fort Leavenworth following the Van Buren raid. He resumed his administrative duties as commander of the District of Kansas, but within six months he was back in the field at the head of the Kansas Division.

In a whirlwind campaign he defeated a Confederate force at Honey Springs, Indian Territory, and finally captured Fort Smith in September 1863. The following year Blunt joined forces with Curtis at Westport. He returned to civilian life after the war but suffered from mental illness, possibly the result of syphilis, and died in 1881. Incensed by Schofield's underhanded machinations, Blunt never missed an opportunity to denounce his former commander as a coward and a miscreant.

Herron remained in Missouri for several months after the close of the Prairie Grove campaign despite an increasingly strained relationship with Schofield. He took part in the siege of Vicksburg and spent the rest of the war in Louisiana and Texas, mostly in administrative positions. After peace was restored, he practiced law in New Orleans and became involved in Reconstruction politics. Herron acquired numerous Confederate documents relating to Prairie Grove, including reports on the battle by Roane, Frost, Fagan, Shaver, Charles Adams, Grinsted, William Adams, and Roberts. He may have intended to write a history of the campaign, but no manuscript has ever been found. Herron later moved to New York where he lived in reduced circumstances. He died in 1902.[10]

The Prairie Grove campaign was the last significant Confederate offensive west of the Mississippi River. It also was the last large-scale military operation atop the Ozark Plateau. Cavalry raids, irregular warfare, and outlawry continued to exact a dreadful toll in lives and property, but after 1862 armies no longer wound through the Boston Mountains or clashed on the Springfield Plain. After Prairie Grove the Civil War in the trans-Mississippi entered a new phase. The Confederates abandoned nearly everything north of the Arkansas River, and the Federals shifted their attention and their resources to other theaters.

Confederate veterans of the Prairie Grove campaign took a measure of pride in the hardships they endured and the obstacles they overcame, but memories of missed opportunities followed them to the grave. Federal veterans suffered as well, but they were comforted by the knowledge that their sacrifices had not been in vain. "Would that they had been as successful in the East as we have been in the West," mused a soldier in the Army of the Frontier.[11]

APPENDIX

Order of Battle

An asterisk (*) indicates that the unit participated in the campaign but was not present at the battle of Prairie Grove.

DEPARTMENT OF THE MISSOURI, U.S.A.

Maj. Gen. Samuel R. Curtis

Army of the Frontier

Brig. Gen. John M. Schofield; Brig. Gen. James G. Blunt

First (Kansas) Division

Brig. Gen. James G. Blunt

FIRST BRIGADE

Brig. Gen. Frederick Salomon

Ninth Wisconsin, Lt. Col. Arthur Jacobi
Sixth Kansas Cavalry and Battery, Col. William R. Judson
Ninth Kansas Cavalry and Battery, Col. Edward Lynde
Second Ohio Cavalry, Col. August V. Kautz *
Third Wisconsin Cavalry and Battery, Maj. Elias A. Calkins
Second Indian Home Guard, Maj. Moses B. C. Wright
Second Kansas Battery, Lt. Edward A. Smith *
Stockton's Ohio Battery, Capt. Job B. Stockton

SECOND BRIGADE

Col. William Weer

Tenth Kansas, Maj. Henry H. Williams
Thirteenth Kansas, Col. Thomas M. Bowen
Third Indian Home Guard, Col. William A. Phillips
First Kansas Battery, Lt. Marcus D. Tenney

THIRD BRIGADE

Col. William F. Cloud

Eleventh Kansas, Col. Thomas Ewing Jr.
Second Kansas Cavalry and Battery, Lt. Col. Owen A. Bassett
First Indian Home Guard, Lt. Col. Stephen H. Wattles
Second Indiana Battery, Capt. John W. Rabb
Hopkins's Kansas Battery ("Trophy Battery"), Capt. Henry Hopkins

Second (Missouri) Division

Brig. Gen. James Totten; Col. Daniel Huston Jr.

FIRST BRIGADE

Col. Daniel Huston Jr.; Col. John G. Clark

Twenty-sixth Indiana, Col. John G. Clark
Eighteenth Iowa, Col. John Edwards *
Seventh Missouri Cavalry, Maj. Eliphalet Bredett
Battery A, Second Illinois Light Artillery, Lt. Herman Borris

SECOND BRIGADE

Col. William M. Dye

Thirty-seventh Illinois, Lt. Col. John C. Black; Maj. Henry N. Frisbie
Twentieth Iowa, Lt. Col. Joseph B. Leake
Sixth Missouri Cavalry, Maj. Samuel Montgomery
Battery F, First Missouri Light Artillery, Capt. David Murphy

Third (Missouri) Division

Brig. Gen. Francis J. Herron

HEADQUARTERS ESCORT

First Missouri Cavalry, Maj. James M. Hubbard

FIRST BRIGADE

Col. Dudley Wickersham; Lt. Col. Henry G. Bertram

Twentieth Wisconsin, Maj. Henry A. Starr
Tenth Illinois Cavalry and Battery, Lt. Col. James Stuart
First Iowa Cavalry, Col. James O. Gower
Second Wisconsin Cavalry, Maj. William H. Miller
Battery L, First Missouri Light Artillery, Capt. Frank Backof

SECOND BRIGADE

Col. William W. Orme

Ninety-fourth Illinois, Lt. Col. John McNulta
Nineteenth Iowa, Lt. Col. Samuel McFarland; Maj. Daniel Kent
Eighth Missouri Cavalry, Col. Washington F. Geiger
Seventh Missouri State Militia Cavalry, Col. John F. Phillips *
Battery E, First Missouri Light Artillery, Lt. Joseph Foust

NOT BRIGADED

First Arkansas Cavalry, Col. M. LaRue Harrison

Fourteenth Missouri State Militia Cavalry, Col. John M. Richardson

---

TRANS-MISSISSIPPI DEPARTMENT, C.S.A.

Lt. Gen. Theophilus H. Holmes

Trans-Mississippi Army (First Corps)

Maj. Gen. Thomas C. Hindman

Shoup's Division

Brig. Gen. Francis A. Shoup

FAGAN'S BRIGADE

Brig. Gen. James F. Fagan

Brooks's Arkansas Infantry, Col. William H. Brooks

King's Arkansas Infantry, Col. James P. King

Pleasants's Arkansas Infantry, Col. Joseph C. Pleasants; Lt. Col. John A. Geoghegan

Hawthorn's Arkansas Infantry, Col. Alexander T. Hawthorn

Chew's Arkansas Sharpshooter Battalion, Maj. Robert E. Chew

Blocher's Arkansas Battery, Capt. William D. Blocher

MCRAE'S BRIGADE

Col. Dandridge McRae

Morgan's Arkansas Infantry, Col. Asa S. Morgan

Glenn's Arkansas Infantry, Lt. Col. John E. Glenn

Hart's Arkansas Infantry, Lt. Col. Robert A. Hart

Young's Arkansas Infantry, Lt. Col. Charles L. Young

Woodruff's Arkansas Battery, Capt. John G. Marshall

Frost's Division

Brig. Gen Daniel M. Frost

PARSONS'S BRIGADE

Brig. Gen. Mosby M. Parsons

Mitchell's Missouri Infantry, Lt. Col. Charles S. Mitchell

Steen's Missouri Infantry, Col. Alexander E. Steen

Hunter's Missouri Infantry, Col. Dewitt C. Hunter

Ponder's Missouri Infantry, Lt. Col. Willis M. Ponder

Caldwell's Missouri Infantry, Col. Josiah H. Caldwell

Pindall's Missouri Sharpshooter Battalion, Maj. Lebbeus A. Pindall

Tilden's Missouri Battery, Capt. Charles B. Tilden

SHAVER'S BRIGADE
Col. Robert G. Shaver

Adams's Arkansas Infantry, Col. Charles W. Adams
Shaler's Arkansas Infantry, Col. James R. Shaler *
Grinsted's Arkansas Infantry, Col. Hiram L. Grinsted
Adams's Arkansas Infantry, Lt. Col. William C. Adams
Roberts's Missouri Battery, Capt. Westly Roberts

ROANE'S BRIGADE (ATTACHED)
Brig. Gen. John S. Roane

Bass's Texas Cavalry, Col. Thomas C. Bass
Stone's Texas Cavalry, Maj. Robert D. Stone
Guess's Texas Cavalry, Lt. Col. George W. Guess
Alexander's Texas Cavalry, Col. Almerine M. Alexander
Clark's Missouri Infantry, Col. John B. Clark Jr.
Reid's Arkansas Battery, Capt. John G. Reid
Shoup's Arkansas Battery, Capt. John C. Shoup

Marmaduke's Division
Brig. Gen. John S. Marmaduke

SHELBY'S BRIGADE
Col. Joseph O. Shelby

Gordon's Missouri Cavalry, Lt. Col. B. Frank Gordon
Thompson's Missouri Cavalry, Col. Gideon W. Thompson
Jeans's Missouri Cavalry, Col. Beal G. Jeans
Elliott's Missouri Cavalry Battalion, Maj. Benjamin Elliott
Bledsoe's Missouri Battery, Capt. Joseph Bledsoe
Quantrill's Band, Lt. William Gregg

CARROLL'S/MONROE'S BRIGADE
Col. Charles A. Carroll; Lt. Col. James C. Monroe

Carroll's Arkansas Cavalry, Maj. Lee J. Thomson
Monroe's Arkansas Cavalry, Lt. Col. James C. Monroe; Lt. Col. James A. Johnson

MACDONALD'S BRIGADE
Col. Emmett MacDonald

Young's Missouri Cavalry, Lt. Col. Merritt L. Young
Crump's Texas Cavalry, Lt. Col. R. Phillip Crump
West's Arkansas Battery, Capt. Henry C. West

Notes

Abbreviations

AHC	Arkansas History Commission, Little Rock
BL	William H. Boyce Letters, Linda Russell Collection, Edmonds, Washington
CU	Columbia University, New York City
CWM	Civil War Museum at Wilson's Creek National Battlefield, Republic, Missouri
CWTI	*Civil War Times Illustrated* Collection, USAMHI
DU	Duke University, Durham, N.C.
DWC	Dale West Collection, Longview, Tex.
HFC	Harris Family Correspondence, Jackson County Historical Society, Independence, Mo.
HL	Huntington Library, San Marino, Calif.
ISHL	Illinois State Historical Library, Springfield
ISL	Indiana State Library, Indianapolis
KSHS	Kansas State Historical Society, Topeka
LC	Library of Congress, Washington, D.C.
LLC	Lewis Leigh Collection, USAMHI
MC	Matt Mathews Collection, Ottawa, Kansas
MHM	Missouri History Museum, St. Louis
NARA	National Archives and Records Administration, Washington, D.C.
NYHS	New-York Historical Society, New York City
OR	U.S. War Department, *The War of the Rebellion: A Compilation of the Official Records of the Union and Confederate Armies. OR* citations take the following form: volume number (part number, where applicable): page number. Unless otherwise indicated, all citations are from series 1.
PGBSP	Prairie Grove Battlefield State Park, Prairie Grove, Arkansas
SHSIDM	State Historical Society of Iowa, Des Moines
SHSW	State Historical Society of Wisconsin, Madison
SMOH	Shiloh Museum of Ozark History, Springdale, Arkansas
SOR	Janet B. Hewitt et al., eds., *Supplement to the Official Records of the Union and Confederate Armies. SOR* citations take the same form as *OR* citations.

UAF	University of Arkansas at Fayetteville
UMC	University of Missouri–Columbia
UND	University of Notre Dame, South Bend, Ind.
USAMHI	U.S. Army Military History Institute, Carlisle, Pennsylvania

Chapter One

1 Shea and Hess, *Pea Ridge.*
2 Neal and Kremm, *Lion of the South,* 1–20.
3 Nash, *Biographical Sketches,* 154, 150.
4 "Personal Recollections of the Late General Thomas C. Hindman," *St. Louis Daily Times,* 4 Oct. 1868.
5 Symonds, *Stonewall of the West,* 35–42.
6 *OR* 13:28.
7 *OR* 13:833, 29, 830.
8 Shea and Hess, *Pea Ridge,* 284–306.
9 Banasik, *Embattled Arkansas,* 59–111.
10 Skinner, *Autobiography,* 299–300.
11 *OR* 13:38–39; Skinner, *Autobiography,* 300–303, 307–9; John W. Brown Diary, 18 July 1862, UAF; *Little Rock True Democrat,* 3 July 1862.
12 "Personal Recollections," *St. Louis Daily Times,* 4 Oct. 1868; Skinner, *Autobiography,* 301, 325; George D. Alexander to Hindman, 10 Mar. 1863, Alexander Papers, CU; *OR* 13:31–34, 38–39, 53:848; Asa S. Morgan to wife, 29 Sept. 1862, Morgan Collection, AHC; John C. Wright, *Memoirs,* 74, 76–77.
13 Banasik, *Missouri Brothers in Gray,* 31–32.
14 *OR* 13:33, 45.
15 Brownlee, *Gray Ghosts,* 76–91; *OR* 13:10.
16 *OR* 13:43.
17 "Personal Recollections," *St. Louis Daily Times,* 4 Oct. 1868; *OR* 53:848; John C. Wright, *Memoirs,* 76.
18 "Personal Recollections," *St. Louis Daily Times,* 4 Oct. 1868.
19 Crist, *Papers of Jefferson Davis,* 163; Robert J. Bell Diary, 12 Aug. 1862, Parsons Papers, MHM.
20 Crist, *Papers of Jefferson Davis,* 360–61; *OR* 13:898–99.
21 Crist, *Papers of Jefferson Davis,* 361; *OR* 13:877; Dandridge McRae to wife, n.d., McRae Papers, AHC. Brigadier General Paul O. Hebert commanded the District of Texas and Major General Richard Taylor, recently arrived from Virginia, commanded the District of Louisiana.
22 *OR* 13:881; Skinner, *Autobiography,* 327; "Personal Recollections," *St. Louis Daily Times,* 4 Oct. 1868; John C. Wright, *Memoirs,* 79.
23 *OR* 13:875, 899; John B. Clark to Hindman, 12 Aug. 1862, Alexander Papers, CU.
24 *OR* 13:46; Carroll to Hindman, 12 Aug. 1862, Alexander Papers, CU.
25 David W. Moore to uncle, 10 Sept. 1862, Moore Letter, AHC; Gilbert, "Confederate Soldier Writes Home," 28; *OR* 13:886.
26 Turnbo Journal, 133, University of Oklahoma; Carroll to Hindman, 21 July 1862, Alex-

ander Papers, CU; Samuel W. Ritchey to aunt, 8 Sept. 1862, HFC; Gilbert, "Confederate Soldier Writes Home," 27–28.

27 Skinner, *Autobiography*, 285.

28 *OR* 13:42, 47; George W. Guess to Sarah Cockrell, 29 July 1862, Guess Letters, University of Texas; Emmett MacDonald to Hindman, 1 Sept. 1862, Alexander Papers, CU.

29 Crist, *Papers of Jefferson Davis*, 362; *OR* 13:889; Holmes to Hindman, 27 Aug. 1862, Alexander Papers, CU; *Little Rock True Democrat*, 10 Sept. 1862.

30 Asa S. Morgan to wife, 7 Oct. 1862, Morgan Collection; *OR* 13:887, 918. While waiting for Hindman to return, Holmes asked President Davis to send a "few *good* Generals" to replace the "many utterly worthless officers" in his command. Crist, *Papers of Jefferson Davis*, 361–62.

31 *OR* 13:42–43.

Chapter Two

1 Connelly, *Schofield*, 12–62.

2 William W. Orme to [?], Davis Papers, ISHL. The less attractive side of Schofield's personality is revealed in his autobiography, *Forty-six Years in the Army*.

3 Hamilton, "Enrolled Missouri Militia"; *OR* 13:8, 10–12.

4 Castel, *Frontier State at War*, 82–85.

5 *Chicago Tribune*, 9 Jan. 1863; Charles N. Mumford to family, 27 Aug., 16 Sept. 1862, Mumford Letters, SHSW; Britton, *Memoirs*, 280; Helm Memoir, LLC, USAMHI.

6 *Daily Missouri Democrat*, 26 Nov. 1862; Furry, *Preacher's Tale*, 101–2.

7 *OR* 13:632.

8 Robert F. Braden to mother, 4 Aug. 1862, Braden Papers, ISL; Schofield to Frederick Steele, 18 Sept. 1862, Schofield Papers, LC.

9 *OR* 13:653–54.

10 *OR* 13:653; Shea and Hess, *Pea Ridge*, 5–7.

11 *OR* 13:654, 656, 666.

12 Schofield to Gamble, 24 Sept. 1862, Gamble Papers, MHM. This letter is also in *SOR* 2(3):91–92.

13 *OR* 13:656, 667–68; Curtis to Francis J. Herron, 6, 11 Oct. 1862, Herron Papers, NYHS. The date of Schofield's message in the *OR* is incorrect; it should be 25 Sept. 1862.

14 *OR* 13:23, 560.

15 Blunt to wife, 23 Sept. 1862, Civil War Letters, MC; *OR* 13:696–97.

16 Blunt to wife, 23 Sept. 1862, Civil War Letters, MC.

17 Q.U.I. letter in *Daily Missouri Democrat*, 17 Nov. 1862; "Jenks" letter in *Des Moines State Register*, 6 Nov. 1862; unidentified letter in *Leavenworth Daily Times*, 11 Nov. 1862; *OR* 13:697.

18 William P. Black to mother, 13 Nov. 1862, Black Family Papers, ISHL; Uriah Eberhart to wife, 11 Nov. 1862, Eberhart Papers, SHSW.

19 Carlson, "Francis Jay Herron"; Stuart, *Iowa Colonels and Regiments*, 205–6.

20 Orme to [?], 29 Sept., 5 Nov. 1862, Davis Papers, ISHL; George W. Root to sister, 22 Nov. 1862, Root Letters, SHSW; Tilley, *Federals on the Frontier*, 35; Office of the Adjutant General, *Report of the Adjutant General and Acting Quartermaster of Iowa*, 2:835.

21 Herron to Curtis, 2 Oct., Herron to Schofield, 10, 13 Oct., Schofield to Herron, 13 Oct., and Curtis to Herron, 11 Oct. 1862, Herron Papers, NYHS; *OR* 13:725.

22 E.H.G. [Eli H. Gregg] letter in *Muscatine Daily Journal*, 22 Dec. 1862.

23 "Typo" letter and unidentified letters in *Keokuk Gate City*, 7, 15, 17 Oct. 1862; Pratt, "Civil War Letters," 254; "Sentinel" letter in *Indianapolis Daily Journal*, 21 Oct. 1862.

24 *OR* 13:46–47; "Second Brigade" letter in *Kansas State Journal*, 23 Oct. 1862; Schofield to Curtis, 5 Oct. 1862, Schofield Papers, LC.

25 *OR* 13:665–66; Bearss, "Army of the Frontier's First Campaign," 283–319.

26 Williams Memoir, 23, *CWTI*, USAMHI; Quesenberry Diary, 11 Oct. 1862, UMC; *OR* 13:311, 333–34.

27 *OR* 13:711, 715–16, 730, 765; Schofield to Curtis and to Blunt, 5 Oct. 1862, Schofield Papers, LC.

28 *OR* 13:725; Tenney, *War Diary*, 36.

29 *OR* 13:729, 732, 735–36; Schofield to Curtis, 5 Oct. 1862, Schofield Papers, LC; "Sentinel" letters in *Indianapolis Daily Journal*, 3, 21 Oct. 1862.

30 *OR* 13:730.

31 "Brief History of 20th Regiment," Farley Papers, SHSW; Tilley, *Federals on the Frontier*, 30–31. The lone holdout was court-martialed and sentenced to work on the Springfield fortifications for a year without pay.

32 Verplanck Van Antwerp letter in *Keokuk Gate City*, 6 Nov. 1862; T.H.S. letter in *Burlington Hawkeye*, 15 Nov. 1862; Tenney, *War Diary*, 38.

33 Kitts, "Civil War Diary," 323; Lindberg and Matthews, "'Eagle of the 11th Kansas,'" 21; Samuel Worthington to sister, 20 Oct. 1862, Worthington Letters, KSHS; Blunt to daughter, 20 Oct. 1862, Civil War Letters, MC.

34 Jacob D. Brewster to wife, 19 Oct. 1862, Brewster Letters, SHSIDM; E.H.G. letter in *Muscatine Daily Journal*, 18 Nov. 1862; Tilley, *Federals on the Frontier*, 32 (McIntyre); unidentified letter in *Keokuk Gate City*, 17 Nov. 1862.

35 Verplanck Van Antwerp letter in *Keokuk Gate City*, 6 Nov. 1862; Worthington to father, 7 Nov. 1862, Worthington Letters, KSHS; Ross to wife, 20 Oct. 1862, Ross Correspondence, KSHS. For more about Federal impressions of the Ozark Plateau, see Shea, "Semi-Savage State," and Bradbury, "Good Water & Wood but the Country Is a Miserable Botch."

36 W.J.S. [William J. Steele] letter in *Davenport Daily Gazette*, 5 Nov. 1862; Q.U.I. letter in *Daily Missouri Democrat*, 10 Nov. 1862; "Jenks" letter in *Dubuque Daily Times*, 6 Dec. 1862; "Boswell" letter in *Bloomington Daily Pantagraph*, 3 Dec. 1862; Lemke, "Miller," 8; unidentified letter in *Emporia News*, 29 Nov. 1862.

37 T.H.S. letter in *Burlington Hawkeye*, 15 Nov. 1862; unidentified letter in *Atchison Freedom's Champion*, 20 Dec. 1862.

38 Lemke, "Miller," 8–10; Worthington to Enos, 28 Oct. 1862, Worthington Letters, KSHS; "Thomas" letter in *Davenport Daily Democrat and News*, 4 Dec. 1862; "Sentinel" letter in *Indianapolis Daily Journal*, 31 Oct. 1862.

39 Orme to [?], 19, 29 Oct. 1862, Davis Papers, ISHL.

40 Orme to [?], 29 Oct. 1862, ibid.; Greene, "Campaigning," 294.

Chapter Three

1 *OR* 13:334, 883, 899. The council of war took place on 14 October at William Holcomb's house in the center of present-day Springdale. The house was located near the intersection of Mill and Johnson streets. An American Legion Post occupies the site today.

2 Cooper to Hindman, 28 Oct. 1862, Alexander Papers, CU; *OR* 13:334.

3 Cooper to Hindman, 28 Oct. 1862, Alexander Papers, CU; *OR* 13:334, 819; *SOR* 3:59; Littlefield and Underhill, "Fort Wayne."

4 Cooper to Hindman, 28 Oct. 1862, Alexander Papers, CU; *OR* 13:334.

5 *OR* 13:747, 749, 755–56; Blunt, "General Blunt's Account," 227–28; Schofield to Herron, 19 Oct. 1862, Schofield Papers, LC.

6 *OR* 13:325–26; Lindberg and Matthews, "'Eagle of the 11th Kansas,'" 21; E.H.G. letter in *Muscatine Daily Journal,* 18 Nov. 1862.

7 *OR* 13:325–26; "More Anon" letter in *Kansas State Journal,* 20 Nov. 1862; Glover, "Accounts of Horace L. Moore."

8 Crawford, *Kansas in the Sixties,* 55–56; Glover, "Accounts of Horace L. Moore."

9 *OR* 13:326–27, 331; "More Anon" letter in *Kansas State Journal,* 20 Nov. 1862; Haas Diary, 25 Oct. 1862, PGBSP.

10 *SOR* 3:65–66; Barker, "Fight at Fort Wayne."

11 *OR* 13:334–35; Haimerl, *Clarkson's Battalion,* 80–83, 93–94; Curtis Payne, *Thundering Cannons,* 35.

12 *OR* 13:327, 330–31; unidentified letter in *Daily Missouri Democrat,* 6 Nov. 1862; Barker, "Fight at Fort Wayne," 71; William H. Haynes to Hindman, 25 Oct. 1862, Alexander Papers, CU; Glover, "Accounts of Horace L. Moore."

13 *OR* 13:327.

14 Crawford, *Kansas in the Sixties,* 59–61; "M" letter in *Leavenworth Daily Times,* 2 Dec. 1862; "More Anon" letter in *Kansas State Journal,* 20 Nov. 1862; E.H.G. letter in *Muscatine Daily Journal,* 18 Nov. 1862; Levinius Harris letter in *Daily Missouri Democrat,* 15 Nov. 1862.

15 Levinius Harris letter in *Daily Missouri Democrat,* 15 Nov. 1862; Barker, "Fight at Fort Wayne," 71; Kitts, "Civil War Diary," 324; "X" letter in *Daily Missouri Democrat,* 15 Nov. 1862.

16 *OR* 13:327, 331; unidentified letter in *Daily Missouri Democrat,* 6 Nov. 1862; Kitts, "Civil War Diary," 324; Farlow and Barry, "Osborne's Civil War," 198.

17 Edmund G. Ross to wife, 25 Oct. 1862, Ross Correspondence, KSHS; "Second Brigade" letter in *Kansas State Journal,* 13 Nov. 1862; Kitts, "Civil War Diary," 324; Farlow and Barry, "Osborne's Civil War," 199; Lindberg and Matthews, "'Eagle of the 11th Kansas,'" 22.

18 Ellithorpe Diary, 8 Nov. 1862, CWM; *OR* 13:336, 328; *SOR* 3:67; Curtis Payne, *Thundering Cannons,* 37–39; Harris letter in *Daily Missouri Democrat,* 15 Nov. 1862; J.B.M. [Josiah B. McAfee] letter in *Leavenworth Daily Conservative,* 13 Nov. 1862; unidentified letter in *Leavenworth Daily Times,* 11 Nov. 1862.

19 E.H.G. letter in *Muscatine Daily Journal,* 18 Nov. 1862.

20 *SOR* 3:66; *OR* 13:335.

21 Hindman to Holmes, 25 Oct., and MacDonald to Hindman, 27 Oct. 1862, Alexander Papers, CU; *SOR* 3:69–70; Haimerl, *Clarkson's Battalion,* 100–102.

22 Cooper to Hindman, 28 Oct. 1862, Alexander Papers, CU.

23 Q.U.I. letter in *Daily Missouri Democrat,* 30 Oct. 1862.

24 *OR* 13:886; Hindman to Holmes, 15 Oct. 1862, Alexander Papers, CU.

25 Hindman to Holmes, 15 Oct. 1862, Alexander Papers, CU; *OR* 13:47.

26 Hindman to Cooper, 20 Oct. 1862, Alexander Papers, CU. Hindman also ordered Colonel John Q. Burbridge at Pittman's Ferry to attack the Federal depot at Rolla with his small Missouri cavalry brigade, but the raid never materialized. *OR* 13:48; *SOR* 3:61.

27 Hindman to Mosby M. Parsons, 20 Oct. 1862, Alexander Papers, CU; *SOR* 3:61–62.

28 *SOR* 3:61, 63; Hindman to John C. Palmer, 21 Oct. 1862, Alexander Papers, CU.

29 *SOR* 3:60, 64; *OR* 13:49; Quesenberry Diary, 22 Oct. 1862, UMC. The junction of present-day Arkansas 16 and 23 is still called "Brashears," though nothing remains of the historic hamlet except a cemetery. A nineteenth-century history states that William Brashears first settled in the area in 1866, but Hindman and other Confederates referred to the junction as "Brashear," "Brashears," or "Brashear's" in 1862. Hindman's correspondence between October 22 and 25 is headed "Camp War Eagle." *History of Benton,* 1083–84.

30 Hindman to Holmes, 22 Oct. 1862, Alexander Papers, CU; *OR* 13:48. Historic Ozark Road south of Brashears is present-day Arkansas 23.

31 *OR* 13:22; Q.U.I. letter in *Daily Missouri Democrat,* 30 Oct. 1862; Vaught, "Diary of an Unknown Soldier," 69; Smith Diary, 20 Oct. 1862, DWC; William H. Boyce to parents, 25 Oct. 1862, BL; Barney, *Recollections,* 70–71; Dolphus Terry letter in *Davenport Daily Gazette,* 11 Nov. 1862.

32 Elder, *Damned Iowa Greyhound,* 24; Vaught, "Diary of an Unknown Soldier," 69; Tilley, *Federals on the Frontier,* 33; Jacob D. Brewster to sister, 25 Oct. 1862, Brewster Letters, SHSIDM. Schofield reported that the Confederates "fled upon our approach" to Huntsville. Colonel Joseph O. Shelby, commanding the Confederate rear guard, claimed that his troopers skirmished heavily with the oncoming Federals and inflicted several casualties. Shelby's account seems exaggerated. *OR* 13:49, 20.

33 *OR* 13:20; Henry C. Crawford to [?], 31 Oct. 1862, Crawford Letters, UMC.

Chapter Four

1 *OR* 13:20; Schofield to Herron, 22 Oct. 1862, Schofield Papers, LC; Leake, "Campaign," 277–78; Elder, *Damned Iowa Greyhound,* 25; Fry, *As Ever Your Own,* 13; Allen, "Three Frontier Battles," 487. Osage Spring is northeast of the intersection of I-540 and Arkansas 94 (New Hope Road) in present-day Rogers. The historic landscape has been obliterated by commercial development.

2 Leake, "Campaign," 278; Barnes, *What I Saw You Do,* 11; Houghland, "19th Iowa," 64; Q.U.I. letter to *Daily Missouri Democrat,* 30 Oct. 1862.

3 "Correspondent" letter in *New York Herald*, 6 Nov. 1862; Jacob D. Brewster to sister, 25 Oct. 1862, Brewster Letters, SHSIDM; Henry C. Crawford to [?], 31 Oct. 1862, Crawford Letters, UMC; Albert J. Rockwell to sister, 15 Nov. 1862, Rockwell Letters, SHSW; Barney, *Recollections*, 85; Aaron P. Mitchell to wife, 25 Oct. 1862, in Sawyer, "Aaron P. Mitchell Letters."

4 Crawford to [?], 31 Oct. 1862, Crawford Letters; *SOR* 35(2):337; Brewster to wife, 29 Oct. 1862, Brewster Letters, SHSIDM; Pratt, "Civil War Letters," 256.

5 *OR* 13:325, 764–66, 20.

6 *OR* 13:760–61, 764–65.

7 *OR* 13:759–60; Samuel R. Curtis letter in *Fairfield Ledger*, 30 Oct. 1862.

8 *OR* 13:760.

9 *OR* 13:762–63.

10 *OR* 13:759.

11 *OR* 13:765. Three decades later, when Curtis was safely in his grave, Schofield professed to have been incensed at the order to pull out of northwest Arkansas. In a draft of his self-serving autobiography, he wrote: "But General Curtis, *apparently thinking that he in St. Louis knew more about the enemy in my front than I did*, ordered me to move north and east with two divisions, leaving Blunt with one division to occupy that country." The italicized clause does not appear in the published version of the autobiography. Perhaps Schofield realized that the truth could be stretched only so far. "General Schofield's Narrative of the Military Operations in Which He Was Engaged during the Civil War," pt. 2:19, Schofield Papers, LC; Schofield, *Forty-six Years in the Army*, 62.

12 *SOR* 3:61, 63, 68–69; Hindman to Holmes, 25, 29 Oct. 1862, Alexander Papers, CU.

13 Lane Memoir, 34–35, UMC.

14 "Personal Recollections," *St. Louis Daily Times*, 4 Oct. 1868; Hindman to Holmes, 22 Oct. 1862, Alexander Papers, CU; Lee, "John Sappington Marmaduke." Marmaduke attended Yale and Harvard before receiving an appointment to the U.S. Military Academy.

15 Marmaduke to Hindman, 25 Oct. 1862, Alexander Papers, CU; *OR* 13:980.

16 *SOR* 3:63, 60; *OR* 13:980; Hindman to Holmes, 26 Oct. 1862, Alexander Papers, CU; Hindman to Marmaduke, 26 Oct. 1862, in Order Book, Fourth Cavalry Division, MHM; Asa S. Morgan to wife, 27 Oct. 1862, Morgan Collection, AHC. The historic junction of Ozark and Huntsville roads is approximated by the intersection of present-day Arkansas 16 and 74. McGuire's Store was one mile east of the junction. The store is gone, but McGuire's two-story house still stands on the north side of Arkansas 74.

17 *OR* 13:766, 20; William P. Black to mother, 27 Oct. 1862, Black Family Papers, ISHL; Q.U.I. letter in *Daily Missouri Democrat*, 5 Nov. 1862.

18 *OR* 13:766; Blunt to Schofield, 29 Oct. 1862, Letters Received, Army of the Frontier, Headquarters, NARA.

19 *SOR* 10(2):682, 16:681, 686, 692, 704, 721, 35:337, 36:41, 74:734, 769. Historic Elm Springs Road is now Arkansas 112.

20 Lothrop, *First Regiment Iowa Cavalry*, 85; Pohl, "From Davenport to Vicksburg," 498–

500; "Jenks" letter in *Daily Missouri Democrat,* 7 Nov. 1862; *SOR* 3:78–79, 34(2):431, 454, 457. Historic Robinson's Crossroads is approximated by the present-day intersection of U.S. 412 and Arkansas 265 (Telegraph Road). The historical marker for Robinson's Crossroads is incorrectly located at an intersection 1.5 miles farther east.

21 Pohl, "From Davenport to Vicksburg," 499–500; "Jenks" letter in *Daily Missouri Democrat,* 7 Nov. 1862; *SOR* 3:78. Historic Oxford Bend no longer exists; it was located on the west bank of the White River opposite present-day Goshen.

22 Pohl, "From Davenport to Vicksburg," 499–500; "Jenks" letter in *Daily Missouri Democrat,* 7 Nov. 1862; *SOR* 3:78. Herron "highly complimented" the officers and men of Company A, Seventh Missouri State Militia Cavalry, for their role in the fight. *SOR* 35(2):421.

23 Hindman to Holmes, 22 Oct. 1862, Alexander Papers, CU; N.A.T. [Nathaniel A. Taylor] letter in *San Antonio Weekly Herald,* 20 Dec. 1862. Cravens was the brigade's third commander in less than a week. Hindman had removed Colonel Thomas C. Bass for being "too much intimidated" and replaced him with Bradfute, who promptly removed himself by falling ill. Hindman to Holmes, 22 Oct. 1862, Alexander Papers.

24 Pohl, "From Davenport to Vicksburg," 500.

25 Lothrop, *First Regiment Iowa Cavalry,* 85; Pohl, "From Davenport to Vicksburg," 500; *SOR* 3:79.

26 *OR* 13:980; Edwards, *Shelby and His Men,* 94; Lothrop, *First Regiment Iowa Cavalry,* 85; Pohl, "From Davenport to Vicksburg," 500–501.

27 *OR* 13:49; Quesenberry Diary, 28 Oct. 1862, UMC. The "strong position" on Ozark Road was midway between present-day Elkins and Durham.

28 Lothrop, *First Regiment Iowa Cavalry,* 85; Stuart, *Iowa Colonels and Regiments,* 548; Pohl, "From Davenport to Vicksburg," 500–501; *OR* 13:20, 344–45; *SOR* 3:76; Elbert M. Heath letter in *Little Rock True Democrat,* 22 Jan. 1863.

29 Hindman to Holmes, 28 Oct., and to Marmaduke, 29 Oct. 1862, Alexander Papers, CU.

30 Mosby M. Parsons to Hindman, 3 Nov., Hindman to Holmes, 29, 31 Oct., and Hindman to William H. Haynes, 31 Oct. 1862, Alexander Papers, CU; Quesenberry Diary, 28 Oct. 1862, UMC. Parsons's movement from Yellville to the Mulberry River is described in the Pinnell Journals, MHM.

31 MacDonald to Hindman, 27 Oct. 1862, Alexander Papers, CU.

Chapter Five

1 Mitchell to wife, 29 Oct. 1862, in Sawyer, "Aaron P. Mitchell Letters"; "Sentinel" letter in *Indianapolis Daily Journal,* 21 Nov. 1862; Smith Diary, 27, 28 Oct. 1862, DWC; Baxter, *Pea Ridge and Prairie Grove,* 173–78.

2 Elder, *Damned Iowa Greyhound,* 36; Tilley, *Federals on the Frontier,* 90–92; "Correspondent" letter in *New York Herald,* 7 Nov. 1862; Q.U.I. letter in *Daily Missouri Democrat,* 5 Nov. 1862; W.J.S. and Dolphus Torrey letters in *Davenport Daily Gazette,* 7, 11 Nov. 1862.

3 *OR* 13:20–21; Schofield to Blunt, 29 Oct. 1862, Schofield Papers, LC.

4 *OR* 13:21, 775–76; Kitts, "Civil War Diary," 325; Blunt to Schofield, 30, 31 Oct. 1862, Letters Received, Army of the Frontier, Headquarters, NARA; Blunt, "General Blunt's Ac-

count," 228; Connelley, *Life of Preston B. Plumb,* 110; Lindberg and Matthews, "'Eagle of the 11th Kansas,'" 23.

5 Schofield to Blunt, 1 Nov. 1862, Letters Sent, Army of the Frontier, Headquarters, NARA.

6 *OR* 13:706, 778; Lindberg and Matthews, "'Eagle of the 11th Kansas,'" 23; Vaught, "Diary of an Unknown Soldier," 74; unidentified letter in *Milwaukee Daily Sentinel,* 10 Nov. 1862. The message from Schofield to Curtis is incorrectly dated 3 October in the *OR*; the correct date is 3 November.

7 *OR* 13:778–79; Elder, *Damned Iowa Greyhound,* 26; unidentified letter in *Daily Missouri Democrat,* 7 Nov. 1862; William H. Boyce to parents, 6 Nov. 1862, BL; Q.U.I. letter in *Daily Missouri Democrat,* 10 Nov. 1862; Vaught, "Diary of an Unknown Soldier," 74.

8 Elder, *Damned Iowa Greyhound,* 27; T.H.S. letter in *Burlington Hawkeye,* 15 Nov. 1862; Thomas Murray to brother, 3 Nov. 1862, Correspondence, University of Missouri—Rolla; Q.U.I. letter in *Daily Missouri Democrat,* 10 Nov. 1862.

9 T.H.S. letter in *Burlington Hawkeye,* 15 Nov. 1862; Fry, *As Ever Your Own,* 16.

10 Q.U.I. letter in *Daily Missouri Democrat,* 10 Nov. 1862; "Thomas" letter in *Davenport Daily Democrat and News,* 17 Nov. 1862.

11 Schofield to Curtis, 6, 7 Nov. 1862, Curtis Papers, SHSIDM.

12 *OR* 13:781; Schofield to Curtis, 7 Nov. 1862, Curtis Papers, SHSIDM.

13 *OR* 13:21; Fry, *As Ever Your Own,* 16; Houghland, "19th Iowa," 64; Pratt, "Civil War Letters," 257.

14 Schofield to Curtis, 7 Nov., and Curtis to Schofield, 8 Nov. 1862, Curtis Papers, SHSIDM; *OR* 13:785; Smith Diary, 10 Nov. 1862, DWC; Leake, "Campaign," 280–81.

15 Schofield, *Forty-six Years in the Army,* 62; Schofield to Curtis, 7, 10 Nov. 1862, Curtis Papers, SHSIDM; *OR* 13:784–85; General Orders Nos. 11 and 13, 8 and 13 Nov. 1862, Army of the Frontier, Headquarters, NARA.

16 Curtis to Schofield, 13 Nov. 1862, Curtis Papers, SHSIDM; Blunt to Schofield, 12 Nov. 1862, Schofield Papers, LC. When Schofield fell ill, Curtis reminded Halleck that "I need more generals." Halleck responded by sending Brigadier General Willis A. Gorman to the Department of the Missouri. *OR* 13:787, 793.

17 Austin Durham to wife, 14 Nov. 1862, Durham Papers, IHS; Schofield to Totten, 14 Nov. 1862, Letters Sent, Army of the Frontier, Headquarters, NARA. This account of Herron's affliction was penned by one of his staff officers: "General Herron has been suffering much recently with inflamed eyes, brought on and aggravated by the sharp winds and insufferable dust which he had to encounter upon the long marches. Fears were entertained at one time that he would be disabled on account of the trouble, but a few days of rest and skillful treatment has nearly effected a cure, and now he is with us once more as vigilant and active as ever." "Jenks" letter in *Dubuque Daily Times,* 6 Dec. 1862.

18 Warren Day to wife, 1, 9 Nov. 1862, Day Correspondence, KSHS; Ellithorpe Diary, 3 Nov. 1862, CWM; E.H.G. letter in *Muscatine Daily Journal,* 22 Dec. 1862; *OR* 13:784, 795; "Nassau" letter in *Daily Missouri Democrat,* 27 Nov. 1862.

19 *OR* 13:783, 358; Blunt to wife, 23 Sept. 1862, Civil War Letters, MC; J.B.M. letter in *Leavenworth Daily Conservative,* 29 Nov. 1862; Tenney, *War Diary,* 42.

20 *OR* 13:358; Ellithorpe Diary, 9 Nov. 1862, CWM; Tenney, *War Diary*, 42; Marmaduke to Hindman, 5, 9 Nov. 1862, and MacDonald to Hindman, 11 Nov. 1862, Alexander Papers, CU. The location of this skirmish cannot be determined, but it probably was near Boonsboro (present-day Canehill).

21 "M" letter in *Leavenworth Daily Times*, 2 Dec. 1862; Tenney, *War Diary*, 42; Glover, "Accounts of Horace L. Moore." Cloud's running fight with MacDonald followed the same route as that of the much larger battle of Cane Hill, fought three weeks later on 28 November. Cane Hill is described in detail in Chapter 7.

22 *OR* 13:358; Tenney, *War Diary*, 42–43.

23 "M" letter in *Leavenworth Daily Times*, 2 Dec. 1862; Tenney, *War Diary*, 43; J.B.M. letter in *Leavenworth Daily Conservative*, 29 Nov. 1862.

24 Marmaduke to Hindman, 5, 9 Nov. 1862, Alexander Papers, CU; Company Book of Company B, 11, 13 Nov. 1862, AHC; *OR* 13:792; Calvin W. Marsh to Curtis, 14 Nov. 1862, Curtis Papers, SHSIDM.

25 *OR* 13:358, 795, 796; Ellithorpe Diary, 14, 16 Nov. 1862, CWM; Tenney, *War Diary*, 43.

26 *OR* 13:792, 794, 800; Calvin W. Marsh to Curtis, 14 Nov., Schofield to Curtis, 16 Nov., and Curtis to Marsh, 15 Nov. 1862, Curtis Papers, SHSIDM.

27 Smith Diary, 17–19 Nov. 1862, DWC; Schofield to Curtis, 20 Nov. 1862, Curtis Papers, SHSIDM; Schofield to Blunt, 16, 18 Nov. 1862, Letters Sent, Army of the Frontier, Headquarters, NARA; *OR* 13:796, 801, 807; Elder, *Damned Iowa Greyhound*, 27–28; Leake, "Campaign," 280.

28 Schofield and Herron to Curtis, 21 Nov. 1862, Curtis Papers, SHSIDM; Daily Journal, 21 Nov. 1862, Army of the Frontier, Second Division, NARA; Herron to Totten, 21 Nov. 1862, Letters Sent, Army of the Frontier, Second Division, NARA; George W. Root to sister, 22 Nov. 1862, Root Letters, SHSW. Schofield also hoped to be present for the birth of his third child. He reached St. Louis on 23 November, and Henry Halleck Schofield entered the world the next day. Sadly, the boy lived only a few months. Connelly, *Schofield*, 41, 349n.

29 Schofield to Curtis and Special Orders No. 53, both 18 Nov. 1862, Curtis Papers, SHSIDM; *Daily Missouri Democrat*, 24 Nov. 1862; General Orders No. 14, 26 Nov. 1862, and Daily Journal, 26 Nov. 1862, Army of the Frontier, Second Division, NARA; Barnes, *What I Saw You Do*, 12; William P. Black to mother, 13 Nov. 1862, Black Family Papers, ISHL. Totten served in staff positions for the rest of the war. He was dismissed from the army for drunkenness in 1870.

30 *OR* 22(1):788–89.

31 Totten to Schofield, 9 Nov. 1862, Letters Received, Army of the Frontier, Headquarters, NARA; Albert J. Rockwell to father, 26 Nov., and to sister, 15 Nov. 1862, Rockwell Letters, SHSW; Q.U.I. letter in *Daily Missouri Democrat*, 20 Nov. 1862; George W. Root to sister, 22 Nov. 1862, Root Letters, SHSW; William H. Horine to brother, 21 Nov. 1862, Horine Letters, McLean County Historical Society, Bloomington, Ill. McCulloch's Spring (also called "McCulloch's Store") was located on Telegraph Road about eight miles southwest of Wilson Creek and about the same distance northeast of Crane Creek.

32 David L. Ash to wife, 12, 23 Nov. 1862, Ash Papers, USAMHI; *Leavenworth Daily Conservative,* 11 Nov. 1862. The sense of befuddlement was not limited to soldiers. Isaac Murphy, the sole member of the 1861 Arkansas secession convention to vote against leaving the Union, was forced into exile in Missouri after the outbreak of war. He accompanied Schofield in hopes of returning to his Huntsville home. Instead, he found himself stranded at Elkhorn Tavern. A frustrated Murphy wrote: "I could not see the wisdom of the see saw movements that have been practiced by the Army of the Frontier." Murphy to William L. Fayel, 13 Nov. 1862, Breckenridge Papers, MHM.

33 Q.U.I. letter in *Daily Missouri Democrat,* 20 Nov. 1862.

34 Rockwell to father, 26 Nov. 1862, Rockwell Letters; "Milwaukee" letter in *Milwaukee Daily Sentinel,* 3 Dec. 1862; Vaught, "Diary of an Unknown Soldier," 81.

35 Herron to Curtis and Curtis to Herron, 24 Nov. 1862, Curtis Papers, SHSIDM; *OR* 22(1):38–39, 794; *SOR* 19(2):63; Lothrop, *First Regiment Iowa Cavalry,* 87–88. Herron reported incorrectly that a battalion of the Second Wisconsin Cavalry also took part in the Yellville raid.

36 Vaught, "Diary of an Unknown Soldier," 80–82; William H. Boyce to parents, 27 Nov. 1862, BL.

37 Bodwell Diary, 14 Nov. 1862, KSHS; unidentified letter, 12 Nov. 1862, "Correspondence of Wisconsin Volunteers," Quiner Papers, SHSW; "More Anon" letter in *Kansas State Journal,* 20 Nov. 1862; unidentified letter in *Emporia News,* 29 Nov. 1862; J.B.M. letter in *Leavenworth Daily Conservative,* 13 Nov. 1862.

38 William P. Black to mother, 3 Jan. 1863, Black Family Papers, ISHL; A.R. letter in *Kansas State Journal,* 20 Nov. 1862; E.H.G. letter in *Muscatine Daily Journal,* 18 Nov. 1862; "M" letter in *Leavenworth Daily Times,* 2 Dec. 1862.

39 *OR* 13:785–86; Samuel Worthington to father, 7 Nov. 1862, Worthington Letters, KSHS; "Nassau" letter in *Daily Missouri Democrat,* 26 Nov. 1862; "Junius" letter in *Janesville Daily Gazette,* 4 Dec. 1862; Daniel H. Loomis to mother, 10 Nov. 1862, Loomis Letters, UMC; Ellithorpe Diary, 6, 7, 12, 18 Nov. 1862, CWM.

40 Kitts, "Civil War Diary," 325; *Buck and Ball,* 15 Dec. 1862; Tenney, *War Diary,* 42; Warren Day to wife, 9 Nov. 1862, Day Correspondence, KSHS; "More Anon" letter in *Kansas State Journal,* 28 Oct. 1862; *OR* 13:785–86.

41 *OR* 13:785–86; Tenney, *War Diary,* 44; "Nassau" letters in *Daily Missouri Democrat,* 26, 27 Nov. 1862; Britton, *Union Indian Brigade,* 108; E.H.G. letter in *Muscatine Daily Journal,* 22 Dec. 1862. The Confederate force at Dutch Mills was Monroe's Arkansas Cavalry. The Rebels "stampeded" when they unexpectedly encountered Phillips's command. Company Book of Company B, 13 Nov. 1862, AHC.

42 *OR* 22(1):790, 807; Blunt to Albert W. Bishop, 22 Nov. 1862, Bishop Collection, Old State House Museum, Little Rock.

43 Unidentified letter, 12 Nov. 1862, "Correspondence of Wisconsin Volunteers," Quiner Papers, SHSW; Bodwell Diary, 20 Nov. 1862, KSHS.

44 J.B.M. letter in *Leavenworth Daily Conservative,* 15 Nov. 1862; unidentified letter in *Emporia News,* 29 Nov. 1862; "Junius" letter in *Janesville Daily Gazette,* 4 Dec. 1862; Blunt, "General Blunt's Account," 229–30.

Chapter Six

1 Hindman to John S. Roane, 3 Nov., and to Holmes, 4 Nov. 1862, Alexander Papers, CU; *OR* 13:911.

2 Hindman to John S. Roane, 1 Nov. 1862, Alexander Papers, CU; *OR* 13:50.

3 Hindman to Holmes and John P. Lockman to Hindman, both 17 Nov. 1862, Alexander Papers, CU.

4 Hindman to R. Phillip Crump, 24 Nov., to Holmes, 31 Oct., 1–4 Nov., and to Douglas H. Cooper, 30 Oct. 1862, Alexander Papers, CU; Hindman letters in *Bloomington Daily Pantagraph*, 20 Jan. 1863; Asa S. Morgan to wife, 13, 15 Nov. 1862, Morgan Collection, AHC. The Hindman letters in the *Daily Pantagraph*, both dated 16 Nov. 1862, were part of a cache of documents seized by Union troops during the Van Buren raid in December.

5 Pleasant M. Cox to parents, 25 Nov. 1862, HFC; George W. Guess to Cockrell, 30 Nov. 1862, Guess Letters, University of Texas; William H. Hoskin Diary, 18–22 Nov. 1862, UMC; Turnbo Journal, 132, University of Oklahoma; Waller Diary, 18–22 Nov. 1862, CWM.

6 Hindman to Marmaduke, 14 Nov., and to John W. Dunnington, 25 Oct., Dunnington to Hindman, 1 Nov., Holmes to Hindman, 2 Nov., George D. Alexander to Hindman, 4, 5, 15, 28 Nov., John B. Lockman to Hindman, 17 Nov., and Daniel M. Frost to Hindman, 30 Nov. 1862, Alexander Papers, CU; *OR* 13:916; N.A.T. letter in *San Antonio Weekly Herald*, 20 Dec. 1862.

7 Cox to family, 25 Nov. 1862, HFC; N.A.T. letter in *San Antonio Weekly Herald*, 20 Dec. 1862; Almerine M. Alexander letter in *Little Rock True Democrat*, 31 Dec. 1862.

8 Circular, 8 Nov., and Holmes to Hindman, 15 Nov. 1862, Alexander Papers, CU; *OR* 13:916.

9 Pinnell Journals, 16 Nov. 1862, MHS.

10 "Personal Recollections," *St. Louis Daily Times*, 4 Oct. 1862; James M. Keller to Hindman, 27 Nov. 1862, Alexander Papers, CU. Keller noted that 83 of the 1,259 patients admitted to the hospital on Mulberry Creek had died during November. Another 37 had deserted, presumably after recovering sufficient strength to outrun pursuers.

11 Lane Memoir, 35–37, UMC; Williams Memoir, *CWTI*, USAMHI.

12 Edwin C. Harris to wife, 11 Nov., and Samuel W. Ritchey to aunt, 25 Nov. 1862, Harris Letters, Gilder Lehrman Collection, NYHS; Special Orders Nos. 45 and 46, 18 and 19 Nov. 1862, Alexander Papers, CU; McCorkle, *Three Years with Quantrill*, 75–76.

13 Hindman to [?] Sparks, 4 Nov. 1862, Alexander Papers, CU.

14 Holmes to Hindman and General Orders No. 17, both 9 Nov. 1862, Alexander Papers, CU; *OR* 13:913. The official title of Hindman's command was "First Corps, Trans-Mississippi Army," but since no Second Corps was ever formed, the term "Trans-Mississippi Army" will suffice for our purposes.

15 Hindman to R. Phillip Crump, 24 Nov. 1862, Alexander Papers, CU; N.A.T. letter in *San Antonio Weekly Herald*, 20 Dec. 1862. The word "northwest" in the N.A.T. letter was printed as "southwest" in the newspaper.

16 Hindman to R. Phillip Crump, 24 Nov., and to John S. Roane, 25 Nov., and Marmaduke to Hindman, 5 Nov. 1862, Alexander Papers, CU.

17 Hindman to R. Phillip Crump, 24 Nov. 1862, Alexander Papers, CU; Asa S. Morgan to wife, 25 Oct. 1862, Morgan Collection; Davis, *Confederate General*, 5:150–51.

18 Hindman to R. Phillip Crump, 24 Nov. 1862, Alexander Papers, CU; Miller, "Daniel Marsh Frost"; Roberts Letter, PGBSP. In November 1862 Frost was infuriated to learn that Union military authorities had confiscated his rental properties in St. Louis. Dipping his pen in vitriol, he described the Lincoln administration as a gang of "negro thieves, house burners, Dutchmen and assassins—a second King of Dahomey for President, and numerous Nena Sahib's for Generals." Personal Journal of Expenses, 13 Nov. 1862, Frost Papers, MHM.

19 Hindman to R. Phillip Crump, 24 Nov., and Marmaduke to Hindman, 25 Nov. 1862, Alexander Papers, CU; *OR* 13:50–51, 898; N.A.T. letter in *San Antonio Weekly Herald*, 20 Dec. 1862.

20 Morgan to wife, 13 Nov. 1862, Morgan Collection; N.A.T. letter in *San Antonio Weekly Herald*, 20 Dec. 1862; Alexander letter in *Little Rock True Democrat*, 31 Dec. 1862.

21 Harris to wife, 4 Nov. 1862, HFC; Hoskin Diary, 24 Nov. 1862, UMC; Ritchey to aunt, 25 Nov. 1862, Harris Letters, Gilder Lehrman Collection, NYHS.

22 *OR* 13:906–7, 914, 918, 921, 926–28, 22(1):898.

23 Holmes to Hindman, 6, 10, 22, 28 Nov. 1862, Alexander Papers, CU; *OR* 13:913, 917.

24 Hindman letter, dated 15 Nov. 1862, in *Daily Missouri Republican*, 6 Feb. 1863; Holmes to Hindman, 24 Nov., and Cooper to Hindman, 27 Nov. 1862, Alexander Papers, CU. The Hindman letter in the *Daily Missouri Republican* was part of a cache of documents seized by Union troops during the Van Buren raid in December.

25 Marmaduke to Hindman, 25, 26 Nov. 1862, Alexander Papers, CU.

26 Marmaduke to Hindman, 24, 25 Nov., and H. M. Peters to Emmett MacDonald, 1 Dec. 1862, Alexander Papers, CU; Tenney, *War Diary*, 41. When he evacuated Fayetteville on 29 October, Schofield had left twenty sick and wounded Union soldiers behind. Instead of paroling these men in the hospital, as was standard practice, MacDonald sent them to Little Rock as prisoners of war. Hindman told Marmaduke to advise Blunt that the captured Federals would be paroled and sent to Helena as soon as possible. Marmaduke chose Stanley to deliver the message. Hindman to Marmaduke, 20 Nov. 1862, Order Book, Fourth Cavalry Division, MHM.

27 Marmaduke to Hindman, 24 Nov. 1862, Alexander Papers, CU; *OR* 13:50. (Marmaduke and Hindman generally spelled the Union general's name "Blount.") Marmaduke estimated the distance from Van Buren to Flint Creek by way of Fayetteville at sixty miles, but it was actually seventy to seventy-five miles by the roads of the day.

28 Hindman to Marmaduke and Marmaduke to Hindman, 25 Nov. 1862, Alexander Papers, CU.

Chapter Seven

1 *OR* 22(1):41–43, 792; Curtis to Herron and Herron to Curtis, 28 Nov. 1862, Curtis Papers, SHSIDM. Blunt sent an identical message to Schofield.

2 Lindberg and Matthews, "'Eagle of the 11th Kansas,'" 23; "Nassau" letter in *Daily Missouri Democrat,* 11 Dec. 1862; Silas H. Marple to wife, 25–26 Nov. 1862, Marple Family Collection, SMOH.

3 "Nassau" letter in *Daily Missouri Democrat,* 11 Dec. 1862; Blunt, "General Blunt's Account," 230; Britton, *Union Indian Brigade,* 108; Robert T. McMahan Diary, 27, 29 Nov. 1862, UMC; Bodwell Diary, 27 Nov. 1862, KSHS. Few traces remain of the historic track west of Wedington Mountain. East of the mountain it is approximated by Washington County Road 68.

4 Farlow and Barry, "Osborne's Civil War," 201; Bodwell Diary, 28 Nov. 1862, KSHS; *OR* 22(1):43. The only surviving fragment of historic Ridge Road is the southernmost two miles of Washington County Road 436.

5 Marmaduke to Hindman, 26, 28 Nov. 1862, Alexander Papers, CU. The site of Kidd's Mill is preserved in a roadside park on the west side of Arkansas 45.

6 General Order, 27 Nov. 1862, Hanway Collection, KSHS; *OR* 22(1):55–56, 58; Clement A. Evans, *Confederate Military History,* 10:138. Historic Fayetteville Road west of Prairie Grove is a combination of U.S. 62, Washington County Road 287, and Arkansas 45. Historic Cincinnati Road is Washington County Road 13 between present-day Lincoln and present-day Canehill (formerly Boonsboro). In the nineteenth century the road bent around the west and south sides of the cemetery and joined historic Fayetteville Road a quarter-mile south of the present-day highway junction. The unpaved section of historic Cincinnati Road adjacent to the cemetery still exists in a form that Marmaduke and Shelby would recognize.

7 *OR* 22(1):43.

8 Ibid.

9 *OR* 22(1):55–56. Shelby later claimed that he had covered both approaches and was not surprised by the appearance of the Federals on Fayetteville Road, but this manifestly was not the case.

10 *OR* 22(1):49; Gardner, "First Kansas Battery," 247; Crawford, *Kansas in the Sixties,* 70; Kitts, "Civil War Diary," 326; "Nassau" letter in *Daily Missouri Democrat,* 11 Dec. 1862.

11 *OR* 22(1):47, 52; Bodwell Diary, 28 Nov. 1862, KSHS. Samuel Crawford (*Kansas in the Sixties,* 68) blamed Blunt rather than Ewing for the fiasco: "The General's order of march for his cavalry and artillery was ill conceived, and his plan of battle was worse. He knew nothing of the enemy's actual position, and went blundering along with his artillery virtually unsupported, in the advance, and his cavalry and infantry all mixed up in the rear, and scattered and straggling back for miles along a muddy road."

12 "Second Brigade" letter in *Kansas State Journal,* 18 Dec. 1862; Bodwell Diary, 28 Nov. 1862, KSHS; Glover, "Accounts of Horace L. Moore"; *OR* 22(1):49.

13 *OR* 22(1):47, 49–51, 56, 58; Bodwell Diary, 28 Nov. 1862, KSHS.

14 Kitts, "Civil War Diary," 327; Gardner, "First Kansas Battery," 247; McMahan Diary, 28 Nov. 1862, UMC; Clement A. Evans, *Confederate Military History,* 10:139; Silas H. Marple to wife, 14 Dec. 1862, Marple Family Collection, SMOH; Richardson, *Early Settlers of Cane Hill,* 56.

15 Clement A. Evans, *Confederate Military History,* 10:139; *OR* 22(1):59, 53.

16 *OR* 22(1):51, 53–55; Clement A. Evans, *Confederate Military History,* 10:139.

17 *OR* 22(1):56–57, 47, 44. Historic Van Buren Road still exists as a combination of Washington County Roads 291, 8, and 284.

18 *OR* 22(1):44, 47, 57, 59; "Nassau" letter in *Daily Missouri Democrat,* 11 Dec. 1862; unidentified letter in *Emporia News,* 20 Dec. 1862; Clement A. Evans, *Confederate Military History,* 10:139.

19 *OR* 22(1):44, 47, 59; Edmond G. Ross to wife, 30 Nov. 1862, Ross Correspondence, KSHS; Bodwell Diary, 28 Nov. 1862, KSHS.

20 *OR* 22(1):53, 55, 59.

21 *OR* 22(1):44–45; "Nassau" letter in *Daily Missouri Democrat,* 11 Dec. 1862; McMahan Diary, 28 Nov. 1862, UMC.

22 *OR* 22(1}:45, 50, 52; Ewing to wife, 2 Dec. 1862, Ewing Family Papers, LC; Bodwell Diary, 28 Nov. 1862, KSHS.

23 Marple to wife, 4 Dec. 1862, Marple Family Collection, SMOH; Lindberg and Matthews, "'Eagle of the 11th Kansas,'" 24.

24 *OR* 22(1):44–45; "Second Brigade" letter in *Kansas State Journal,* 18 Dec. 1862; unidentified letter in *Emporia News,* 20 Dec. 1862.

25 *OR* 22(1):55, 59.

26 *OR* 22(1):44–45; Kitts, "Civil War Diary," 327; Ewing to wife, 2 Dec. 1862, Ewing Family Papers, LC; Bodwell Diary, 28 Nov. 1862, KSHS; Ross to wife, 30 Nov. 1862, Ross Correspondence, KSHS.

27 *OR* 22(1):45, 50. "Second Brigade" letter in *Kansas State Journal,* 18 Dec. 1862; "Nassau" letter in *Daily Missouri Democrat,* 11 Dec. 1862; Crawford, *Kansas in the Sixties,* 71.

28 *OR* 22(1):45, 53, 57, 59; Clement A. Evans, *Confederate Military History,* 10:140. Cove Creek Road south of Morrow's is approximated by Washington County Road 285. The historic road ran along the valley floor, but few traces remain.

29 *OR* 22(1):45, 54, 59; "Nassau" letter in *Daily Missouri Democrat,* 11 Dec. 1862; Britton, *Union Indian Brigade,* 114; "Letters of Samuel James Reader," 169–170n.

30 *OR* 22(1):45, 54, 58; Clement A. Evans, *Confederate Military History,* 10:140; Americus V. Rieff Memoir, Cory Papers, KSHS; "Second Brigade" letter in *Kansas State Journal,* 18 Dec. 1862; "Nassau" letter in *Daily Missouri Democrat,* 11 Dec. 1862; Britton, *Union Indian Brigade,* 114. Shelby allowed an alcoholic newspaperman named John N. Edwards to write his reports beginning in the fall of 1862. Edwards produced an appalling mishmash of fact and fiction. In his melodramatic account of the final action on Cove Creek Road, Edwards failed to mention Carroll, substituted Shelby's Missouri regiments for Carroll's Arkansas regiments, and gave Shelby full credit for turning back the Federal pursuit. Shelby endorsed Edwards's lies and Marmaduke accepted them, a fact that reflects badly on both men. Five years later Edwards distorted the truth even more in his so-called history of Shelby's Brigade. *OR* 22(1):58; Edwards, *Shelby and His Men,* 103.

31 *OR* 22(1):45; Clement A. Evans, *Confederate Military History,* 10:140–41; "Second Brigade" letter in *Kansas State Journal,* 18 Dec. 1862.

32 *OR* 22(1):45, 54, 58; Americus V. Rieff Memoir, Cory Papers, KSHS; Clement A. Evans, *Confederate Military History,* 10:141.

33 *OR* 22(1):45–46, 48, 52; "Second Brigade" letter in *Kansas State Journal,* 18 Dec. 1862;

"Nassau" letter in *Daily Missouri Democrat*, 11 Dec. 1862; Bodwell Diary, 28 Nov. 1862, KSHS; Silas H. Marple to wife, 4 Dec. 1862, Marple Family Collection, SMOH. Captain Harrell denied that the Confederates sent in a flag of truce, but the evidence for a flag is strong. Clement A. Evans, *Confederate Military History*, 10:141.

34 *OR* 22(1):46, 55, 57, 59; "Second Brigade" letter in *Kansas State Journal*, 18 Dec. 1862; List of Killed and Wounded, [30 Nov. 1862], Order Book, Fourth Cavalry Division, MHM; "Letters of Samuel James Reader," 170n. Jewell and other wounded Federals were taken to Robert Moore's house in Newburg. Richardson, *Early Settlers of Cane Hill*, 16. An officer on Marmaduke's staff wrote that ten Confederates were killed and fifty wounded, but he may not have included slightly wounded men. Robert H. Smith to wife, 30 Nov. 1862, Smith-Mendenhall Family Papers, Montana State University.

35 Marmaduke to Hindman, Hindman to Frost, Shoup, and Roane, and Hindman to R. Phillip Crump, 28 Nov. 1862, Alexander Papers, CU; *OR* 22(1):899; Weddle, *Plow-Horse Cavalry*, 78; N.A.T. letter in *San Antonio Weekly Herald*, 20 Dec. 1862.

36 Marmaduke to Hindman, 29 Nov. 1862, Alexander Papers, CU; Robert H. Smith to wife, 1 Dec. 1862, Smith-Mendenhall Family Papers, Montana State University.

37 Daily Journal, 28 Nov. 1862, Army of the Frontier, Second Brigade, First Division, NARA; Blunt to Curtis, 28 Nov. 1862, Letters Sent, Army of the Frontier, First Division, NARA; Blunt to Schofield, 28 Nov. 1862, Schofield Papers, LC; Curtis to Blunt, 1 Dec. 1862, Curtis Papers, SHSIDM; Schofield to Blunt, 6 Dec. 1862, Letters Sent, Army of the Frontier, Headquarters, NARA; *OR* 22(1):41, 795.

38 Crawford, *Kansas in the Sixties*, 72; unidentified letter in *Emporia News*, 20 Dec. 1862; Gurden E. Beates to William S. Blakely, 3 Dec. 1862, Martin Collection, KSHS.

39 "Second Brigade" letter in *Kansas State Journal*, 18 Dec. 1862; Edmund G. Ross to wife, 1 Dec. 1862, Ross Correspondence, KSHS.

40 Ellithorpe Diary, 24 Nov. 1862, CWM.

41 Ibid., 1 Dec. 1862; Edmund G. Ross to wife, 30 Nov. 1862, Ross Correspondence, KSHS; Silas H. Marple to wife, 14 Dec. 1862, Marple Family Collection, SMOH.

42 *Buck and Ball*, 15 Dec. 1862; Blunt to Salomon, Weer, and Cloud, 29 Nov. 1862, Letters Sent, First Division, and Salomon to Blunt, 1 Dec. 1862, Letters Sent, First Brigade, First Division, Army of the Frontier, NARA; McMahan Diary, 28 Nov. 1862, UMC.

43 McMahan Diary, 28 Nov. 1862, UMC; Bodwell Diary, 30 Nov. 1862, KSHS.

44 Scott, "Fighting Printers of Company E." Ross was publisher of the *Kansas State Record* (Topeka) before the war.

45 Edmund G. Ross to wife, 1 Dec. 1862, Ross Correspondence, KSHS; *OR* 22(1):42–43, 795.

Chapter Eight

1 Marmaduke to Hindman, 29 Nov. 1862, Alexander Papers, CU.

2 *OR* 22(1):899–900.

3 Marmaduke to Hindman, 29 Nov., and Robert C. Newton to Marmaduke, 30 Nov. 1862, Alexander Papers, CU. The "Topographical Engineer" was identified only as a Mr. Lawrence.

4 Marmaduke to Hindman, 29 Nov., 1 Dec. 1862, Alexander Papers, CU; Hindman to

Marmaduke, 30 Nov. 1862, Order Book, Fourth Cavalry Division, MHM; Hindman to Holmes, 1 Dec. 1862, in *Daily Missouri Republican*, 6 Feb. 1863. The Confederate telegrams published in the *Daily Missouri Republican* were part of the booty seized by Union soldiers during the Van Buren raid at the end of 1862.

5 Hindman to Robert W. Lee, 30 Nov. 1862, Alexander Papers, CU.

6 Pinnell Journals, 29, 30 Nov., 1 Dec. 1862, MHM; Waller Diary, 29, 30 Nov., 1 Dec. 1862, CWM; Daniel M. Frost to Hindman, 30 Nov., Hindman to John B. Clark Jr. and George D. Alexander to Hindman, 1 Dec. 1862, Alexander Papers, CU; Turnbo Journal, 137, University of Oklahoma.

7 Holmes to Hindman, 29, 30 Nov. 1862, Alexander Papers, CU.

8 "Conversation by telegraph between Generals Holmes and Hindman," 1 Dec. 1862, Alexander Papers, CU; Hindman letter printed in *Daily Missouri Republican*, 6 Feb. 1863.

9 Farlow and Barry, "Osborne's Civil War," 202–3; Cloud to Ellithorpe, 1 Dec. 1862, Ellithorpe Family Papers, KSHS; Ellithorpe Diary, 2 Dec. 1862, CWM; Hindman to Roane, Shoup, Frost, and Marmaduke, 1 Dec., and Marmaduke to Hindman, 2 Dec. 1862, Alexander Papers, CU; *OR* 22(1):146. Hindman instructed Marmaduke to provide an escort for messengers on Cove Creek Road, Telegraph Road, Frog Bayou Road, and the Line Road. "It is unsafe to send unarmed couriers," he warned. Hindman to Marmaduke, 25 Nov. 1862, Correspondence of Marmaduke, Collection of Confederate Records, NARA.

10 *OR* 22(1):900; Hindman to Cooper, 1 Dec. 1862, Order Book, Fourth Cavalry Division, MHM; Cooper to Hindman, 2 Dec. 1862, Alexander Papers, CU; Cooper to Jerome P. Wilson, 3 Dec. 1862, Wilson Papers, Emory University, Atlanta.

11 Waller Diary, 1–4 Dec. 1862, CWM; Hoskin Diary, 29 Nov.–4 Dec. 1862, UMC; Lane Memoir, 37, UMC; Hindman to Marmaduke, 3 Dec. 1862, Alexander Papers, CU. Historic Telegraph Road from Van Buren to Dripping Springs (the actual springs and not the present-day hamlet of the same name) is Arkansas 59 and Old Uniontown Road; from Dripping Springs to Cedarville, it is Arkansas 220 and Arkansas 59; from Cedarville to Lee Creek, it is approximated by Arkansas 59 (the historic road parallels the modern highway about a half-mile to the east for three miles), then it is Arkansas 220.

12 Holmes to Hindman, 5 Dec. 1862, Alexander Papers, CU.

13 *OR* 22(1):805; Blunt to Commanding Officer, 2 Dec. 1862, Letters Sent, Army of the Frontier, First Division, NARA; Bishop, *Loyalty on the Frontier*, 67; *SOR* 4:29. Blunt did not know Herron was in command because there was no communication between the two wings of the Army of the Frontier from 20 November, the day Schofield left Springfield, to 3 December, a total of thirteen days.

14 Helm Memoir, LLC, USAMHI; Circular, 2 Dec. 1862, General Orders, Army of the Frontier, First Division, NARA; Daily Journal, 3–6 Dec. 1862, Army of the Frontier, Second Brigade, First Division, NARA; *OR* 22(1):71–72; "Nassau" letter in *Daily Missouri Democrat*, 27 Dec. 1862.

15 McMahan Diary, 3–6 Dec. 1862, UMC; Kitts, "Civil War Diary," 328; Bodwell Diary, 3–7 Dec. 1862, KSHS; Titcomb Diary, 3–5 Dec. 1862, HL; Greene, "Campaigning," 297.

16 Allen, "Three Frontier Battles," 489.

17 Blunt, "General Blunt's Account," 231.

18 Crawford, *Kansas in the Sixties*, 72–73; Glover, "Accounts of Horace L. Moore." Crawford stated that he personally rode to Boonsboro and informed Blunt of the Confederate approach, but his egocentric version of events on 6–7 December is contradicted by other accounts.

19 Blunt to Herron, 5 Dec. 1862, Letters Sent, Army of the Frontier, First Division, NARA; Blunt to wife, 5 Dec. 1862, Civil War Letters, MC. Italics added to the Blunt quotation.

20 Blunt to Salomon, 5 Dec. 1862, Letters Sent, Army of the Frontier, First Division, NARA.

21 Titcomb Diary, 4 Dec. 1862, HL; Kitts "Civil War Diary," 328; Ellithorpe Diary, 3 Dec. 1862, CWM; Thomas Ewing to wife, 2 Dec. 1862, Ewing Family Papers, LC; McMahan Diary, 2 Dec. 1862, UMC.

22 *OR* 22(1):83. The address was headed "In the field, December 4, 1862," but it must have been printed in Van Buren a day or two earlier. Some Union accounts give the impression that the Prairie Grove battlefield was littered with copies of the address, but the acute scarcity of paper in the Confederate army meant that only a limited number of sheets were printed. The terms "tories" and "hired Dutch" referred to Loyalists and Hessians in the War of Independence, barely eighty years in the past.

23 *OR* 22(1):140.

24 Bull Memoir, 59–60, MHS; Pinnell Journals, 6 Dec. 1862, MHM; Company Book of Company B, 5 Dec. 1862, AHC; *Dallas Herald*, 13 Dec. 1862. Information about the eclipse was provided by the MacDonald Observatory, Fort Davis, Tex. Edwards (*Shelby and His Men*, 95) stated incorrectly that the eclipse took place on the night of 6 December.

25 *OR* 22(1):71, 149.

26 *OR* 13:458, 22(1):147, 154; *SOR* 4:75.

27 *OR* 13:458, 22(1):154; *SOR* 4:75; Farlow and Barry, "Osborne's Civil War," 203.

28 *OR* 13:458, 22(1):154, 94; *SOR* 4:75; Spencer H. Mitchell to parents, 30 Jan. 1863, Mitchell Letter, UMC; Bodwell Diary, 6 Dec. 1862, KSHS.

29 *OR* 22(1):147, 154; *SOR* 21(2):176; Bodwell Diary, 6 Dec. 1862, KSHS; Farlow and Barry, "Osborne's Civil War," 204; Clement A. Evans, *Confederate Military History*, 10:143.

30 *OR* 22(1):154; Clement A. Evans, *Confederate Military History*, 10:142–43; Helm Memoir, LLC, USAMHI; Kitts, "Civil War Diary," 328.

31 Company Book of Company B, 6 Dec. 1862, AHC; *OR* 22(1):154, 147, 140; Kitts, "Civil War Diary," 328.

32 Spencer H. Mitchell to parents, 30 Jan. 1863, Mitchell Letter, UMC; Lane Memoir, 37, UMC; *OR* 22(1):140.

33 *OR* 22(1):812–13.

34 *OR* 22(1):72, 124, 126–27.

35 *OR* 22(1):140. Some accounts state that Holmes warned Hindman of Herron's approach. This is incorrect. Holmes telegraphed Hindman on 6 and 7 December to ad-

vise him that Union forces in southwest Missouri were heading his way, but these warnings were based on faulty information from a civilian source who claimed to have seen Union columns leave Springfield on 27 and 28 November. More to the point, the telegrams did not reach Hindman until *after* the battle of Prairie Grove. *OR* 22(1):902; Holmes to Hindman, 7 Dec. 1862, Alexander Papers, CU. The Morrow house was moved to Prairie Grove Battlefield State Park in the 1950s.

36 *OR* 22(1):140.

37 Pittman Memoir, UAF; Pinnell Journals, 7 Dec. 1862, MHM; *OR* 22(1):140.

Chapter Nine

1 *OR* 22(1):806–7, 794; Herron to Curtis, 1 Dec. 1862, Curtis Papers, SHSIDM. Curtis asked Brigadier General Egbert B. Brown, commanding militia forces in southwest Missouri, whether he had "spare forces" with which to assist Blunt. Brown did not, nor did anyone else. Curtis to Brown and Brown to Curtis, 3 Dec. 1862, Curtis Papers, SHSIDM.

2 Barnes, *What I Saw You Do*, 15–16; unidentified letter in *Keokuk Gate City*, 31 Dec. 1862; H.I.H. letter in *Daily Missouri Democrat*, 22 Dec. 1862.

3 Jacob D. Brewster to wife, 3 Dec. 1862, Brewster Letters, SHSIDM.

4 Andrews, *Civil War Diary*, 3; Monnett, "Yankee Cavalryman," 292; Smith Diary, 4 Dec. 1862, DWC; Barney, *Recollections*, 110. A division-size camp sprawled across a large area, and the distance marched by a given regiment might vary considerably from the distance marched by another regiment in the same division.

5 Pratt, "Civil War Letters," 264; Barney, *Recollections*, 111; Tilley, *Federals on the Frontier*, 55; Bonnell Diary, 3–5 Dec. 1862, USAMHI.

6 Monnett, "Yankee Cavalryman," 293; Vaught, "Diary of an Unknown Soldier," 83–85; Arthur Diary, 5 Dec. 1862, UND.

7 Daily Journal, 3–5 Dec. 1862, Army of the Frontier, Second Division, NARA.

8 Herron to Curtis, 5 Dec. 1862, Curtis Papers, SHSIDM; *OR* 22(1):809–10.

9 Williams Diary, 5 Dec. 1862, KSHS; Blunt to Herron, 5 Dec. 1862, Letters Sent, Army of the Frontier, First Division, NARA.

10 *OR* 22(1):123–27, 812; Ingersoll, *Iowa and the Rebellion*, 363; Francis Springer Diary, 6 Dec. 1862, Springer Papers, ISHL; unidentified letter in *Keokuk Gate City*, 31 Dec. 1862.

11 *OR* 22(1):813.

12 Vaught, "Diary of an Unknown Soldier," 86; Tilley, *Federals on the Frontier*, 57; Bonnell Diary, 6 Dec. 1862, USAMHI; Houghland, "19th Iowa," 64; Dungan, *Nineteenth Regiment Iowa*, 52.

13 Bonnell Diary, 6 Dec. 1862, USAMHI; Houghland, "19th Iowa," 64; Vaught, "Diary of an Unknown Soldier," 86; Baxter, *Pea Ridge and Prairie Grove*, 180. The junction of historic Telegraph and Fayetteville roads is approximated by the present-day intersection of Sixth Street and Razorback Road. University of Arkansas athletic facilities now occupy the cove where Herron's men rested along Town Branch.

14 Daily Journal, 5, 6 Dec. 1862, Army of the Frontier, Second Division, NARA; Adams, "Battle of Prairie Grove," 452–54; Barney, *Recollections*, 111–12.

15 Prentis, *Kansas Miscellanies,* 19.

16 Leake, "Campaign," 283; Eugene B. Payne, "Prairie Grove," 6; Barney, *Recollections,* 109–10; Tilley, *Federals on the Frontier,* 55–56; Bonnell Diary, 4 Dec. 1862, USAMHI. Leake provided additional information: "During the stay at Camp Lyon the men [of the Twentieth Iowa] were provided with everything they needed for comfort except shoes and stockings. Only 100 pairs of shoes, 180 pairs of infantry boots, and 108 pairs of socks could be obtained. These were distributed through the regiment to those who were most in need of them." *SOR* 4:43–44.

17 Arkansas 170 approximates the route of historic Fayetteville Road between present-day Farmington and Prairie Grove. The winding sections of the highway follow the original roadbed.

18 *SOR* 4:34; *OR* 22(1):102, 105, 137; Thomas H. Moore letter in *National Tribune,* 6 Nov. 1884.

19 Bishop, *Loyalty on the Frontier,* 67–68; *SOR* 4:29–30; Harrison to Blunt, 6 Dec. 1862, Letters Received, Army of the Frontier, First Division, NARA; "One Who Was There" letter in *Daily Missouri Democrat,* 27 Jan. 1863. Blunt accused Harrison of cowardice, but the evidence supports Harrison's contention that his horses were in poor condition and that he kept Blunt fully informed of his progress and problems. Moreover, Blunt's order sending Harrison to Rhea's Mill is straightforward and contains no hint of displeasure. For Blunt's diatribe against Harrison, see *OR* 22(1):72.

20 Blunt to "Commanding Officer of the Advance Cavalry of General Herron's Command," 6 Dec. 1862, Herron Papers, NYHS; "One Who Was There" letter in *Daily Missouri Democrat,* 27 Jan. 1863.

21 *OR* 22(1):113; Monnett, "Yankee Cavalryman," 295; Jewett, *Failed Ambition,* 166–67.

22 *SOR* 4:30; "One Who Was There" letter in *Daily Missouri Democrat,* 27 Jan. 1863; Office of the Adjutant General, *Report of the Adjutant General of Arkansas,* 55–56.

23 *OR* 22(1):147, 149–50.

24 Ibid.

25 *OR* 22(1):113–14, 147, 150.

26 *OR* 22(1):113, 147, 150; Ford Memoir, 16–17, MHM; Jewett, *Failed Ambition,* 168; George W. Williams to wife, 10 Dec. 1862, Williams Letters, LLC, USAMHI; McCorkle, *Three Years with Quantrill,* 78; Henry Worthen and William T. McKee letters in *National Tribune,* 30 Oct. 1884, 8 Sept. 1927; Monnett, "Yankee Cavalryman," 298–99.

27 *OR* 22(1):154; Mock Letter, PGBSP. MacDonald's report in the *OR* should read "northeasterly" instead of "northwesterly." No trace of what MacDonald called the "right-hand road" survives, but it appears on two Union maps, one of which correctly identifies it as "Neighborhood Road." Arthur Diary, UND; Ward Map, PGBSP.

28 *OR* 22(1):154–57.

29 *SOR* 4:30–31; "One Who Was There" letter in *Daily Missouri Democrat,* 27 Jan. 1863; Charles F. Eichacker to Bryant, 31 Dec. 1862, Bryant Collection, Chicago Historical Society; Ford Memoir, 16–17, MHM; Ellis Steverson letter in *National Tribune,* 19 July 1913. McNulta, "Incidents of a Battle," is largely fiction and should be used with caution.

30 *OR* 22(1):154–55; Ford Memoir, 18, MHM; Office of the Adjutant General, *Report of*

the Adjutant General of Arkansas, 56; *SOR* 4:31; Jewett, *Failed Ambition,* 168; MacDonald to Marmaduke, 24 Dec. 1862, Alexander Papers, CU. A First Arkansas Cavalry officer explained that the regiment was caught off guard because the "information contained in the order [to proceed to Rhea's Mill], together with the fact that troops had passed through all night undisturbed, made it a matter of entire surprise to us to find the enemy there at all, and especially in force." "One Who Was There" letter in *Daily Missouri Democrat,* 27 Jan. 1863.

31 *SOR* 4:31. Harrison reported that "the officers of my command, with one or two exceptions, did all in their power to stay the stampeded troops at the commencement of the battle, and through the day exhibited great coolness." *SOR* 4:33.

32 *OR* 22(1):102–3, 156–57; Ford Memoir, 17–18, MHM.

33 *OR* 22(1):156–57. Edwards's (*Shelby and His Men,* 117–18) postwar account of this episode fails to mention MacDonald, Young, or Crump. Another source claims that Shelby was rescued by Gregg's guerrillas. Crittenden, *Crittenden Memoirs,* 239.

34 *OR* 22(1):147, 155–57; Duncan, "Soldiers Fare," 50–51; N.A.T. letter in *San Antonio Weekly Herald,* 10 Jan. 1863; Henry Worthen letter in *National Tribune,* 30 Oct. 1884; Jewett, *Failed Ambition,* 170.

35 *OR* 22(1):85, 123, 137, 147, 150; *SOR* 4:22; Henry Worthen letter in *National Tribune,* 30 Oct. 1884. Union casualty lists contain discrepancies, so the numbers in the text should be considered approximate rather than definitive. Confederate losses cannot be determined because Marmaduke's Division suffered additional casualties during the day.

36 *OR* 22(1):141, 147, 155.

37 Brewster to wife, 9 Dec. 1862, Brewster Letters, SHSIDM; *OR* 22(1):102–3; *SOR* 4:34.

38 Vaught, "Diary of an Unknown Soldier," 86–87; Baldridge Memoir, PGBSP; Barney, *Recollections,* 118–19; Prentis, *Kansas Miscellanies,* 19; Tilley, *Federals on the Frontier,* 71.

39 Dungan, *Nineteenth Regiment Iowa,* 52; Elder, *Damned Iowa Greyhound,* 36–37; F. T. Hawley letter in *National Tribune,* 21 July 1887.

40 "Brief History of 20th Regiment Wisconsin Volunteers," Farley Papers, SHSW; *OR* 22(1):103, 105, 132, 136, 147, 150.

Chapter Ten

1 Samuel P. Pittman account in *Prairie Grove Herald,* 10 Dec. 1914; "Thomas" letter in *Davenport Daily Democrat and News,* 1 Jan. 1863.

2 Gatewood, "Prairie Grove Valley," 19–20; Edmund G. Ross to wife, 12 Dec. 1862, Ross Correspondence, KSHS. The historic church was located just north of the present-day white frame Presbyterian church on Buchanan Street (U.S. 62). The Buchanan house was a few hundred yards northeast of the historic church, but it, too, is gone. When the postwar town of Prairie Grove was laid out, the meandering historic roads and lanes were "straightened" to conform to the standard plat or grid. The historic junction of Fayetteville and Cove Creek roads was located near the intersection of Mock and Bush streets, about three blocks north of the traffic light on Buchanan Street.

3 Pratt, "Civil War Letters," 267; "Jenks" letter in *Daily Missouri Democrat,* 18 Dec. 1862; Britton, *Memoirs,* 52–53.

4 Dan P. Thomas to wife, 18 Dec. 1862, Thomas Letter, PGBSP; Lane Memoir, 38, UMC; Spencer H. Mitchell to parents, 30 Jan. 1863, Mitchell Letter, UMC; Williams Memoir, *CWTI,* USAMHI; Cornelius Buckler to wife, 15 Dec. 1862, Watkins Collection, AHC.

5 Pittman Memoir, UAF; William J. Wright, "Charge at Prairie Grove," *Daily Missouri Republican,* 3 Apr. 1886.

6 *OR* 22(1):141, 53:459; *SOR* 4:55, 75–76, 88; Pinnell Journals, 7 Dec. 1862, MHM.

7 *OR* 22(1):141.

8 Ibid.; Hindman to Holmes, 12 Dec. 1862, Alexander Papers, CU.

9 Edwards, *Shelby and His Men,* 98; Woodruff, *With the Light Guns,* 84–85.

10 *SOR* 4:58–59, 63; William J. Wright, "Charge at Prairie Grove," *Daily Missouri Republican,* 3 Apr. 1886.

11 *OR* 22(1):150–51, 155, 158; *SOR* 4:58–59, 64, 72; Woodruff, *With the Light Guns,* 85.

12 *OR* 22(1):147–48, 155.

13 *OR* 22(1):140.

14 *OR* 22(1):141.

15 Ibid. Major William E. Woodruff, Shoup's artillery commander, stated that Shoup learned of Herron's approach from Marmaduke and that Shoup passed that information to Hindman when the two generals conferred on the Ridge. Shoup concocted a different story in his report. He claimed that Shelby told him Herron was "halted a short distance ahead" and that the Federals were "in no considerable force." Because both Marmaduke and Shelby were falling back before Herron's rapid advance, it is highly unlikely either man would have made such a statement. Shoup then presented a convoluted and implausible explanation of his subsequent decision to halt: "As I should have to cross the creek, which involved delay, and as I believed I would be following an inconsiderable force while the main body of the enemy was in the opposite direction, and as the position on the ridge offered an excellent defense, I thought that the position should be held by a part of my command, while the rest should join in a movement on General Blunt, whom I supposed to be moving from Cane Hill." None of this squares with what Shoup told Hindman on the Ridge, as confirmed by both Hindman and Woodruff. *SOR* 4:57–58; Woodruff, *With the Light Guns,* 84–85.

16 *OR* 22(1):73, 87–88, 141, 459–60; Jewett, *Failed Ambition,* 168.

17 Unidentified letter in *Arkansas State Gazette,* 14 Feb. 1863.

18 Brandenburg Memoir, Mock Letter, and Pyeatt Memoir, PGBSP; Staples Memoir, AHC.

19 *OR* 22(1):103, 106; *SOR* 4:34–35.

20 *OR* 22(1):103, 105–6, 132, 136; *SOR* 4:35.

21 *OR* 22(1):105–6, 136; *SOR* 4:35, 58, 64, 72.

22 *SOR* 4:35, 51; *OR* 22(1):103; unidentified letter in *Arkansas State Gazette,* 27 Dec. 1862; Fred T. Hawley letter in *National Tribune,* 21 July 1887; Charles D. Thompson to father, Dec. 21, 1862, Thompson Letters, McLean County Historical Society, Bloomington, Ill.

23 *SOR* 4:35; Jacob D. Brewster to wife, 9 Dec. 1862, Brewster Letters, SHSIDM.

24 *OR* 22(1):109, 111; Payne Journal, 21, University of Michigan; Edwin B. Messer letter in *Waukegan Weekly Gazette*, 27 Dec. 1862; Henry Heitahrends letter in *Rock Island Weekly Union*, 31 Dec. 1862; Tilley, *Federals on the Frontier*, 72.

25 *OR* 22(1):106. The downstream ford is now known as "Taylor Ford."

26 *OR* 22(1):106, 109, 115, 118, 120, 123; *SOR* 4:44–45.

27 *SOR* 4:59, 72; *OR* 22(1):123.

28 *OR* 22(1):107, 123; "Jenks" letter in *Des Moines State Register*, 23 Dec. 1862; Woodruff, *With the Light Guns*, 85.

29 *SOR* 4:59.

30 *OR* 22(1):112, 128–29, 136, 151. The relocation of U.S. 62 in the 1950s severely damaged the knoll. Engineers cut a "notch" fifteen feet deep and fifty feet wide through the center of the knoll to accommodate a two-lane highway. Construction of a house atop the knoll a few years later resulted in additional damage.

31 *SOR* 4:72; Ruffner, "Sketch of First Missouri Battery," 417–18.

32 *OR* 22(1):103, 118, 129; Ruffner, "Sketch of First Missouri Battery," 418; Pratt, "Civil War Letters," 265.

33 William H. Jaques letter in *Fairfield Ledger*, 8 Jan. 1863; Prentis, *Kansas Miscellanies*, 20; William S. Pierce letter in *National Tribune*, 26 June 1890.

34 Barney, *Recollections*, 120; Messer letter in *Waukegan Weekly Gazette*, 27 Dec. 1862.

35 *OR* 22(1):136, 142, 158; *SOR* 4:73; Barney Seaman, "Prairie Grove," *Daily Missouri Republican*, 13 Feb. 1886; unidentified letter printed in *Arkansas State Gazette*, 27 Dec. 1862.

36 Edwards, *Shelby and His Men*, 100; *OR* 22(1):158; *SOR* 4:73; Woodruff, *With the Light Guns*, 87; J.L.C. letter in *Daily Missouri Republican*, 19 Dec. 1862; "By One Who Was In It" letter in *Indianapolis Daily Journal*, 29 Dec. 1862; Britton, *Memoirs*, 49; William P. Black to mother, 9 Dec. 1862, Black Family Papers, ISHL.

37 McRae to Shoup (McRae's report), 9 Dec. 1862, Herron Papers, NYHS; McRae to wife, [? Dec. 1862], McRae Papers, AHC; Edwards, *Shelby and His Men*, 100.

38 Duncan, "Soldiers Fare," 51; William J. Wright, "Charge at Prairie Grove," *Daily Missouri Republican*, 3 Apr. 1886; Elliott, *Garden of Memory*, 69; Rockwell Memoir, UMC.

39 Jewett, *Failed Ambition*, 170.

40 *SOR* 4:35; *OR* 22(1):101, 104, 123–24; Leake, "Campaign," 284; Adams, "Battle of Prairie Grove," 456.

41 *OR* 22(1):816.

Chapter Eleven

1 *OR* 22(1):132, 134.

2 *OR* 22(1):136.

3 Pratt, "Civil War Letters," 256.

4 *OR* 22(1):130, 134–35; Tilley, *Federals on the Frontier*, 66; Vaught, "Diary of an Unknown Soldier," 87.

5 *OR* 22(1):132; William H. Horine to cousin and to brother, 8, 25 Jan. 1863, Horine Letters, and Charles D. Thompson to father, 21 Dec. 1862, Thompson Letters, McLean County Historical Society, Bloomington, Ill.; Joseph B. Weaver letter in *Bloomington*

Daily Pantagraph, 27 Dec. 1862. Among the casualties was Henry C. Greenman, the only member of the Ninety-fourth Illinois killed outright at Prairie Grove. The historic east cornfield is south of present-day U.S. 62 and lies outside the park. A housing development occupies the site.

6 *OR* 22(1):132, 151; Weaver letter, unidentified letter, and J.K.M. letter in *Bloomington Daily Pantagraph*, 27, 29, 31 Dec. 1862.

7 *OR* 22(1):106, 128, 130, 134; *United States Biographical Dictionary*, 555; Pratt, "Civil War Letters," 266; unidentified letter in *Bloomington Daily Pantagraph*, 29 Dec. 1862. Orme remained near the Ninety-fourth Illinois throughout the battle. His constant presence annoyed McNulta, who emphasized in his report and postwar writings that it was he, not Orme, who commanded the regiment at Prairie Grove.

8 Adams, "Battle of Prairie Grove," 457; *SOR* 4:36, 65; "W" letter in *Arkansas Patriot*, 25 Dec. 1862.

9 Fred T. Hawley letter in *National Tribune*, 21 July 1887; *Army of the Frontier*, 5–6.

10 *OR* 22(1):128; *Soldiers' and Citizens' Album of Biographical Record*, 2:775–76; Prentis, *Kansas Miscellanies*, 21; E.G.M. [Edward G. Miller] letter in *Wisconsin State Journal*, 26 Dec. 1862. Fagan stated that Blocher fired "grape and canister" at the approaching Federals, but Blocher made no such claim and no one in the Twentieth Wisconsin mentioned coming under fire. Fagan's report is riddled with inaccuracies and should be used with caution. *SOR* 4:65.

11 *SOR* 4:73; unidentified letter in *Arkansas State Gazette*, 27 Dec. 1862. The lone artillery piece atop the Ridge today supposedly represents Blocher's position, but it is too far forward. The four (later three) Confederate guns were located in Borden's lane, which is now a paved walkway. Stand a few yards south of the walkway and you can see what Blocher saw. On a related subject, one of Blocher's gunners asserted that "*we had not a shadow of support from the commencement to the close of the fight*," evidence of the distance between the military crest on the brow of the Ridge, where Blocher was posted, and the location of the infantry on the natural crest. The gunner also stated that all twelve horses belonging to his gun and caisson were killed. He noted that his "gun-team was composed of six fine grey horses, that had just been purchased for us, and presented a splendid target for the enemy to play on." Blocher lost forty-three horses at Prairie Grove, by far the highest toll experienced by any battery on either side. Unidentified letter in *Arkansas State Gazette*, 27 Dec. 1862.

12 *SOR* 4:73; Prentis, *Kansas Miscellanies*, 21; Rundle Memoir, SHSW; "B" letter in *Milwaukee Daily Sentinel*, 8 Jan. 1863; E.G.M. letter in *Wisconsin State Journal*, 26 Dec. 1862; Gilbert F. Wilson and Hawley letters in *National Tribune*, 28 Nov. 1912, 21 July 1887.

13 *SOR* 4:59; McRae to Shoup, 9 Dec. 1862 (McRae's report), Herron Papers, NYHS; Jewett, *Failed Ambition*, 168.

14 Morgan to McRae (Morgan's report), 9 Dec. 1862, Morgan Collection, AHC.

15 *SOR* 4:65; Alexander T. Hawthorn letter in *Mobile Advertiser and Register*, 31 Jan. 1863.

16 *SOR* 4:63–65.

17 Hawthorn letter in *Mobile Advertiser and Register*, 31 Jan. 1863.

18 *SOR* 4:66, 69–71; Hawthorn letter in *Mobile Advertiser and Register*, 31 Jan. 1863;

John C. Wright, *Memoirs*, 97–98. Polk was a nephew of Confederate lieutenant general Leonidas Polk and a more distant relative of former president James K. Polk.

19 William S. Pierce letter in *National Tribune*, 26 June 1890; Charles E. Steven letter, 25 Dec. 1862, and Henry E. Thompson letter, 9 Dec. 1862, "Correspondence of Wisconsin Volunteers," Quiner Papers, SHSW; Rundle Memoir, SHSW; Prentis, *Kansas Miscellanies*, 21–22; Henry A. Starr letter in *Milwaukee Daily Sentinel*, 27 Dec. 1862; E.G.M. letter in *Wisconsin State Journal*, 26 Dec. 1862; *OR* 22(1):128; Egbert A. Sprague to aunt, 5 Jan. 1863, Sprague Papers, SHSW.

20 Prentis, *Kansas Miscellanies*, 21–22; E.G.M. letter in *Wisconsin State Journal*, 26 Dec. 1862; Rundle Memoir, SHSW. Herron told Blunt that the Third Division captured "four caissons complete, and filled with ammunition." In like manner, he informed Curtis that the haul included "four caissons filled with good ammunition and everything in good style." *OR* 22(1):104, 107; *SOR* 4:37. Herron, of course, was not on the Ridge. A member of Blocher's Battery reported that the Confederates retained all four guns but only two caissons. The two missing caissons were presumed captured. Unidentified letter in *Arkansas State Gazette*, 27 Dec. 1862. Blocher's report is full of evasions and omissions; it includes this wonderfully disingenuous statement: "Two of my caissons I could not find, supposed to have been carried to the rear by our own men." *SOR* 4:73–74. Readers may draw their own conclusions.

21 *OR* 22(1):134–35; Vaught, "Diary of Unknown Soldier," 87; Tilley, *Federals on the Frontier*, 59, 67; William H. Jaques letter in *Fairfield Ledger*, 8 Jan. 1863.

22 Elder, *Damned Iowa Greyhound*, 35–39; *SOR* 4:65; Jaques letter in *Fairfield Ledger*, 8 Jan. 1863; Herron letter in *Mt. Pleasant Home Journal*, 14 Feb. 1863.

23 Elder, *Damned Iowa Greyhound*, 35; S.B.G. [Samuel B. Guernsey] letter in *Fort Madison Plain Dealer*, 2 Jan. 1863; "19th Ioway or the Prairie Grove Fight," 65, State Historical Society of Iowa, Iowa City.

24 *OR* 22(1):135; Elder, *Damned Iowa Greyhound*, 35–39; Jaques letter in *Fairfield Ledger*, 8 Jan. 1863; Will S. Brooks letter in *Burlington Hawkeye*, 14 Jan. 1863.

25 William J. Wright, "Charge at Prairie Grove," *Daily Missouri Republican*, 3 Apr. 1886.

26 Columbus H. Gray to father, 12 Dec. 1862, Gray Letter, PGBSP.

27 *SOR* 4:66; *Little Rock True Democrat*, 4 Feb. 1863; Gray to father, 12 Dec. 1862, Gray Letter, PGBSP.

28 *OR* 22(1):130–31, 135; S.B.G. letter in *Fort Madison Plain Dealer*, 2 Jan. 1863.

29 *OR* 22(1):110, 112, 123–24, 129, 136.

30 "Jenks" letter in *Daily Missouri Democrat*, 18 Dec. 1862.

31 Barney Seaman, "Prairie Grove," *Daily Missouri Republican*, 13 Feb. 1886; Eugene B. Payne, "Prairie Grove," 12; "Jenks" letter in *Daily Missouri Democrat*, 18 Dec. 1862; "19th Ioway and the Prairie Grove Fight," 65; Ingersoll, *Iowa and the Rebellion*, 327.

32 *OR* 22(1):106, 136; Wilson letter in *National Tribune*, 28 Nov. 1912; Jaques letter in *Fairfield Ledger*, 8 Jan. 1863.

33 *OR* 22(1):142; *SOR* 4:59–60, 70.

34 *SOR* 4:436; Uriah Eberhart to wife, 10 Dec. 1862, Eberhart Papers, SHSW.

35 E.G.M. letter in *Wisconsin State Journal*, 26 Dec. 1862; *OR* 22(1):85; Henry Thompson letter, 9 Dec. 1862, Nathan Cole letter, n.d., and Henry A. Starr letter, 9 Dec. 1862,

"Correspondence of Wisconsin Volunteers," Quiner Papers, SHSW; Prentis, *Kansas Miscellanies*, 22; Starr letters in *Milwaukee Daily Sentinel*, 23, 27 Dec. 1862.

36 "Jenks" letter in *Daily Missouri Democrat*, 18 Dec. 1862; *OR* 22(1):86; "NED" letter in *Mt. Pleasant Home Journal*, 21 Feb. 1863; Jaques letter in *Fairfield Ledger*, 8 Jan. 1863.

37 *OR* 22(1):86, 131–33; Tilley, *Federals on the Frontier*, 59; Cook, *Immortal Blue*, 14. The Ninety-fourth Illinois was composed entirely of men from Bloomington and McLean County.

38 *SOR* 4:36.

Chapter Twelve

1 *OR* 22(1):109; William P. Black letter in *Chicago Tribune*, 25 Dec. 1862.

2 "By One Who Was In It" letter in *Indianapolis Daily Journal*, 29 Dec. 1862; Black letter in *Chicago Tribune*, 25 Dec. 1862; William P. Black to mother, 9 Dec. 1862, Black Family Papers, ISHL.

3 *OR* 22(1):109; Leake, "Campaign," 285.

4 *OR* 22(1):111; "By One Who Was In It" letter in *Indianapolis Daily Journal*, 29 Dec. 1862; Mullins, *Fremont Rifles*.

5 "By One Who Was In It" letter in *Indianapolis Daily Journal*, 29 Dec. 1862; *SOR* 4:67; Ezra W. Border letter in *National Tribune*, 18 Dec. 1913; William P. Black to mother, 9 Dec. 1862, Black Family Papers, ISHL; Adams, "Battle of Prairie Grove," 458. The Confederates who occupied the Borden homestead and briefly slowed Huston's advance may have been Captain Samuel Gibson's company of Morgan's Arkansas Infantry. Asa S. Morgan to Dandridge McRae, 9 Dec. 1862 (Morgan's report), Morgan Collection, AHC.

6 Eugene B. Payne, "Prairie Grove," 13; Heaton Memoir, PGBSP.

7 *OR* 22(1):109, 111; Border letter in *National Tribune*, 18 Dec. 1913; "By One Who Was In It" letter in *Indianapolis Daily Journal*, 29 Dec. 1862.

8 *OR* 22(1):150–51; "By One Who Was In It" letter in *Indianapolis Daily Journal*, 29 Dec. 1862.

9 *OR* 22(1):142; *SOR* 4:60, 76–77. Shoup may have been influenced by McRae, who erroneously believed Huston was heading in his direction in "overwhelming force" and called for help. McRae to Shoup (McRae's report), 9 Dec. 1862, Herron Papers, NYHS.

10 *SOR* 4:88, 91; Ruffner, "Sketch of First Missouri Battery," 417–18.

11 *OR* 22(1):110, 115, 123; *SOR* 4:88, 91–92; Roberts Letter, PGBSP; Ruffner, "Sketch of First Missouri Battery," 418. Roberts submitted a letter of resignation two months after the battle. Frost endorsed the letter as follows: "Captain Roberts is totally ignorant of the duties of an artillery officer, although in other respects a brave and worthy man and soldier." Roberts Letter, 12 Feb. 1863, PGBSP.

12 *SOR* 4:80–82, 90; Maddox, *Hard Trials*, 7.

13 *SOR* 4:81–82; Spears, "Autobiography," 62.

14 *OR* 22(1):151; *SOR* 4:82; Courtland E. Whitsit letter in *Indianapolis Daily State Sentinel*, 22 Dec. 1862; W.W.M. letter in *Aurora Commercial*, 1 Jan. 1863. Adams misidentified Elliott's Missourians as Crump's Texans in his report.

15 Border letter in *National Tribune,* 18 Dec. 1913; *OR* 22(1):111; Robert F. Braden to mother, 12 Dec. 1862, Braden Papers, ISL; William P. Black to mother, 9 Dec. 1862, Black Family Papers, ISHL.

16 McFarland, "John C. Black"; Border letter in *National Tribune,* 18 Dec. 1913.

17 *OR* 22(1):118; Payne Journal, 22, University of Michigan; David L. Ash to wife, 10 Dec. 1862, Ash Papers, USAMHI.

18 *OR* 22(1):118–19; William P. Clark letter in *Chicago Tribune,* 25 Dec. 1862; John C. Black testimony, Black Court of Inquiry, Army of the Frontier, NARA; Eugene B. Payne to wife, 9 Dec. 1862, Payne Papers, Wilder Collection, Teaneck, N.J.; Morse Journal, 7 Dec. 1862, PGBSP; Edwin B. Messer letter in *Waukegan Weekly Gazette,* 27 Dec. 1862.

19 *SOR* 4:82–83; Charles W. Adams to Robert G. Shaver, 14 Dec. 1862, Alexander Papers, CU; Maddox, *Hard Trials,* 7–8. Adams also praised Major James H. Williams for his "gallantry, daring, and very efficient services; he was everywhere present in the thickest of the fire, cheering, encouraging, and urging the men forward, and in the confusion which ensued, [he] exerted himself almost to exhaustion to rally the men." *SOR* 4:83–84.

20 *OR* 22(1):119; Morse Journal, 7 Dec. 1862, PGBSP; John C. Black testimony, John C. Black Court of Inquiry, Army of the Frontier, NARA; William P. Black to mother, 9 Dec. 1862, Black Family Papers, ISHL; William D. McCord letter in *Illinois Gazette,* 7 Jan. 1863; Alexander T. Hawthorn letter in *Mobile Advertiser and Register,* 31 Jan. 1863.

21 Daniel Huston testimony, John C. Black Court of Inquiry, Army of the Frontier, NARA.

22 Robert F. Braden to mother, 12 Dec. 1862, Braden Papers, ISL; *OR* 22(1):85, 112; Courtland E. Whitsit letter in *Indianapolis Daily State Sentinel,* 22 Dec. 1862.

23 *OR* 22(1)1:85; William P. Black to mother, 9 Dec. 1862, Black Family Papers, ISHL. Henry Frisbie wrote an anonymous letter to a St. Louis newspaper in which he indirectly accused Colonel Black of cowardice. Black requested a Court of Inquiry to clear his name. The court found that Black was a "very excellent officer" who saved his regiment from "annihilation" and that a "more gallant soldier never faced an enemy." For good measure, the court denounced the author of the letter as "conniving, unscrupulous, and malicious" and recommended that he be brought up on charges. Schofield approved the decision of the court. "F" letter in *Daily Missouri Democrat,* 1 Jan. 1863; General Orders No. 12, 17 Feb. 1863, Army of the Frontier, NARA.

24 Eugene B. Payne, "Prairie Grove," 15–16; *OR* 22(1):106; *SOR* 4:36; J.L.C. letter in *Daily Missouri Republican,* 24 Dec. 1862.

25 William P. Black to mother, 9 Dec. 1862, Black Family Papers, ISHL; Hawthorn letter in *Mobile Advertiser and Register,* 31 Jan. 1863; "By One Who Was In It" letter in *Indianapolis Daily Journal,* 29 Dec. 1862; *OR* 22(1):124.

26 *SOR* 4:70; William P. Black to mother, 9 Dec. 1862, Black Family Papers, ISHL; Black letter in *Chicago Tribune,* 25 Dec. 1862; David L. Ash to wife, 10 Dec. 1862, Ash Papers, USAMHI; Smith Diary, 7 Dec. 1862, DWC; Morse Journal, 7 Dec. 1862, PGBSP.

27 *OR* 22(1):110, 112, 124, 129.

28 *OR* 22(1):136, 151; *SOR* 4:90; Barney Seaman, "Prairie Grove," *Daily Missouri Republican,* 13 Feb. 1886.

29 *OR* 22(1):131, 133, 135, 148, 155. Charles Adams claimed that his regiment (or what remained of it) took part in the advance, but MacDonald did not mention Adams in his report. *SOR* 4:82.

30 *OR* 22(1):104, 110, 112, 129, 131, 133.

31 Monnett, "Yankee Cavalryman," 295–96.

32 *SOR* 4:60, 67, 70. Parsons reported encountering Marmaduke "immediately in the rear of my line" around 4:30 P.M. or shortly after the close of action east of Fayetteville Road. What Marmaduke was doing there at that time is not known. *OR* 53:460.

33 *SOR* 4:62, 69, 71; Columbus H. Gray to father, 12 Dec. 1862, Gray Letter, PGBSP. Young and Crump reported twenty-eight of MacDonald's troopers killed, wounded, and missing for the entire day, including the morning cavalry fight and the late afternoon skirmish on Viney Grove Road. *OR* 22(1):156–57.

34 *OR* 22(1):116. Dye reported that the Second Brigade had been "entirely broken up by orders, which never reached us, and the parts sent to widely separated portions on the field." He explained that because those orders "were constantly being sent directly to officers under my command, I soon abandoned all hope of harmonizing the movements of the brigade, as such, with those of other bodies, and devoted the greater part of my attention to the movements of the Twentieth Iowa."

35 *OR* 22(1): 123, 109–10, 115, 120.

36 *OR* 22(1):120–21; *SOR* 4:45; Barney, *Recollections,* 121; Leake, "Campaign," 285; E.N.B. [Ellsworth N. Bates] letter in *Cedar Valley Times,* 25 Dec. 1862. Huston chose not to criticize Dye for his flagrant disregard of orders. He reported only that "by some mistake in conveyance of an order" the Twentieth Iowa was "without my knowledge brought into action beyond the extreme right of the line." Moreover, he praised Dye, a fellow West Pointer, as an "old, tried, and gallant soldier." *OR* 22(1):109–10.

37 McRae to Shoup (McRae's report), 9 Dec. 1862, Herron Papers, NYHS; *SOR* 4:85–86, 88–89; *OR* 22(1):115–16, 120–21; Barney, *Recollections,* 122. Grinsted left his two "best companies" deployed as skirmishers along Cove Creek Road. Those seventy-six officers and men constituted one-fourth of his strength; their absence may have been the reason for the poor performance of his skirmishers against the Twentieth Iowa. *SOR* 4:88.

38 *OR* 22(1):115–16; Bearss, *Civil War Letters,* 89; E.N.B. letter in *Cedar Valley Times,* 25 Dec. 1862; Leake, "Campaign," 285; W.J.S. letter in *Davenport Daily Gazette,* 22 Dec. 1862.

39 *OR* 22(1):123–24; E.N.B. letter in *Cedar Valley Times,* 25 Dec. 1862.

40 Joseph B. Weaver letter in *Bloomington Daily Pantagraph,* 27 Dec. 1862; Pratt, "Civil War Letters," 266; "Jenks" letter in *Des Moines State Register,* 23 Dec., and *Daily Missouri Democrat,* 18 Dec. 1862; Pohl, "From Davenport to Vicksburg," 504; *SOR* 4:36.

41 *OR* 22(1):103, 116, 121, 124; *SOR* 4:36. The staff officer was Captain William H. Clark. He had made the three-day journey from Missouri lying flat on his back in a supply wagon, too ill to ride, but on 7 December he mounted his horse and stayed in the saddle all day. *SOR* 4:36.

Chapter Thirteen

1 *OR* 22(1):140, 147, 154.

2 *OR* 22(1):71–72. Historic Hogeye Road west of Blair Creek is Washington County Road 14; east of the creek it is Washington County Road 18. Hogeye Road east of historic Hogeye Crossing was abandoned after the war, and few traces remain today. As a result of this and other changes, the historic crossroads is now an oddly shaped three-way junction.

3 *OR* 22(1):72–73, 87; Blunt, "General Blunt's Account," 231. Brigadier General Egbert B. Brown, the Union commander in Springfield, ordered Richardson to Blunt's relief. Accompanied by a company of the First Arkansas Cavalry, Richardson and his small command left Cassville late on 3 December and reached Cane Hill late on 5 December, a ride of seventy-three miles in forty-eight hours.

4 *OR* 22(1):72, 87; Blunt, "General Blunt's Account," 231; Titcomb Diary, 7 Dec. 1862, HL. Richardson reported that Coleman said the Confederates "were marching up the Cove Creek road in great force," but this clearly is hindsight because Coleman never saw the enemy column. Richardson's dispatches to Blunt have not been found. *OR* 22(1):87.

5 *OR* 22(1):72–73; Farlow and Barry, "Osborne's Civil War," 205; *Military History of Kansas Regiments*, 96; Glover, "Accounts of Horace L. Moore."

6 Prentis, *Kansas Miscellanies*, 30–31; Porter Journal, 7 Dec. 1862, SHSW.

7 *OR* 22(1):72–73; Helm Memoir, LLC, USAMHI.

8 *OR* 22(1):73; Blunt to Herron, 7 Dec. 1862, Letters Sent, Army of the Frontier, First Division, NARA. Blunt's couriers ran into Thompson's Missouri Cavalry near Muddy Fork.

9 *OR* 22(1):73.

10 "Nassau" letter in *Daily Missouri Democrat*, 27 Dec. 1862; *Military History of Kansas Regiments*, 97; Titcomb Diary, 7 Dec. 1862, HL; Prentis, *Kansas Miscellanies*, 31; Bodwell Diary, 7 Dec. 1862, KSHS. Blunt would accuse Richardson of incompetence and cowardice, but he never heard Richardson's side of the story. Because the Fourteenth Missouri State Militia Cavalry was not part of the Army of the Frontier, Richardson submitted his report to the Adjutant General of Missouri, not Blunt. *OR* 22(1):72.

11 Prentis, *Kansas Miscellanies*, 31–32; unidentified letter, "Correspondence of Wisconsin Volunteers," Quiner Papers, SHSW.

12 *Military History of Kansas Regiments*, 98, 327–28; *OR* 22(1):94.

13 Blunt to wife, 9 Dec. 1862, Civil War Letters, MC; Ellithorpe Diary, 7 Dec. 1862, CWM; Palmer, "Outing in Arkansas," 221; Ireneus C. Myers to brother, 26 Dec. 1862, Myers Family Papers, KCPL. I have silently corrected Blunt's punctuation.

14 *OR* 22(1):73, 87–88; Britton, *Memoirs*, 39–40.

15 Blunt to Salomon and to Cloud, 7 Dec. 1862, Letters Sent, Army of the Frontier, First Division, NARA.

16 *OR* 22(1):73–74, 124. Historic Bottom Road branched off from historic Fayetteville Road about 1.8 miles west of Muddy Fork and followed a tributary of Moore's Creek toward Rhea's Mill. The road was prone to flooding (hence the name) and was abandoned after the war. Only fragments remain today.

17 Furry, *Preacher's Tale,* 26–27.

18 McMahan Diary, 7 Dec. 1862, UMC; Porter Journal, 7 Dec. 1862, SHSW; "Nassau" letter in *Daily Missouri Democrat,* 27 Dec. 1862.

19 *OR* 22(1):74, 124–25; W.P.A. [William P. Allen] letter in *Burlington Hawkeye,* 29 Dec. 1862.

20 Titcomb Diary, 7 Dec. 1862, HL; McMahan Diary, 7 Dec. 1862, UMC; Bodwell Diary, 7 Dec. 1862, KSHS.

21 Furry, *Preacher's Tale,* 6.

22 *OR* 22(1):74; Daily Journal, 7 Dec. 1862, Army of the Frontier, Second Brigade, First Division, NARA; "Caliban" letter in *Atchison Freedom's Champion,* 3 Jan. 1863.

23 *OR* 22(1):94–95; Glover, "Accounts of Horace L. Moore"; Prentis, *Kansas Miscellanies,* 32.

24 Prentis, *Kansas Miscellanies,* 32–33; "Caliban" letter in *Atchison Freedom's Champion,* 3 Jan. 1863; *Military History of Kansas Regiments,* 98–99, 329; Lindberg and Matthews, "'Eagle of the 11th Kansas,'" 25–26; Daily Journal, 7 Dec. 1862, Army of the Frontier, Second Brigade, First Division, NARA.

25 *OR* 22(1):125; "Iowa" letter in *Burlington Hawkeye,* 23 Dec. 1862; Allen, "Three Frontier Battles," 491–92. The route of historic Viney Grove Road is approximated by Washington County Roads 62 and 80. In his report Wickersham called Viney Grove Road the "old Fayetteville road." *OR* 22(1):125.

26 *OR* 22(1):156.

27 *OR* 22(1):125–26; Lothrop, *First Regiment Iowa Cavalry,* 89–90; W.P.A. letter in *Burlington Hawkeye,* 29 Dec. 1862; "Iowa" letter in *Burlington Hawkeye,* 23 Dec. 1862. Wickersham incorrectly reported that he reached the Alexander Marrs farm. The Marrs farm was located more than half a mile south of the Wilson farm and remained behind Confederate lines throughout the battle.

28 *OR* 22(1):125; "Iowa" letter in *Burlington Hawkeye,* 23 Dec. 1862.

29 *OR* 22(1):74; Blunt to wife, 9 Dec. 1862, Civil War Letters, MC. Blunt stated in various documents that he reached Prairie Grove at "1.45 o'clock," "two o'clock P.M.," and "between one and two o'clock P.M." Either his watch was slow or he fudged the time. *OR* 22(1):74; Blunt to wife, 9 Dec. 1862, MC; Blunt, "General Blunt's Account," 232. The West family still farms the land cleared by their pioneer ancestors. The historic house has been replaced by a modern structure, but little else has changed. Even the fence lines remain essentially the same.

30 "By One Who Was In It" letter in *Indianapolis Daily Journal,* 29 Dec. 1862; Heaton Memoir, PGBSP; H.I.H. letter in *Daily Missouri Democrat,* 22 Dec. 1862; *OR* 22(1): 106–7.

31 *OR* 22(1):74; Blunt to wife, 9 Dec. 1862, Civil War Letters, MC; Blunt, "General Blunt's Account," 232; Allen, "Three Frontier Battles," 491–92; Tilley, *Federals on the Frontier,* 60.

32 *OR* 22(1):74, 96, 99; Allen, "Three Frontier Battles," 492. Historic Viney Grove Road was located three hundred yards east of present-day Viney Grove Road north of its junction with present-day Jenkins Road. The historic road and the present-day road are essentially the same south of Jenkins Road.

33 "Nassau" letter in *Daily Missouri Democrat*, 27 Dec. 1862; *OR* 22(1):74, 96, 99; Palmer, "Outing in Arkansas," 222.

Chapter Fourteen

1 *OR* 22(1):141.

2 *OR* 22(1):150–51. Parsons reported that Thompson "engaged the enemy's scouts" on Fayetteville Road but did not encounter "determined resistance." If that was the case, why didn't Thompson push on toward Boonsboro? *OR* 53:459.

3 *OR* 53:156, 460.

4 *SOR* 4:76; *OR* 22(1):142, 53:460; Lane Memoir, 38, UMC.

5 *OR* 53:142, 460–61; *SOR* 4:77; Miller, "Mosby M. Parsons." The Prairie Grove School District owns nearly all of the property above the Morton house. The historic vegetation has been replaced by a sprawling complex of buildings, athletic facilities, playgrounds, and parking lots. Fortunately, the historic terrain seems to have survived the educational onslaught in reasonably good condition. Parsons's initial position was located near the crest of the hill in the vicinity of present-day Douglas Street and Shady Acres Lane, immediately south of the school complex.

6 *SOR* 4:55–56, 77. Although Roane's position cannot be determined with precision, his right probably was located near the present-day high school building on the east side of Viney Grove Road. His left ran down the west slope of the hill toward Muddy Fork.

7 *SOR* 4:55–56; *OR* 22(1):158; unidentified letter in *Arkansas State Gazette*, 14 Feb. 1863. The number and caliber of guns in Shoup's Battery is a matter of dispute. My estimate is on the conservative side. The location of the Confederate artillery on Viney Grove Road cannot be determined.

8 *SOR* 4:77.

9 *OR* 22(1):121; *SOR* 4:46; Ellithorpe Diary, 7 Dec. 1862, CWM.

10 *OR* 22(1):74, 96, 99; "Nassau" letter in *Daily Missouri Democrat*, 27 Dec. 1863; Palmer, "Outing in Arkansas," 222; Spencer H. Mitchell to parents, 30 Jan. 1863, Mitchell Letter, UMC.

11 "Camp Follower" letter in *Daily Missouri Republican*, 8 Mar. 1863; Prentis, *Kansas Miscellanies*, 36.

12 *OR* 22(1):75, 98–99.

13 *OR* 22(1):93; *SOR* 4:85–86; Elliott, *Garden of Memory*, 69. Ninety members of the First Indian remained behind to hold the horses. The regiment may have drifted to the left because of the presence of a large ravine on its right.

14 *OR* 22(1):74–75, 92, 95, 116, 121; Barney, *Recollections*, 123–25; unidentified letter in *Cedar Valley Times*, 8 Jan. 1863; W.J.S. letter in *Davenport Daily Gazette*, 22 Dec. 1862.

15 *OR* 22(1):93–94, 121.

16 *SOR* 4:86, 89. McRae's account of this stage of the battle is vague and lends credence to Grinsted's claim that he was elsewhere. McRae to Shoup (McRae's report), 9 Dec. 1862, Herron Papers, NYHS.

17 *SOR* 4:86, 88–89; Elliott, *Garden of Memory*, 69; McRae to Shoup (McRae's report), 9 Dec. 1862, Herron Papers, NYHS; unidentified letter in *Cedar Valley Times*, 8 Jan.

1863; Barney, *Recollections*, 124. After his death, command of Young's Arkansas Infantry should have passed to Major Lucian C. Gause, but his name does not appear in surviving accounts. It is not known who led the regiment during the final hours of the battle.

18 *SOR* 4:86; *OR* 22(1):92, 116, 121; unidentified letter in *Cedar Valley Times*, 8 Jan. 1863; Leake, "Campaign," 286.

19 *SOR* 4:86.

20 *OR* 22(1):92, 96, 100; *SOR* 4:86; W.J.S. letter in *Davenport Daily Gazette*, 22 Dec. 1862; Barney, *Recollections*, 127.

21 *OR* 22(1):92, 96, 100, 117; unidentified letter in *Cedar Valley Times*, 8 Jan. 1863; Bearss, *Civil War Letters*, 89–90; Barney, *Recollections*, 125–26.

22 *OR* 22(1):85, 94; Bearss, *Civil War Letters*, 91. Wattles stated that the Indians "report no wounds but such as the necessities of the case demand." *OR* 22(1):94.

23 *SOR* 4:87; Banasik, *Embattled Arkansas*, 513, 515.

Chapter Fifteen

1 *OR* 22(1):75, 89, 95, 97.

2 *OR* 22(1):75, 92, 99; "Nassau" letter in *Daily Missouri Democrat*, 27 Dec. 1862; Gardner, "First Kansas Battery," 250; Helm Memoir, LLC, USAMHI; "Caliban" letter in *Atchison Freedom's Champion*, 3 Jan. 1863. Moonlight later wrote that "with shout after shout we took the woods driving everything before us," but Moonlight remained on the valley floor with the left wing of the Eleventh Kansas and did not participate in the attack. None of the Federals who went up the hill mentioned cheering, and a soldier in the Thirteenth Kansas specifically stated that his regiment advanced "in silence." Lindberg and Matthews, "'Eagle of the 11th Kansas,'" 26; "Caliban" letter in *Atchison Freedom's Champion*, 3 Jan. 1863.

3 Ireneus C. Myers to brother, 26 Dec. 1862, Myers Family Papers, KCPL; Helm Memoir, LLC, USAMHI. The opposing lines collided where present-day Staggs Drive is located. Staggs Drive winds through the public school complex along the north side of the football stadium and baseball field.

4 Blunt, "General Blunt's Account," 232–33; unidentified letter and "Caliban" letter in *Atchison Freedom's Champion*, 3 Jan. 1863; Farlow and Barry, "Osborne's Civil War," 206–7; "Union" letter in *Oskaloosa Independent*, 27 Dec. 1862.

5 Lane Memoir, 38, UMC; Spencer H. Mitchell to parents, 30 Jan. 1863, Mitchell Letter, UMC.

6 *OR* 53:460; *SOR* 4:56.

7 *OR* 22(1): 112, 116, 124, 136.

8 Bearss, *Civil War Letters*, 89; Christian Keller to wife, 17 Dec. 1862, Keller Letter, PGBSP; W.J.S. letter in *Davenport Daily Gazette*, 22 Dec. 1862; W.P.A. letter in *Burlington Hawkeye*, 29 Dec. 1862; Charles S. Adair to parents, 10 Dec. 1862, Adair Family Collection, KSHS; Prentis, *Kansas Miscellanies*, 34; unidentified letter in *Atchison Freedom's Champion*, 3 Jan. 1863; Silas H. Marple to wife, 11 Dec. 1862, Marple Family Collection, SMOH; Thomas H. Murray letter in *Dallas Herald*, 7 Jan. 1863.

9 Lane Memoir, 38; N.A.T. letter in *San Antonio Weekly Herald,* 10 Jan. 1863; "Nassau" letter in *Daily Missouri Democrat,* 27 Dec. 1862.

10 Tilley, *Federals on the Frontier,* 60; Pinnell Journals, 7 Dec. 1862, MHM; "Caliban" letter in *Atchison Freedom's Champion,* 3 Jan. 1863; William J. May letter in *National Tribune,* 5 Feb. 1891; Blunt to wife, 9 Dec. 1862, Civil War Letters, MC; "Nassau" letter in *Daily Missouri Democrat,* 27 Dec. 1862; Warren Day to wife, 10 Dec. 1862, Day Correspondence, KSHS; Myers to brother, 26 Dec. 1862, Myers Family Papers, KCPL.

11 Staples Memoir, AHC; Baxter, *Pea Ridge and Prairie Grove,* 182. The historic Morton house was demolished sometime after 1911, but the site on the north side of present-day Jenkins Road is inside the park and is marked.

12 Thomas H. Murray letter in *Dallas Herald,* 7 Jan. 1863; unidentified letter in *Natchez Daily Courier,* 14 Feb. 1863; *OR* 22(1):89; A. C. Pierce to William S. Blakely, 10 Dec. 1862, Martin Collection, KSHS. I have silently adjusted the punctuation in the Parsons quote.

13 *OR* 22(1):75, 89, 95, 97; *Military History of Kansas Regiments,* 99; Pierce to Blakely, 10 Dec. 1862, Martin Collection, KSHS; Helm Memoir, LLC, USAMHI.

14 *OR* 53:461; Bull Memoir, 61, MHM.

15 *OR* 22(1):75, 89, 91, 95; *Military History of Kansas Regiments,* 99. Some Federals failed to halt at the fence and fled to the far side of Crawford's Prairie. Weer expressed the hope that these "disgraceful exceptions" would redeem themselves at a later time. Weer was a lawyer, not a geologist, and he used the terms "brow" and "brow of the hill" to refer to the drop-off from the bench to the valley floor at the foot of the hill. *OR* 22(1):89.

16 *OR* 22(1):75, 89, 91–92, 97; Pierce to Blakely, 10 Dec. 1862, Martin Collection, KSHS; Myers to brother, 26 Dec. 1862, Myers Family Papers, KCPL; Silas H. Marple to wife, 11 Dec. 1862, Marple Family Collection, SMOH. The "orchard lane" appears on one Union map as a pair of parallel fence lines several yards apart. Possibly Morton was expanding his orchard and wanted to complete the new fence before dismantling the old one.

17 Lane Memoir, 38; "Caliban" letter in *Atchison Freedom's Champion,* 3 Jan. 1863; Silas H. Marple to wife, 11 Dec. 1863, Marple Family Collection, SMOH.

18 *OR* 22(1):75–76, 90–91; Gardner, "First Kansas Battery," 250–51.

19 *OR* 22(1):89–91; William J. May letter in *National Tribune,* 5 Feb. 1891; Glover, "Accounts of Horace L. Moore"; E.H.G. letter in *Muscatine Daily Journal,* 3 Jan. 1863.

20 Thomas O. Adkins to Chambers Baird, [?] Dec. 1862, Baird Papers, DU; Helm Memoir, LLC, USAMHI; *OR* 22(1):77, 91, 95; Farlow and Barry, "Osborne's Civil War," 207. Ewing reported that he remained in the "orchard lane" until the battle was over, but his wing of the Eleventh Kansas retreated to the artillery line along with everyone else. *OR* 22(1):97–98.

21 *OR* 53:460–61. Parsons's report makes confusing reading because he treated the Confederate movement down the hill and across the valley floor as a single continuous event.

22 Lane Memoir, 38, UMC.

23 Allardice, *More Generals in Gray*, 215–17; *OR* 53:461; John F. Howes to Mrs. Steen, 17 Dec. 1862, Steen Collection, MHM; Palmer, "Outing in Arkansas," 222.

24 William J. May letter in *National Tribune*, 5 Feb. 1891; Lothrop, *First Regiment Iowa Cavalry*, 90; Spencer H. Mitchell to parents, 30 Jan. 1863, Mitchell Letter, UMC; Pinnell Journals, 7 Dec. 1862, MHM; Helm Memoir, LLC, USAMHI; Gardner, "First Kansas Battery," 250–51; *OR* 22(1):75–76; Thomas J. Lewis to wife, 14 Dec. 1862, Lewis Letters, SHSIDM.

25 *OR* 22(1):96, 100; Warren Day to wife, 10 Dec. 1862, Day Correspondence, KSHS; Adkins to Baird, [?] Dec. 1862, Baird Papers, DU; Lothrop, *First Regiment Iowa Cavalry*, 90; E.H.G. letter in *Muscatine Daily Journal*, 3 Jan. 1863; Thomas O. Adkins letter in *Ripley Bee*, 29 Jan. 1863.

26 *OR* 22(1):89, 92, 100; John F. Howes to Mrs. Steen, 17 Dec. 1862, Steen Collection, MHM; Palmer, "Outing in Arkansas," 222–23; Blunt, "General Blunt's Account," 233; Silas H. Marple to wife, 11 Dec. 1862, Marple Family Collection, SMOH; Lothrop, *First Regiment Iowa Cavalry*, 90; Glover, "Accounts of Horace L. Moore"; Adkins to Baird, [?] Dec. 1862, Baird Papers, DU; Crawford, *Kansas in the Sixties*, 81.

27 Spencer H. Mitchell to parents, 30 Jan. 1863, Mitchell Letter, UMC; Prentis, *Kansas Miscellanies*, 34; Helm Memoir, LLC, USAMHI; Britton, *Memoirs*, 41; Gardner, "First Kansas Battery," 251; Farlow and Barry, "Osborne's Civil War," 207.

28 *OR* 22(1):84–85, 96, 98; Ewing to wife, 10 Dec. 1862, Ewing Family Papers, LC; Laune, "Avra P. Russell." Ewing officially reported 4 dead and 28 wounded, but in a letter to his wife dated two days earlier he listed 5 killed and 33 wounded.

29 *OR* 22(1):84–85, 100; Gardner, "First Kansas Battery," 251. The *OR* lists eight wounded in the Second Indiana Battery, but that may be the result of a transcription error.

30 *OR* 22(1):125–27; Sidney H. Nichols to parents, 10 Dec. 1862, "Correspondence of Wisconsin Volunteers," Quiner Papers, SHSW; *Army of the Frontier*, 12.

31 *OR* 53:461.

32 Ibid.; *SOR* 4:57; Banasik, *Embattled Arkansas*, 514–15, 520–26. I have treated Clark's Missouri Infantry as a part of Parsons's Brigade.

Chapter Sixteen

1 Duncan, "Soldiers Fare," 52.

2 *OR* 22(1):142–44.

3 *SOR* 2(2):805; Walker, "Battle of Prairie Grove," 360; Lane Memoir, 39, UMC; Pinnell Journals, 7 Dec. 1862, MHM; Ruffner, "Sketch of First Missouri Battery," 418; Duncan, "Soldiers Fare," 52; N.A.T. letter in *San Antonio Weekly Herald*, 10 Jan. 1863.

4 *OR* 22(1):142, 144, 53:461; *SOR* 4:61, 68, 78; Hoskin Diary, 8–9 Dec. 1862, UMC; Pinnell Journals, 8–9 Dec. 1862, MHM; Waller Diary, 9 Dec. 1862, CWM; Farlow and Barry, "Osborne's Civil War," 210; McRae to wife, [?] Dec. 1862, McRae Papers, AHC.

5 Bull Memoir, 61–62, MHM; Waller Diary, 7–8 Dec. 1862, CWM; Farlow and Barry, "Osborne's Civil War," 207–8.

6 *OR* 22(1):66–67, 152, 154–55; Clement A. Evans, *Confederate Military History*, 10:144; Yeary, *Reminiscences*, 781. Monroe paroled the Union surgeon and patients at the

"General Hospital" in Boonsboro but ungenerously confiscated their medical supplies. He also rounded up a group of refugee slaves who had elected not to accompany the Kansas Division to Rhea's Mill. Marmaduke took the women to Van Buren and employed them as "cooks, nurses, and laundresses" in his division hospital. The fate of any men in the group is unknown. Marmaduke to Hindman, 17 Dec. 1862, Alexander Papers, CU.

7 Gray Letter, 12 Dec. 1862, PGBSP; Samuel P. Pittman, "Prairie Grove Battle," *Prairie Grove Herald*, 10 Dec. 1914.

8 Barney, *Recollections*, 127; John Gere to mother, 12 Dec. 1862, Gere Letter, *CWTI*, USAMHI.

9 *Army of the Frontier*, 23; Tilley, *Federals on the Frontier*, 62–63; Thomas O. Adkins to Chambers Baird, 12 Dec. 1862, DU.

10 Yeary, *Reminiscences*, 780–81.

11 *OR* 22(1):103; Eugene B. Payne to wife, 9 Dec. 1862, Payne Papers, Wilder Collection, Teaneck, N.J.; Pratt, "Civil War Letters," 266; Henry N. Frisbie Letter, 4 Nov. 1889, PGBSP; Blunt to Hindman, 8 Dec. 1862, Alexander Papers, CU; Blunt to wife, 9 Dec. 1862, Civil War Letters, MC. The parley took longer than expected; Hindman, becoming anxious about Marmaduke's safety, sent a note across the lines inquiring about the delay. Herron assured Hindman that Marmaduke was in good hands. "General Marmaduke is now with me awaiting an answer [from General Blunt], which is expected in a few moments. General Marmaduke of course will only remain until the answer is received. General Blunt is one third of a mile from me, which will account for the delay." Herron to Hindman, 8 Dec. 1862, Alexander Papers, CU.

12 *OR* 22(1):76, 101, 103, 144; Blunt to Hindman, 8 Dec. 1862, Alexander Papers, CU; Jacob D. Brewster to wife, 8 Jan. 1863, Brewster Letters, SHSIDM; "Nassau" letter in *Daily Missouri Democrat*, 10 Dec. 1862; unidentified letter, 9 Dec. 1862, "Correspondence of Wisconsin Volunteers," Quiner Papers, SHSW. One Union participant claimed that Frost and MacDonald were also present. MacDonald was a possibility because his brigade was still on the battlefield, but Frost was long gone. J.L.C. letter in *Daily Missouri Republican*, 19 Dec. 1862.

13 Blunt to wife, 9 Dec. 1862, Civil War Letters, MC; Blunt, "General Blunt's Account," 233; *OR* 22(1):78–79; "Jenks" letter in *Daily Missouri Democrat*, 18 Dec. 1862.

14 George W. Guess to Sarah H. Cockrell, 16 Dec. 1862, Guess Letters, University of Texas; Alexander T. Hawthorn letter in *Mobile Advertiser and Register*, 31 Jan. 1863; Thomas Letter, 18 Dec. 1862, PGBSP; Phillip Smith Letter, 12 Dec. 1862, PGBSP; James Edmondson letter in *Fort Smith Bulletin*, 17 Dec. 1862; Duncan, "Soldiers Fare," 51.

15 Pinnell Journals, 12 Dec. 1862, MHM; Thomas Letter, 18 Dec. 1862, PGBSP; Quesenberry Diary, 11, 16 Dec. 1862, UMC.

16 McRae to wife, [? Dec. 1862], McRae Papers, AHC; Alexander T. Hawthorn letter in *Mobile Advertiser and Register*, 31 Jan. 1863; "Personal Recollections of the Late General Thomas C. Hindman," *St. Louis Daily Times*, 4 Oct. 1868.

17 "General Hindman's Address" in *Dallas Herald*, 31 Dec. 1862; Hindman circular, 15 Dec., Charles W. Adams to Robert G. Shaver, 14 Dec., William H. Brooks to James F.

Fagan, 21 Dec., John W. Wallace to James P. King, 23 Dec., and Emmett MacDonald to John S. Marmaduke, 24 Dec. 1862, Alexander Papers, CU. A handful of nominations have survived, each accompanied by a "full statement of the circumstances," but the names of the three finalists are unknown.

18 Edwards, *Shelby and His Men*, 91; "W" letter in *Arkansas Patriot*, 25 Dec. 1862; N.A.T. letter in *San Antonio Weekly Herald*, 10 Jan. 1863; Pinnell Journals, 7 Dec. 1862, MHM; editorials in *Little Rock True Democrat*, 17 Dec. 1862, 14 Jan. 1863.

19 "General Hindman's conversation by telegraph: Talk with General Holmes, Dec. 12, 1862," Alexander Papers, CU.

20 Turnbo Journal, 141–42, University of Oklahoma; Hoskin Diary, 20 Dec. 1862, UMC; Pinnell Journals, 20 Dec. 1862, MHM.

21 Pinnell Journals, 22 Dec. 1862, MHM; *OR* 22(1):171; Weddle, *Plow-Horse Cavalry*, 85; Lotspeich Memoir, 12, AHC; Turnbo Journal, University of Oklahoma; 145; Hindman to Holmes, 14 Dec. 1862, in *Daily Missouri Republican*, 6 Feb. 1863; Holmes to Thomas Reynolds, 29 Dec. 1862, Jones Papers, DU; Crist, *Papers of Jefferson Davis*, 585. The Confederate telegrams published in the *Missouri Republican* were part of the booty seized by Union soldiers during the Van Buren raid at the end of 1862.

22 *OR* 22(1):905; Hindman to John B. Lockman and to Holmes, 13 Dec. 1862, Alexander Papers, CU.

23 Editorial in *Fort Smith Bulletin*, 17 Dec. 1862; Hindman to Holmes, 15 Dec., and Anthony S. Lonigan to U.S. Hill and Augustus M. Ward, 17 Dec. 1862, Alexander Papers, CU; Hindman to [?] Pritchard, 17 Dec. 1862, in *Daily Missouri Republican*, 6 Feb. 1863.

24 Thomas Letter, 18 Dec. 1862, PGBSP; Weddle, *Plow-Horse Cavalry*, 85; Edwin E. Harris to wife, 7 Jan. 1863, Harris Letters, Gilder Lehrman Collection, NYHS; Hindman to Caleb Dorsey, 18 Dec., and Dorsey to Hindman, 21 Dec. 1862, Alexander Papers, CU.

25 Phillip Smith to wife, 12, 19 Dec. 1862, Smith Letters, PGBSP.

26 Hindman to Holmes, 23 Dec. 1862, Alexander Papers, CU; Holmes to Reynolds, 29 Dec. 1862, Jones Papers, DU.

27 Hindman to Holmes, 14 Dec. 1862, in *Daily Missouri Republican*, 6 Feb. 1863; *OR* 22(1):171–72.

Chapter Seventeen

1 Unidentified letter in *Atchison Freedom's Champion*, 3 Jan. 1863; Farlow and Barry, "Osborne's Civil War," 207; Baldridge Memoir, PGBSP; William P. Black to mother, 9 Dec. 1862, Black Family Papers, ISHL; Helm Memoir, LLC, USAMHI; Tilley, *Federals on the Frontier*, 60.

2 William Black letter in *Chicago Tribune*, 25 Dec. 1862; Thomas O. Adkins to Chambers Baird, 12 Dec. 1862, Baird Papers, DU; Palmer, "Outing in Arkansas," 223; McLaughlin Letter, 12 Mar. 1863, PGBSP; Thomas O. Adkins letter in *Ripley Bee*, 29 Jan. 1863.

3 Pyeatt Memoir, PGBSP; James G. Blunt to Frederick Salomon, 8 Dec. 1862, Letters Sent, Army of the Frontier, First Division, NARA; McMahan Diary, 8 Dec. 1862, UMC; Greene, "Campaigning," 299; Titcomb Diary, 8 Dec. 1862, HL.

4 Houghland, "19th Iowa," 65; Arthur Diary, 8 Dec. 1862, UND; Joseph B. Weaver letter

in *Bloomington Daily Pantagraph*, 27 Dec. 1862; Courtland E. Whitsit letter in *Indianapolis Daily State Sentinel*, 22 Dec. 1862; Barney, *Recollections*, 128.

5 *OR* 22(1):69–70, 100–102, 821; Pratt, "Civil War Letters," 266.

6 Curtis to Blunt, 10 Dec. 1862, Herron Papers, NYHS; *OR* 22(1):68–69, 22(2):11.

7 *OR* 22(1):853, 13:21.

8 Schofield to McClernand, 8 Dec. 1862, and to Halleck, 12 Dec. 1862, Schofield Papers, LC.

9 James C. Dungan letter in *Muscatine Daily Journal*, 30 Jan. 1863; Gad Bryan letter in *Dubuque Daily Times*, 13 Jan. 1862; Austin Durham to wife, 10 Dec. 1862, Durham Papers, IHS.

10 Silas H. Marple to wife, 23 Dec. 1862, Marple Family Collection, SMOH; George W. Williams to wife, 10 Dec. 1862, Williams Letters, LLC, USAMHI; Joseph Eaton letter in *Rock Island Weekly Argus*, 7 Jan. 1863.

11 William H. Boyce to parents, 11 Dec. 1862, BL; Monnett, "Yankee Cavalryman," 301; Lemke, "Miller," 12.

12 Greene, "Campaigning," 300; Barney, *Recollections*, 129–30.

13 Curtis to Blunt and to Herron, 11 Dec. 1862, Herron Papers, NYHS; *OR* 22(1):829–30; Blunt to Curtis, Letters Sent, Army of the Frontier, First Division, NARA; Forman, *Western Sanitary Commission*, 61.

14 Baxter, *Pea Ridge and Prairie Grove*, 186–89; Uriah Eberhart Diary, 11–12 Dec. 1862, Eberhart Papers, SHSW; Robert F. Braden to mother, 3 Jan. 1863, Braden Papers, ISL; George W. Williams to wife, 10 Dec. 1862, Williams Letters, LLC; L. S. Blake letter, [? Dec. 1862], "Correspondence of Wisconsin Volunteers," Quiner Papers, SHSW; Shea, "Aftermath of Prairie Grove," 348–50; Forman, *Western Sanitary Commission*, 61–62; Carpenter, *Genealogical Notes*, 141. Despite a mountain of evidence to the contrary, Hubbard insisted that "supplies of medical and hospital stores were abundant." He was removed as medical director two months after the battle. Hubbard, "Second Extract," 1:341; Russell, "Extract," 1:343.

15 Charles E. Stevens letter, 25 Dec. 1862, "Correspondence," Quiner Papers, SHSW.

16 Blunt to Curtis, 10 Dec. 1862, Letters Sent, Army of the Frontier, First Division, NARA; *OR* 22(1):829; William Fithian to wife, 25, 28 Dec. 1862, Black Family Papers, ISHL; Calkins, "Wisconsin Cavalry," 180–81.

17 Shea, "Aftermath of Prairie Grove," 349–50; Carpenter, *Genealogical Notes*, 140–41; William Fithian to wife, 8 Jan. 1863, Black Family Papers, ISHL. Carpenter ran into his old college roommate, Thomas Ewing, shortly after arriving in Fayetteville. The two men had not seen each other since graduating from the University of Pennsylvania in 1849.

18 Carpenter, *Genealogical Notes*, 140; Robert F. Braden to mother, 3 Jan. 1863, Braden Papers, ISL; George W. Williams to wife, 10 Dec. 1862, Williams Letters, LLC, USAMHI; Ira Russell letter in *Cedar Valley Times*, 5 Feb. 1863.

19 Edmond G. Ross to wife, 12 Dec. 1862, Ross Correspondence, KSHS; H.I.H. letter in *Daily Missouri Democrat*, 22 Dec. 1862; Barney, *Recollections*, 130; Alfred J. Gillespie letter in *Ottumwa Weekly Courier*, 8 Jan. 1863.

20 Warren Day to wife, 14 Dec. 1862, Day Correspondence, KSHS; Blunt to wife, 9 Dec.

1862, Civil War Letters, MC; Morse Journal, 9 Dec. 1862, PGBSP; Weer to Blunt, 13 Dec. 1862, and Blunt to Weer, 14 Dec. 1862, Letters Sent, Army of the Frontier, Second Brigade, First Division, NARA. Another source listed 639 Confederate wounded in Union hands. Some of the wounded were still convalescing at Cane Hill in March 1863. Russell, "Extract," 1:342; Britton, *Memoirs*, 174.

21 Edwin B. Messer letter in *Waukegan Weekly Gazette*, 27 Dec. 1862; unidentified [Charles E. Stevens] letter in Lowell *Daily Citizen and News*, 2 Feb. 1863; Monnett, "Yankee Cavalryman," 301; George B. Pickett letter in *Rock Island Weekly Argus*, 7 Jan. 1863; "Union" letter in *Oskaloosa Independent*, 27 Dec. 1862; Britton, *Memoirs*, 56–57.

22 William D. McCord letter in *Illinois Gazette*, 7 Jan. 1863; "Nassau" letter in *Daily Missouri Democrat*, 27 Dec. 1862; Ransom S. Phillips to family, 15 Dec. 1862, Phillips Letter, PGBSP.

23 Unidentified letter in *Emporia News*, 10 Jan. 1863; Baldridge Memoir, PGBSP; Pratt, "Civil War Letters," 270.

24 *OR* 22(1):84–86, 140, 142; Williams Diary, 7 Dec. 1862, KSHS; Palmer, "Outing in Arkansas," 225. Here and elsewhere I have referred to Banasik's analysis of troop strength and casualties in his *Embattled Arkansas*, 455–57, 512–46.

25 Tilley, *Federals on the Frontier*, 68; Guyer, "Journal and Letters," 576; unidentified letter, 9 Dec. 1862, "Correspondence," Quiner Papers.

26 Arthur Diary, 7 Dec. 1862, UND; Fry, *As Ever Your Own*, 24; Pratt, "Civil War Letters," 267; Robert F. Braden to mother, 12 Dec. 1862, Braden Papers, ISL.

27 George W. Root to sister, 15 Nov., 24 Dec. 1862, Root Letters, SHSW.

28 Staples Memoir, AHC; Brandenburg Memoir, PGBSP.

29 Brandenburg Memoir and Mock Letter, PGBSP.

30 Tilley, *Federals on the Frontier*, 72–74; Robert F. Braden to mother, 12 Dec. 1862, Braden Papers, ISL; "Jenks" letter in *Dubuque Daily Times*, 10 Jan. 1863; Smith Diary, 7 Dec. 1862, DWC.

31 H.I.H. letter in *Daily Missouri Democrat*, 22 Dec. 1862; "Nassau" letter in *Daily Missouri Democrat*, 27 Dec. 1862; *OR* 22(1):77, 81.

32 Glover, "Accounts of Horace L. Moore"; Adams, "Battle of Prairie Grove," 463–64; Bishop, *Loyalty on the Frontier*, 70. An influential Iowa postwar history described Herron's actions at Prairie Grove as "extremely audacious—perhaps unwise and unsafe." Byers, *Iowa in War Time*, 188–89.

33 Blunt, "General Blunt's Account," 234; Lothrop, *First Regiment Iowa Cavalry*, 95–96; William F. Cloud letter in *Leavenworth Daily Conservative*, 28 Dec. 1862; editorial in *Bloomington Daily Pantagraph*, 13 Dec. 1862.

34 Blunt to Salomon, 8 Dec. 1862, Letters Sent, Army of the Frontier, First Division, NARA; Blunt to wife, 9 Dec. 1862, Civil War Letters, MC; Tilley, *Federals on the Frontier*, 79; *OR* 22(1):829–30, 22(2):7; Silas H. Marple to wife, 9 Jan. 1863, Marple Family Collection, SMOH; Fry, *As Ever Your Own*, 24; Barney, *Recollections*, 158.

35 Silas H. Marple to wife, 14 Dec. 1862, Marple Family Collection, SMOH; Scott, "Fighting Printers of Company E," 278–79. Because the front page of the *Buck and Ball* was printed before the evacuation of Boonsboro on 6 December, that date appeared on the masthead.

36 "Jenks" letter in *Dubuque Daily Times,* 10 Jan. 1863; Ellithorpe Diary, 16 Dec. 1862, CWM; Shea, "Aftermath of Prairie Grove," 349; Sidney H. Nichols to parents, 10 Dec. 1862, "Correspondence," Quiner Papers.

37 McMahan Diary, 25 Dec. 1862, UMC; Bonnell Diary, 25 Dec. 1862, USAMHI; Blunt to Herron, 23 Dec. 1862, Herron Papers, NYHS; Thomas E. Wright, "Capture of Van Buren," 79; Pompey, *Keep the Home Fires Burning,* 39.

38 Hindman to A. J. Maginnis, 14 Dec., and Blunt to Hindman, 17 Dec. 1862, Alexander Papers, CU; Thomas E. Wright, "Capture of Van Buren," 76–78; Jewett, *Failed Ambition,* 172–77; Francis M. Emmons to his sister, 25 Dec. 1862, Emmons Letters, UMC; Smith Diary, 8 Dec. 1862, DWC; William D. McCord letter in *Illinois Gazette,* 7 Jan. 1863; Alfred J. Gillespie letter in *Ottumwa Weekly Courier,* 8 Jan. 1863; Alfred C. Pierce to William S. Blakely, 10 Dec. 1862, Martin Collection, KSHS; Barney, *Recollections,* 131.

Chapter Eighteen

1 *OR* 22(1):858, 867; Schofield to Blunt, 22 Dec. 1862, Letters Sent, Army of the Frontier, NARA; Cloud to Blunt, 21 Dec. 1862, Letters Received, Army of the Frontier, First Division, NARA; *Daily Missouri Republican,* 20 Dec. 1862.

2 *OR* 22(1):875; Blunt, "General Blunt's Account," 235; Curtis to Schofield, 26 Dec. 1862, Curtis Papers, SHSIDM.

3 *OR* 22(1):169, 875; Blunt, "General Blunt's Account," 235; Curtis to Blunt, 11 Dec. 1862, Herron Papers, NYHS; Lindberg and Matthews, "'Eagle of the 11th Kansas,'" 28.

4 Blunt, "General Blunt's Account," 235; Tilley, *Federals on the Frontier,* 81; Ireneus C. Myers to brother, 26 Dec. 1862, Myers Family Papers, KCPL; Jacob D. Brewster to wife, 31 Dec. 1863, Brewster Letters, SHSIDM.

5 Britton, *Memoirs,* 58–59; Thomas E. Wright, "Capture of Van Buren," 80–81; Bonnell Diary, 27 Dec. 1862, USAMHI; *OR* 22(1):167, 169; "Thomas" letter in *Davenport Daily Democrat and News,* 22 Jan. 1863; Robertson, "Civil War Letter," 82.

6 Greene, "Campaigning," 301–2; Myers to brother, 8 Jan. 1863, Myers Family Papers, KCPL; McMahan Diary, 27 Dec. 1862, UMC; Lindberg and Matthews, "'Eagle of the 11th Kansas,'" 28; Bodwell Diary, 27 Dec. 1862, KSHS.

7 "Thomas" letter in *Davenport Daily Democrat and News,* 22 Jan. 1863; Jacob D. Brewster to wife, 31 Dec. 1862, Brewster Letters, SHSIDM; *OR* 22(1):168; Barney, *Recollections,* 143; Thomas E. Wright, "Capture of Van Buren," 82–83.

8 Blunt, "General Blunt's Account," 236; Britton, *Memoirs,* 61–62; J.S.R. letter in *Atchison Freedom's Champion,* 31 Jan. 1863; Dungan, *Nineteenth Regiment Iowa,* 66; Farlow and Barry, "Osborne's Civil War," 211.

9 Thomas E. Wright, "Capture of Van Buren," 83; Robertson, "Civil War Letter," 83; Hindman to Crump, 14 Dec. 1862, Alexander Papers, CU; Jacob D. Brewster to wife, 31 Dec. 1862, Brewster Letters, SHSIDM; J.S.R. letter in *Atchison Freedom's Champion,* 31 Jan. 1863.

10 Titcomb Diary, 28 Dec. 1862, HL; Jacob D. Brewster to wife, 31 Dec. 1862, Brewster Letters, SHSIDM; Crawford, *Kansas in the Sixties,* 87–89; "Nassau" letter in *Daily Missouri Democrat,* 20 Jan. 1863; J.S.R. letter in *Atchison Freedom's Champion,* 31 Jan. 1863; Lindberg and Matthews, "'Eagle of the 11th Kansas,'" 28–29.

11 "Camp Follower" letter in *Daily Missouri Republican,* 20 Jan. 1863; Jacob D. Brewster to wife, 31 Dec. 1862, Brewster Letters, SHSIDM; *OR* 22(1):169; Lothrop, *First Regiment Iowa Cavalry,* 371; unidentified letter in *Keokuk Gate City,* 21 Jan. 1863; Titcomb Diary, 28 Dec. 1862, HL.

12 *OR* 22(1):167; Guyer, "Journal and Letters," 580; "Camp Follower" letter in *Daily Missouri Republican,* 20 Jan. 1863.

13 Rowland S. Mantor to parents, 5 Jan. 1863, Mantor Letters, UMC; J.S.R. letter in *Atchison Freedom's Champion,* 31 Jan. 1863; "Camp Follower" letter in *Daily Missouri Republican,* 20 Jan. 1863; Titcomb Diary, 28 Dec. 1862, HL.

14 Jacob D. Brewster to wife, 31 Dec. 1862, Brewster Letters, SHSIDM; Britton, *Memoirs,* 64–66; Rowland S. Mantor to parents, 5 Jan. 1863, Mantor Letters, UMC; Lindberg and Matthews, "'Eagle of the 11th Kansas,'" 28–29; "Camp Follower" letter in *Daily Missouri Democrat,* 20 Jan. 1863.

15 Thomas E. Wright, "Capture of Van Buren," 84; H.J.S. letter in *Daily Missouri Democrat,* 16 Jan. 1863. Local legend has it that the steamboat *Ben Carson* outdistanced the Federals and escaped. Circumstantial evidence indicates that the *Ben Carson* left Van Buren earlier that day and was long gone by the time the Army of the Frontier arrived. *Little Rock True Democrat,* 31 Dec. 1862.

16 H.J.S. letter in *Daily Missouri Democrat,* 16 Jan. 1863; unidentified letter in *Keokuk Gate City,* 21 Jan. 1863; Alfred J. Gillespie letter in *Ottumwa Weekly Courier,* 12 Feb. 1863. The *Frederic Notrebe* was a 190-ton packet built in Ohio in 1860. It was described as a "handsome packet, with an elegantly furnished cabin, and everything else to correspond." "Nassau" letter in *Daily Missouri Democrat,* 20 Jan. 1863.

17 *OR* 22(1):167, 170–72; *SOR* 34:419; Herron to Curtis, 31 Dec. 1862, Curtis Papers, SHSIDM; Farlow and Barry, "Osborne's Civil War," 212. The *Key West* was a 170-ton packet built in Pennsylvania in 1857. I have been unable to find information about the *Rose Douglas* and the *Violet.*

18 *OR* 22(1):167; Britton, *Memoirs,* 64–66; Alfred J. Gillespie letter in *Ottumwa Weekly Courier,* 12 Feb. 1863; Blunt, "General Blunt's Account," 236; H.J.S. letter in *Daily Missouri Democrat,* 16 Jan. 1863. Captain Jacob D. Brewster of Herron's staff gained possession of the flag and told his wife that he intended to keep it as a "curiosity." Brewster to wife, 8 Jan. 1863, Brewster Letters, SHSIDM.

19 *OR* 22(1):172.

20 Robert G. Shaver, "Raid on and Capture of Van Buren," 12–13, Shaver Papers, AHC; Turnbo Journal, 148, University of Oklahoma; unidentified letter in *Keokuk Gate City,* 21 Jan. 1863; Rowland S. Mantor to parents, 5 Jan. 1863, Mantor Letters, UMC; *OR* 22(1):169, 172.

21 Rowland S. Mantor to parents, 5 Jan. 1863, Mantor Letters, UMC; unidentified letter in *Keokuk Gate City,* 21 Jan. 1863; Thomas E. Wright, "Capture of Van Buren," 84–85; Clint M. Turner letter in *Burlington Hawkeye,* 27 Jan. 1863; H.J.S. letter in *Daily Missouri Democrat,* 16 Jan. 1863; Robert G. Shaver, "Raid on and Capture of Van Buren," 20, Shaver Papers.

22 Thomas E. Wright, "Capture of Van Buren," 85; Jacob D. Brewster to wife, 31 Dec. 1862, Brewster Letters, SHSIDM.

23 Turnbo Journal, University of Oklahoma, 149.

24 Herron to Curtis, 31 Dec. 1862, Curtis Papers, SHSIDM; *OR* 22(1):169; Rowland S. Mantor to parents, 5 Jan. 1863, Mantor Letters, UMC; "Camp Follower" letter in *Daily Missouri Republican*, 20 Jan. 1863; Titcomb Diary, 28 Dec. 1862, HL; Britton, *Memoirs*, 67. The only confirmed fatality was Henry H. Hiatt, Second Kansas Cavalry, who was killed by a shell fragment early in the bombardment.

25 Bodwell Diary, 28 Dec. 1862, KSHS; Haas Diary, 28 Dec. 1862, PGBSP; Morse Journal, 28 Dec. 1862, PGBSP.

26 Britton, "Day with Colonel W. F. Cloud," 314–15; Rowland S. Mantor to parents, 5 Jan. 1863, Mantor Letters, UMC; Pinnell Journals, 28 Dec. 1862, MHM; Quesenberry Diary, 29 Dec. 1862, UMC.

27 *OR* 22(1):172.

28 McMahan Diary, 29 Dec. 1862, UMC; Haas Diary, 27–29 Dec. 1862, PGBSP; Lothrop, *First Regiment Iowa Cavalry*, 371; Guyer, "Journal and Letters," 580–81; Robertson, "Civil War Letter," 84.

29 Thomas E. Wright, "Capture of Van Buren," 86; Barney, *Recollections*, 144; Eugene B. Payne to wife, 2 Jan. 1863, Payne Papers, Wilder Collection, Teaneck, N.J.; Greene, "Campaigning," 303–4.

30 Thomas E. Wright, "Capture of Van Buren," 86.

31 H.J.S. letter in *Daily Missouri Democrat*, 16 Jan. 1863; Greene, "Campaigning," 307; Barney, *Recollections*, 145; Tilley, *Federals on the Frontier*, 85; Fry, *As Ever Your Own*, 25. Jacob Haas and other soldiers from the Ninth Wisconsin found a group of slaves locked in a barn. "We set them at liberty and for joy they jumped like crickets. Afterward they went with us." Haas Diary, 27 Dec. 1862, PGBSP.

32 Tilley, *Federals on the Frontier*, 84–85; Bodwell Diary, 28 Dec. 1862, KSHS; Thomas E. Wright, "Capture of Van Buren," 85; "Camp Follower" letter in *Daily Missouri Republican*, 20 Jan. 1863; H.J.S. letter in *Daily Missouri Democrat*, 16 Jan. 1863.

33 *OR* 22(1):170; unidentified letter in *Kansas Chief*, 8 Jan. 1863; Herron to Curtis, 31 Dec. 1862, Curtis Papers, SHSIDM.

34 H.J.S. letter in *Daily Missouri Democrat*, 16 Jan. 1863; "Waucassie" letter in *Houston Tri-Weekly Telegraph*, 30 Jan. 1863. Blunt and Herron did not tell Curtis of their harebrained jaunt. The story "leaked" a few weeks later when a participant published an account in a St. Louis newspaper.

35 Tilley, *Federals on the Frontier*, 86–87; "Arkansaw" letter in *Bloomington Daily Pantagraph*, 12 Jan. 1863; Thomas E. Wright, "Capture of Van Buren," 86–87; Bonnell Diary, 29 Dec. 1862, USAMHI; *OR* 22(1):170; Allen, "Three Frontier Battles," 492. Schofield crossed the Boston Mountains from Fayetteville to Lee Creek, a distance of thirty-one miles, in the remarkable time of three hours and five minutes. His escort of seventy-five troopers of the First Iowa Cavalry was led by Captain Alexander G. McQueen. "General Schofield was greatly pleased and complimented us highly," reported McQueen. Lothrop, *First Regiment Iowa Cavalry*, 95.

36 Greene, "Campaigning," 308; Titcomb Diary, 29 Dec. 1862, HL; Britton, *Memoirs*, 68–69; *OR* 22(1):168–69.

37 Titcomb Diary, 30 Dec. 1862, HL; "Camp Follower" letter in *Daily Missouri Republican*,

20 Jan. 1863; Uriah Eberhart to wife, 2 Jan. 1863, Eberhart Papers, SHSW; Lindberg and Matthews, "'Eagle of the 11th Kansas,'" 29; Shea, "Aftermath of Prairie Grove," 356, 358.

38 Blunt, "General Blunt's Account," 238; Jacob D. Brewster to wife, 31 Dec. 1862, Brewster Letters, SHSIDM; Thomas E. Wright, "Capture of Van Buren," 87–88; *OR* 22(1):170; Lemke, "Miller," 12.

39 "Arkansaw" letter in *Bloomington Daily Pantagraph*, 12 Jan. 1863; Lemke, "Miller," 12.

40 *OR* 22(1):168.

41 *OR* 22(1):168–69; Bonnell Diary, 31 Dec. 1862, USAMHI; Bodwell Diary, 31 Dec. 1862, 1 Jan. 1863, KSHS; Thomas E. Wright, "Capture of Van Buren," 88. The Indians somehow got their hands on a supply of whiskey. A Wisconsin soldier reported that they "made some noise but it was all got over with out any trouble." Robertson, "Civil War Letter," 84.

42 "C" letter in *Chicago Tribune*, 20 Jan. 1863; *SOR* 4:97; Clint M. Turner letter in *Burlington Hawkeye*, 27 Jan. 1863.

43 "Jenks" letter in *Dubuque Daily Times*, 10 Jan. 1863; *OR* 22(1):882–85; Curtis to Blunt and Herron, 29 Dec. 1862, Curtis Papers, SHSIDM; unidentified letter in *Keokuk Gate City*, 21 Jan. 1863; *Little Rock True Democrat*, 14 Jan. 1863.

Chapter Nineteen

1 *OR* 22(1):796, 53:867; Edwin E. Harris to wife, 26 Jan. 1863, Harris Letters, Gilder Lehrman Collection, NYHS; Skinner, *Autobiography*, 325.

2 Editorial in *Chicago Tribune*, 19 Jan. 1863.

3 *OR* 53:848, 22(2):780, 784, 787, 803.

4 Lotspeich Memoir, AHC; William D. Blocher et al., letter in *Little Rock True Democrat*, 11 Mar. 1863.

5 Neal and Kremm, *Lion of the South*, 161–246.

6 Dungan, *Nineteenth Regiment Iowa*, 72; Silas H. Marple to wife, 21 Jan. 1863, Marple Family Collection, SMOH.

7 *OR* 22(1):6; General Orders No. 1, 1 Jan. 1863, Army of the Frontier, NARA.

8 In the final draft of his memoirs, Schofield denounced Blunt as "probably the lowest specimen of humanity that ever disgraced a general's stars in this or perhaps any other country." This passage does not appear in the published version. "General Schofield's Narrative," 2:84–86, Schofield Papers, LC.

9 Curtis to brother, 14 Dec. 1862, Curtis Papers, HL.

10 Herron did not make the reports available to the editors of the *OR*. They were finally published (with some transcription errors) in the *SOR*. The originals are in the Herron Papers, NYHS.

11 Morse Journal, 31 Dec. 1862, PGBSP.

Bibliography

Manuscripts

Arkansas

Arkansas History Commission (Little Rock)
- C. B. Lotspeich Memoir
- Dandridge McRae Papers
- Company Book of Company B, Monroe's Arkansas Regiment
- David W. Moore Letter
- Asa S. Morgan Collection
- Robert G. Shaver Papers
- Nancy Morton Staples Memoir
- Raymond Watkins Collection

Butler Center for Arkansas Studies (Little Rock)
- George W. M. Reid Daybook

Old State House Museum (Little Rock)
- Albert W. Bishop Collection

Prairie Grove Battlefield State Park
- Samuel Baldridge Memoir
- Caledonia Ann Borden Brandenburg Memoir
- Henry N. Frisbie Letter
- Columbus H. Gray Letter
- Jacob Haas Diary
- Jesse W. Heaton Memoir
- Christian Keller Letter
- James P. King Letter
- Thomas King Letter
- William McLaughlin Letter
- Margaret Rogers Mock Letter
- Alexander O. Morse Journal
- Ransom S. Phillips Letter
- Julia West Pyeatt Memoir
- Westly Roberts Letter

Phillip Smith Letters
Dan P. Thomas Letter
James Ward Map
Shiloh Museum of Ozark History (Springdale)
Marple Family Collection
University of Arkansas at Fayetteville
John W. Brown Diary
Samuel P. Pittman Memoir
William H. H. Shibley Papers
Jacob M. J. Smith Journals

California

Huntington Library (San Marino)
Samuel R. Curtis Papers
George Titcomb Diary

District of Columbia

Library of Congress
Thomas Ewing Family Papers
John M. Schofield Papers
National Archives and Records Administration
Records of the War Department
Army of the Frontier, Headquarters (RG 393)
General Orders, October 1862–April 1863
Letters Received, 1862
Letters Sent, September 1862–June 1863
Army of the Frontier, First Division
General Orders, August–December 1862
Letters Received, July–December 1862
Letters Sent, August–December 1862
Army of the Frontier, First Brigade, First Division
General Orders, August 1862–June 1863
Letters Sent, September 1862–May 1863
Special Orders, August 1862–June 1863
Army of the Frontier, Second Brigade, First Division
Daily Journal, October 1862–March 1863
Letters Sent, September 1862–February 1864
Army of the Frontier, Second Division
Daily Journal, November 1862–June 1863
General Orders, August–December 1862
Letters Sent, October 1862–March 1863
John C. Black Court of Inquiry (RG 94)
Collection of Confederate Records (RG 109)

Confederate States Army Casualties
Thomas C. Hindman Papers
John S. Marmaduke Correspondence

Georgia

Emory University (Atlanta)
Jerome P. Wilson Papers

Illinois

Chicago Historical Society
Cyrus Bryant Collection
Illinois State Historical Library (Springfield)
John C. Black Family Papers
David Davis Papers
William E. McMullen Letter
Francis Springer Papers
McLean County Historical Society (Bloomington)
William H. Horine Letters
William W. Orme Papers
Charles D. Thompson Letters

Indiana

Indiana Historical Society (Indianapolis)
Austin Durham Papers
Indiana State Library (Indianapolis)
Robert F. Braden Papers
University of Notre Dame (South Bend)
David B. Arthur Diary

Iowa

Iowa State University (Ames)
Charles W. Chapman Diary
State Historical Society of Iowa (Des Moines)
Jacob D. Brewster Letters
Samuel R. Curtis Papers
Charles W. Huff Diary
Thomas J. Lewis Letters
William G. Thompson Letters
State Historical Society of Iowa (Iowa City)
Frank M. Bykrit Diary
"The 19th Ioway or the Prairie Grove Fight"
University of Iowa (Iowa City)
Edward E. Davis Letters

Kansas

Kansas State Historical Society (Topeka)
Samuel L. and Florella B. Adair Family Collection
Sherman Bodwell Diary
Leman G. Chellis Papers
William E. Connelley Papers
Charles E. Cory Papers
Warren and Mary A. Day Correspondence
Charles W. DeWolf Diary
Ellithorpe Family Papers
James Hanway Collection
William C. Hayes Letters
Josephine B. Martin Collection
Preston B. Plumb Papers
Edmund G. Ross Correspondence
John S. Williams Diary
Samuel Worthington Letters
Matt Mathews Collection (Ottawa)
Civil War Letters

Michigan

University of Michigan (Ann Arbor)
Eugene B. Payne Journal

Minnesota

Minnesota Historical Society (St. Paul)
Adrian Schweizer Diary

Missouri

Jackson County Historical Society (Independence)
Harris Family Correspondence
Kansas City Public Library
Myers Family Papers
Missouri History Museum (St. Louis)
William C. Breckenridge Papers
William Bull Memoir
Civil War Collection
J. C. Dwyer Reminiscences
Salem H. Ford Memoir
Daniel M. Frost Papers
Hamilton R. Gamble Papers
Order Book, September 1862–June 1864, Fourth Cavalry Division, First Army Corps, Trans-Mississippi Department

Mosby M. Parsons Papers
Ethan A. Pinnell Journals
Thomas L. Snead Collection
Alexander E. Steen Collection
University of Missouri–Columbia
Henry C. and William H. Crawford Letters
Francis M. Emmons Letters
William H. Hoskin Diary
Peter D. Lane Memoir
Daniel H. Loomis Letters
Robert McMahan T. Diary
Rowland S. Mantor Letters
Spencer H. Mitchell Letter
John P. Quesenberry Diary
Jacob H. Rockwell Memoir
University of Missouri–Rolla
Thomas Murray Correspondence
Civil War Museum at Wilson's Creek National Battlefield (Republic)
Albert C. Ellithorpe Diary
John D. Waller Diary

Montana

Montana State University (Bozeman)
Smith-Mendenhall Family Papers

New Jersey

Jeremy H. Wilder Collection (Teaneck)
Eugene B. Payne Papers

New York

Columbia University (New York City)
Peter W. Alexander Papers
New-York Historical Society (New York City)
Francis J. Herron Papers
Gilder Lehrman Collection
Edwin E. Harris Letters

North Carolina

Duke University (Durham)
Chambers Baird Papers
Charles C. Jones Papers
University of North Carolina (Chapel Hill)
John Perkins Papers

Oklahoma

University of Oklahoma (Norman)
  Silas C. Turnbo Journal

Pennsylvania

U.S. Army Military History Institute (Carlisle)
  David L. Ash Papers
  John C. Bonnell Diary
  Civil War Times Illustrated Collection
    John N. Gere Letter
    John C. Williams Memoir
  Lewis Leigh Collection
    Thomas M. Helm Memoir
    George W. Williams Letters
  Roger D. Ruddick, "From the Hayfields to the Battlefields"

Texas

Barker Texas History Center, University of Texas (Austin)
  George W. Guess Letters
Dale West Collection (Longview)
  Edward H. Smith Diary

Washington

Linda Russell Collection (Edmonds)
  William H. Boyce Letters

Wisconsin

State Historical Society of Wisconsin (Madison)
  Uriah Eberhart Papers
  James Farley Papers
  Almerin Gillette Papers
  Jacob McLaughlin Papers
  Charles N. Mumford Letters
  Emanuel Munk Correspondence
  Charles W. Porter Journal
  Edwin B. Quiner Papers
  Albert J. Rockwell Letters
  George W. Root Letters
  Joseph P. Rundle Memoir
  George B. Sprague Papers
  Jonathan D. Stevens Letters
  Cornelius Vanansdall Letters

University of Wisconsin at Whitewater
George Barnett Collection

Internet and Electronic Media

Glover, James A., ed. "The Accounts of Horace L. Moore of the Battles of the Second Kansas Volunteer Cavalry." *Second Kansas Volunteer Cavalry*, <http://home.kscable.com/balocca/cavalry.html>. December 2002.

Payne, Curtis. *Thundering Cannons: Howell's Texas Battery in the Indian Nations*. CD, 1995.

Sawyer, Phillip R., ed. "Aaron P. Mitchell Letters." *Iowa in the Civil War*, <http://www.iowa-counties.com/civilwar/20th_inf/aaron_mitchell/index.htm>. November 2004.

Newspapers

Arkansas Patriot (Little Rock)
Arkansas State Gazette (Little Rock)
Arkansas Traveler (Cane Hill)
Atchison Freedom's Champion (Kansas)
Aurora Commercial (Indiana)
Bloomington Daily Pantagraph (Illinois)
Buck and Ball (Cane Hill, Ark.)
Burlington Hawkeye (Iowa)
Cannelton Daily Reporter (Indiana)
Cedar Valley Times (Cedar Rapids, Iowa)
Chicago Tribune
Clinton Herald (Iowa)
Daily Missouri Democrat (St. Louis)
Daily Missouri Republican (St. Louis)
Dallas Herald
Davenport Daily Democrat and News (Iowa)
Davenport Daily Gazette (Iowa)
Des Moines State Register
Dubuque Daily Times (Iowa)
Emporia News (Kansas)
Fairfield Ledger (Iowa)
Fort Madison Plain Dealer (Iowa)
Fort Scott Bulletin (Kansas)
Fort Smith Bulletin (Arkansas)
Galveston Tri-Weekly News
Houston Tri-Weekly Telegraph
Illinois Gazette (Lacon)
Indianapolis Daily Journal
Indianapolis Daily State Sentinel
Janesville Daily Gazette (Wisconsin)
Kansas Chief (White Cloud)
Kansas State Journal (Lawrence)
Keokuk Gate City (Iowa)
Lawrence Republican
Leavenworth Daily Conservative (Kansas)
Leavenworth Daily Times (Kansas)
Liberty Tribune (Missouri)
Little Rock True Democrat (Arkansas)
Lowell Daily Citizen and News (Massachusetts)
Milwaukee Daily Sentinel
Mobile Advertiser and Register (Alabama)
Mt. Pleasant Home Journal (Iowa)
Muscatine Daily Journal (Iowa)
Natchez Daily Courier
National Tribune (Washington, D.C.)
New York Herald
Oskaloosa Independent (Kansas)
Ottumwa Weekly Courier (Iowa)
Prairie Grove Herald (Arkansas)
Ripley Bee (Ohio)
Rock Island Weekly Argus (Illinois)
Rock Island Weekly Union (Illinois)
San Antonio Weekly Herald
St. Louis Daily Times
Washington Telegraph (Arkansas)
Waukegan Weekly Gazette (Illinois)
Wisconsin State Journal (Madison)
Wyandotte Commercial Gazette (Kansas)

Published Sources

Adams, Henry C. "Battle of Prairie Grove." *War Papers Read before the Indiana Commandery, Military Order of the Loyal Legion of the United States*. Indianapolis: Commandery, 1898.

Allardice, Bruce S. *More Generals in Gray*. Baton Rouge: Louisiana State University Press, 1995.

Allen, William P. "Three Frontier Battles." *Glimpses of the Nation's Struggle: Papers Read before the Minnesota Commandery of the Military Order of the Loyal Legion of the United States*. St. Paul: St. Paul Book and Stationary, 1897.

Andrews, Alva, ed. *Civil War Diary of M. S. Andrews*. Seymour, Iowa: N.p., n.d.

Army of the Frontier: Commemorating the Fiftieth Anniversary of the Battle of Prairie Grove, Ark. Milwaukee: N.p., 1912.

Banasik, Michael E. *Embattled Arkansas: The Prairie Grove Campaign of 1862*. Wilmington, N.C.: Broadfoot, 1996.

———, ed. *Missouri Brothers in Gray: The Reminiscences and Letters of William J. Bull and John P. Bull*. Iowa City: Camp Pope Bookshop, 1998.

———, ed. *Serving with Honor: The Diary of Captain Eathan Allen Pinnell of the Eighth Missouri Infantry*. Iowa City: Camp Pope Bookshop, 1999.

Barker, Thomas S. "The Fight at Fort Wayne, Ind. T." *Confederate Veteran* 15 (February 1907): 70–71.

Barnes, Joseph D. *What I Saw You Do: A Brief History of the Battles, Marches, and Sieges of the Twentieth Iowa Volunteer Infantry*. Port Bryan, Ill.: Owen and Hall, 1896.

Barney, Chester. *Recollections of Field Service with the Twentieth Iowa Infantry Volunteers; or, What I Saw in the War*. Davenport, Iowa: Gazette, 1865.

Baxter, William. *Pea Ridge and Prairie Grove; or, Scenes and Incidents of the War in Arkansas*. Cincinnati: Poe and Hitchcock, 1864.

Bearss, Edwin C. "The Army of the Frontier's First Campaign: The Confederates Win at Newtonia." *Missouri Historical Review* 61 (1966): 283–319.

———. "The Army of the Frontier Invades Washington County." Washington County Historical Society *Flashback* 20 (February 1970): 1–20.

———. "The Federals Raid Van Buren and Threaten Fort Smith." *Arkansas Historical Quarterly* 26 (1967): 123–42.

———, ed. *The Civil War Letters of Major William G. Thompson of the 20th Iowa Infantry Regiment*. Fayetteville, Ark.: Washington County Historical Society, 1966.

Bishop, Albert W. *Loyalty on the Frontier; or, Sketches of Union Men of the South-West: With Incidents and Adventures in Rebellion on the Border*. St. Louis: Studley, 1863.

Blunt, James G. "General Blunt's Account of His Civil War Experiences." *Kansas Historical Quarterly* 1 (1932): 211–65.

Bradbury, John F., Jr. "'Buckwheat Cake Philanthropy': Refugees and the Union Army in the Ozarks." *Arkansas Historical Quarterly* 57 (1998): 233–54.

———. "'Good Water & Wood but the Country Is a Miserable Botch': Flatland Soldiers Confront the Ozarks." *Missouri Historical Review* 90 (1996): 166–86.

Braden, Robert F. "Selected Letters of Robert F. Braden, 1861–1863." *Indiana History Bulletin* 41 (1964): 110–21.

Britton, Wiley. *The Civil War on the Border*. 2 vols. New York: Putnam, 1899.

———. "A Day with Col. W. F. Cloud." *Chronicles of Oklahoma* 3 (1927): 311–21.

———. *Memoirs of the Rebellion on the Border, 1863*. Chicago: Cushing and Thomas, 1882.

———. *The Union Indian Brigade in the Civil War*. Kansas City: Hudson, 1922.

Brophy, Patrick, ed. *In the Devil's Dominions: A Union Soldier's Adventures in "Bushwhacker Country."* Nevada, Mo.: Vernon County Historical Society, 1998.

Brownlee, Richard S. *Gray Ghosts of the Confederacy: Guerrilla Warfare in the West, 1861–1865*. Baton Rouge: Louisiana State University Press, 1958.

Byers, Samuel H. M. *Iowa in War Times*. Des Moines: Condit, 1888.

Cain, Marvin R., and John F. Bradbury, Jr. "Union Troops and the Civil War in Southwestern Missouri and Northwestern Arkansas." *Missouri Historical Review* 88 (1993): 29–47.

Calkins, Elias A. "The Wisconsin Cavalry Regiments." *War Papers Read before the Commandery of the State of Wisconsin, Military Order of the Loyal Legion of the United States*. Milwaukee: Burdick, Armitage, and Allen, 1896.

Carlson, Gretchen. "Francis Jay Herron." *Palimpsest* 11 (1930): 141–50.

Carpenter, Seymour D. *Genealogical Notes of the Carpenter Family*. Springfield: Illinois State Journal, 1907.

Castel, Albert. *A Frontier State at War: Kansas, 1861–1865*. Ithaca: Cornell University Press, 1958.

Collins, Robert. *General James G. Blunt: Tarnished Glory*. Gretna, La.: Pelican, 2005.

Conkling, Roscoe P., and Margaret B. Conkling. *The Butterfield Overland Mail, 1857–1869*. 2 vols. Glendale, Calif.: Arthur H. Clark, 1947.

Connelley, William E. *The Life of Preston B. Plumb*. Chicago: Browne and Howell, 1913.

Connelly, Donald B. *John M. Schofield and the Politics of Generalship*. Chapel Hill: University of North Carolina Press, 2006.

Cook, Theo M. *Immortal Blue: Co. H 19th Iowa Volunteer Infantry, 1862–1865*. Bonaparte, Iowa: Record-Republican, 1966.

Cory, Charles E. "The Sixth Kansas Cavalry and Its Commander." *Collections of the Kansas State Historical Society, 1909–1910* 2 (1910): 217–38.

Crawford, Samuel J. *Kansas in the Sixties*. Chicago: McClurg, 1911.

Crist, Lynda L., ed. *The Papers of Jefferson Davis*. Vol. 8. Baton Rouge: Louisiana State University Press, 1995.

Crittenden, Henry H. *The Crittenden Memoirs*. New York: Putnam, 1936.

Davis, William C. "The Battle of Prairie Grove." *Civil War Times Illustrated* 7 (July 1968): 12–19.

———, ed. *The Confederate General*. 6 vols. Harrisburg: National Historical Society, 1991.

Denison, William W. "Battle of Prairie Grove." *Collections of the Kansas State Historical Society, 1923–1925* 16 (1925): 586–90.

Donovan, Timothy P., and Willard B. Gatewood, eds. *The Governors of Arkansas: Essays in Political Biography*. Fayetteville: University of Arkansas Press, 1981.

Dougan, Michael B. *Confederate Arkansas: The People and Policies of a Frontier State in Wartime*. University: University of Alabama Press, 1976.

Duncan, J. S., ed. "A Soldiers Fare Is Rough: Letters from A. Cameron in the Indian Territory." *Military History of Texas and the Southwest* 1 (1974): 39–61.

Dungan, J. Irvine. *History of the Nineteenth Regiment Iowa Volunteer Infantry*. Davenport, Iowa: Luse and Griggs, 1865.

Eberhart, Uriah. *History of the Eberharts in Germany and the United States*. Chicago: Donohue and Henneberry, 1891.

Edwards, John N. *Shelby and His Men; or, The War in the West*. Cincinnati: Miami, 1867.

Elder, Donald C., III, ed. *A Damned Iowa Greyhound: The Civil War Letters of William Henry Harrison Clayton*. Iowa City: University of Iowa Press, 1998.

Elliott, M. A., comp. *The Garden of Memory: Stories of the Civil War as Told by Veterans and Daughters of the Confederacy*. Camden, Ark.: Brown, 1911.

Evans, Clarence, ed. "Memoirs, Letters, and Diary Entries of German Settlers in Northwest Arkansas, 1853–1863." *Arkansas Historical Quarterly* 6 (1947): 226–49.

Evans, Clement A., ed. *Confederate Military History: A Library of Confederate States History*. 12 vols. Atlanta: Confederate, 1899.

Farlow, Joyce, and Louise Barry. "Vincent B. Osborne's Civil War Experiences." *Kansas Historical Quarterly* 10 (1952): 108–33, 187–223.

Forman, Jacob G. *The Western Sanitary Commission; A Sketch of Its Origin, History, Labor for the Sick and Wounded of the Western Armies, and Aid Given to Freedmen and Union Refugees, with Incidents of Hospital Life*. St. Louis: Studley, 1864.

Fry, Laurie, ed. *As Ever Your Own: The Civil War Letters of B. B. Sanborn*. Arlington, Va.: Naptime, 1997.

Furry, William, ed. *The Preacher's Tale: The Civil War Journal of Rev. Francis Springer, Chaplain, U.S. Army of the Frontier*. Fayetteville: University of Arkansas Press, 2001.

Gardner, Theodore. "The First Kansas Battery: An Historical Sketch, with Personal Reminiscences of Army Life, 1861–65." *Collections of the Kansas State Historical Society, 1915–1918* 14 (1918): 235–82.

Gatewood, Willard B. "The Prairie Grove Valley and Its Communities." Washington County Historical Society *Flashback* 53 (Winter 2003): 1–28.

Gilbert, Lucian D. "A Confederate Soldier Writes Home." Washington County Historical Society *Flashback* 24 (November 1974): 28–29.

Greene, Albert R. "Campaigning in the Army of the Frontier." *Collections of the Kansas State Historical Society, 1915–1918* 14 (1918): 283–310.

Guyer, Max H., ed. "The Journal and Letters of Corporal William O. Gulick." *Iowa Journal of History and Politics* 28 (1930): 194–267, 390–455, 543–603.

Haimerl, David L. *Clarkson's Battalion C.S.A.: A Brief History and Roster*. Independence, Mo.: Two Trails, 2005.

Hamilton, James A. "The Enrolled Missouri Militia: Its Creation and Controversial History." *Missouri Historical Review* 69 (1975): 413–32.

Herr, George W. *Episodes of the Civil War: Nine Campaigns in Nine States.* San Francisco: Bancroft, 1890.

Hewitt, Janet B., et al., eds. *Supplement to the Official Records of the Union and Confederate Armies.* 100 vols. Wilmington, N.C.: Broadfoot, 1994–99.

History of Benton, Washington, Carroll, Madison, Crawford, Franklin, and Sebastian Counties, Arkansas. Chicago: Goodspeed, 1889.

Houghland, James E. "The 19th Iowa in Battle and in Prison." *The National Tribune Scrap Book: Stories of the Camp, March, Battle, Hospital and Prison Told by Comrades.* Washington: National Tribune, 1909.

Hubbard, George H. "Second Extract from a Narrative of His Services on the Medical Staff." *The Medical and Surgical History of the War of the Rebellion, 1861–1865.* 6 vols. Washington, D.C.: Government Printing Office, 1870–88.

Ingenthron, Elmo. *Borderland Rebellion: A History of the Civil War on the Missouri-Arkansas Border.* Branson, Mo.: Ozarks Mountaineer, 1980.

Ingersoll, Lurton D. *Iowa and the Rebellion.* Philadelphia: Lippincott, 1866.

Jewett, Tom, ed. *Failed Ambition: The Civil War Journals and Letters of Cavalryman Homer Harris Jewett.* College Station, Tex.: Virtualbookworm.com, 2004.

Johnston, Dorothy M. *History of Rhea Community, Washington County, Arkansas.* Lincoln, Ark.: Johnston, 1987.

Jones, Samuel. "The Battle of Prairie Grove." *Southern Bivouac* 1 (1885): 203–11.

Kitts, John H. "The Civil War Diary of John Howard Kitts." *Collections of the Kansas State Historical Society, 1915–1918* 14 (1918): 318–32.

Laune, Seigniora R. "Avra P. Russell." *Collections of the Kansas State Historical Society, 1915–1918* 14 (1918): 84–88.

Leake, Joseph B. "Campaign of the Army of the Frontier." *Military Essays and Recollections: Papers Read before the Commandery of the State of Illinois, Military Order of the Loyal Legion of the United States.* Vol. 2. Chicago: McClurg, 1891.

Lee, John F. "John Sappington Marmaduke." *Collections of the Missouri Historical Society* 2 (1906): 26–40.

Lemke, Walter J., ed. "Captain Edward Gee Miller of the 20th Wisconsin: His War, 1862–1865." *Bulletin of the Washington County Historical Society* 37 (1960).

———, ed. "Federal Army Orders, 1863–1864." Washington County Historical Society *Flashback* 8 (January 1958): 1–8.

———, ed. "Old Hermannsburg: Civil War Violence on the Border." Washington County Historical Society *Flashback* 9 (October 1959): 1–6.

———, ed. "Special Issue in Commemoration of the 100th Anniversary of the Battle of Prairie Grove, December 7, 1862." Washington County Historical Society *Flashback* 12 (December 1862).

———, ed. "W. H. Rhea Totals His Losses before and after the Battle of Prairie Grove." Washington County Historical Society *Flashback* 6 (May 1956): 17–18.

"The Letters of Samuel James Reader, 1861–1863." *Kansas Historical Quarterly* 9 (1940), 26–174.

Lindberg, Kip, and Matt Matthews, eds. "'The Eagle of the 11th Kansas': Wartime

Reminiscences of Colonel Thomas Moonlight." *Arkansas Historical Quarterly* 62 (2003), 1–41.

Littlefield, Daniel F., and Lonnie E. Underhill. "Fort Wayne and the Arkansas Frontier, 1838–40." *Arkansas Historical Quarterly* 35 (1976): 334–59.

Logan, Robert R., ed. "Addresses at Dedication of Prairie Grove Battlefield Monument, December 7, 1956." *Arkansas Historical Quarterly* 16 (1957): 257–80.

Lothrop, Charles H. *A History of the First Regiment Iowa Cavalry Veteran Volunteers.* Lyons, Iowa: Beers and Eaton, 1890.

Love, William D. *Wisconsin in the War of the Rebellion; A History of All Regiments and Batteries the State Has S1ent to the Field.* Chicago: Church and Goodman, 1866.

Maddox, George T. *Hard Trials and Tribulations of an Old Confederate Soldier.* Van Buren, Ark.: Argus, 1897.

Martin, Amelia. "United Confederate Veterans." Fort Smith Historical Society *Journal* 5 (September 1981): 2–4.

Mathes, J. A. "Battles in Trans-Mississippi Department." *Confederate Veteran* 2 (March 1894): 79.

McCorkle, John. *Three Years with Quantrill.* Norman: University of Oklahoma Press, 1992.

McDonough, James L. *Schofield: Union General in the Civil War and Reconstruction.* Tallahassee: Florida State University Press, 1972.

McFarland, Bill. "John C. Black: Biography of a Medal of Honor Winner from Illinois." *Military Images* 8 (March/April 1987): 13–15.

McGhee, James E. *Guide to Missouri Confederate Units, 1861–1865.* Fayetteville: University of Arkansas Press, 2008.

———. *Missouri Confederates: A Guide to Sources for Confederate Soldiers and Units, 1861–1865.* Independence, Mo.: Two Trails, 2001.

McNulta, John. "Incidents of a Battle." McLean County Historical Society *Transactions* 1 (1899): 467–76.

Military History of Kansas Regiments during the War for the Suppression of the Great Rebellion. Leavenworth, Kans.: Burke, 1870.

Miller, Robert E. "Daniel Marsh Frost, C.S.A." *Missouri Historical Review* 85 (1991): 381–401.

———. "General Mosby M. Parsons: Missouri Secessionist." *Missouri Historical Review* 80 (1985): 33–57.

Monnett, Howard N., ed. "A Yankee Cavalryman Views the Battle of Prairie Grove." *Arkansas Historical Quarterly* 21 (1962): 289–304.

Montgomery, Don. *The Battle of Prairie Grove.* Prairie Grove, Ark.: Prairie Grove Battlefield State Park, 1996.

Morrison, W. L. "Letter." *Confederate Veteran* 5 (July 1897): 367–68.

Mullins, Michael A. *The Fremont Rifles: A History of the 37th Illinois Veteran Volunteer Infantry.* Wilmington, N.C.: Broadfoot, 1990.

Nash, Charles E. *Biographical Sketches of Gen. Pat Cleburne and Gen. T. C. Hindman.* Little Rock: Tunnah and Pittard, 1895.

Neal, Diane, and Thomas W. Kremm. *Lion of the South: General Thomas C. Hindman.* Macon, Ga.: Mercer University Press, 1993.

Office of the Adjutant General. *Report of the Adjutant General of Arkansas for the Period of the Late Rebellion, and to November 1, 1866.* Washington, D.C.: Government Printing Office, 1867.

———. *Report of the Adjutant General of the State of Illinois Containing Reports for the Years 1861–1866.* 8 vols. Springfield: Rokker, 1886.

———. *Report of the Adjutant General of the State of Indiana.* 8 vols. Indianapolis: Conner, 1865–69.

———. *Report of the Adjutant General and Acting Quartermaster General of Iowa.* 2 vols. Des Moines: Palmer, 1863.

———. *Report of the Adjutant General of the State of Kansas, 1861–1865.* Topeka: Kansas State Printing, 1896.

Palmer, Henry E. "An Outing in Arkansas; or, Forty Days and a Week in the Wilderness." *Civil War Sketches and Incidents: Papers Read by Companions of the Commandery of the State of Nebraska, Military Order of the Loyal Legion of the United States.* Omaha: Commandery, 1902.

Payne, Eugene B. "Prairie Grove." *Military Order of the Loyal Legion of the United States: Commandery of the District of Columbia: War Papers, No. 52.* Washington: Commandery, 1904.

Phillips, Charles J. "Alvin Woods' Retreat from Prairie Grove." *Chronicles of Oklahoma* 7 (1929): 170–71.

Pitcock, Cynthia D., and Bill J. Gurley, eds. *I Acted from Principle: The Civil War Diary of Dr. William M. McPheeters, Confederate Surgeon in the Trans-Mississippi.* Fayetteville: University of Arkansas Press, 2002.

Pohl, James W., ed. "From Davenport to Vicksburg: The Odyssey of a Soldier in the Civil War." *Annals of Iowa* 40 (1971): 494–517.

Pompey, Sherman L. *Keep the Home Fires Burning: A History of the Seventh Regiment Missouri State Militia Cavalry in the Civil War.* Warrensburg, Mo.: Johnson County Historical Society, 1962.

Pratt, Hary E., ed. "Civil War Letters of Brigadier General William Ward Orme, 1862–1866." *Journal of the Illinois State Historical Society* 23 (1930): 246–315.

Prentis, Noble L. *Kansas Miscellanies.* Topeka: Kansas Publishing, 1889.

Quiner, Edwin B. *The Military History of Wisconsin: A Record of the Civil and Military Patriotism of the State in the War for the Union.* Chicago: Clarke, 1866.

Rechow, Theodore G. *Autobiography.* Bolivar, Mo.: 1929.

Richardson, Ellen E. *Early Settlers of Cane Hill.* Cane Hill, Ark.: ARC Press, 1988.

Roberts, Bobby L. "General T. C. Hindman and the Trans-Mississippi District." *Arkansas Historical Quarterly* 32 (1973): 297–311.

Robertson, Brian K., ed. "A Civil War Letter: Benjamin Fullager's Account of the Union Expedition against Van Buren," *Arkansas Historical Quarterly* 61 (2002): 80–87.

Roster of Wisconsin Volunteers, War of the Rebellion, 1861–1865. 2 vols. Madison: Democrat, 1886.

Ruffner, Samuel T. "Sketch of First Missouri Battery, C.S.A." *Confederate Veteran* 20 (September 1912): 417–20.

Russell, Ira. "Extract from a Report on the Operations of the Medical Department during the Battle of Prairie Grove, Arkansas." *The Medical and Surgical History of the War of the Rebellion, 1861–1865*. 6 vols. Washington, D.C.: Government Printing Office, 1870–88.

Sanders, L. T. "Incidents in the Battle of Prairie Grove." *Confederate Veteran* 24 (January 1916): 16.

Schofield, John M. *Forty-six Years in the Army*. New York: Century, 1897.

Scott, Kim A. "A Diminished Landscape: The Life and Death of Major Robert Henry Smith." *Missouri Historical Review* 91 (1997): 353–72.

———. "The Fighting Printers of Company E, Eleventh Kansas Volunteer Infantry." *Arkansas Historical Quarterly* 46 (1987): 261–81.

———. "The Preacher, the Lawyer, and the Spoils of War." *Kansas History* 13 (1990–91): 206–17.

Scott, Kim A., and Stephen Burgess. "Pursuing an Elusive Quarry: The Battle of Cane Hill, Arkansas." *Arkansas Historical Quarterly* 56 (1997): 26–55.

Shea, William L., ed. "The Aftermath of Prairie Grove: Union Letters from Fayetteville." *Arkansas Historical Quarterly* 47 (1988): 345–61.

———. "A Semi-Savage State: The Image of Arkansas in the Civil War." *Arkansas Historical Quarterly* 48 (1989): 309–28.

Shea, William L., and Earl J. Hess. *Pea Ridge: Civil War Campaign in the West*. Chapel Hill: University of North Carolina Press, 1992.

Skinner, James L., ed. *The Autobiography of Henry Merrell: Industrial Missionary to the South*. Athens: University of Georgia Press, 1991.

Soldiers' and Citizens' Album of Biographical Record. 2 vols. Chicago: Grand Army, 1890.

Spears, Pleasant H. "Autobiography of Pleasant H. Spears." *Newton County Family History, Vol. 2*. Jasper, Ark.: Newton County Historical Society, 1999.

Stark, Andrew, ed. *The Kansas Annual Register for the Year 1864*. Leavenworth, Kans.: Bulletin, 1864.

Stuart, Addison A. *Iowa Colonels and Regiments: Being a History of Iowa Regiments in the War of the Rebellion*. Des Moines: Mills, 1865.

Symonds, Craig L. *Stonewall of the West: Patrick Cleburne and the Civil War*. Lawrence: University Press of Kansas, 1998.

Tenney, Luman H. *War Diary of Luman H. Tenney, 1861–1865*. Cleveland: Evangelical, 1914.

Tilley, Nannie M., ed. *Federals on the Frontier: The Diary of Benjamin F. McIntyre, 1862–1864*. Austin: University of Texas Press, 1963.

The United States Biographical Dictionary and Portrait Gallery of Eminent and Self-made Men. Wisconsin Volume. Chicago: American Biographical, 1877.

U.S. War Department. *The War of the Rebellion: A Compilation of the Official Records of the Union and Confederate Armies*. 128 vols. Washington, D.C.: Government Printing Office, 1880–1901.

Vaught, Elsa, ed. "Diary of an Unknown Soldier." *Arkansas Historical Quarterly* 18 (1959): 50–89.

Walker, Charles W. "Battle of Prairie Grove." *Publications of the Arkansas Historical Association* 2 (1908): 354–61.

———. "Gen. James F. Fagan." *Confederate Veteran* 25 (September 1917): 402–4.
Weddle, Robert S. *Plow-Horse Cavalry: The Caney Creek Boys of the Thirty-fourth Texas.* Austin: Madrona, 1974.
Wilder, Jeremy H. "The Thirty-seventh Illinois at Prairie Grove." *Arkansas Historical Quarterly* 49 (1990): 3–19.
Wilson, Juanita. *Cincinnati, Arkansas, 1836–1986.* Siloam Springs, Ark.: Siloam Springs, 1986.
Wiswell, George E., and Essie Wiswell. *Prairie Grove, Arkansas: Centennial History, 1888–1988.* Siloam Springs, Ark.: Siloam Springs, 1988.
Woodruff, William E. *With the Light Guns in '61–'65: Reminiscences of Eleven Arkansas, Missouri and Texas Light Batteries, in the Civil War.* Little Rock: Central, 1903.
Wright, John C. *Memoirs of Colonel John C. Wright.* Pine Bluff: Rare Book, [1982?].
Wright, Thomas E., ed. "The Capture of Van Buren, Arkansas, during the Civil War: From the Diary of a Union Horse Soldier." *Arkansas Historical Quarterly* 38 (1979): 72–89.
Yeary, Mamie. *Reminiscences of the Boys in Gray, 1861–1865.* Dayton: Morningside, 1986.

Index